D0975347

A Manual of Style

A Manual of Style

Twelfth Edition, Revised

FOR AUTHORS, EDITORS, AND COPYWRITERS

The University of Chicago Press

CHICAGO AND LONDON

International Standard Book Number: 0-226-77008-7
Library of Congress Catalog Card Number: 6-40582
The University of Chicago Press, Chicago 60637
The University of Chicago Press, Ltd., London W.C. 1

First Edition published 1906. Twelfth Edition 1969
Third Impression 1970
Printed in the United States of America
Designed by Cameron Poulter

Contents

Preface

The twelfth edition of the University of Chicago Press *Manual of Style* is by far the most complete revision of this well-known volume ever undertaken. Because of the many changes—technological, social, economic—that have occurred in publishing since the last major revision, in 1949, a very different kind of book seems called for. Scholarly and scientific investigation is ever more specialized, and scholars and scientists are consequently less steeped in the humanistic disciplines; editors increase daily in numbers and their average experience consequently decreases, so that the practical wisdom of the profession is ever more attenuated; publishers and printers are called upon to produce ever more books on closer schedules in a world of ever-rising costs. In the face of these changes, the editors of this manual have attempted to stress fundamentals that in the past may have been taken for granted, to illustrate every principle enunciated as fully as possible, and in all instances to advocate the simple and economical in place of the elaborate and expensive.

The chief reason for any style book, of course, is to ease the work of the writer, the editor, and the typesetter in achieving clarity and consistency within a publication. To say, for instance, that *Congress* is always spelled with an initial capital letter and that the titles of plays are given in italics is to remove two cases from the list of those that must be decided on their own merits—such decisions to be remembered from the beginning to the end of the work. When style rules go beyond their role of achieving clarity and consistency, when they become precious or merely doctrinaire, they must be changed or eliminated. The editors of this volume have tried to do precisely that with many rules that have outlived their usefulness. They have also added a great many new rules which they hope will be examined and tested by authors and fellow editors for their usefulness in achieving the goals specified.

Although this twelfth edition is essentially a new book, its editors have built upon foundations laid down by their predecessors. The earliest of these foundations were probably coeval with the establishment of the Press itself, in 1891. A single sheet of typographic style fundamentals drawn up by the first proofreader for his own guidance had by 1901 become a slender "Style Book: Adopted and in Use for University Publications." The first published version of the Press's style rules, no doubt issued in response to demands from outside the university community for such a book, appeared in 1906:

Manual of Style
Being a Compilation of the Typographical Rules
In Force at the University of Chicago Press
To Which Are Appended
Specimens of Type in Use

Since the publication of that first edition of the *Manual of Style* sixty-three years ago much has changed at the Press. Authors are no longer advised that manuscripts "should be either typewritten or in a perfectly clear handwriting." The leaf-entwined art nouveau typographic ornaments and initial letters that graced early Press publications have disappeared, as has also, alas, two-color printing throughout the Press's own *Manual*. Some things, however, have not changed. What was said in the preface to the first edition about the philosophy of a style manual is as true today as it was then, and cannot be said better by the present editors:

> Rules and regulations such as these, in the nature of the case, cannot be endowed with the fixity of rock-ribbed law. They are meant for the average case, and must be applied with a certain degree of elasticity. Exceptions will constantly occur, and ample room is left for individual initiative and discretion. They point the way and survey the road, rather than remove the obstacles. Throughout this book it is assumed that no regulation contained therein is absolutely inviolable. Wherever the peculiar nature of the subject-matter, the desirability of throwing into relief a certain part of the argument, the reasonable preference of a writer, or a typographical contingency suggests a deviation, such deviation may legitimately be made. Each case of this character must largely be decided upon its own merits. Generally it may be stated that, where no question of good taste or good logic is involved, deference should be shown to the expressed wishes of the author.

This revision of the *Manual of Style* was begun some years ago at the urging of Roger W. Shugg, then director of the University of Chicago Press, and completed under the present director, Morris Philipson, who freed the two editors chiefly involved from some of their other responsibilities to give them time for work on the *Manual*. Preparation of the volume has been in the general charge of Bruce Young, assisted by Catharine Seybold; these two editors also wrote the basic text for thirteen of its twenty chapters. Present and former members of the Press staff who contributed materially are Margaret Flack, Irene Grad, John Grossman, Ann Jacobs, John Jennings, John Kendrick, Cameron Poulter, Linda Rankin, Nancy Romoser, and Margot Schutt. Other contributors are Joan Ryan, Harvard University Press; Edward A. Shaw, director, University of Oklahoma Press; J. G. Bell, Stanford University Press; and Curt Johnson.

Many persons, too numerous to mention by name, have contributed suggestions that have been reflected in the final draft of this book. These persons include members of the University of Chicago faculty; authors of books published by this press; and editors at other university presses, especially those of Cornell, Harvard, Illinois, Indiana, Oklahoma, Minnesota, Toronto, and Wisconsin.

The text of this volume was set by the University of Chicago Printing Department. The editors are grateful to the entire staff for their expert work, especially to Greer Allen, manager, for typographical suggestions and to George Batruel, chief proofreader, and Marilyn Faull for a critical reading of the proof and for many helpful suggestions.

Part 1

Bookmaking

1 *The Parts of a Book*

OUTLINE OF MAJOR DIVISIONS

1.1   A book usually consists of three major divisions: (1) the *front matter* or *preliminaries* (prelims), (2) the *text*, and (3) the *back matter* or *end matter* or *reference matter*. An appropriate sequence for all the parts is shown in the following outline. Few books have all these parts, of course, and some books have other parts not shown in the outline, for example, a list of abbreviations. Note that front-matter pages here are numbered with lowercase roman numerals (but see par. 1.76). Note too that each page is counted although no folio (page number) is *expressed* (printed) on display pages or blank pages (i–vi). A *recto* page is a right-hand page; a *verso* page is a left-hand page. Recto folios are odd numbers; verso folios, even numbers.

1. Placement of the contents page is discussed in par. 1.26.

PRELIMINARIES

HALF TITLE

1.2 The half title (p. i) normally consists only of the main title. The subtitle is omitted, and the author's name does not appear.

FACING TITLE PAGE

1.3 The verso of the half title (p. ii) is often blank, or the designer may wish to make the title page a two-page spread (pp. ii–iii).

1.4 If the book is in a series, the title of the series, the volume number, if any, in the series, and the name of the editor or general editor of the series should appear here:

>The Chicago History of American Civilization
>Daniel J. Boorstin, Editor

Note that the title of a series editor follows his name (never "Edited by ———").

1.5 In a multiauthor book—more than three contributors but fewer than, say, fifteen—the contributors may be listed, in alphabetical order, on page ii. (A long list of contributors or a list of conference participants should be placed in the back matter.)

1.6 If the book is a publication of the proceedings of a symposium, the title of the symposium, the name of the city where it was held, and the date may appear on page ii. Sometimes the committee that planned the symposium and edited the volume may be added here; sometimes also the name of the sponsor of the symposium.

1.7 Some publishers list an author's previous publications on page ii; the University of Chicago Press generally lists these on the jacket, rarely inside the book.

1.8 In a book printed by the offset process a frontispiece, either a line cut or a halftone plate, may appear on page ii. In a letterpress book in which plates are printed separately from the text a halftone frontispiece must be tipped in (see par. 11.4) and hence cannot occupy page ii.

TITLE PAGE

1.9 The title page (p. iii) presents the full title of the book, the name of the author, editor, or translator (if any), and the name of the publishing house. The designer usually specifies a type size or style for the subtitle different from that of the main title; therefore, no colon or other mark of punctuation is needed to separate the two parts of the title.

1.10   If the book is a new edition of a work previously published, as is this manual, the number of the edition ("Third Edition") or "Revised Edition" may also appear on the title page, usually following the title.

1.11   The author's name should be printed in the form he specifies; given names should not be shortened to initials unless, like H. G. Wells and others, this is how the author prefers to be known. European authors, many of whom are accustomed to using only one initial and their surnames, may usually be persuaded by their American publishers to permit the spelling out of their given names on the title page. Affiliations and degrees appearing after the author's name in the manuscript are omitted from the printed page, with the exception of "M.D.," which may be retained for an author of a book in the field of medicine.

1.12   The form for an editor's name on the title page is:

Edited by John Doe (*not* John Doe, Editor)

1.13   The publisher's full name should be given on the title page, sometimes followed by the name of the city (or cities) where the principal offices are located. The publisher's device (*colophon*) may appear on the title page as an embellishment. Some publishers give the year of publication on the title page; the University of Chicago Press does not.

COPYRIGHT PAGE

1.14   The most important item on the copyright page (p. iv) is, of course, the copyright notice. Section 20 of the Copyright Law of the United States of America reads:

> The notice of copyright shall be applied, in the case of a book or other printed publication, upon its title page or the page immediately following, or if a periodical either upon the title page or upon the first page of text of each separate number or under the title heading, or if a musical work either upon its title page or the first page of music. One notice of copyright in each volume or in each number of a newspaper or periodical published shall suffice.[2]

The form of the copyright notice is as follows: copyright symbol (©) in books published since the Universal Copyright Convention

2. Quoted in Margaret Nicholson, *A Manual of Copyright Practice*, p. 233.

of 1955, date (year only), name of copyright holder (publishing house, author, or other):

© 1968 by The University of Chicago

The word *copyright* may be spelled out (as it was before the UCC) and used in place of the symbol, but why lengthen the notice? Since the copyright does not take effect until the day the book is published, the year specified in the copyright notice must also be the year in which the book was first published. The name of the copyright holder is given in the contract drawn up for a particular work, and therefore the contract should always be consulted by the person who prepares the copyright page for the printer.[3]

1.15   Subsequent *editions* (not impressions) of a book are each copyrighted, and the date of each normally appears in the copyright notice.

1.16   The date of copyright renewal or a change in the name of the copyright holder (rights may be assigned to the author or someone else after the initial copyright has been registered and printed in the first impression) should be inserted in the copyright notice if the book is reprinted. If the book is not reprinted, any reassignment of copyright or renewal is legally valid, even though it does not appear on the copyright page.

1.17   Following the specific copyright notice, most United States publishers print "All rights reserved." This is to comply with the requirement of all countries belonging to the Buenos Aires Convention (the United States and most Latin American countries) that to be protected a published work must contain, in any language, "a statement of reservation of property rights."[4]

Standard Book Number: 226-30204-0

Library of Congress Catalog Card Number: 62-12633

The University of Chicago Press, Chicago 60637
The University of Chicago Press, Ltd., London

© 1962 by The University of Chicago. All rights reserved
Published 1962. Fourth Impression 1969
Printed in the United States of America

Fig. 1.1 Copyright page for the fourth impression of Robert T. Golembiewski's *The Small Group: An Analysis of Research Concepts and Operations*.

---

3. For further information about copyright see chapter 4.

4. Nicholson, p. 140.

1.18   The publishing history of a book usually follows the copyright notice, although it may appear elsewhere on the copyright page, or it may be omitted altogether. The sequence of items is as follows: date (year) of first publication; date of second (or other) edition; date of impression if other than the first. These items may each be on a separate line or may be run together. There should be no period at the end of a line.

1.19   The publisher's mailing address—and sometimes the addresses of his overseas agents—is usually given on the copyright page.

1.20   The Standard Book Number and the Library of Congress Catalog Card Number should appear on the copyright page, on successive lines. The SBN is assigned by the publisher, under a system administered by the R. R. Bowker Co., and uniquely identifies the particular book. The "LC number"[5] is assigned by the Library of Congress upon application of the publisher.

1.21   The name of the country where the book was actually *printed* must appear in the book (not just on the jacket) and is usually placed on the copyright page:

> Printed in the United States of America
> Printed in Great Britain

Originally published in 1932 as Histoire de la philosophie:
La philosophie moderne. III: Le XIXe siècle. Période
des systèmes (1800–1850)
Copyright 1932, Presses universitaires de France

*The present bibliography has been revised and enlarged to include
recent publications. These have been supplied by Wesley Piersol*

Standard Book Number: 226-07228-2
Library of Congress Catalog Card Number: 63-20912
The University of Chicago Press, Chicago 60637
The University of Chicago Press, Ltd., London
Translation © 1968 by The University of Chicago
All rights reserved. Published 1968
Printed in the United States of America

Fig. 1.2. Copyright page for volume 6 of Emile Bréhier's *The History of Philosophy*, showing the title of the original French publication with its copyright date. Note that the Library of Congress Catalog Card Number is the one assigned when volume 1 was published; the same number is used for all volumes in a single work.

---

5. The Library of Congress Catalog Card Number is not the same as the call number assigned later when the finished book is cataloged.

1.22   If the book is a translation, the original title, publisher, and copyright information are customarily recorded on the copyright page (fig. 1.2). The copyright notice of the translation may then read:

> English translation © 1968 by John Doe
> *or:*
> Translation © 1968 by John Doe

DEDICATION

1.23   Whether a book includes a dedication at all, to whom it is dedicated, and the phrasing of the dedication are matters for the author to determine. It may be suggested, however, that the word "Dedicated" is superfluous; a simple "To" is sufficient. It is not necessary to identify (or even to give the whole name of) the person to whom the work is dedicated, nor is it necessary to give the life dates of a person who has died; but both are permissible. Extravagant dedications are things of the past. A dedication intended to be humorous will very likely lose its humor with time and so is inappropriate in a serious book destined to take a permanent place in the literature. The dedication (p. v) is usually followed by a blank verso page (p. vi).

EPIGRAPH

1.24   An author may wish to include an epigraph—a pertinent quotation—at the beginning of his book. If he has no dedication, the epigraph may be placed on page v. When there is also a dedication, the epigraph may follow on a new recto page (p. vii), or, to save space, it may be put on page vi or on a blank verso page facing the first page of the text. Less customary but possible in certain books is the placement of an epigraph on the title page or even on the half title.

1.25   The source of a quotation used in this way is given on a line following the quotation and is usually set flush right, with no parentheses or brackets. Only the author's name (and only his last name if he is well known) and, usually, the title of the work need appear. No page or line numbers and no bibliographical details are necessary. Since an epigraph is not part of the text, its source should never be given as a footnote. And when an author feels compelled to explain the relevance of his epigraph, he should do so in his preface or other introductory material, not in a note on the epigraph page.

TABLE OF CONTENTS

1.26 The table of contents (often titled simply Contents) begins on page v, or, if there is a dedication or an epigraph, on page vii. This is a departure from the convention that advocates placing the contents page at the end of all preliminary pages, so that it immediately precedes the text. The logic of the older convention is that such matter as prefaces, acknowledgments, and so on are not part of the text and thus usually should not be listed in the table of contents, the assumption being that anything preceding the contents is not listed in it. The University of Chicago Press is not alone in now observing another kind of logic: (1) In a book containing many preliminary pages—for example, a foreword, an editor's preface, an author's preface, and acknowledgments—just finding the contents page can be a frustrating experience for the reader. (2) Although the preliminaries are not part of the subject matter of the text, they are part of the book and thus deserve a listing in the table of contents. Henceforth, therefore, readers of new University of Chicago Press books will find the table of contents preceding the prefatory matter (foreword or preface), with subsequent parts of the book listed in it.

1.27 The table of contents should include the title and beginning page number of each section of the book: front matter, text divisions, and back matter, including the index. If the book is divided into parts as well as chapters, the part titles should appear in the contents, but their page numbers are not essential if the page number of the chapter following each part title is sufficient indication of where the part begins. Page numbers in the manuscript and galley proofs of the table of contents are indicated by "000," the actual numbers being inserted after all pages have been made up. Subheads within chapters may be included in the table of contents, particularly in technical books and in books with long chapters divided into sections defined by meaningful subheads. When subheads are included in the contents, they are usually indented under the chapter titles and often set in smaller type (fig. 1.3). In a long table of contents they may be run in, each followed by its page number.

1.28 In a volume consisting of papers, or chapters, by different authors, the name of each author should be given in the table of contents with the title of his chapter:

Contents

Fig. 1.3. Partial table of contents for a scientific work, showing chapter titles, *A*- and *B*-level subheads, and back matter.

1.29 The list of illustrations (now often titled Illustrations) begins on a recto page following the table of contents. It should match the table of contents in type size and general style. In books containing various kinds of illustrations, the list may be subdivided into sections headed, for example, Maps, Charts, Figures, Plates. Page numbers are given for all illustrations printed with the text, even when folios are not expressed on the page (see par. 1.79). Since plates in a letterpress book are commonly inserted between the signatures and are therefore unpaginated, the words *Facing page* or *Following page* should appear in small type above the column of page numbers applying to them. *Facing page* is used when each insert is only one leaf, both sides of which face a page of text. *Following page* is used when the inserts consist of four or more pages and the inner plates therefore do not "face" a page of text (see pars. 11.39–40). *Following page 000* may be centered above a group of illustration titles so that the same page number need not be repeated for each. The page indication for a frontispiece, whether the frontispiece is tipped in or printed on page ii, is simply *Frontispiece*.

1.30 The titles of illustrations given in the list need not correspond exactly to the legends printed with the illustrations themselves. If the legends are long, shortened forms should be given in the list of illustrations.

1.31 In a book with very few illustrations or one with many illustrations, such as charts and graphs, tied closely to the text, it is not essential to list them in the front matter. Multiauthor books, proceedings of symposia, and the like commonly do not carry lists of illustrations.

LIST OF TABLES

1.32 A list of tables (often titled Tables) begins on a recto page following the table of contents or, if there is one, the list of illustrations. Listing tables in the front matter is helpful mainly in technical books carrying many tables and with frequent textual references to them. The titles may be shortened if necessary.

FOREWORD

1.33   The terms *foreword* and *preface* are now increasingly differentiated, a foreword being a statement by someone other than the author, a preface the author's own statement about his work. Both are set in the same size and style of type as the text. A foreword normally runs only two to four pages, and its author's name appears at the end, usually in caps and small caps and indented one em from the right. His title may appear under his name, often in italics; or his affiliation may be given, in smaller type and on the left side of the page. If a foreword ends on a recto page, the verso of that page should be left blank so that the following section may begin on a recto page.

PREFACE AND ACKNOWLEDGMENTS

1.34   Material normally included in an author's preface consists of his reasons for undertaking the work, his method of research (only if this has some bearing on the reader's understanding of the text), acknowledgments, and, sometimes, permissions granted for the use of previously published material (see par. 4.12). If his acknowledgments are lengthy, they may be put in a separate section following the preface; or if a preface consists only of acknowledgments, its title should be changed to Acknowledgments. Acknowledgments are sometimes put at the back of a book, preceding the index.

1.35   Material essential to the text, material that the reader should see before he reads the book—an account of the historical background of the subject of the book, for example—should not be relegated to a preface but should be printed as an *introduction* at the beginning of the text proper. Text matter should not be mixed with acknowledgments, methodology or history of a research project, or other matter concerning the writing of the book.

1.36   A preface should be signed by its author (name at the end, as described above for the author of a foreword) only when there might be some doubt about who wrote it. The reader logically assumes that an unsigned preface was written by the author whose name appears on the title page. The University of Chicago Press discourages the inclusion of place (city) and date at the end of a preface or a foreword. When these facts are given, they are set flush left and in a type size smaller than that of the text (usually 8-point).

1.37   When a new preface is written for a new edition, it precedes the original preface, which is usually retitled Preface to First Edition. In a book containing both an editor's preface and a preface by the author, the editor's preface comes first and the editor's name is appended to it.

OTHER FRONT MATTER

1.38   The parts of a book so far described are those found in the front matter of most books. Edited texts and other kinds of scholarly works often require more material in the preliminary pages—biographical information about the author of an edited text, for example, or any explanation of editorial procedures or peculiarities of apparatus that the reader needs to understand before encountering the text proper.

1.39   *Introduction.* A relatively long substantive introduction not part of the subject matter of the text itself should be paginated with the preliminaries. An introduction written by an author to set the scene for his text, however, such as the historical background of his subject, should be part of his text, paginated with arabic folios.

1.40   *List of abbreviations.* In some heavily footnoted books, especially where there are many references to a few easily abbreviated sources, it may be a convenience to the reader to give a list of abbreviations for these sources before the text rather than in the back matter. If no more than one page long, such a list may be placed on the verso page facing the first page of text; if longer, it should begin on a recto page at the end of the prelims. A long list of abbreviations used in footnotes and bibliography, and sometimes in the text, is generally best placed in the back matter, preceding the bibliography.

1.41   *Editorial method.* An explanation of an editor's method or a discussion of variant texts, often necessary in scholarly editions, may constitute a large part of an editor's preliminary pages. Any such material is essential for the user of edited texts and is therefore often placed at the end of the prelims, just before the text proper. Short, uncomplicated remarks about editorial method, however—such as the fact that the spelling and capitalization have been modernized—should be incorporated in the editor's preface, not put in a separate section.

14

TEXT

1.42 In general, the preliminary pages of a book serve as a guide to the contents and nature of the book, and the back matter provides reference material.[6] The text proper should contain everything the author expects his readers to learn about his subject. The organization of the text material can help or hinder comprehension of it. The author who does little more than copy his research notes in the sequence he filed them, or who feels compelled to use every nugget panned in the library, will seldom produce a clearly organized work. The ideal author keeps his prospective audience in mind and presents his material in a logical pattern, selecting what is essential and omitting what is nonessential or repetitious. The following paragraphs deal with divisions commonly found in most books, not with substantive organization of text material. Details of handling special elements in the text—quotations, illustrations, tables, mathematics, and footnotes—are discussed in part 2.

CHAPTERS

1.43 Most prose works are divided into chapters, preferably, though not necessarily, of approximately the same length. Chapter titles should be similar in tone, if not in length. Each title should give a reasonable clue to what is in the chapter; whimsical titles in a serious book, for example, can be misleading. Many potential readers scan a table of contents to determine whether a book is worth their time (and money). Relatively short titles are preferable to long, ungainly ones, both for appearance on the page and for use in running heads.

1.44 In the printed book, each chapter normally starts on a new page, verso or recto,[7] and its opening page carries a drop folio and no running head. The chapter display usually consists of the chapter number[8] and the chapter title. In titles of two or more lines, punctuation should be omitted at the end of a line unless it is essential for clarity. Footnote reference numbers or symbols should not appear anywhere in the chapter display.

6. In a book containing many preliminary pages a second half title introducing the text proper is helpful to the reader (see par. 1.78).

7. When offprints of individual chapters are planned, each chapter in a book should begin on a recto page so that the printer need not reimpose pages for offprints but can simply gather them together.

8. By Press preference the word *chapter* is omitted.

1.45   In multiauthor books (each chapter by a different author) chapter numbers are sometimes omitted. The author's name is given in the display, but his affiliation, or other identification, is usually not considered part of the display but is put in an unnumbered footnote on the first page of his chapter (see par. 15.22) or in a list of contributors. The source of previously published material (e.g., in an anthology) may also be given in an unnumbered footnote on its opening page (see par. 15.21). When both an author's identification and a source reference appear, the author's identification is given first.

PARTS

1.46   When text material may be logically divided into sections larger than chapters, the chapters may be grouped in parts. Each part may be numbered and is normally given a part title, as in this manual. The part number and title appear on a separate page preceding the part, in bookmaking called the *part title*. Chapters within parts are numbered consecutively through the book (*not* beginning over with 1 in each part).

1.47   Each part may have an introduction, usually short, and titled, for example, Introduction to Part 2. A text introduction to an entire book that is divided into parts precedes part 1 and needs no part-title page to introduce it. Also, no part title need precede the back matter of a book divided into parts.

OTHER DIVISIONS

1.48   *Poetry.* In a book of previously unpublished poetry, each poem usually begins on a new page. Any part titles provided by the poet need not be numbered but should appear on a separate page preceding the poems grouped under them.

1.49   *Letters and diaries.* Correspondence and journals are usually presented in chronological order, seldom conducive to division into chapters or parts. Dates, used as guidelines rather than titles, are often inserted above relevant diary entries. The names of the sender and the recipient of a letter may serve the same function in published correspondence. In a collection of letters written by (and to) a single person, however, the name of that person is not used each time. For example, in *The Papers of James Madison*, "To Edmund Randolph" and "From Edmund Randolph" are sufficient. The date of a letter may be included in the guideline

16

if it does not appear in the letter itself. Such guidelines in diaries and correspondence do not begin a new page in the book unless page makeup demands it.

SUBHEADS

1.50   In prose works where the chapters are long and the material complicated, the author (or the editor) may insert *subheads*, or *subheadings*, in the text as guides to the reader. Subheads should be kept short, succinct, and meaningful; and, like chapter titles, they should be similar in sense and tone.

1.51   Many scholarly works require only one degree (level) of subhead throughout the text. Some, particularly scientific or technical works, require sub-subheads and even further subdivisions. Where more than one degree of subhead is used, the subheads are referred to as the *A-level* subhead (the principal subhead), the *B-level* subhead (the secondary subhead), the *C-level*, and so on. Only in the most complicated works does the need for more than three levels arise.

1.52   Subheads, except the lowest level, are each set on a line separate from the text, the levels differentiated by type and placement (specified by the book designer; see par. 19.27). The lowest level is often set at the beginning of a paragraph, in italics and followed by a period, where it is referred to as a *run-in side head* (rather than *C*-level, for example).

1.53   In some works the number of levels of subheads required may vary from chapter to chapter; that is, one or two chapters may need three levels, the rest only one or two. The fact that one chapter or part or section of a chapter contains three levels does not mean that every chapter, part, or section must contain the same number. Some material may require identifying side heads, for example, while the rest of the book is clear, and better off, without them. Again, it is not necessary that the *A*-level heading be used in every chapter. Depending upon the importance and complexity of the material presented in a given chapter, *B*-level headings may well serve to mark the major divisions of one chapter whereas *A*-level headings are required for another.

1.54   Unless sections in a chapter are referred to in cross-references elsewhere in the text, numbers are usually unnecessary with subheads. Also, in general, subheads are more useful to a reader than numbers alone.

1.55   In scientific and technical works, however, the numbering of sections, subsections, and sometimes sub-subsections makes for easy reference and may be a real convenience to the reader. There are various ways to number sections. The most common of these is the *double numeration* system, in which the number of a section consists of the number of the chapter, a decimal point, and the number of the section within a chapter. The number 4.8, for example, signifies the eighth section in chapter 4. A subsection might be numbered 4.8.3. Another system, used in some monographs, is to ignore the chapter number (which should here be a roman numeral to prevent confusion) and to number *A*-level subheads consecutively through the book, *B*-level subheads consecutively under each *A*-level, and subsections under the *B*-level: 25.10.7 thus might occur in chapter V. This manual employs still another system—chapter number followed by paragraph number to facilitate cross-referencing.

1.56   No footnote reference number should appear in or following a subhead.

1.57   The first sentence of text following a subhead should not contain a pronoun referring back to a word in the subhead; the word itself should be repeated where necessary. For example:

> SECONDARY SPONGIOSA
> The secondary spongiosa is a vaulted structure . . .

> *not:*
> SECONDARY SPONGIOSA
> This is a vaulted structure . . .

BACK MATTER

APPENDIX

1.58   Although an appendix is of course not an essential part of every book, the possibilities and the uses of the device are many. Some kinds of material properly relegated to an appendix are: explanations and elaborations too long for footnotes and not essential parts of the text but helpful to a reader seeking further clarification; texts of documents, laws, etc., illustrating the text; long lists or charts or tables. The appendix should not be a repository for odds and ends of the author's research that he was unable to work into his text.

1.59   When more than one appendix appears in a book, each should be numbered like chapters (Appendix 1, Appendix 2, etc.) or desig-

18

nated by letters (Appendix A, Appendix B, etc.), and each should be given a title as well. The first appendix begins on a recto page; subsequent appendixes may begin verso or recto. In multiauthor books an appendix to a specific chapter is placed (beginning verso or recto) at the end of that chapter rather than at the end of the book.

1.60 The text of appendixes is usually, though not always, set in smaller type than the text proper, often the same as that used for excerpts in the text. The appendix, however, is always set full measure, even when excerpts are indented.

NOTES

1.61 A section of notes or references in the back matter begins on a recto page following any appendix material and preceding a bibliography. If the notes are arranged by chapters, with references to them in the text, chapter numbers, and usually titles, must appear above each relevant group of notes. These are treated as *A*-level subheads (see par. 1.51). Each group of notes does not begin a new page, but enough space should be inserted between groups to enable the reader to find his way.[9]

GLOSSARY

1.62 A glossary is a useful tool for the reader in a book on a subject necessitating many foreign words or in a technical work intended for the general reader who may be puzzled by words and phrases not in the common vocabulary (such as this manual). Words to be defined in a glossary should be arranged in alphabetical order, each on a separate line and followed by its definition. No period is used at the end of the definition—except where some or all of the definitions consist of more than one sentence. A glossary begins on a recto page and usually precedes the bibliography, if there is one.

BIBLIOGRAPHY

1.63 A bibliography begins on a recto page. The form of a bibliography varies with the nature of the book, the inclination of the author, and sometimes the guidance or suggestion of the publisher. It may be a single listing of sources, arranged alphabetically by author.

9. For notes in the back matter as opposed to footnotes see par. 15.2. For unnumbered back notes and notes keyed to line numbers see par. 19.41. For running heads to a section of notes see par. 1.72.

It may be broken into sections, by subject or by kinds of materials (primary and secondary sources, etc.). It may be a selected bibliography (preferable, as a rule, in a published book as opposed to a doctoral dissertation). It may be an annotated bibliography, the annotations sometimes indented under each entry and set in smaller type. Or it may be a discursive "bibliographical essay" in which the author discusses the sources most useful to his study.

1.64 Bibliographies are normally set in a type size smaller than that of the text and in flush-and-hang style (except the essay kind) with extra space between entries. (For examples see chapter 16.)

INDEX

1.65 The index, or the first of several indexes, should begin on a recto page; subsequent indexes may begin verso or recto. If there are two indexes, name and subject, the name index precedes the subject index. (For acceptable kinds and forms of indexes see chapter 18.) Indexes are normally set two or more columns to a page and in a type size smaller than that of the text (see pars. 19.42–44).

COLOPHON

1.66 An embellishment sometimes added on the last page (usually recto) of a specially designed and produced book is the colophon, in

---

The Papers of James Madison

DESIGNED BY JOHN B. GOETZ
COMPOSED BY THE UNIVERSITY OF CHICAGO PRESS
IN LINOTYPE JANSON WITH DISPLAY LINES IN
MONOTYPE JANSON AND CASLON OLD STYLE
PRINTED BY THE UNIVERSITY OF CHICAGO PRESS
ON WARREN'S UNIVERSITY TEXT, A PAPER WATERMARKED
WITH JAMES MADISON'S SIGNATURE AND MADE EXPRESSLY
FOR THE VOLUMES OF THIS SET
PLATES PRINTED BY MERIDEN GRAVURE COMPANY
BOUND BY RAND MC NALLY IN COLUMBIA BAYSIDE LINEN
AND STAMPED IN GENUINE GOLD

Fig. 1.4. Colophon used at the end of each volume of *The Papers of James Madison*, edited by William T. Hutchinson and William M. E. Rachal and published by the University of Chicago Press.

this sense not simply the publisher's device but an inscription including the facts of production (fig. 1.4). This practice is not so common in book publishing today as it once was.

RUNNING HEADS

1.67 Running heads, the headings at the tops of pages in a book, are signposts telling the reader where he is. For this purpose running heads are useful in most scholarly works, textbooks, and the like. They may be omitted where they serve no practical purpose—in a book of poems, for example.

FRONT MATTER

1.68 Running heads should never be used on display pages (half title, title, copyright, dedication, epigraph) or on the first page of a table of contents, preface, etc. An element in the prelims that runs more than one page must carry running heads if the design calls for running heads in the text. Each element in the front matter normally carries the same running head on verso and recto pages.

VERSO	RECTO
Contents	Contents
Preface	Preface

TEXT

1.69 Running heads in the text are governed chiefly by the structure and nature of the book. The recto and verso running heads usually differ, but the chapter title may be used for both. The tradition of running the *book* title on the verso page throughout seems to be crumbling. Reasons against the use of the book title are (1) that the title may be changed while the book is going through production and (2) that most readers presumably know what book they are reading and prefer running heads indicating part, chapter, or section. Some acceptable arrangements are:

VERSO	RECTO
Part title	Chapter title
Chapter title	Subhead
Chapter title	Chapter title
Author [multiauthor books]	Chapter title

(For preparation of running-head copy see pars. 2.108–10.)

1.70   Where subheads in the text are used as recto running heads and where several subheads appear on a page, the last one on the page is used as the running head.

BACK MATTER

1.71   Some acceptable arrangements for running heads in the back matter are:

VERSO	RECTO
Appendix A	Title of appendix
Appendix	Appendix [if no title]
Glossary	Glossary
Bibliography	Bibliography
Bibliography	Section title
Index	Index
Subject Index	Subject Index

1.72   A section of notes in the back of the book presents a special problem. As a definite convenience to readers, the running heads should give the inclusive page numbers of the text where the relevant note references are to be found. Thus, two facing running heads might read:

VERSO	RECTO
Notes to Pages 2–10	Notes to Pages 11–25

OMISSION OF RUNNING HEADS

1.73   In addition to display pages in the front matter (see par. 1.1) running heads are omitted from part titles, chapter openings, and any page containing only an illustration or a table. A running head should be used on a page containing both an illustration (or a table) and lines of text.

PAGE NUMBERS

1.74   All modern books are paginated consecutively, and all leaves in a book (except end papers) are counted in the pagination, whether folios are expressed or not. There are various locations on the page acceptable for the folio. The most common, and perhaps the most easily found, is at the top of the page, flush outside (left on verso pages, right on recto pages). The folio may also be printed at the bottom of the page, and in that location it is called a *drop folio*. Drop folios may appear flush outside or in the center or indented from the outside.

FRONT MATTER

1.75   The preliminary pages of a book usually, especially in United States publications, are paginated with lowercase roman numerals (see outline, par. 1.1). The practice is due partly to tradition and partly to expedience: some of these pages (those containing the table of contents and the lists of illustrations and tables) cannot be finally made up until the text is in page proofs, and others (those containing the preface, acknowledgments, and dedication) are often heavily revised or even added by the author at the last moment, after the rest of the book is in pages. Thus, separate numeration for the prelims makes good sense.

1.76   This is not the only system, however. In some books arabic numbering begins with the first page (half title) and continues straight through the book. This system, more common in Great Britain than here, should be held in mind as a sometimes useful alternative to the better-known system. When prelims are unusually long, use of arabic numerals eliminates the awkwardness of roman folios running up through xlviii, xlix, etc. But since this system affects the pagination of the entire book, the author must understand that there is no possibility of adding a dedication page or an additional page of acknowledgments once paging has begun.

1.77   Whether roman or arabic folios are used, no folio is expressed on display pages (half title, title, copyright, dedication, epigraph), and a drop folio (or none) is used on the opening page of each of the following sections of the prelims.

TEXT AND BACK MATTER

1.78   Following the prelims, arabic numerals are used throughout the book (in rare instances an index may be paginated with roman folios, in sequence with the roman folios of the prelims). When roman folios are used in the prelims, the text begins with arabic folio 1. If the text begins with a second half title (same as that on page i) or with a part title, the half title or part title counts as folio 1, its verso page as folio 2, and the first folio to be expressed is the drop folio 3 on the first page of text. If there is no part- or half-title page, the first page of the text proper becomes page 1.

1.79   The opening page of each chapter and of each section in the back matter carries a drop folio. Folios are not usually expressed on pages containing only illustrations or tables, except in books containing long sequences of figures or tables.

2 *Manuscript Preparation*

INTRODUCTION

2.1   The preparation of a *manuscript*—alternatively called *typescript* or *copy*—suitable for use by publisher and printer is mainly the author's responsibility. It is his final draft. In it he has said what he wants to say and provided any necessary apparatus and illustrative material. In preparing his manuscript, the author who wants his book published with the least possible confusion and delay should keep in mind relevant suggestions in this chapter. And the manuscript editor, who prepares the author's manuscript for the printer, should be thoroughly aware of all points raised in this chapter, whether they are his responsibility or not.

AUTHOR TO PUBLISHER

CONTENTS OF MANUSCRIPT

2.2   The parts of a book outlined in chapter 1 (par. 1.1) are, in general, what the publisher expects to find in a manuscript submitted for publication. Some of the preliminary pages may be added later—such as the dedication, foreword, preface, or acknowledgments—but the publisher wants to know what preliminaries are to come and approximately when. There is no excuse, however, for an author's failing to provide a title page and especially a table of contents for any manuscript; if the table of contents is incomplete, the author has not finished his manuscript and should not be submitting it to a publisher. The publisher will furnish the copyright page and the copy for running heads. The rest of the manuscript is normally the author's responsibility. In short, the author's manuscript submitted in final form to his publisher must include:

Title page
Table of contents
List of illustrations
List of tables
Any other preliminaries (or notification of what is to come)

All text matter
Footnotes, if any, on separate pages
Tables, if any, on separate pages

Bibliography or list of references (unless none is planned)
Any other end matter, except index[1]

All illustrations (or notification of what is missing)
Legend copy for illustrations, on separate pages

ARRANGEMENT OF MANUSCRIPT

2.3   As the above outline indicates, the way a manuscript is assembled for the printer is usually not the way the printed book will appear. Preliminary pages and the body of the text and the back matter should be arranged in the order in which they will appear in the book. But other matter requiring different treatment by the printer should be grouped together by category and separated from the text. Such matter includes footnotes, tables, line drawings, halftones, and legends for illustrations.

1. The index is also the author's responsibility, unless other arrangements are made with the publisher. The index manuscript cannot of course be completed until the author has all his page proofs. For suggestions concerning appendixes see par. 1.58.

2.4   *Footnotes,* typed on separate pages and labeled by chapter, should be placed all together at the end of the manuscript. The footnote pages should be numbered consecutively with the text pages (see par. 2.9).

2.5   *Tables,* typed or pasted on separate sheets, should be placed together. Pages of tables are not numbered with the manuscript pages, but each table must bear an indication—the manuscript page number—of where it should appear in the printed book.

2.6   *Illustrations* should be put in a separate envelope and protected by a sheet or sheets of stiff cardboard. Clips, staples, or pins should never be used to fasten illustrations. And illustrations intended as final artwork should never be folded; illustrations too large to be placed in an envelope should be rolled and sent in mailing tubes.

2.7   *Legends* should be typed on pages separate from the illustrations and put in the envelope containing the illustrations.

NUMBERING PAGES

2.8   The author need number his preliminary pages only if an element, such as a preface, occupies more than one manuscript page. The sequence of pages within this element may then be indicated by ordinary arabic numerals. Before the manuscript goes to the printer, the editor will number the preliminaries as they are to appear in the printed book (see par. 2.92), indicating any verso pages that are to remain blank.

2.9   All the manuscript pages containing text, back matter, and footnotes must be numbered consecutively from the first page to the last page (not by chapter or section). The numbers should be placed in the upper right corner of each page, clearly separated from the text. A hand numbering machine with a freshly inked pad is best for this operation and certainly less time-consuming than writing each number. If the author does not number his pages consecutively, the editor will do so for him, because the publisher must know how many manuscript pages he has in order to estimate the length of the printed book.

2.10   Tables and illustrations are estimated separately and therefore are not numbered consecutively with the manuscript pages. The estimate for these is based on the number and complexity of each.

2.11   Index copy, prepared by the author after all the rest of his book has been made up in pages, is of course numbered separately. And even though an index is in alphabetical order (the sequence of pages presumably obvious), its manuscript pages (or cards) must be numbered.

NUMBER OF COPIES

2.12   Many publishers, including the University of Chicago Press, request two copies of a manuscript submitted for publication—the ribbon, or first, copy and a legible carbon or machine copy.[2] The ribbon copy is marked by the editor and becomes the copy from which type is set. The second copy goes to the production department for design and estimate.[3] Editorial and preliminary production processes may thus take place simultaneously. Only one set of illustrations—halftones or prepared artwork—is necessary. And the publisher normally requires only one copy of the index manuscript, since he has estimated its probable length in advance.

TYPING THE MANUSCRIPT

2.13   The physical appearance of a manuscript is of immense importance to the whole publishing process. A well-prepared manuscript is very likely to influence the publisher's readers in its favor. Later, when accepted for publication, a tidy manuscript facilitates the work of the editor, the designer, the cost estimator, the typesetter, and the proofreader. Badly prepared copy makes for delays at every step and adds to the cost of printing the book and therefore to its price to the public—to say nothing of frayed nerves all around.

PAPER

2.14   It is essential that the first copy, and desirable that the carbon copy as well, be typed on good-quality paper of standard size—8½ by 11 inches. The kind of paper called "erasable" (available under various trade names) is *not* recommended for manuscripts which are to go through the publishing process; the "erasable" characteristic of such paper leads to the blurring and sometimes the actual disappearance of the type under the slight pressure of a hand—and many hands touch a manuscript before it becomes a book.

2. The author should always retain a third copy for himself.

3. For acceptability of machine copies see par. 2.33. The copy used by editor and typesetter in producing the book should never be a carbon copy.

TYPEWRITER

2.15   Whenever possible, the same typewriter or at least the same type size (pica, being larger, is better than elite) should be used for an entire manuscript. The type bars should be clean and the ribbon fresh.

2.16   A correct letter should not simply be typed over an incorrect one; either erase the error and insert the correction or strike out the incorrect letter and type (or write) the correct one above it.

2.17   A typewriter equipped with diacritical marks and symbols occurring frequently in a manuscript is most desirable. A capital *L* with a hyphen through it may be used to represent a British pound sign, a double quotation mark may be typed above a letter to indicate an umlaut, and a comma under a letter may indicate a cedilla; but a single quotation mark used to indicate an accent is ambiguous—it could be either a grave or an acute accent, and the typesetter should not be asked to decide which is correct. Any diacritical marks or symbols not available on the typewriter must be inserted by the author or his typist—in ink and accurately placed. A handwritten Greek letter or a possibly ambiguous symbol should be identified by its name, written and circled in the margin next to the line where it occurs (*alpha, sigma, times* or *mult* for an *x* used as a multiplying sign, etc.; for typing mathematics see chapter 13). The typist should know that the figure 1 on a typewriter is not a capital *I* but a lowercase *l* and that the zero key (0) is different from that for the letter *o*.

SPACING

2.18   All copy intended for publication should be typed *double space*, or triple space—never single space. Single-spaced material is not only impossible to edit clearly but it is difficult for the typesetter to follow. The rule about double spacing applies to the text and also to block quotations, or extracts, within the text, to footnotes, to appendix material, to bibliographies and indexes—in other words to all parts of the manuscript. Double space means a full blank line *between all typed lines*, not just between notes or between items in a bibliography.

2.19   Generous *margins*—at least an inch—should be left on either side and at the top and bottom of every page. Chapter openings should be at least three inches from the top of the page.

CHAPTER TITLES AND SUBHEADS

2.20   Chapter titles and subheads in the text will be set in a style specified by the book designer. He may decide to have them printed in full capitals or in capitals and lowercase, in italic or in roman or in boldface type. The typist, not knowing what style will be selected, should type them with initial capitals only—that is, capitalize the first letter of each word except prepositions, articles, and coordinate conjunctions. Chapter titles and subheads should not be underlined. It is easier for the editor who marks the manuscript to indicate capitals or italic type than to delete the typed underlining or to lowercase many capitals.

2.21   Subheads of different levels (see par. 1.51) may be differentiated in typescript by their placement on the page. The most important subhead—the *A*-level subhead—may be centered on the page; the second, the *B*-level, subhead may be typed flush left. A subhead that begins a paragraph should be followed by a period. No period follows a subhead typed on a line by itself.

EXTRACTS

2.22   Block quotations, or extracts, should be double-spaced and set off from the text by indenting them a few spaces from the left and leaving extra space above and below. Poetry extracts should be centered on the page, the indention of lines and space between stanzas reflecting the original pattern. An omitted line (or lines) of poetry is indicated by a single line of spaced periods approximately the length of the line above it. (For omissions in prose extracts see pars. 10.20–27, 10.31–35.)

FOOTNOTES

2.23   Footnotes should be typed, double space, on separate sheets, never at the foot of the pages or interlineated with the text. Typing footnotes on separate pages is, incidentally, much easier for the typist than trying to fit them in at the bottom of pages.[4] Each footnote should begin on a new line, with a paragraph indention, and each should end with a period.

4. In dissertations and other academic papers not intended for publication, footnotes are commonly typed single space at the foot of the pages for the convenience of the readers.

2.24 Footnotes to the text are numbered consecutively through each chapter (beginning with 1 for the first note in a chapter). Footnote numbers in the text are typed above the line, with no parentheses, periods, or slash marks. The numbers introducing the footnotes themselves should be typed on the line and followed by a period.

TABLES

2.25 Tables should be typed on pages separate from the text. The word *Table* and the table number, an arabic figure, are centered on a line above the table. The table title is centered on the line(s) below the number. The title should be typed with only initial capital letters— that is, all words should be capitalized except coordinate conjunctions, prepositions, and articles. Table titles, in other words, should never be typed in full capitals, nor should a period follow a title. Explanatory matter applicable to the entire table, such as "In Millions," should be enclosed in parentheses and centered below the title.

2.26 Brief tabular material—not more than, say, four lines and two columns—if it does not include vertical lines, braces, and the like (which cannot easily be set by a Linotype operator), may be typed with the text. Longer lists of one or two columns that may be broken (continued on the next page) should also be typed with the text. Any such matter will be treated as extracts and set in the type size specified for extracts.

2.27 Columns in a table must be precisely aligned; column headings and stub entries must leave no doubt about what belongs with what. All rules must be solid lines, either typed or drawn with a ruler.

2.28 Table footnotes are typed below the table and indicated by symbols or letters (see par. 12.30).

GLOSSARIES AND LISTS OF ABBREVIATIONS

2.29 All words to be defined in a glossary or abbreviations to be explained in a list should be typed flush left, in alphabetical order and with no period following them. Leave about four spaces between the longest word or abbreviation and its definition, and align all definitions. Runover lines in definitions should be indented under the beginning line of the definition. If some definitions contain more than one sentence, all should end with a period. If all definitions are one sentence or less, no periods are used after them.

BIBLIOGRAPHIES AND REFERENCE LISTS

2.30 Each item in a bibliographical list should begin flush left (with no paragraph indention). In entries requiring more than one line, runover lines should be indented about three spaces. All bibliographical material must be typed *double space*, and it is well to leave two blank lines between items.

2.31 Authors' names in an alphabetical list are typed last name first. If several works by the same author are listed, a dash (three or four typed hyphens) is used in place of the author's name for each item following the first. If a period follows the author's name in the first item, a period follows the dash as well. (For capitalization, punctuation, and other matters of bibliographical style see chapter 16.)

INDEXES

2.32 After the indexer's cards or slips have been alphabetized and edited (see pars. 18.48–79), the index should be typed double space, and one column to a page, on regular manuscript pages. The author should retain a copy of his index manuscript and all his index cards until the index has been printed. Typesetters *can* set type from cards, but the process is more costly because of time spent in handling cards and is generally discouraged by publishers. Before shipping his box(es) of index cards, therefore, the author should consult his publisher.

MACHINE COPIES

2.33 As the equivalent of good typescript, most publishers will accept machine copies (such as Xerox) made from clean typescript or from original masters or stencils (such as Multilith or Mimeograph). The image must be crisp, not blurred, and the paper of good quality and suitable for marking with the editor's blue pencil. Xerox copies of printed matter—for anthologies or other works containing excerpts from previously published material—are also acceptable, provided the image is clear and the type lines straight (see par. 2.118). Xerox or other machine copies of artwork are not acceptable unless the artwork is to be redrawn.

CORRECTIONS

2.34   An author who can check his final typescript without wanting to make at least a few changes is a rare bird indeed. Last-minute changes on a manuscript are quite acceptable to publisher and printer, provided the author shows consideration for those who must read his alterations.

2.35   An added or altered word or phrase may be written—in ink and in a legible hand (not printed in capital letters)—directly *above* the manuscript line where it is to be inserted. Words, sentences, or whole paragraphs may be deleted by a firm line drawn through them. Pages containing such corrections need not be retyped.

2.36   Corrections too lengthy to be written above the line must be typed and inserted where they belong. The best way to insert such material is to cut the page where the insertion is to be made and paste, or tape,[5] the pieces of text in the desired order on fresh sheets of paper. Because of the typesetting process it is highly desirable that all manuscript material in a given type size, such as the text, be arranged in the order in which it is to be printed. And although all pages of a manuscript should be the same size, the amount of material on them may vary from page to page. It is not necessary to renumber pages of an entire manuscript as a result of a few added pages, but any added page should bear an indication of where it belongs—two extra pages between pages 24 and 25, for example, should be numbered 24a and 24b.

2.37   Corrections made on manuscripts in any of the following ways are *unacceptable* to most publishers and printers:

> Writing or typing on the reverse of pages
> Writing up or down the margins
> Typing inserts on slips attached to pages
> Pasting an addition to the bottom of a page and folding it up
> Directing the typesetter to insert a passage from another page
> Writing illegibly or with blurred pencil

The physical appearance of a well-prepared manuscript will attest not only to the typist's skill but to the author's concern about the accuracy and grace of his finished work as well as his awareness of the requirements of the publishing process.

5. It is best to use transparent tape with a dull finish that can be written upon with a pencil; staples, pins, or paper clips should never be used to fasten manuscript material intended for a printer.

CORRELATING PARTS OF A MANUSCRIPT

2.38   References in one part of a manuscript to other parts of the manuscript provide a fertile ground for error, as any copy editor well knows. The careful author will check his *final* typescript for any discrepancies that may have crept in during the various stages of preparation. It is also the duty of the manuscript editor to check all such references and to query the author regarding any discrepancies found in them.

TABLE OF CONTENTS AND CHAPTER TITLES

2.39   The table of contents lists the titles of all sections of the book (see pars. 1.26–28) and must therefore be checked against the text to see that the wording is identical in both places and that nothing has been omitted from the table of contents. If a later decision is made to alter a chapter title, to add or delete an appendix, the change must also be made in the table of contents.

2.40   Manuscript page numbers in the table of contents are sometimes helpful to the publisher and his readers. If the author supplies them, however, the editor must remember to circle them before the manuscript goes to the typesetter so that they will not be set. The printed page numbers will of course be quite different and cannot be added to the table of contents until the entire book is in page proofs. Page numbers to be supplied are normally indicated by zeros (000) in manuscript and galley proofs.

CROSS-REFERENCES

2.41   Any reference in the text to a specific part of the work—a chapter, a section, an appendix—should be verified. A chapter number, or its title, may have been changed or an appendix dropped after the author made reference to it. References to tables, figures, or plates must be checked carefully against the actual table or figure. Cross-references in the footnotes, from one note to another, are especially hazardous because footnotes are frequently renumbered in the course of preparing a manuscript.

2.42   Cross-references to specific pages in a book should be kept to a minimum. They cannot be filled in until pages have been made up, and then, in Linotype composition, an entire line must be reset to accommodate each one—a costly process. Wherever possible it is best to refer, if reference must be made, to a chapter or a section.

An author addicted to multiple cross-references of this sort might do well to ask himself whether he has organized his material as efficiently as possible and whether his reader would not rather use the index to find related material than have his reading interrupted by frequent admonitions to turn to another page. If the author feels that a page reference is absolutely necessary, he indicates it by zeros or dashes (e.g., see p. 000) not by manuscript page number. Zeros in the text not only alert the proofreader to the fact that a number is to be inserted in final page proof but also reserve space in the printed line for that number. Some printers use black en quads for this purpose. If someone other than the author is to insert the page numbers in the page proofs, the author should give the appropriate manuscript page number, and circle it, in the margin of his manuscript next to the line including the reference.

FOOTNOTES AND FOOTNOTE REFERENCES

2.43   In a work containing numbered notes to the text—either at the foot of the pages or at the back of the book—there must of course be a number in the text referring to each note and a note corresponding to each number. Obvious as this seems, all notes should be checked against the text to make sure that every note has a corresponding number in the text and that each note is the one intended for that spot in the text. Note numbers are often inadvertently omitted when a manuscript is retyped, and the sequence of notes may be affected by any rearranging of material. No note should have more than one text reference to it, and no two notes should bear the same number, such as 15 and 15*a*.

NOTES AND BIBLIOGRAPHIES

2.44   In a work containing both footnotes and a bibliography, sources cited in the notes should be checked against the bibliography. If the same source appears in both places, the footnote citation may be shortened (see par. 15.9). The author's name and the title of the work must be spelled and punctuated the same way in both places.

TEXT REFERENCES AND BIBLIOGRAPHIES

2.45   In a work using the system of citing references in parentheses in the text (see par. 16.46), each citation must be checked against the bibliography or the list of references, where it should appear in full. The author's name and the date of publication must agree.

TABLES AND TEXT

2.46 Tables typed or pasted on separate sheets must be marked with the manuscript page number of the text that each is to accompany. The manuscript text page also must have the table number noted in the margin next to the passage where the author wishes it to appear in the printed book. A table is usually placed near the first reference to it. Text references to tables must be by table number, not by a phrase such as *the following table* or *the above table*. Nor should a colon be used to introduce a table. In making up pages the printer may not be able to put a table exactly where the author wants it, but he will put it as close to the spot as possible.

2.47 A final check of tables in a manuscript will ascertain that (1) they are numbered consecutively (through the entire book or through each chapter), (2) that each bears the manuscript page of the relevant text, and (3) that the placement of each is accounted for by a marginal directive in the text. If there is a list of tables in the front of the book, this should also be checked against the tables themselves (see par. 1.32).

ILLUSTRATIONS, LEGENDS, AND TEXT

2.48 Line drawings—figures to be printed with the text—are handled in much the same way as tables, described above. Marginal notes in the text (e.g., fig. 1, fig. 2) must indicate where each belongs. Since, unlike table titles, figure legends (titles) are typed on pages separate from the figures themselves, each drawing must bear a penciled notation showing the figure number and the manuscript page number of the text passage where it belongs. Such notations should of course never be written within the boundaries of the drawing itself, but in the upper or lower margins. If the figure is a glossy print, the notation may be written either with a grease pencil in the outside margin or with a plain soft pencil very lightly on the back of the print. Care should be taken that no mark made on the back of a print shows through on the front, for it will mar the finished work.

2.49 In a letterpress book, halftone illustrations must usually be printed on paper of a quality different from that used for the text. They cannot therefore be placed at specific spots in the text but must be inserted between, or wrapped around, signatures of text (see fig. 11.1). If such illustrations are referred to in the text, they

37

are usually called *plates* and numbered consecutively. They may
be called figures only if there are no line drawings or other figures
to be printed with the text, because they cannot be numbered consecutively with text figures. If they are not referred to in the text,
they need not be numbered in the printed book. For identification
by editor and printer, however, each illustration and its legend
must be numbered—very lightly on the back of each print and a
circled number next to each legend. Also, if there is any room for
doubt, the word *top* should be written at the top, either front or
back, of an illustration.

2.50 A final check of illustrations will ascertain that each has a legend
and that each bears a number corresponding to that of its legend.
If there is a list of illustrations in the front of the book, this too
should be checked against the legends of the illustrations (see
pars. 1.29–31).

ABBREVIATIONS

2.51 If a list of abbreviations is included in a book (see par. 1.40), any
abbreviation used in notes, bibliography, or elsewhere should be
checked against the list. If an author intends to abbreviate a title,
he should do so consistently, neither spelling it out occasionally
nor using more than one form of abbreviation for it. Other indications, aside from a list of abbreviations, of intent to abbreviate—
such as "hereafter cited as . . . " (see par. 15.44)—should also be
checked by the author and the editor: are all subsequent references
indeed abbreviated, or shortened, as the author stipulates?

PUBLISHER TO AUTHOR

2.52 After a manuscript has been accepted for publication, the various
processes entailed in making it into a book may commence. The
carbon, or second, copy goes to the production department for
design and cost estimate. The first copy, the one from which type
will be set, goes to the editorial department where it is assigned to
a manuscript editor, sometimes called a copy editor (here called
simply the editor).

2.53 The editor will send the edited manuscript back to the author,
either in parts or all at once, usually letting the author know in
advance when he may expect it. When he receives the manuscript,
the author should answer all queries from the editor written in the
margins of the manuscript pages, on a separate query sheet, or in

38

the editor's covering letter. He should also read the manuscript again with an eye for any changes he might wish to make in it. Any final alterations in the text, any rechecking of quoted material, should be done at this stage of the publishing process. Alterations made after type is set—on galley or page proofs—are costly and time-consuming, and often result in errors in the finished book. Hence the publisher's fervent wish that an author return his edited manuscript with all final changes on it. (For author's alterations on proofs, and charges therefor, see pars. 3.31–35.)

2.54 When the editor sends the manuscript to the author, he will give a date, a *deadline*, by which he expects it back from the author. The author must meet this deadline, or if he knows it will be impossible for him, he should notify his editor at once. His manuscript is by this time usually scheduled to go to the printer on a specific date, promised by the editor to the production department, and if the author misses his deadline his book must be rescheduled (see par. 3.5).

2.55 Finally, in checking his edited manuscript the author should realize that the publisher's editor is his ally. The editor is usually the first person, after the author and his typist, to read every letter, every word, every mark of punctuation in the manuscript. His editorial eye is likely to catch discrepancies in style and sometimes facts, faulty syntax, unclear phrasing, ambiguous pronouns, and other matters often overlooked by an author.

THE EDITORIAL FUNCTION

2.56 The editor's duties are, in general, twofold. First, he (more often she) tries to carry out the author's wishes and edit the manuscript to his satisfaction. Second, the editor marks the manuscript following the designer's layout—often working with the designer in the process—and sees that all parts of the manuscript are easily readable by the printer's typesetter. The editor thus becomes the liaison between the author and the production department. But his first and most important job is to edit the manuscript. What does this mean?

MECHANICAL EDITING

2.57 The editorial function is in effect two processes. The first, for want of a better term, may be called *mechanical* editing, though no machine has yet been devised to do it. The process involves a close reading of the manuscript with an eye to such matters as consistency of capitalization, spelling, and hyphenation; agreement of verbs and subjects; beginning and ending quotation marks and parentheses; number of ellipsis points; numbers given as figures or written out; and many other details of style.

STYLE

2.58 The word *style* means two things to an editor. The first meaning is that implied in the title *A Manual of Style*. Publishers refer to style in this sense as *house style* or *press style*—rules regarding the mechanics of written communication detailed in part 2 of this manual. Authors more often think of style in its other sense, as a way of writing, of literary expression. Editors are of course also aware of this meaning of style when they undertake the second, nonmechanical process of editing.

SUBSTANTIVE EDITING

2.59 This second editorial process may be called *substantive* editing— rewriting, reorganizing, or suggesting other ways to present material. The editor will know by instinct and learn from experience when and how much of this kind of editing to do on a particular manuscript. An experienced editor will never inflict his own way of writing on an author who has a quite different style. He will recognize, and not tamper with, unusual figures of speech and idiomatic usage. He will know when to make an editorial change and when simply to suggest it, when to delete a repetition and when simply to point it out to the author, and many other matters. Since every manuscript is unique in the amount and kind of substantive editing desirable, no rules can be devised for the editor to follow. Except for certain magazine publishers, no publishing house has a *house literary style*.

COPY EDITING

2.60 Copy editing—also, mainly in newspaper offices, called *copy-reading*—is the editor's most important and most time-consuming task. It requires close attention to every detail in a manuscript, a thorough knowledge of what to look for and of the style to be followed,[6] and the ability to make quick, logical, and defensible decisions.

6. For rules regarding style see the chapters in part 2 of this manual.

Editing a manuscript from which type is to be set requires a (different method) than that used in correcting proof. A correction or an operational sign are is inserted in a line of type or above not in the margins as in proof reading. The operator follows each looks at every line of the manuscript as he sets type and so any editors change must be in its proper place and clearly written.

Specific marks

A caret between two words shows where additional material is to be inserted. three lines under a lowercase letter tell the typesetter to make it a capital; 2 lines mean a small capital (A.D. 90); one line means italic; a wavy line means boldface; and a stroke through a capital letter means lowercase. Unwanted underlining in a manuscript is taken out thus. A small circle around a comma indicates changes it to a period. A straight line between parts of a closed compound word will make it two words—to be doubly sure, use a space mark as well; two short parallel lines mean a hyphen in copy edited manuscript.

A circle around an abbrev or a figure tells the typesetter to spell it out (abbreviations ambiguous or not likely to be recognized by a typesetter should be spelled out by the editor [Biol.=Biology or Biological; gen.=gender, genitive, or genus], as should figures that might be spelled more than one way [2500=twenty-five hundred or two thousand five hundred].) Dots under a crossed-out word or passage mean stet (let it stand). Whenever it is ambiguous, an end-of-line hyphen should be underlined or crossed out so that the printer's typesetter will know whether to keep the hyphen in the typeset line or to close up the word. Dashes other than hyphens should always be marked; otherwise a hyphen may appear between continuing numbers such as 15-25 (see p. 125).   (2)

Ink or Pencil

Typesetters prefer ink to pencil for editorial changes: faint pencil marks are indicative of the "timid editor." Green ink is favored by editors who dare to make changes boldly. Editors who use colored pencil (because erasing is easier than with ink) must write so that the typesetter can see what they have done.

Fig. 2.1. Example of edited manuscript

2.61   Most editors prefer to read quickly through a manuscript before they begin editing it. The kind, and amount, of editing to be done depends on the nature of the material, the audience for whom it is intended, and the author's skill in preparing his manuscript—all factors that can be determined by a first reading, or sampling. Also helpful to the editor before he begins editing are correspondence between author and publisher and any readers' reports on the manuscript. These should be examined for comments applicable to the editing. The editor should of course know whether the manuscript is part of a series with a particular style of its own. And, certainly, if the manuscript is, say, volume 4 of an author's magnum opus, the first three volumes of which may have been published a number of years before, the editor will, insofar as possible, follow the style of the earlier volumes, regardless of current changes in house style.

ESTIMATING TIME

2.62   In many publishing houses editors are required to estimate the amount of time they will need to complete the editing on each manuscript. No editor should attempt such an estimate until he has actually begun work on a manuscript. The appearance of a manuscript may be deceptive; a cleanly typed manuscript may prove to be full of flaws, whereas a visually untidy manuscript, with many alterations, may be eminently readable and leave little for the editor to do. Until he has edited to his satisfaction at least twenty-five pages of an average manuscript and closely examined the footnotes and other apparatus, the editor cannot, with any degree of accuracy, prophesy how many hours the whole will take.

QUERIES TO AUTHORS

2.63   What to ask an author about his manuscript—and how and when to query him—is an important part of editing. First, the editor should not usually query matters of house style—capitalization, spelling, etc. If, however, the editor has found it necessary to lowercase words consistently capitalized by the author, it might be well to explain in his covering letter why he has done so; and if there are many such editorial changes, the editor may want to send the author a copy of his *style sheet* (see par. 2.72). But where the editor has not changed the author's pattern of capitalization, etc., but has only tried to bring consistency to the manuscript, no mention need be made of these details.

2.64 Second, the editor should avoid writing long notes explaining his changes. Most authors readily understand, and appreciate, an editorial correction of a dangling modifier, a misplaced pronoun, a repeated word or phrase, a misalliance between subject and verb, and the like. An editor should of course know why he makes any such emendation but should not explain it unless challenged by the author.

2.65 Third, no query to an author should sound stupid, naïve, or pedantic. Nor should a query be phrased so that it seems to reflect upon the author's scholarly ability or powers of interpretation. Humorous remarks, even when addressed to an author the editor knows will appreciate them, are generally better omitted. Every author has a right to expect conscientious, intelligent help from his editor. Unintelligent queries, as well as sloppy editing, will quite rightly make him lose faith in his editor and prejudice him against the publisher as well.

2.66 The editor should call the author's attention to any discrepancies in facts. For example, if a meeting is said, on page 13, to have taken place on 10 May 1896, and the same meeting is mentioned on page 87 as occurring in 1897, the editor (if he is sharp-eyed enough to catch it) will lightly circle each date and will write "1897? see p. 87" in the margin of page 13, and, on page 87, "1896? see p. 13." Similarly, possibly unintentional repetition of material, sometimes on widely separated pages, should be pointed out: "Repetition intentional? see p. 25." A missing quotation mark or footnote reference number: "Where does quote begin?" "Where is fn. 87?" Or, if the editor inserts the missing item where he thinks it belongs and wants the author to verify it: "OK?"

2.67 Some editors prefer to write queries not in the margins of the manuscript but on separate slips, or fliers, that are gummed on one end so that they can be attached to the underside of the edge of a manuscript page. The slips are detached by the editor after the author returns the edited manuscript and before it goes to the printer. The advantage of this method is that the margins of the manuscript remain clean; thus, in a manuscript requiring many queries or many suggestions for sentence revision, it is usually better to use separate slips (pins, not paper clips or staples, may be used if the slips are not gummed). The disadvantage is that the author may detach the slips, with or without answering the question, and the editor thus has no record of what he queried. A second possible disadvantage is that, after the editor has removed the slips and sent the manuscript to the printer, a proofreader may ask the same question on the galley proofs, not knowing that the author has already given an answer.

2.68   Whichever method of querying an author is used—slips or marginal notes—the editor should always ask the author *not* to detach slips or *not* to erase any queries. When the manuscript is returned by the author, the editor, as he checks the author's answers, will detach any slips or cross out any marginal queries before releasing the manuscript for typesetting.

2.69   Manuscripts requiring extensive revision—heavy rewriting, deleting, rearranging—that has not been agreed upon by the author before the editor begins his work demand a more cautious approach. The editor may send a preliminary letter explaining his proposed editorial changes and how he thinks they will improve the manuscript. He may then send one or two edited chapters and wait for the author's approval of these before proceeding with the entire manuscript.

2.70   The editor will save time later if, while the editing progresses, he notes on a separate piece of paper any general questions, suggestions, or explanations he may wish to incorporate in his letter to the author accompanying the edited manuscript.

EDITING TEXT

2.71   An editor will usually edit one kind of material at a time, beginning with the text. (Footnotes should be edited together, tables together, legends together, because to edit similar matter in a manuscript in a continuous process lessens the chance of variations in style.)[7] To check spelling and meaning in editing the text the editor must have a dictionary at his elbow and other reference works nearby. The spelling of unfamiliar names and words should be checked, as well as some commonly misspelled familiar ones (e.g., Apennines, Pyrenees, stratagem, improvise).

2.72   *Style sheet.* In addition to checking reference works, to ensure consistency in the style used in a particular manuscript, the editor usually finds it helpful if not imperative to keep for each manu-

---

7. This system is of course impractical for a long manuscript such as a book of readings or a collection of papers that goes through the publishing process in separate sections.

script a running account of special words to be capitalized, odd spellings, compound words with or without hyphens, and the like. For easy reference this style sheet should be in rough alphabetical order, and the manuscript page number of at least the first occurrence of a word should be noted beside it. If there is any chance that the editorial mind will change late in the manuscript—say, about hyphenating a particular compound—it is well to note the page number of each occurrence. One, and perhaps the tidiest, way to keep such an editor's style sheet is to rule off a blank page allowing enough space (a guess) for each letter of the alphabet. The abbreviated sample style sheet shown in figure 2.2 may serve as an example. The editor should consult and add to his style sheet throughout the copy-editing process, remembering that a word added from the middle or end of a manuscript may well have escaped his attention in earlier pages. A final, quick rereading of the entire manuscript is desirable to catch any such slips. The style sheet should also be consulted in editing discursive footnotes and legends to illustrations and in checking names on maps, words in figures, tables, and the like.

2.73   A style sheet not only aids the editor's memory while he is actually editing a manuscript. It may be indispensable in the later stages of production. Few editors can give their time exclusively to one manuscript. An editor is usually responsible for at least six and often twenty or so manuscripts in various stages of production. He cannot be expected to remember the particular style for each when he checks the manuscript returned from the author, the galley proofs, the page proofs, the index, months after editing the original. Also, another editor may have to substitute for him at some stage of production, and that editor will need to know the style followed. Therefore, the style sheet should remain in the editor's file until the book is bound.

2.74   *Watching for lapses.* In addition to regularizing details of style, the editor is expected to catch errors or infelicities of expression that mar an author's prose. Such matters include dangling modifiers, unclear antecedents, redundancies, split infinitives (a debatable "error"), lack of agreement of verb with subject, faulty attempts at parallel construction, misplaced modifiers, overuse of an author's pet word or phrase, unintentional repetition of words, and so on. He should also consider, insofar as possible, the logical flow of argument and suggest moving a sentence or a paragraph, deleting irrelevant material, or adding a transitional sentence where he thinks such emendations would improve the sequence of

ABCD Article 20 of the constitution (ber.) 14 chief executive 17 Bundestag 19 about-face 21 Allies 25	MNOP parliament 3 power-seeker 14 ministry of education 26 Philistine 37 neonationalism 41 Napoleonic wars 45 the occupation 50
EFGH grass-roots party 7 Free Democrat 10 eastern zone 15 5 percent clause 30 great-power status 31 Great Powers 32	QRST troublemakers 6 Stone Age 9 Realpolitik 13 rightists 18 Red menace 21
IJKL imperial monarchy 5 kaiser 6 ICBM's 31 insofar 40	UVWXYZ Western tradition 4 well-being 5 Zeitgeist 27 worldwide 86 un-Christian 88

Fig. 2.2. Manuscript editor's style sheet

thought. Also, special terms or little-known persons should usual-ly be defined or identified the first time they appear in the book; and first names of persons should normally be given the first time they are mentioned. The editor must here recognize that a term unfamiliar to him may be commonly accepted in the author's field and thus need no definition for prospective readers. And first names of well-known persons (e.g., Disraeli, Shakespeare) should not be inserted by an editor.

2.75   *Subheads.* Subheads in the text should be checked for uniformity and pertinence. Does each give an accurate indication of what is in the following text? Are they too long and can they be short-ened? Does the first sentence of text following a subhead refer to a word in the subhead without repeating it? (See par. 1.57.)

2.76   *Cross-references.* All references in the text to tables, charts, figures, maps, appendixes, lists of references, or other parts of the book should be verified by the editor, even if the author has also done so (see pars. 2.38–49). If the author, for example, mentions the gross national product for 1965 in the text and refers the reader to table 4, which the editor finds gives figures only through 1964, the editor should query the author about the discrepancy. Again for ex-ample, place names on a map intended to illustrate the text must be spelled as they are in the text. When an author uses an exces-sive number of cross-references to specific pages, the editor should advise him of the desirability of eliminating most of them (see par. 2.42).

2.77   Some authors need to be discouraged from distracting the reader and interrupting the subject matter by frequent remarks on the structure of their work—the "this is what I did earlier in my book, this is what I am doing now, and this is what I will do later" syndrome. A clear organization of material, a good index, and, where absolutely necessary, a footnote reference to relevant ma-terial elsewhere in the book will obviate the need for any such remarks in the text.

2.78   *Quotations.* Aside from adjusting quotation marks and ellipsis points to conform to house style (see pars. 10.20–27, 10.31–35), the editor must do nothing to material quoted by an author from an-other source. Interpolations (in square brackets) by the author and translations by the author of foreign language material, however, may be edited for style. Misspelled words and apparent errors in transcribing a quotation (obvious omission of a word, for ex-ample) should be queried to the author.

47

EDITING FOOTNOTES

2.79 In editing manuscripts with many footnote citations it is helpful to keep a separate list, arranged by chapter and note number, of the first citation of each work. The last name of the author is usually sufficient here. To provide a shortened form for subsequent citations to a work it is often necessary to check its first appearance, which is easy to find if the editor has noted it on his list.

2.80 The editor must be sure that every reference to a work is given the same way. Shortened titles or abbreviations, for example, once decided upon, must be the same every time they appear. If a volume number is given with one or more references to a journal, the volume number should be given for every reference to that journal.

2.81 Before making sweeping changes affecting the style of an author's footnotes, the editor is often well advised to consult the author, explaining his reasons for wishing to make such changes and obtaining his concurrence. An author who has prepared his notes with meticulous care, with the necessary information in each citation and consistency of style throughout, is likely to be dismayed by editorial efforts to force house style upon his work. In such cases the author should be allowed to keep his own style (unless his work is part of a volume containing chapters by other authors as well and thus a variety of styles that must be made uniform). In other cases the author and editor may work out a compromise system acceptable to both.[8]

2.82 Discursive material in footnotes is edited like the text and should be read as carefully as the text. The editor should ask the author to cut any excessively long note, either by deleting material in it or by adding parts of it to the text. The chief reason for cutting long footnotes, apart from the reader's possible annoyance and the effect on the printed page, is the makeup problem caused by runover footnotes. Long lists, long tables, and the like are better placed in the text or in an appendix.

2.83 The editor should always check footnote reference numbers in the text against the footnotes themselves. Checking the numbers, or renumbering footnotes, should be an operation in itself. If the editor attempts to renumber footnotes while editing the text or the notes, he runs the risk of skipping or repeating a number. When

8. For detailed rules about footnote style and examples see chapter 15.

renumbering is necessary, the old number should be crossed out and the new one inserted in the text and before the footnote simultaneously.

2.84   An editor's judgment is sometimes helpful to an author unsure or careless about his use of citations. The source of any direct quotation in a scholarly text should be made clear to the reader, either in what the author says about it in the text or in a note. Paraphrases of other writers' ideas should be acknowledged and sources of little-known facts given. Well-known facts, easily ascertainable from many sources, of course need no documentation. The editor, however, must be cautious and entirely sure of his ground before asking an author to alter his documentation.

2.85   In a work containing a bibliography as well as footnotes, each citation in the notes should be checked against the bibliography. Any discrepancy in spelling, date of publication, and the like should either be resolved by the editor or queried for the author's attention. Since works peripheral to the subject of the manuscript may be cited in a note but, quite properly, not listed in the bibliography, the editor should not question the omission of such items from the bibliography. His function is to see that a source not in the bibliography is given with full bibliographical details in the note. Nor should an editor try to determine whether every entry in a bibliography is cited somewhere in the notes, even when the author titles his bibliography "Works Cited."

EDITING BIBLIOGRAPHIES

2.86   The editor's task in editing a bibliography or reference list is to make each entry conform to the same style: the order of the items in each entry, the capitalization of titles, abbreviations, punctuation.[9] Alphabetically arranged lists should be checked to see that every entry is in the right place. If the list is chronological, the dates should be checked, and so on. Discrepancies or omissions found in correlating source citations in the text or footnotes with the bibliography should be queried and the manuscript page number of the citation in question given so that the author can easily compare the two.

EDITING TABLES

2.87   If the author has typed his tables on pages with his text, the editor should cut them out and paste them on separate pages, making

9. For various bibliographical styles see chapter 16.

sure that he puts the text page number on the new page containing the table and the number of the table in the margin of the text page. If the author has prepared his tables on separate pages, the editor need only check to see that the author has noted the placement of each in his text.

2.88 The editor will then check for uniformity of style in tables containing similar material: wording in titles, box headings, and stub entries; abbreviations; use of leaders; and other matters.[10] The sequence of symbols or letters referring to footnotes should be noted (see par. 12.30). Commas may need to be added in figures of four or more digits, columns brought into proper alignment, vertical or horizontal lines drawn or deleted, and so on. And sometimes the editor will find it necessary to recast an entire table to provide a clearer representation of its material.

PREPARING ILLUSTRATIONS AND LEGENDS

2.89 When an author fails to identify his illustrations or to type legends on separate sheets, the editor must do so for him (see par. 2.48). The editor will often find it convenient to have a copy of the legends in his file for future reference; he may in some instances have to check engraver's proofs of the illustrations without the printer's proofs of the legends, for example.

2.90 The editor should examine the illustrations themselves, primarily to see that the spelling of words and names, the form of figures, and the like agree with the style used in the text. He may also work with the production department on cropping and scaling illustrations, arranging them on a page, and so on. If a map or other illustration containing words to be set in type must be redrawn, the editor will usually provide a typed list of all such words. Place names on a map should be arranged by category—countries, states, cities, rivers, mountains, etc.—since each category will be set in a different type size.[11]

PREPARING FRONT MATTER

2.91 The editor normally provides copy for the half title of a book, the series title, if any, and the copyright page. To prepare the copyright page, the editor needs to read the contract to determine the copyright holder and to examine any correspondence between au-

10. For various styles used in setting tables see chapter 12.
11. For further suggestions on illustrations and legends see chapter 11.

thor and publisher relating to permissions, translations, new editions, and the like. Any oversight or inaccuracy on the copyright page is attributable to the editor, not to the author. Often the editor will need to retype (or supply) copy for the title page, table of contents, and list of illustrations. The editor should check the table of contents carefully to see that it includes all parts of the manuscript (including the index) and that the wording of titles matches that of the text.[12]

2.92 *Numbering.* The manuscript pages of front matter should be arranged in the order in which they will appear in the printed book. Any missing part should be indicated by a sheet of paper inserted at the appropriate point and marked with the name of what is missing (e.g., "Dedication to come"; "Preface approx. 3 MS pp. to come"). The pages up to and including the first page of the table of contents are numbered with lowercase roman numerals, usually at the *foot* of the page, circled, since they are not to be printed. Blank pages are noted also; if, for example, page ii is blank, the half-title page would be marked "p. i (p. ii blank)." Where an editor cannot determine what page an element (such as the preface) will fall on when the pages are made up, the words *recto page* on the first manuscript page will tell the printer how to paginate it. (Normally, each element of the prelims following the copyright page begins on a recto page.) The manuscript pages of a preface or foreword are also numbered serially in the usual way, but with some flag to prevent their being taken for text pages (e.g., "Pref.-1, Pref.-2, Pref.-3, etc.").

2.93 In place of any material not yet received from the author, the editor should insert a sheet indicating what is to come and, if possible, when. Front matter often goes straight into pages (no galleys), and the printer needs to know about any missing matter so that he can allow for it in paging the front matter.

EDITING INDEXES

2.94 When the index manuscript arrives on the editor's desk, he should edit and mark it for the printer at once. The rest of the book is now in pages, some of it perhaps even being printed, and the index must be set in type as soon as possible. If the author has prepared his index in a logical fashion, the editor need only check alphabetization of main entries and cross-references, arrangement

12. For sequence and form of preliminary pages see chapter 1.

of subentries, sequence of page numbers ("74–74" or "85, 50, 97" obviously require consulting the pages cited), and punctuation in each entry. If the index is excessively long or so illogically planned that it would be difficult to use, the editor is in trouble. He must either repair the matter himself as quickly as possible or again consult the author. Specific instructions given an author *before* he prepares his index, will usually, but not always, prevent such traumatic editorial experiences.[13] To aid the printer, the editor should note, on the first page of the index manuscript, the page in the book on which the index begins (i.e., the recto folio following the last number of the page proofs).

SENDING MANUSCRIPT TO AUTHOR

2.95   An edited manuscript is a unique copy of that manuscript, representing a considerable investment of editorial time and thought. It must not be lost. A manuscript sent by mail should be carefully wrapped with cardboard and strong wrapping paper, sealed, marked for first-class mail, and insured or registered. Illustrations should not be returned to the author, unless there is a question about them, until proof is ready for him to check.

COVERING LETTER

2.96   The editor will send, with the manuscript or separately, a letter containing any needed explanation of what he has done to the manuscript, general questions about the manuscript, and a request that the author answer all queries in the margins of the manuscript itself. The author will also need to know by what specific date he is expected to return the manuscript to the editor and, if possible, approximately when he may expect galley proofs. The editor should inquire to what address the author wants his proofs sent and tell him how many sets of galleys and pages he will receive (he may require more than the customary number). Finally, if it is the author's first book, the editor may offer to send him suggestions about preparing his index before that stage arrives in the production process. A well-written, gracious, and informative letter accompanying a carefully edited manuscript will assure an author of the editor's ability and concern for his book and therefore make for easy cooperation between editor and author throughout the publishing process.

13. For suggestions on index style see chapter 18.

MARKING FOR THE PRINTER

2.97   In many publishing houses, including the University of Chicago Press, the editor marks the manuscript with type specifications indicated on the designer's layout (see chap. 19) or from a list of specifications furnished by the designer. Care must be exercised to follow the specifications exactly and to mark like parts alike. The layout does not show all parts of a book but does give a sample of each type size to be used in text and display matter.

TYPE SPECIFICATIONS

2.98   The type size, leading, typeface, and type width to be used in the text proper should be written in the margin of the first page of each chapter or other division of text. The type size and leading and amount of indention, if any, should be placed beside the first extract in each chapter. Poetry extracts, unless the design specifies otherwise, are generally marked "center on longest line." If all material to be set as extracts is marked carefully with a red vertical line at the left, it is not necessary to mark type sizes for extracts after the first in each chapter. Similarly, the type specifications for the subheads need to be marked only at the first occurrence of each level in a chapter, if all subheads are marked *A*, *B*, etc.—the letter circled—to indicate which level is intended. An italic subhead that begins a paragraph (run-in side head) should not be marked, except to be underlined for italics, since it will be set in the same type size as the text. In marking and designating the levels of subheads, the editor should (1) check the capitalization of the subhead, (2) delete a period or other punctuation following a subhead set on a line by itself, (3) mark the placement of the subhead (center, flush left, etc.), and (4) mark the first line of text following a subhead if the design calls for it to begin flush left or with an indention other than that used for a regular paragraph.

2.99   If a manuscript has footnotes typed on text pages, a blue vertical line at the left of each note will tell the printer what is to be set as a footnote, and the type size needs to be given only with the first note in each chapter. Footnotes typed on separate pages need no blue line; the type size should be given at the beginning of each chapter's notes. An unnumbered footnote to be set on the first page of a chapter should be labeled as such. The editor should indicate also whether footnote numbers are to be superior or on the line, whether each note begins with a paragraph indention or flush left, whether any extra space is to be inserted between notes, and the length of any rule to be set above notes on a page.

2.100   Each line of a chapter opening (chapter number, title, etc.) should be marked for type size and placement, and any ornamental rule or other device used in the design should be noted on the manuscript. The first line of a chapter often begins flush left or with a special indention or with a display initial, any of which should be indicated in each chapter opening. Where small caps are specified for the initial word or phrase of a chapter, the editor should indicate how much is to be set in small caps by drawing two lines below.

2.101   Bibliographies, indexes, and any other matter to be set in flush-and-hang style should be marked for the amount of indention of runover lines—"flush and hang runovers 1 em," for example. Material to be set in outline style (see par. 8.39) should be marked "outline style" in addition to any special type designations (outlines in the text may often be set in a reduced type size specified for extracts). "Outline style" will tell the typesetter to set any runover lines flush with the first word of the line above.

IDENTIFICATION AND PLACEMENT OF MATERIAL

2.102   When a manuscript goes to a printer it is usually separated into parts for both the typesetting and proofreading processes. The printer will mark parts so divided with his own job number or other identification, but it is helpful to all concerned, including the editor himself, to have identification marked by the editor at the top right corner of the first page of each chapter or other part of the manuscript. The author's last name and the part are usually sufficient: "Jones, chap. 3," "Jones, Bibliog." At the bottom of the last page of text of a chapter or other part the editor may write "End chap. 3." At the end of the last chapter he should tell the printer what follows in the book: "End chap. 10. Appendix A follows," for example. Each section of the back matter should be so marked, and the last page of the last section of a book should indicate whether an index is to come: "End Bibliog., Index to follow," or, for example, "End chap. 15 & book. *No* index." All such notes to the printer should be circled, indicating that they are not to be set in type.

2.103   In marking the manuscript for the printer, the editor should also make sure that the placement of every table and figure is clearly indicated. Footnotes, having corresponding reference numbers in the text, need not be marked for placement in the manuscript, other than indicating the chapter number at the head of each group of notes.

NUMBERING PAGES

2.104   If the author has not numbered his manuscript pages consecutively, the editor must do so (see pars. 2.8–11). If the author has numbered his pages, the editor should check the numbers and indicate to the printer any added or missing page numbers. For example, two pages added after page 54 are numbered 54*a* and 54*b;* on page 54, next to the page number, the editor notes: "54*a–b* follow." Similarly, if, say, pages 22–24 have been deleted, a note should be written on page 21: "p. 25 follows."

2.105   The editor should always note on the manuscript where the arabic folios are to begin in the book. A part title or a second half title preceding the text counts as page 1, and page 2 is normally blank. The editor will therefore mark the part title with a figure 1 at the bottom of the page, circling the number to indicate that it is not to be set, and will also, on the same page, note "p. 2 blank." The first page of the text will then be marked "folio 3," indicating to the printer that 3 is the first folio to be set. If there is no part title or half title, the editor should indicate the beginning of the arabic folios by writing "folio 1" on the first page of text. The proofreader will normally transfer such notations to the galley proofs.

EDITOR TO PRINTER

2.106   In addition to the manuscript edited and marked with type specifications, the editor should supply on separate sheets any special information that will aid the typesetter, compositor, and proofreader in the production of a particular manuscript. Such material includes spine (and cover) copy, running heads, list of special characters, style sheet for the proofreader, and a transmittal sheet telling what is included and what is yet to come.

SPINE COPY

2.107   The layout should be consulted for what the designer has specified for the stamping on the spine of the cloth cover and for what, if anything, is planned for the front cover. The editor then prepares copy accordingly.[14] Copy must also be prepared for the spine and cover of the book jacket. Normally the editor furnishes copy only for the author's name, title of the book, and the publisher's name. The sales or publicity department provides flap copy and any other material for the front and back of a jacket. If the layout gives no specification for the spine, the editor will supply copy anyway, giving the last name of the author, the main title of the book, and the publisher's name, usually in shortened form ("Chicago" instead of "The University of Chicago Press").

RUNNING HEADS

2.108   The editor must provide copy from which running heads will be set.[15] This is usually typed in two columns, one for verso, the other for recto running heads. A running head for any preliminary matter that will occupy more than one printed page must be included, as well as the running head for the index. Since, except in special cases provided for by the designer, a running head must be short enough to fit in a single line, usually containing the page number (folio) as well, the editor must often shorten a title to fit. To do this he must first determine from the designer's layout how many characters (letters, punctuation marks, and spaces between words) he is allowed for the running head. Second, he must select the most meaningful words in a title, considering the subject of the entire book and the significance of the chapter title within it. (If titles must be drastically shortened as running heads, it is best to submit the list to the author for his approval before type is set.) In shortening foreign language titles the editor must avoid omitting a word governing the case ending of another word included in the running head. Third, the editor will mark the running-head copy with the type specifications and will note also the specification for the folios—for example, "9 pt. Janson drop folios, flush outside, O.S. figs."

2.109   Running-head copy is usually sent with the edited manuscript to the production department and the printer. It may, in some cases, be sent with galley proofs returned to the printer for page makeup.

2.110   In a work where the running head reflects what is on a given page, running heads cannot be prepared and set in type until pages have been made up (see par. 1.70).

14. *Never* should the designer's layout be used as copy for typesetting.
15. For selection of material to be used in running heads see pars. 1.68–71.

2.111   The printer's typesetter usually needs to know what *special characters* he will have to provide for a particular manuscript. Special characters normally are Greek letters, isolated mathematical or other symbols, diacritical marks (except French accents and the German umlaut). The editor should prepare a separate list of such characters, including the manuscript page number where each first appears, the type size in which it is to be set, and whether it is italic or roman.

STYLE SHEET FOR PROOFREADER

2.112   The professional proofreader, either in the printing house or in the publishing establishment, finds it helpful to have, from the editor, a list of any departures from the usual house style in a particular manuscript. If the proofreader is thus advised of the editor's intentions, he will not query the editor on galley proofs.

TRANSMITTAL SHEET

2.113   The last thing an editor usually does before turning an edited manuscript over to the production department to be sent to the printer is to make a list of what is in the package. The University of Chicago Press has a form called "Editor's Checklist" for this purpose, which the editor fills out in triplicate—one for the editor's file, two to go with the manuscript (one for the production department, the other for the printer). In addition to the author's full name, the correct title of his work, and the editor's name, this form lists all possible parts of a book, followed by two blank columns, one headed "Herewith," the other "To Come." The editor checks the relevant items in the proper column and crosses out items irrelevant to the work concerned. The form also lists items not part of the work itself but necessary to the production of it and so provided by the editor where necessary. These include layout, spine copy, running-head copy, list of special characters, and editor's style sheet for the proofreader. At the end of the transmittal sheet, space is provided for instructions about the number of sets of proof needed by the author and the editor and, if the editor is not to mail proofs, the author's address and any special mailing instructions.

2.114   If a manuscript goes to production in piecemeal fashion, a complete transmittal sheet should accompany the first batch released, indicating what is yet to come. Successive batches should each be accompanied by a partial transmittal sheet (listing only what is being transmitted) so that the editor has a record of when all parts of the manuscript were released.

PREPARING MANUSCRIPT FROM PRINTED MATERIAL

USING COPIES OF THE ORIGINAL

2.115 Manuscript for anthologies, collected works, and other books containing previously published material should not be retyped unless the material has been substantially rewritten. The editor, compiler, or author of the volume must have two clean copies of the printed material to make one copy of the manuscript. Each page should be pasted or taped (not stapled) to a standard sheet of paper (8½ by 11 inches), so that the "manuscript" pages are of uniform size and the typesetter can follow the copy as he would a typed manuscript. A Xerox or other machine copy may be made of the pasted-up pages to provide a second copy of the manuscript.

2.116 Footnotes on the original pages may remain at the foot of the pasted-up pages, because to cut them apart and paste them on separate pages is to run the risk of losing some of them. If much editing must be done on the footnotes or if an editor's notes are intermingled with the original notes, all footnotes should be pasted, or typed, on separate sheets.

2.117 Unless there is ample space to insert corrections above printed lines in the original, any corrections made in the original should be put in the margins, the method used in correcting proofs (see par. 3.14). Corrections squeezed between closely set lines are usually hard to see and often quite illegible.

MACHINE COPIES

2.118 When two clean copies of the original are not available for making the manuscript copy to be used by the typesetter, clear Xerox or other machine copies will serve the purpose, provided:

1. The lines of type do not turn up at the ends, reflecting the curve of a book's page as it is being copied.

2. All words at the ends of lines are present and clearly decipherable.

3. The image is not blurred and is neither too dark nor too light.

4. The paper on which the copy is made can be written upon with pencil.

Machine copies must be pasted on standard-size sheets, just as pages from an original.

2.119 Machine copies of original illustrations are unacceptable for reproduction. The editor or compiler should make every effort to procure glossy prints of the original illustration. Failing that, the publisher can usually have a reproduction made from the illustration in the original publication—without destroying the book or journal in which it appears.

SOURCE NOTES

2.120 Each selection of previously published material should be accompanied either by a headnote before the text begins or by an unnumbered footnote on the first page of text giving the source of the selection (see par. 1.45) and the name of the copyright holder (see chap. 4). If the title has been changed, the original title should appear in the note.

2.121 Some selections in anthologies may have been previously published in several places and in several versions. The source note should give as much of the publishing history as necessary and, where there are several versions, state which version is used.

2.122 Many complications may arise in seeking permissions from copyright holders and in phrasing source notes, and the compiler of an anthology may well need the advice of an expert. The matter should never be ignored or left to the last minute.

EDITING

2.123 Usually only certain alterations are permissible, without explanation, in editing material previously published. Footnotes may be renumbered consecutively throughout a selection or a chapter in a selection. Cross-references to parts of the original work not reprinted should be deleted. Obvious typographical errors, inadvertent grammatical slips, and unintentional inconsistencies in modern works may be corrected. Single quotation marks may be changed to double quotation marks, and double to single, following American practice (see par. 10.20), and periods and commas put inside a quotation mark (see par. 5.8). Words set in full capitals in the text should be marked for small capitals. Other typographical oddities should not be reproduced unless they contribute to the sense of the original. An old title page, for example, should not be set in type approximating the original type face but should be reproduced from a photograph of the original.

2.124   Unless the editor or compiler explains—in his preface or elsewhere—what kinds of changes he has made in the original text, all other matters of style should be retained: British or archaic spelling; excessive punctuation, or lack of punctuation; capitalization in the text and notes; style of footnotes (in some instances this may need slight modification for clarity). Any internal deletion in a selection should be indicated by ellipsis points (see par. 10.31).

2.125   The copy editor will need specific information from the editor or compiler of the volume concerning what changes he has made and what he wants the copy editor to do. The copy editor should read all material for sense; there is always the chance that material has been pasted up out of order, that something has been omitted, that meaningless cross-references have not been deleted. Ambiguous hyphens at the ends of lines should be marked so that the typesetter will know when to keep the hyphen and when to close up the word. Discrepancies and apparently incorrect sentences should be queried, but no changes made without calling the volume editor's attention to them.

HANDLING SYMPOSIUM VOLUMES

2.126   Volumes in which each chapter is by a different author usually multiply, often magnify, the problems normally encountered by a publisher in producing a one-author book. Even when the copy editor does not have to deal directly with each author, to cope with from five to sixty-five or more styles—not only of the writing itself but of spelling and capitalization, footnotes or references in text, bibliographies, subheads, and tables, graphs, charts, or other artwork—can be a nightmare. Symposia, particularly papers read before a conference of scholars learned in a highly specialized subject, usually require the most time and effort. And because the proceedings of a particular conference reflect the current state of research in that subject, it is highly desirable that they be published as soon after the conference as possible. A sense of urgency must be maintained through all stages of publishing the book.

PRELIMINARY PLANNING

2.127   Many problems and delays may be avoided and costs reduced through careful planning by the publisher (including the copy editor) and the volume editor together before the manuscript has been submitted for publication. The functions and responsibilities of each should be clearly defined and understood.[16] The publisher, having agreed to publish the manuscript, will draw up the contract, arrange for the physical production of the volume, and send offprints and complimentary copies to contributors. Some of the functions listed below, as ideally the responsibility of the volume editor, may in particular cases be undertaken by the publisher, and these are the decisions to be made in the planning stage.

VOLUME EDITOR'S RESPONSIBILITIES

2.128   The term *volume editor* as used here does not refer to a member of the publisher's staff but to the scholar selected, usually by the contributors to the symposium or the sponsors of it, to collect the papers for the volume and to work with the publisher. The competence and availability of the volume editor can affect the publication process at every stage. Ideally, the volume editor will undertake, and carry out, the following responsibilities, where applicable:

1. Getting manuscripts, including illustrations, from all contributors well before the date set for submitting the volume to the publisher.

2. Sending a consent-to-publish form (provided by the publisher) to each contributor (see par. 4.27).

3. Getting written permission from copyright holders to reproduce any material previously copyrighted: papers published elsewhere, illustrations, tables, and the like taken from another work (see chap. 4).

4. Editing each paper, especially those written by foreign-born authors, for sense and grammar, and checking lists of references and other apparatus for uniformity of style.

5. Sending edited or rewritten manuscripts to the contributors for their approval *before* the volume goes to the publisher.

16. If there is more than one volume editor, the exact responsibilities of each editor must be spelled out in advance. Two or more editors attempting to perform the same functions during the publication process will delay production and may easily frustrate the copy editor with conflicting directives.

6. Editing any discussions to be included in the volume and getting any necessary approvals from the discussants.

7. Providing a list of contributors, with their affiliations, to be printed in the volume, or an identifying note for each contributor to be printed as an unnumbered footnote on the first page of his paper.

8. Providing copy for the title page and the table of contents and writing, or providing, any necessary prefatory material.

9. Sending the manuscript to the publisher, either complete or chapter by chapter, in a form acceptable for publication.

10. Checking the manuscript after it has been edited by the publisher's copy editor and answering the copy editor's queries.

11. Reading the master galley proofs.

12. Sending each contributor a copy of his galley proofs (if the contributors are to see proofs), asking the contributors to return their proofs to him by a specific date, and transferring their corrections to the master proofs.

13. Checking master page proofs against corrected galleys.

14. Preparing the index.

15. Asking each contributor how many offprints (reprints) he will want (the publisher usually has a form for this) and providing the publisher with a list of mailing addresses to which offprints should be sent.

2.129   In general, the volume editor should take responsibility for keeping the production schedule set by the publisher and for seeing that each contributor returns edited manuscript or proof by the date stipulated; one dilatory contributor may delay the entire project. The volume editor should also answer any questions and settle any complaints from individual contributors.

2.130   Since the volume editor is usually a busy professor for whom the task of editing the proceedings of a symposium is an added chore, he will seek to lighten the burden. A competent secretary is of course invaluable. Notifying contributors ahead of time about what is expected of them may save time. If possible, the volume editor should inform the contributors, before they prepare their papers, of the publisher's requirements concerning manuscripts acceptable for publication, including a uniform style for listing references. He will also notify them of what they may expect to see in the way of proofs (or, sometimes, edited manuscript) and approximately when. And he will know where the contributors can be reached at all times during the publication process.

COPY EDITOR'S RESPONSIBILITIES

2.131   The publisher's copy editor may find it necessary to perform some of the functions outlined above, if the volume editor is unable or unwilling to do so. It is very important, therefore, that the exact division of responsibility for a particular volume be decided at the preliminary planning stage. And the copy editor should be fully aware of everyone's responsibilities, not just his own, since it is usually a function of the copy editor to see that the volume goes through the publication process as quickly as possible, and he must know what is happening to all parts of the volume at all times.

2.132   The copy editor must also copy edit the entire manuscript. The volume editor cannot usually be expected to bring about consistency in capitalization, spelling, abbreviations, and so forth. Rewording or substantive editing should be kept to an absolute minimum, especially when contributors are not to see copy-edited manuscripts. Queries, also kept to a minimum, should be addressed to the volume editor and the copy-edited manuscript sent to him, unless other arrangements have been made in advance.

2.133   Such volumes often come to the copy editor not complete but chapter by chapter and not necessarily in sequence. To keep track of matters, the copy editor will need to prepare a schedule sheet for his own use. The left-hand column should list the chapters in the order in which they will appear in the finished volume. Columns are then provided in which to record the specific dates when (1) copy is received, (2) edited copy goes to volume editor, (3) edited copy returns from volume editor, (4) manuscript goes to printer, (5) galleys are received and sent to volume editor, (6) galleys are returned from volume editor, (7) page proofs go out, and (8) pages are returned. Where pertinent, it is helpful also to note the number of illustrations and tables in each chapter. Both illustrations and tables are numbered consecutively in each chapter, not throughout the volume—that is, the first figure in each chapter is figure 1, the first table is table 1.[17] To save time, manuscript

17. All illustrations and separate tables should be identified by the name of the author of the chapter as well as by the name of the volume editor and the number of the item, to avoid confusion in makeup.

may be sent to the printer out of sequence so that type may be set and galleys pulled and sent out.[18] Galley proofs returned from the volume editor should be held until chapters can be returned in sequence for page makeup.

FOR FURTHER REFERENCE

2.134   Nearly all the works listed in the Bibliography of this manual are helpful to editors and authors. Among the most useful are: H. W. Fowler, *A Dictionary of Modern English Usage*, 2d ed. revised by Sir Ernest Gowers, for refined distinctions regarding English usage, with entertaining and informative examples; Theodore M. Bernstein, *The Careful Writer*, for acceptable modern idiom and for avoiding jargon and other forms of bad writing; Porter G. Perrin, *Writer's Guide and Index to English*, for grammar and syntax.

18. A copy of the complete table of contents, even if it is tentative, should accompany the first batch of manuscript sent to the printer so that he will know what to expect.

3 *Proofs*

INTRODUCTION

3.1   To produce a book requires the work of many craftsmen, each trained in a special field: designer, estimator, typesetter, compositor, proofreader, page makeup man, paper manufacturer, printer, binder, as well as production personnel to coordinate the various functions and business personnel to take care of the charges. Where do the author and the editor fit into the production process?

3.2   The editor works closely with the production department at all stages of production, and, in a small publishing house, may also perform the functions of a production controller, dealing with the designer, the printer, and others. Most publishers send proofs to an author, usually both galley and page proofs. If a manuscript goes straight into pages, the author will of course see only the page proofs and will be asked to make no change that would affect the length of a page.[1]

3.3   Since the end of World War II the printing industry has been experimenting with new ways of producing the printed word. More and more revolutionary changes are yet to come. Authors, and presumably editors, at least of scholarly books, will still be necessary parts of the operation, though the form in which they see material to be checked may change radically as machines take over more of the functions traditionally performed by man. It is not the purpose of this chapter—or of this manual—to prognosticate the problems of proofreading in the future or even to deal specifically with the already available departures from traditional methods. If the author and the editor know how to cope with proofs in the traditional and still most widely used and accepted way, they can adapt their knowledge to foreseeable contingencies. For the layman, the few technical terms found in this chapter are defined in the Glossary.

1. The omission of galley proofs in the production of a book saves time and costs. It is not recommended, however, for complicated material—many footnotes, text illustrations, tables, etc.—because any error in makeup may require extensive revision of the pages. When the publisher decides to put a book straight into pages, the editor should notify the author in advance—preferably when the edited manuscript is sent to him—so that he will know he cannot make changes after type is set.

SCHEDULES

3.4   After an edited manuscript is sent to the production department, it is given a schedule stipulating dates for receipt and return of galley proofs, page proofs, index, and, depending on the printing process to be used, any further steps in the production process requiring the publisher's attention. The final date on the schedule is the *delivery* date, the day finished books are to be delivered by the printer to the publisher's warehouse. The schedule is affected by various factors, a major one being the printer's work load—when he can promise to begin and finish the typesetting and when he can print the book. Among other factors are the proximity of the author to the publisher (mailing time must be accounted for), the complexity of the book, and when the publisher wants to issue it (*publication* date, some weeks after delivery date).

3.5   Most publishers send an author a schedule of dates applicable to him: when he will receive galleys and pages and when he will be expected to return them. If an author knows he will be unable to meet the specified deadlines, he should inform his editor at once. Proofs returned even a few days late may delay production of the book for weeks. A busy printing house schedules its work far ahead, and when a certain time has been allotted for making up pages of a book and the author's galleys have not been returned in time, the process must be rescheduled for a later (sometimes *much* later) date. When the delivery date (and therefore the publication date) is put off, the sales and publicity departments are also affected, since their plans for distributing the book must be timed to coincide with its actual appearance. Production schedules are therefore very important; they are not to be filed and forgotten.

GALLEY PROOFS

MASTER PROOFS

3.6   Printing houses differ in whether they send galleys as they finish portions of a book or send them all at once after the whole work has been typeset. The former seems to be the more common practice, and most authors prefer it. Normally two copies of the galley proofs are sent to the author, along with the manuscript from which type was set. One, called the *master proofs*, or *marked proofs*, carries the proofreader's corrections, if any, and is the copy to be returned to the publisher with the author's corrections marked on it. The other set of galleys, unmarked by the proofreader, is to be retained by the author for reference. He may wish to transfer corrections to this copy. Many publishers do not send master proofs to authors, partly for safety's sake and partly because some authors correct their proofs in such a way that the printer has difficulty in deciphering the author's intentions. Instead, the editor transfers the proofreader's corrections to another copy—the author's copy—and sends this, along with an unmarked copy, for the author to read. When the author returns his proofs, the editor then transfers the author's corrections to the master copy. Only *one* copy of proofs—the master copy with *all* corrections on it—should be returned to the printer.

DEAD MANUSCRIPT

3.7 The edited manuscript is called the *dead manuscript*, or *dead copy*, after type has been set from it. The University of Chicago Press—as do most other publishers—sends the dead manuscript to the author along with the galley proofs and requests that it be returned with the marked galleys. The author is expected to read his galley proofs against the manuscript and to put corrections only on the galleys. No correction—no mark at all—should ever be made on the dead manuscript by the author or his editor. The manuscript must be kept, for the record, exactly as it went to the typesetter.[2]

READING PROOFS

FOR TYPOGRAPHICAL ERRORS

3.8 The printer's proofreader is usually the only person who has read the proofs word for word before the author sees them. Some proofreaders are better than others, but no proofreader is infallible (see par. 3.30). Therefore it is advisable for the author (or some other person) to read his galleys against his manuscript, word for word, again. To attain the greatest accuracy possible, a second person, a copyholder, should read from the manuscript while the author follows the proof. (Never read from proof to manuscript, always from manuscript to proof.) For one person to try to read both proof and manuscript at once is hard on the eyes and not so

2. Publishers usually keep manuscripts, and corrected proofs, for a certain length of time after the book has appeared—a year, or until the printer's bill has been received—in case of controversy over charges or to check errors found in the printed book.

accurate. If a word or line has been omitted, the text may still make sense—though not what the author intended—and the omission may not be detected without careful comparison with the original manuscript.

3.9   *Punctuation marks.* Punctuation should be read by the copyholder as well as the words of the text. Opening and closing quotation marks and parentheses should be observed; one or the other is sometimes omitted, or reversed. Commas, periods, and apostrophes, being small, sometimes get out of place or disappear. The author should recognize the difference in print between a hyphen and an en dash and an em dash (see par. 5.89). Errors in punctuation may change the sense of a sentence and are thus as important to correct as misspelled words.

3.10   *Numbers.* All figures in text, tables, mathematical copy, and so forth should receive special attention. The omission, or addition, of three zeros, for example, if not caught in proofreading can bring down the scorn of a reviewer on an author whose manuscript was in fact correct.

3.11   *Word division.* In addition to misspelled words, misplaced punctuation, omissions, and so forth, the author or the editor should check word divisions at the ends of printed lines. The typesetter will have used the American (or British) system of word division for common words in the English language (see chap. 6). Where he is most likely to err is in dividing proper names and words in foreign languages (for example, *Khrush-chev* should be *Khru-shchev*). In text and footnotes, therefore, the author should pay particular attention to a foreign word that has been divided at the end of a line (see chap. 9).

3.12   *Broken type and wrong font.* Both broken type and pieces of type from a font other than that used in the text are almost always marked by the printer's proofreader, who is trained to recognize such matters. To the practiced eye a smudged or lightly printed letter is not the same as a broken one, where the line of the letter is clearly bent, or broken so that white space appears in the middle of it. Blurred or faint passages in proof do not indicate broken type and should not be marked as such. Galley proofs with dozens of x's written by the author in the margins because he thinks type might be broken are a nuisance for the printer, who knows that the imperfect impression is simply the result of too little or too much ink when the galley proof was pulled. And, in threading his way through the needless x's, he may well miss a legitimate correction. A wrong font (*wf*), a letter in the wrong type face or size, is usually almost as obvious as a letter turned upside down and rarely goes unmarked by the printer's proofreader.

FOR SENSE

3.13 Reading galley proofs for sense should usually be an operation separate from reading against copy for typographical errors. It is the author's absolutely last chance to confirm his data and to be sure that he has said exactly what he intended to say. He should, of course, have checked all his sources and made his final changes in the edited manuscript (see par. 2.53), but there may be instances where errors of fact go unnoticed until galley proofs and must then be corrected. Such changes are usually few and are quite permissible. But authors in today's costly publishing world should refrain from rewriting their text in any way save to correct an error of fact (see pars. 3.31–35).

CORRECTING PROOFS

3.14 Unlike corrections on the original manuscript, corrections on proofs must always be put in the margin, left or right, next to the line of type in which the correction is to be made. A mark in the line—a caret for an addition, a line through a letter or word to be deleted—will indicate where the correction is to be made. Never should a correction, or addition, be written above a line of type. The typesetter responsible for making corrections scans the margins only and will not see writing buried in lines of type. Where more than one alteration is to be made in a line, corrections should be marked in the margin in the order they are to be made in the line, reading from left to right; a vertical or slant line separates one correction from the next. Both margins of the galley may be used when there are a number of corrections in a line. Guidelines (lines drawn from the point in the line where the correction is to be made to the explanation of it in the margin) are unnecessary, and undesirable, unless the correction cannot be put next to the line. When guidelines are used, they should never cross each other; if they must cross—as in transposing several items in an index, for example—a different color pencil should be used for each.

3.15 In correcting proofs, authors and editors should use a color different from that used by the proofreader. Either a clear, sharp

70

pencil or a pen is acceptable; soft, easily blurred pencil marks and barely legible handwriting are two undesirable ways to make corrections on proofs.

3.16   Book master galleys to be returned to the printer must never be cut apart for any reason. Material to be transposed from one galley to another should be so marked in the margin; for example, a paragraph on galley 4 to be moved to galley 5 would be marked "tr to gal. 5," and the place where it is to be inserted on galley 5 would be marked "tr from gal. 4." When a dummy of a book is made from galleys (a process rarely involving an author, or an editor), an unmarked set of galleys, not the master set, is used for the purpose.

PROOFREADERS' MARKS

3.17   With the first set of proofs sent to the publisher some printers include elaborate instructions on how to make corrections on the galleys. These should be followed if possible; they will differ little from the instructions given here. Symbols and marks explained in the following paragraphs and illustrated in figure 3.1 are universally understood by printers of publications in the English language. For purposes of discussion and for easier comprehension by those unfamiliar with them, proofreaders' marks may be classified as (1) operational signs, (2) typographical signs, and (3) signs clarifying certain punctuation marks to be inserted.

3.18   *Operational signs.* The *delete* sign is used only when something is to be removed from a line—a letter, a word or more, a whole line—without substitution. It is *not* used when another letter, word, or line is to be inserted in place of the deleted matter. A diagonal line through a letter to be deleted, a straight line through a word or more to be deleted, indicates where the deletion is to be made. Matter to be deleted from a typeset line should not be obliterated to the extent that the printer cannot see what to take out. The form of the delete sign written in the margin need not be exactly as shown in figure 3.1, but it should be made in such a way as not to be confused with any handwritten letter, such as *d*, *e*, or *l*. Where a letter is to be deleted from the middle of a word, the delete sign may be written within close-up marks (*delete and close up*), although this is not necessary unless there might be some doubt in the printer's mind, such as what to do with a word from which a hyphen has been deleted.

71

PROOFREADERS' MARKS

OPERATIONAL SIGNS

ℐ	Delete
◡	Close up; delete space
ℐ	Delete and close up
#	Insert space
eq #	Make space between words equal; make leading between lines equal
hr #	Insert hair space
ls	Letterspace
¶	Begin new paragraph
no ¶	Run paragraphs together
⊏⊐	Move type one em from left or right
⊐	Move right
⊏	Move left
⊐⊏	Center
⊓	Move up
⊔	Move down
=	Straighten type; align horizontally
∥	Align vertically
tr	Transpose
(sp)	Spell out
stet	Let it stand
⌄	Push down type

TYPOGRAPHICAL SIGNS

lc	Lowercase capital letter
cap	Capitalize lowercase letter
sc	Set in small capitals
ital	Set in italic type
rom	Set in roman type
bf	Set in boldface type
wf	Wrong font; set in correct type
X	Reset broken letter
⊘	Reverse (type upside down)

PUNCTUATION MARKS

⋀	Insert comma
⋁	Insert apostrophe (or single quotation mark)
⟨⟨ ⟩⟩	Insert quotation marks
⊙	Insert period
(?) ?	Insert question mark
;	Insert semicolon
:	Insert colon
=	Insert hyphen
M	Insert em dash
N	Insert en dash

Fig. 3.1

72

ctr / lc

flush ⌐ The Author As Proofreader ⌐

["I don't care what kind of type you use for my
book," said a myopic author to his publisher, but please
print the galley proofs in large type. Perhaps in the
future such a request will not sound so ridiculous ⌐ ⌐

i to those familar with the printing process. Today, *cap*
however, type once set is not reset except to correct *tr*
errors.[1]

1. Type may be reduced in size, or enlarged photographically when a
book is printed by offset.

Proofreading is an Art and a craft. Every author *lc / stet*
should know the rudiments thereof, though no
printer expects him to be a master. He should watch
printer expects him to be a master. He should watch *e*
not only for misspelled or incorrect works (often a *d*
e /) most illusive error but also for misplace dspaces, "un- *c / #*
tr closde" quotation marks and parenthesis, and im- *eq. # / e*
tr porper paragraphing; and he should recognize the
difference between an em dash—used to separate an
interjectional part of a sentence—and an en dash used
tr commonly between continuing numbers (e.g., pp.
lc / N / = 5–10; A.D. 1165/70) and the word dividing hyphen.
Sometimes, too, a letter from a wrong font will creep *wf*
tr / 9 a mathematical formula. Whatever is *underlined* in *rom*
into the printed text, or a boldface k or d turn up in *ll / bf / roman*
(sp) / ↑ a MS. should of course, be *italicized* in print. To find *ital / ¶* *in*
the errors overlooked by the printer's proofreader is
the authors first problem in proof reading. The sec- *c*
ond problem is to make corrections, using the marks *by*
and symbols, devized by proffessional proofreaders, *s / S*
t that any trained printer will understand. The third—
1/M and most difficult problem for the author proofreading his own work is to resist the temptation to rewrite *=*
when at last he sees his words in print.

Manuscript editor ▢ *c + sc / ▢*

3.19   Too much space between letters is indicated by the *close-up* sign, used in the line as well as in the margin. Sometimes the last letter of a word appears at the beginning of the next word; when this happens, the close-up mark followed by a space mark is written in the margin, and a close-up mark and a vertical line indicating the space are inserted in the line.

3.20   The *space* mark is used to indicate omission of space between words; a vertical line shows where the space is to be inserted. The space mark may also be used to show where extra space (leading) is needed between lines. Words in the same line should be separated by the same amount of space. When the word spaces in a single line are unequal, the *equal-space* sign is written in the margin and carets are inserted in the line to mark the difficulty. Note that spacing between words in two adjacent lines is not necessarily equal in justified type (see par. 19.25). Hair spaces, thin spaces, and letter spaces are generally matters of design and need not concern an author unless he notices inconsistency in setting similar material.

3.21   A *paragraph* sign in the margin tells the printer to begin a new paragraph; in the line either another paragraph sign before the first word of the new paragraph or, more common, an L-shaped mark to the left and partly under the word will show him where to begin the paragraph. To run two paragraphs together, a *no paragraph* sign is written in the margin and a line drawn from the end of one paragraph to the beginning of the next.

3.22   Indention of a line one em from the left or right margin is indicated by a small, open square drawn in the left or right margin next to the line to be moved; another square, or a caret, is drawn next to the material itself. An indention of two or more ems may be indicated either by two or more squares in a row or by the desired figure written inside one square.

3.23   The signs for *moving* type *right* or *left* or for *centering* are used when a line of type is printed too far to the left or right—when a subtitle, an item in a table, or a letter has been set in the wrong place horizontally. Signs for moving type *up* or *down* are used when something has been set on the wrong line—is vertically out of place. All these signs are used in the line as well as written in the margin.

3.24   The sign for *aligning horizontally*—marked in the line as well as in the margin—is used when one or more letters have slipped

74

slightly above or below the line. The sign for *vertical* alignment should be used sparingly in correcting proof; the left and right type margins are often slightly irregular in galley and page proofs because the type itself has not yet been locked in place for printing. The sign should be used mainly to indicate inaccurate alignment in tabular matter.

3.25 The sign for *transposing* is used for letters, words, phrases, lines, paragraphs, or any other material to be moved from one place to another. The indication of where the transposition is to be made in the line is drawn in the same way as in editing a manuscript, but *tr* must appear in the margin in proofs so that the printer will see the change.

3.26 When abbreviations or figures set in type are to be spelled out, they should be circled in the line and the *spell-out* sign written in the margin. Note that to spell out something in the text means that the line will be longer, and therefore several lines may have to be reset unless compensation is made for the extra space (see par. 3.34). Also, the full word should be written in the margin, instead of the sign, if there is any ambiguity about the spelling of the word (for an example of this in edited manuscript see fig. 2.1).

3.27 The word *stet* is used to tell the printer not to take out something earlier marked for deletion. Dots under the crossed-out material indicate what is to remain. Where a note in the margin is also crossed out, *stet as set* will clarify what to let stand.

3.28 *Typographical signs.* Letters set in the wrong kind of type are corrected as follows. To make a capital letter lowercase, draw a diagonal line through the letter and write *lc* in the margin. To capitalize a lowercase letter, draw three lines under the letter (or letters) and write *cap* (*caps*) in the margin. Indicate small capitals by two lines under the letter and *sc* in the margin. To italicize, draw one line under the word and write *ital* in the margin. To have an italicized word reset in roman type, circle the word and write *rom* in the margin. Indicate boldface type by a wavy line under the letter or word and *bf* in the margin. For errors in type such as wrong font (*wf*), broken type (*x*), or a letter turned upside down, circle the letter and write the appropriate symbol in the margin (but see par. 3.12).

3.29 *Punctuation marks.* To change a punctuation mark—from a comma to a semicolon, for example—draw a vertical line through the mark and write the correct one in the margin. To supply a mark where none appears, place a caret at the spot and the correct mark in the margin. Since a handwritten comma, apostrophe, and parenthesis may be confused one with another, a comma written in the margin should have a caret mark over it; an apostrophe, or quotation mark, should have a reversed caret under it, indicating its superior position; a parenthesis should simply be made large enough not be taken for one of the smaller marks. Hyphens and en and em dashes should be differentiated by their appropriate symbols (see fig. 3.1). A period, being small, should be circled. Semicolons, colons, question marks, and exclamation points, if written clearly, need no further identifying marks, except that a question mark that might be mistaken for a query should be followed by *set* with a circle around it.

PRINTER'S ERRORS

3.30   A typesetter's job is to *follow copy*, to reproduce in type exactly what he sees on the manuscript. He can follow alterations correctly made in the manuscript and knows the meaning of editorial marks and directions. He does not, and should not have to, read the manuscript for sense. Unlike a typist, he cannot see the results of what he is doing while he is doing it. Being human, he is almost certain, sooner or later, to make a mistake—to omit a letter, a word, sometimes a whole line, to misspell a word, or, worse, to substitute another word (*country* for *county*, for example). In the publishing business these errors are called *typos* (typographical errors). The printer's proofreader tries to catch any such slips and to correct them before proof goes to the author. Proofreaders, also being human, sometimes miss an error made by the typesetter. It is hoped that the author, though not a trained proofreader, will catch these residual errors. When an author or an editor spots and corrects a printer's error, he should point out that the matter was correct in the manuscript by circling "PE" (printer's error) or "as in copy" next to the correction in the margin. An alternative method of differentiation is to correct the printer's errors in one color and to make other alterations in another; neither color should be the same as that used by the proofreader.

AUTHOR'S ALTERATIONS

3.31   Any change made in proofs that cannot be attributed to the printer counts as an *author's alteration* (AA). Usually the contract between author and publisher stipulates how much of the cost of alterations in proofs (including both galleys and pages) the publisher is to pay—for example, 10 percent of the cost of setting the original type. Costs in excess of this amount are charged to the author and are usually taken out of his royalties.

3.32   Authors with little publishing experience do not realize how very costly their alterations may be. (1) Printers' charges are based mainly on the time required to carry out an operation. To reset a line of type takes considerably longer than to set it in the first place. The line of type marked for correction must be found, removed from the galley tray or made-up page, reset, put back in its place, and proofread again. (2) The insertion, or deletion, of even a comma in Linotype means that the entire line must be reset. (3) The insertion or deletion of a word at the beginning or in the middle of a paragraph means resetting all the rest of the paragraph. (4) Changing anything in a figure or a plate means that the line cut or halftone plate must be remade.

3.33   Publishers, especially production and editorial departments, are most happy with those authors who make very few changes on their proofs and most unhappy with those who feel they must rewrite extensively when they see their work in print. That an author may be willing to pay hundreds of dollars for excess alterations does not minimize the fact that the time-consuming tasks involved in carrying out his last-minute changes of mind will throw his book off schedule.

3.34   The author who finds it necessary to make changes in galley or page proofs should make them in such a way as to require the least possible resetting of lines. For example, if he *adds* a word, he should count the letters in it and try to delete a word with the same number of letters from that line or from the line above or below, thus making it possible to reset only one or two lines instead of the remainder of the paragraph. Similarly, if he *deletes* a word or a phrase in the middle of a paragraph, he should try to add the same number of characters (letters and spaces) nearby to compensate for the deletion.

3.35   Additions too long to be written next to the line where they are to be inserted should be typed on separate slips and attached, with a straight pin or tape, to the galley. They should never be written up or down the margins of the galleys.[3] The spot where an at-

---

3. If there is room at the foot of the galley, an addition or correction may be typed or written in the space and a guideline drawn from it to the spot where it is to be inserted.

tached addition is to be inserted should be marked with a caret and "Insert attached" written and circled in the margin. A circled note on the slip will tell the printer where it belongs should the slip become detached from the galley—for example, "Insert gal. 4." If more than one such insert must be made on a single galley, each should be identified by letter: Insert A, gal. 4; Insert B, gal. 4; etc. The note in the margin of the galley then reads: Insert A attached, etc. To save resetting type, any such addition should be a separate paragraph or should be added to the end of an existing paragraph.

GALLEY NUMBERS

3.36   Printers number galley proofs straight through a book. The number appears in the slug at the top of each galley. This slug is for the printer's convenience in identifying the galley; it usually includes the author's name, a partial title, sometimes the type size of the text and the date when type was set, as well as the galley number. The author who observes that his name is misspelled or his title given wrongly in the slug should not waste time correcting the error, since the slug will be dropped when the pages are made up. The only thing in the slug that need concern the author is the galley number. Depending on the printer, the galley number is the last number given at the right of the slug, or the first number at the left. When an author needs to refer to a galley by number, a cursory examination of a sequence of galleys will tell him which is the galley number. Sometimes galleys bear another number, usually in boldface type, above the slug. This is the *rack* number, which tells the printer where he has stored the type for the galley; it is *not* the galley number and should not be used by authors or editors in referring to specific galleys (rack numbers are sometimes in sequence, sometimes not). The University of Chicago Printing Department numbers galleys not only throughout the book but also through each chapter, each galley thus having two numbers, the first applying to the book, the second to the chapter.

PAGE PROOFS

3.37   Two sets of page proofs are sent to the author, one marked *master* or *corrected* copy, to be returned to the publisher, the other to be retained by the author and used in making the index. Pages are usually sent in batches rather than all at once so that the author, or his indexer, may begin work on the index as soon as possible. The corrected galleys, now called *foul galleys*, are sent with the page proofs and should be returned to the publisher with the master pages. As with dead manuscript (see par. 3.7), no mark whatever should be made on the foul galleys.

CHECKING AGAINST GALLEYS

3.38   To check page proofs, the author should put galley and page side by side and read carefully, on the page, each line that has a correction marked on the galley, his own correction or the proofreader's. He should make sure not only that the correction has been made but that no other error has been introduced in resetting the line. He should also check the lines above and below to see that the reset line has been reinserted in its proper place. Occasionally, because of broken type or other accidents in the plant, a printer may have to reset lines not marked for correction on the galleys. He should, and most printers do, indicate any such lines by writing *reset* in the margin of the galley, so that the printer's proofreader and the author will check these lines in the page proof.

3.39   Although the printer's proofreader has usually done so, it is advisable for the author also to check the top and bottom line of each page to make sure no line has been dropped in making up pages. It is sometimes desirable also to check the sequence of all lines of a page, especially if material has been marked for transposition on the galleys. And, although page makeup men are usually experts, two galleys might be reversed (a rare error), thereby garbling the pages, or a footnote overlooked and left in the text where it appeared in galleys. The author will find any instance of the latter error in makeup when he checks his footnotes to see that each appears on the same page as the text reference to it. A long footnote may run over to the next page, but it must begin on the page that carries its reference.

ADJUSTING PAGE LENGTH

3.40   The length of the type page, specified by the book designer and carefully observed by the printer, need concern the author or the editor only when the makeup man runs into difficulties. In regular text material it is permissible to let *facing pages* (verso and recto; pp. 68 and 69, for example) each run one line long or one line short to avoid a widow (short line at the end of a paragraph) at the top of a page or to fit footnotes and their references on the same page. It is also permissible—indeed necessary—to let one page run short if a subhead would fall at the bottom of the page. Sometimes, however, the printer, with all his ingenuity, is unable to make a page come out right and will ask the author or the editor to *save a line* (*lose a line*) or to *add a line*. To save a line, one looks for the paragraph with the shortest last line—preferably only a word or two—on the page and deletes enough characters from the last sentence of the paragraph (from elsewhere in the paragraph if the last sentence will not permit deletion) to accommodate the last line of the paragraph at the end of the line above. To add a line is to add a phrase or a longer word, preferably toward the end of a paragraph, to make the last line of a paragraph run over to a new line.

CROSS-REFERENCES

3.41   In his page proofs the author must provide the numbers for all references to specific pages in his book ("see p. 225," for example). Usually the proofreader has queried each such reference in the margins of the page proofs so that the author will not overlook any of them. Only at this stage does many an author admit the practicality of his editor's suggestion—at the manuscript stage— to avoid cross-references to pages. Each line containing a cross- reference must be reset, a costly process for an author who has already used up his 10 percent allowance for alterations. Cross- references at the beginning of the book to pages toward the end cannot of course be supplied until the author has all his pages. Therefore, unless his publisher allows him to retain the master pages until he has all of them, he must keep a list of the pages con- taining unfilled cross-references and send his editor the numbers to be supplied as soon as he has received the final batch of pages. The editor must then insert the numbers on pages from an extra set of proofs, mark them *2d corrected proof*, and send them to the printer. Page proofs of books with many such cross-references are best held (not returned to the printer) until all references have been supplied.

AUTHOR'S ALTERATIONS

3.42   Any change introduced by the author in page proofs will cost even more than changes introduced in galleys (see pars. 3.31–35). If he must make a change, it is not only desirable but essential that he compensate for any characters added or deleted so that the length of the page will not be affected.

80

RUNNING HEADS AND FOLIOS

3.43 Running heads and folios on every page must be checked, usually by the editor when page proofs are returned from the author. It is best to do this as a separate operation, not while checking the text pages. A running head may be missing altogether, the wrong running head may have been inserted through part of a chapter, a word may suddenly turn up misspelled in a running head halfway through a chapter. Running heads and folios should be deleted by the editor from any page containing *only* a table or an illustration (see pars. 1.73, 1.77). Careful, undivided attention is thus required to check running heads. Folios are usually accurate but sometimes one is omitted or set in the wrong place or the type is broken; and, in very rare instances, folios may somehow have got out of sequence (if this should happen, the author or his indexer must be notified of the correct pagination).

3.44 When a section of notes at the back of a book requires page numbers in the running heads (see par. 1.72), the editor should insert the numbers or should check all numbers supplied by the author.

3.45 When running heads cannot be supplied until pages have been made up, as in this manual, a list, with page numbers, must be supplied by the editor to the printer.

TABLE OF CONTENTS

3.46 Page numbers are inserted, usually by the editor, in the table of contents after all pages (except the index) have been received from the printer. The page on which the index will start is the first recto page after the end of the page proof. If more than one index is to be included, the page numbers for any index other than the first cannot be determined until index page proof has been received. When someone other than the editor—the printer or the author, for example—has inserted page numbers in the table of contents, the editor should check each number carefully against the final page proofs.

3.47 The wording of chapter titles and other parts of the book in the table of contents should also be checked carefully against page proofs. In checking the table of contents, the editor should look at each page of the page proofs to make sure nothing has been

omitted from the table of contents that should be in it; this is particularly important in checking tables of contents that include
subheads as well as chapter titles.

3.48   Any list of illustrations, figures, or tables should be carefully
checked in the same way as the table of contents, and page numbers supplied when they are missing. Although some printers do
supply page numbers in contents and lists in the preliminary pages,
no printer should be expected to do so, and certainly not after corrected page proofs have been returned to him by the publisher.

PRELIMINARY PAGES

3.49   Display preliminary pages (pp. i–iv; see pars. 1.1–22) should be
checked carefully by production department and designer for
fidelity to the design specified; by the person in charge of contracts
(permissions secretary or other) for information on the copyright
page; and by the editor and author for typographical errors of
any kind. A misspelled word in these pages—the author's name
for instance—is an inexcusable catastrophe in a printed book.

INDEX PROOFS

3.50   The urgency of preparing and editing indexes on schedule has
been pointed out elsewhere (par. 2.94). Most printers also feel a
sense of urgency about setting type on and proofreading an index
when they receive manuscript copy. Usually an index goes straight
to pages—no galley proofs. Except in rare instances, the University of Chicago Press sends neither the edited manuscript nor the
proofs of an index to the author. When an editor has a question
or finds extensive editing necessary, he consults the author by
telephone or letter before sending the index manuscript to the
printer. The editor reads the index proofs carefully, with a copyholder, as soon as he receives them; he should be able to return
them to the printer in less than twenty-four hours.

ILLUSTRATIONS

3.51   Illustrations that are to be printed with the text often appear in
the galley proofs if the cuts have been made at the time galleys
are pulled. If they are not in the galleys, the proofreader will note
the placement of each in the margins of the galley. All such illus-

trations should be in place in page proofs. Any alteration marked on the figure itself will necessitate remaking the entire cut. Authors are thus to be discouraged from changing their minds about their artwork at the proof stage. When a publisher has artwork made from the author's rough sketch, the final drawing should be sent to the author and the editor for approval before a cut is made; it is at this stage that any necessary correction should be indicated.

3.52   Legends to illustrations are proofread like the text. Figures should be checked to see that they have been inserted right side up and that each is accompanied by the correct legend.

3.53   Halftones or other illustrations to be printed as inserts are not included with galley or page proofs. Such illustrations are sent to the author either on engraver's proofs or on blueprints (see par. 3.57). The quality of reproduction on an engraver's proof is the same as that in the finished book and is the best that can be made from the original plate. (For further discussion of handling illustrations see chapter 11.)

OTHER PROOFS

3.54   Page proofs are normally the last proofs seen by an author. If the book is to be printed from type, they are the last proofs furnished by the printer to the publisher. If the book is to be printed by one of the various offset processes, the publisher will probably see proofs of the final stage before printing. The editor should check these to see that all corrections in page proofs have been made, that all material is there and in the correct order.

REPRODUCTION PROOFS

3.55   Reproduction proofs, or *repros* as they are usually called, are the actual camera copy from which the book will be photographed and printed. Repros are printed on coated paper and represent the quality of image to be achieved in the final printing. The editor should not make any changes on repros except to correct typographical errors. Any such corrections should be made in the margin with a light *blue* pencil, a color that the camera does not pick up. Only the faintest of blue marks should be made on the type area itself. A list of page numbers on which such corrections have been made should go to the production department with the corrected repros. The art department can often make corrections by cutting letters from another set of repros (two sets are usually furnished by the printer) and pasting them carefully in place on the set to be used as camera copy. Unwanted marks can be whited out at the same time. Further resetting of type at this stage should be avoided if humanly and mechanically possible.

TYPEWRITER COMPOSITION

3.56 When a book is to be printed from typewriter composition, conventional galley proofs and page proofs are impossible. Instead, the author usually sees a copy of each typed page, upon which his corrections should be made in the same way he would correct printed page proofs. If the original copy, from which the book is to be printed, goes to the author, a tissue overlay should be taped to each page and any corrections made on the overlay, not on the page itself.

BLUEPRINTS

3.57 Blueprints (*blues*), vandykes (brown prints), silver prints, Ozalids (white prints), are all different forms of photographic prints made from negatives to be used in offset printing. They do not show the quality of image to be attained in the final printing, but they provide a means of checking the accuracy of the contents. As with repros and pages of typewriter composition, the editor should check to see that all parts are in place and all corrections made. Corrections made on these prints mean type must be reset and inserted, the pages made up again, and new repros pulled and photographed. Such prints should be checked by the editor the moment they arrive from the printer, who is often waiting for a final OK by telephone from the production department.

3.58 In cases where the author has not seen his text illustrations in place, these proofs must be sent to him, with the understanding that he return them at once or that he telephone any corrections he feels must be made. Any revised prints should be checked by the editor.

FOLDED SHEETS

3.59 Folded sheets (sometimes folded and stitched) are not proofs but the first printed sheets of a book. The production department checks the quality of the printing; the editor checks quickly, especially the preliminary display pages, for a missing or broken letter or other mishap possible in the printing process. The editor also checks the sequence of material to see that no signature has been printed twice, or omitted altogether. Since the book is usually being printed when folded sheets arrive, presses must stop running if a correction is to be made. Any typographical error in the text discovered at this stage must remain (until the second impression). Only an egregious error in the display pages or misplaced material justifies stopping the presses or canceling and reprinting pages.

CASE AND JACKET

3.60   The editor should always check proofs of the *die copy*—names, titles, and ornaments to be stamped on the spine of a book and (sometimes) on the cover. Normally the editor also sees proof of copy for the jacket—front, back, spine, and flaps—at some stage in the production of the jacket. The author usually sees copy written for the jacket flaps but is not asked to check proofs of the jacket.

FINISHED BOOK

3.61   When the folded sheets reach the bindery, one or two copies of the bound book from the first run are sent to the publisher's production department, where the book is checked for flaws in binding or assembling. Normally, neither author nor editor sees the book at this stage, but if they happen to be present they may be allowed to hold it for a while. When books arrive in the warehouse on the delivery date, the courteous publisher will send the author his first free copy at once and by the fastest courier available. The rest of the free copies stipulated in the author's contract will be sent to him from the warehouse at a somewhat later date. If the author finds any typographical errors in the finished book, he should note them on the flyleaf of his copy against the day his publisher notifies him that a second impression is imminent and that he may correct any such errors he has found in the book.

FOR FURTHER REFERENCE

3.62   Some publishers have their own manuals of style containing instructions for proofreading, and some printers send instructions
with proof (see par. 3.17). Marshall Lee's *Bookmaking: The Illustrated Guide to Design and Production* gives lucid descriptions of
the various processes used in modern bookmaking and explains
how to deal with the many different kinds of proofs available.

4 *Rights and Permissions*

4.1   Some knowledge of legal restrictions involved in publishing is a peripheral but highly necessary part of being an author of a published work. The author must know what to expect of his publisher and what his publisher expects of him. The following paragraphs, far from exhaustive, are intended for authors and editors of scholarly books and articles (see par. 4.29).

PUBLISHER'S RESPONSIBILITY

COPYRIGHT

4.2   It is the publisher's responsibility to see that the correct copyright notice appears in each copyrightable book he publishes.[1] To make this notice valid he must also file an application for registration of a claim to copyright with the Register of Copyrights in Washington, D.C., and comply with all regulations this entails.

1. See pars. 1.14–22.

Under the present law copyright protection begins on the day of publication, the first day of public distribution, and remains in force for twenty-eight years, to the day. The publisher may apply for a renewal of copyright, ordinarily in the name of the author, at any time during the year preceding the expiration date, and it is his responsibility to keep a record of this date. The renewal period is also twenty-eight years. Under United States law, therefore, the total time a book may be protected by copyright is fifty-six years. After that, it enters the public domain.

GRANTING PERMISSION TO REPRINT

4.3 A publisher with a relatively large backlist of books and journals, such as the University of Chicago Press, may receive an average of twenty letters a day from authors or compilers or other publishers requesting permission to use material from one or another of his publications. These requests range from whole books or journal articles to snippets of prose from a scholarly monograph. Large requests are granted only with the approval of the author, and any fee charged for the use of the material will be divided with the author or his heirs. Before any request, large or small, is granted, however, the publisher should check the material in question to determine whether he is indeed the original copyright holder of *all* the material in it. To be unequivocally sure of his ground the publisher needs to have had the author's initial cooperation when the book or article was first published.

4.4 Before he will give consent to reprinting from his books, a publisher may ask the requester to fill out a somewhat elaborate form covering any contingencies that may arise (see fig. 4.1).

AUTHOR'S RESPONSIBILITY

GUARANTEE OF AUTHORSHIP

4.5 In signing a contract with his publisher an author guarantees that the work is original, that he owns it, that no part of it has been previously published, and that no other agreement to publish it or part of it is outstanding. If a chapter or other significant part by the same author has been published elsewhere—as a journal article, for example—written permission to reprint it must be secured from the copyright holder of the original publication and sent to the publisher to be filed with the contract of the book in which it is reprinted.

88

Fig. 4.1

REQUEST FOR PERMISSION TO REPRINT

TO: *The University of Chicago Press*
     5750 Ellis Avenue
     Chicago, Illinois 60637

                                                                                (Date)

FROM:_____
        (Name)

_____
        (Address)

I hereby request permission to reprint the following material from your publication:

*Author and full title*_____
Please give below precise details of the material desired, specifying page numbers, paragraphs, approximate number of words and other identifying information, using the reverse side of this form if necessary.

These quotations are to appear without change in the following volume:

                                    (Author and full title)   *(Approx. No. of pages)*
Publisher_____

Probable date of publication_____ Form of publication_____
                                                  (Book, syllabus, etc.)

Probable list price_____ Edition_____
                                            (Text or trade or both)

To be circulated as follows_____
                           (Countries, special markets, etc.)

The undersigned agrees as follows:

1. Full credit will be given The University of Chicago Press, and copyright notice imprinted on the copyright page of the publication or on the first page of each quotation covered by this permission, on every copy manufactured, all in the form specified below.

2. Payment of the required fee will be made on or before date of publication.

3. One copy of the work will be forwarded upon publication to The University of Chicago Press, <u>addressed to the Permissions Department.</u>

4. This permission covers only the use specified above and does not cover translation, digest, abridgment, or selections which may be made of the publication. <u>This permission does not allow use of this material in any edition other than above specified,</u> or in any edition produced by or for a book club with a membership of more than ten thousand, or by other means of reproduction, including motion pictures, sound tapes, and phonograph records.

5. This permission is contingent upon approval of the author, which must be obtained by the requestor.

*[Signed]*_____

APPROVAL OF REQUEST

The foregoing application is hereby approved, subject to the conditions stated above and subject to payment of $_____ as the permission fee, and provided that the following form of credit and copyright notice is used as specified in paragraph 1 above:

> The following phrase should appear, giving full identification of author and title (and series and translator, if any): "Reprinted from [title of book] by [author] by permission of The University of Chicago Press." This phrase should be followed by the identical copyright notice appearing in our publication.

This application and approval contain all the terms relating to said permission to reprint.

*Date of Approval*_____   *Approved:* THE UNIVERSITY OF CHICAGO PRESS

                                               *By*_____

4.6   Notice of the original copyright and permission to reprint must appear either on the copyright page of the book or in a footnote on the first page of the reprinted material or in a special list of acknowledgments. If the original copyright is in the name of the same author, written permission to reprint is not necessary, but the fact of prior publication should be noted in the book. Certainly, unless the material has been substantially changed, the publisher needs to know what parts of a book have appeared (or will appear) in published form elsewhere. Not only might such reprinted parts affect the sale of the book, but, if the publisher is not the original copyright holder of the material, he cannot in the future grant, or refuse to grant, permission to anyone who might wish to quote from the material in another publication; he must refer any such request to the original copyright holder. It is thus the author's legal as well as ethical responsibility to apprise his publisher of just how much of his material is, and how much is not, original and therefore copyrightable by the publisher.

REQUESTING PERMISSION TO REPRINT

4.7   It is the author's responsibility to request any permission required for the use of material owned by others.[2] When the author has received all his permissions, he should send them, or copies of them, to his publisher, who will note, and comply with, any special provisions contained in them. The publisher should preserve such permissions in his file for consultation in the event of future editions or requests for permission to reprint from the work. The publisher does not have the right to grant future requests to reprint from a specific book illustrative entities either taken from another, copyrighted work or procured from a picture agency, library, or museum. The author must therefore provide accurate information regarding the source of any such material in his work.

4.8   Permission for the use of such entities as poems, musical works, or illustrations, even when no fee is charged, is normally granted only for the first edition of a book. New editions, paperback reprints, serialization in a periodical, and so forth will require renewed permissions.

4.9   While writing his book, the author will do well to keep a record of any copyright holder whose permission may be necessary before

2. For kinds of material for which permission is necessary see par. 4.13. Before he requests permission to use any particular item, however, he should pause to consider whether he really needs permission—or whether the use he wishes to make of the passage falls under the heading of "fair use." See pars. 4.16–18.

his book is published. For a work containing many illustrations, long prose passages, or poetry, the process of obtaining permissions may take weeks, sometimes months, to complete. For example, an American publisher may inform the author that he holds rights only for distribution in the United States and that a British publisher holds the European and British Commonwealth rights. The author, wishing worldwide distribution for his book (*world rights*), must then write to the British publisher as well, informing him that he has obtained permission from the American publisher. Again, if a copyright is in the name of an author or his heirs, or, in the case of unpublished material, protected by common-law rights (see par. 4.20), a voluminous correspondence may be necessary before an heir can be found. The author, therefore, should begin requesting permissions as soon as his manuscript is accepted for publication.[3] Ideally, the publisher should have all the author's permissions in hand before type is set on his book.

FEES

4.10   The author is responsible for any fees charged by grantors of permission to reproduce, unless other arrangements are made, in writing, with his publisher. A publisher may agree to pay the fees and to deduct them from the author's royalties, or he may split the fees with the author. If a publisher decides that a book would be enhanced by illustrations not provided by the author, he may (with the author's consent) undertake not only to find the illustrations but to pay any fees involved.

4.11   Fees paid for reproducing material, especially illustrations procured from a picture agency, normally cover one-time use only—in, say, the first edition of the book. If an illustration is used also on the jacket or in advertising, a higher fee is customary. Also, if a book is reprinted as a paperback or goes into a second edition, another fee is usually charged.

ACKNOWLEDGMENT OF PERMISSIONS

4.12   Whether or not he needs permission to use any material not his own, an author should give the exact source of such material: in a footnote or internal reference in the text, in a source note to a table, in a credit line with an illustration (see pars. 11.30–33). Where permission has been granted, the author should, within reason, follow any special wording stipulated by the grantor. For

3. For when to ask permission to reprint selections in anthologies see par. 4.27.

a text passage complete in itself, such as a poem, or for a table, the full citation to the source may be followed by:

Reprinted by permission of the publisher.

A credit line under an illustration may read:

Courtesy of the Newberry Library, Chicago, Illinois.

In a work necessitating many permissions, acknowledgments may be grouped together in a special section called Acknowledgments in the preliminary pages of the book. Citation to the source should, however, be made on the page containing the relevant material.

MATERIAL REQUIRING PERMISSION

COPYRIGHTED MATERIAL

4.13 The author of an original book (not an anthology or edited work; see par. 4.27) must have written permission to use any copyrighted material that is complete in itself: short story, essay, chapter from a book, article, poem, table, chart, graph, map, picture, musical composition, and so forth. He should also seek permission to use more than one line of a short poem still in copyright or any words or music of a popular song.

4.14 No permission is required, of course, for quoting from works in the public domain—works on which the copyright has expired or never existed (such as most United States government publications). The original text of a classic reprinted in a modern edition is in the public domain, but recent translations, edited text, and editorial introductions, notes, or other apparatus are protected by copyright. Whether or not he needs permission to use material, however, the author should give credit to his sources.

4.15 In determining whether a work published in the United States is still in copyright, an author should assume that the copyright has been renewed, whether the renewal date is specified in the copyright notice or not (see par. 4.2).

"FAIR USE"

4.16 The doctrine of fair use is a concept of the common law; its limits are nowhere spelled out exactly.[4] Essentially it implies that an author may quote from another author's work to illustrate or buttress his own points. He should transcribe the quotation accurately and give credit to its source. He should not quote the other author out of context, should not make him seem to be saying

4. Pending legislation may provide a definition.

something opposite to, or different from, that which he intended. And an author should not quote at such length from another source that he diminishes the value of that source. In the latter instance proportion is more important than the absolute length of a quotation: to quote 500 words from an essay of 5,000 is bound to be more serious than to quote the same number of words from a work of 50,000.

4.17 Although neither the Copyright Act nor the court decisions upon which common law is based define fair use in terms of length, publishers tend to do so. One publisher may wish to be asked permission to quote as few as 150 words scattered through several passages from one of his publications; others may set upper limits of 500 or 1,000 words. A single publisher may try to be more strict about the use of some well-known author's work than about that of a lesser-known writer. It should be remembered that no such rules have any validity outside the publishing house walls: the courts, not publishers, decide fair use. The rules exist (1) to give an overworked permissions department, which is seldom in a position to decide whether a proposed use of a quotation is actually fair or not, something to use as a yardstick and (2) also, perhaps, to intimidate unscrupulous would-be users of their authors' works.

4.18 Fair use is use that is fair—simply that. If the quoted passage is from a published work in prose and not an entity of any sort within a larger work and if its use does not detract from the value of the original, the author should probably *not* ask permission to use it, regardless of length. The right of fair use is a valuable one and should not be allowed to decay through failure of scholars to employ it boldly. In borderline cases the author should pause before seeking permission to quote when he has reason to think that rights have passed to heirs who probably cannot be found. Far from establishing his good faith and protecting him from suit or unreasonable demands, it may have just the opposite effect. By seeking permission, his tacit admission may be damaging to his case if litigious heirs ever do make an appearance. Finally, the author and his publisher should both remember that for an injured copyright holder to recover damages from an unfair user of his material, he must *prove* that the use was unfair. The first burden of proof is on the copyright holder, not on the user.

AAUP RESOLUTION

4.19 In a collective effort to reduce the number of permissions—so common in university press publishing—the Association of American University Presses adopted the following resolution in 1961. The resolution of course has no standing in law, but it represents an attempt to underscore the doctrine of fair use for scholars and hence should be more widely known.

> We, the undersigned members of the Association of American University Presses, believe that it is in the interests of publishers and scholars alike to facilitate and spread the use and to increase the value of all scholarly publications by allowing scholars to quote without prior permission from published sources whatever they legitimately need to make their scholarly writings complete, accurate, and authenticated. We believe that such use of the work of others should be subject only to the scholar's obligation to give full credit to the author and publisher of the work quoted, and the further obligation to avoid quoting in such amounts, over and beyond scholarly needs, as to impair or destroy the property rights and financial benefits of their fellow scholars and the original publishers from whose work they are quoting.
>
> Therefore, we, the undersigned members of the Association of American University Presses, agree as follows:
>
> 1. That publications issued under our imprints may be quoted without specific prior permission in works of original scholarship for accurate citation of authority or for criticism, review, or evaluation, subject to the conditions listed below.
> 2. That appropriate credit be given in the case of each quotation.
> 3. That waiver of the requirement for specific permission does not extend to quotations that are complete units in themselves (as poems, letters, short stories, essays, journal articles, complete chapters or sections of books, maps, charts, graphs, tables, drawings, or other illustrative materials), in whatever form they may be reproduced; nor does the waiver extend to quotation of whatever length presented as primary material for its own sake (as in anthologies or books of readings).
> 4. The fact that specific permission for quoting of material may be waived under this agreement does not relieve the quoting author and publisher from the responsibility of determining "fair use" of such material.

For internal reasons a few presses belonging to the association were unable to sign the resolution. Those that have signed it, through 1968, are:

> The University of Arizona Press
> Bollingen Foundation
> The Brookings Institution
> Brown University Press
> University of California Press

The Press of Case Western Reserve University
The University of Chicago Press
Columbia University Press
Cornell University Press
Duke University Press
Duquesne University Press
Fordham University Press
The University of Georgia Press
University of Hawaii Press
The University of Illinois Press
Indiana University Press
The Iowa State University Press
The Johns Hopkins Press
The University Press of Kansas
University of Kentucky Press
Louisiana State University Press
McGill University Press
The University of Massachusetts Press
The M.I.T. Press
The Metropolitan Museum of Art
University of Miami Press
The Michigan State University Press
University of Missouri Press
University of Nebraska Press
The University of New Mexico Press
New York University Press
University of North Carolina Press
Northwestern University Press
University of Notre Dame Press
Ohio University Press
Ohio State University Press
University of Pennsylvania Press
Pennsylvania State University Press
The University of Pittsburgh Press
Princeton University Press
Smithsonian Institution
University of South Carolina Press
Southern Illinois University Press
Southern Methodist University Press
Stanford University Press
Syracuse University Press
University of Tennessee Press
University of Texas Press
University of Toronto Press
Vanderbilt University Press
University Press of Virginia
University of Washington Press
Wayne State University Press
The University of Wisconsin Press
Yale University Press

UNPUBLISHED MATERIAL

4.20   Unpublished correspondence, archives, dissertations (unless on microfilm), are not protected by the copyright law as are published works. They are, however, protected by common-law copyright, which in some ways is more restrictive than statutory copyright. For one thing, there is no fixed duration to the protection it affords. A document under common-law copyright is protected in perpetuity or until (1) it is published and registered for statutory copyright[5] or (2) rights in the work are formally assigned by the author or his heirs to someone else—a corporation, a library, trustees, or the like. For another thing, the doctrine of fair use does not apply to common-law copyright, and even the briefest snippet of, say, an unpublished letter should not be published without permission of the rights holder.

4.21   An author whose research includes the use of such material, whether in private collections or in public depositories, must be informed of any regulations governing its reproduction in a published work. The curator of a collection is normally the source of such information—that is, he knows the regulations governing use of the material and what permissions must be sought and from whom; he cannot, as a rule, himself grant permission.

4.22   With personal correspondence, unless otherwise stipulated, the recipient of a letter owns the letter itself. The right to permit its reproduction, however, belongs to the writer of the letter or his heirs, not to the recipient. The author of a dissertation or of any other unpublished paper is the owner of it (not the library where it is housed) and also has the sole right to permit reproduction.

HOW TO ASK PERMISSION

4.23   All requests for permission to reprint must be sent to the copyright holder (1) in writing and (2) in duplicate. In granting permission the copyright holder will sign and return one copy of the request to the author, retaining the other for his files.

4.24   The request must contain explicit information. First, the title of the original work, the exact passage(s)[6] or a figure or table number, and the page number(s) where the material appears in the

5. Some works, including sermons and speeches, may be registered by the author *without* being published.

6. For long prose passages the first and last words may be given.

original work. Second, information about the publication in which the author wishes to reproduce the material: title, approximate number of printed pages, form of publication (book—clothbound or paperback—or journal), publisher, probable date of publication, probable list price (if available). Third, what kind of rights are requested: if the author's publisher plans worldwide distribution for the book, the author should request *non-exclusive world rights in the English language* for reproducing any material in it.

4.25 Picture agencies will want to know the nature of the work (text, trade book, etc.) and whether the author (or the publisher) intends to use an illustration elsewhere than in the text proper.

4.26 Some publishers who receive many requests for permission to reprint may ask an author requesting such permission from them to fill out a form devised to suit their particular circumstances (see the University of Chicago Press form reproduced in fig. 4.1).

COMPILATIONS

MULTIAUTHOR BOOKS

4.27 A book made up of chapters by different authors, such as the proceedings of a symposium, requires not only a contract signed by the general editor or sponsor of the volume but also a *written* consent to publish from each contributor.[7] Normally, the publisher will provide the volume editor with the appropriate number of forms to be signed by the contributors (fig. 4.2). The editor will then obtain a signed consent from each contributor and send all consents to the publisher to be filed with the contract for the volume.

ANTHOLOGIES

4.28 A book made up entirely of previously published, copyrighted materials—stories, essays, poems, documents, selections from larger works—can be brought into being in part only by permissions granted by copyright holders. The compiler of such a volume, therefore, must begin seeking his permissions as soon as he has selected his materials and before he submits his manuscript to a publisher. Permission may be refused for a selection, or the fee

7. This assumes no prepublication and that the contributor has procured all necessary permissions for the use of any copyrighted material in his chapter.

THE UNIVERSITY OF CHICAGO PRESS

5750 ELLIS AVENUE, CHICAGO, ILLINOIS 60637

DEAR..:

The University of Chicago Press is pleased to have the privilege of publishing
your contribution..
to the Work now entitled..
edited by...

In order that we may accept your contribution for publication, it is essential that
you grant us the copyright to your contribution. After publication of the work, upon
your request, we will assign to you the right to publish your contribution in
scholarly or professional journals when you wish to do so. Thus, this agreement will
in no way impede the rapid dissemination of research material.

The following terms of Publication are accordingly submitted for your consideration.

Consent To Publish

Whereas the University of Chicago, through its Press, is undertaking to publish
the Work named above, of which the undersigned is Author of one or more parts,
the Author transfers and assigns to the University the copyright therein and all
rights protected by copyright. After publication of the Work by the University,
upon your request the right of republication of your contribution in any scholarly
or professional journal will be assigned to you, subject only to receiving proper
credit in the Journal to book publication of the contribution by the University of
Chicago Press.

Previous Publication

The Author guarantees that the material furnished for the Work has not been previously published elsewhere, or that if it has been previously published in whole or
in part, permission has been obtained for publication in the Work. The Author will
submit copy for credit lines with his manuscript for any previously published material.

The Author warrants that the contribution is original and that he is the sole
author and owner of the contribution and has full power to make this license.

Proofreading

The Author will be given an opportunity to read and correct galley proofs, but if
he fails to return them to the Editor of the volume by the date set by the Editor,
production and publication will proceed without the Author's approval of proof.

Compensation

The Author shall receive one (1) free copy of the published Work, and may buy
additional copies by direct order to the Publisher at 40 per cent discount from list
price. The Author shall receive no royalty or other monetary return from the University for the use of his material.

Reprints

The Author may order reprints of his part or parts of the Work, to a maximum
quantity of one hundred (100) copies of each part, at rates listed on the enclosed
order form. Reprints are printed as a part of the press run of the complete Work;
consequently the order form must be returned no later than the date set for the
return of galley proofs.

If the foregoing terms are satisfactory, please sign and date this agreement, re-
turning the white copy to the Publisher and retaining the blue copy for your own
files.

Morris Philipson

DIRECTOR OF THE UNIVERSITY OF CHICAGO PRESS

AUTHOR
_____

Date:
_____

Address to which free copy should be sent:

_____

_____

charged may be so high that the compiler is forced to drop a selection and substitute another. Until all permissions have been received and all fees agreed upon, the table of contents cannot be final.

FOR FURTHER REFERENCE

4.29   This chapter on rights and permissions is intended only to give authors and editors an idea of the major requirements. Publishers' permissions secretaries and others who need more information should consult the standard handbook in the field: Margaret Nicholson, *A Manual of Copyright Practice*, 2d edition. Here will be found full explanations of the complexities of copyright laws, regulations governing works published outside the United States, including variations in the duration of copyright, and other pertinent matters. Also helpful are Philip Wittenberg, *The Law of Literary Property*, written by a professor of law for "the layman in law"; Paul P. Ashley, *Say It Safely: Legal Limits in Publishing, Radio and Television*, 3d edition; and Lowell H. Hattery and George P. Bush, eds., *Reprography and Copyright Law*. These volumes are fully listed in the Bibliography.

Fig. 4.2. Consent-to-publish form currently sent to contributors to multiauthor volumes by the University of Chicago Press. (Shown here is the revised form in use in 1970.)

Part 2

Style

5 *Punctuation*

5.1 The punctuation guidelines offered in this chapter apply largely to running text. For the special punctuation recommended in notes, footnotes, bibliographies, indexes, and so on, see the appropriate chapters in this manual.

5.2 Punctuation marks should generally be printed in the same style or font of type as the word, letter, character, or symbol immediately preceding them:

Luke 4:16*a;*   **Point:** one-twelfth of a pica

Italic or boldface parentheses or brackets, however, should not be used in such situations:

(see paragraph 6*a*)   (see **12b**)   [*Continued*]   [*sic*]

MULTIPLE PUNCTUATION

5.3 The use of more than one mark of punctuation at the same location in a sentence (multiple punctuation) is, for the most part, limited to instances involving quotation marks, parentheses, brackets, or dashes. An abbreviating period, however, is never omitted before a mark of sentence punctuation unless the latter is the period terminating the sentence:

O. D., who had apparently just heard the report, came over to our table in great agitation.
The study was funded by Mulvehill & Co.

When two different marks of punctuation are called for at the same location in a sentence, the stronger mark only is retained:

Who shouted, "Up the establishment!"
"Have you read the platform?" asked Williams in distress.

PERIOD

TERMINAL PUNCTUATION

5.4   A period is used to indicate the end of a declarative or an imperative sentence:

> The two men faced each other in silence.   Wait here.

5.5   A period should be omitted at the end of a sentence that is included within another sentence:

> The snow (I caught a glimpse of it as I passed the window) was now falling heavily.
>
> Gilford's reply, "I do not trust the man," was unexpected.

LISTS

5.6   Omit the period after items in a vertical list unless one or more of the items are complete sentences.

5.7   Use a period without parentheses after numerals or letters used to enumerate items in a vertical list:

> 1. strigiformes   *a.* the Korean War
> 2. caprimulgiformes   *b.* the Eisenhower administration

Numerals or letters enumerating items in a list within a paragraph should be enclosed in parentheses and should not be followed by a period (see par. 5.97).

PERIODS WITH QUOTATION MARKS, PARENTHESES,
AND BRACKETS

5.8   Periods should be placed within the quotation marks except when single quotation marks are used to set off special terms (see pars. 6.41, 6.47). When parentheses or brackets are used to enclose an independent sentence, the period belongs inside. If the enclosed matter is part of an including sentence, the period should be placed outside the parentheses or brackets:

> Emerson replied, "There is no reason to doubt the president's statement."
>
> He had not defined the term 'categorical imperative'.
>
> "I have just read 'A Good Man Is Hard to Find.' "
>
> They had been requested to sing "The Sounds of Silence."
>
> Forelli insisted on rewriting the paragraph. (I had encountered this intransigence on another occasion.)
>
> The driver glanced at his rear-view mirror to observe the passenger (the one in the derby hat).

105

DISPLAY LINES, HEADINGS, AND LEGENDS

5.9   Omit the period after display lines, running heads, centered head-
lines, sideheads set on separate lines, cut-in heads, boxheadings
in tables, one-line superscriptions and legends, date lines heading
communications, and signatures.

OMISSIONS AND LACUNAE

5.10   Periods may be used to mark the omission of letters in mutilated
manuscripts or inscriptions, or lacunae in original writings. Use
one period for each letter lacking, with space as between words:

$$[.\,.\,.\,.\,.\,.]\alpha\sigma[\text{---}]$$
$$[K\alpha\rho\kappa\acute{\iota}]\nu os\;\Delta|$$
$$['A\sigma\tau]\upsilon\delta\acute{a}\mu as\;\ulcorner||\;[\text{---}?]$$
$$[\Theta\epsilon o]\delta\acute{\epsilon}\kappa\tau as\;\ulcorner||$$

$[Ai]\sigma\chi\acute{\upsilon}[\lambda os\text{---}]$ $['A\phi a]\rho\epsilon\acute{\upsilon}s\;||$
$[E\acute{\upsilon}]\acute{\epsilon}\tau\eta s\;|$ $[.\,.\,.\,.\;\omega]\nu\;||$ $A|$
$[\Pi o]\lambda\upsilon\phi\rho\acute{a}\sigma\mu[\omega\nu\text{---}]$ $.\,.\,.\,.\,.\,.$ $\Phi\rho\text{-}$
$[N\acute{o}\theta]\iota\pi\pi os\;|$ $.\,.\,.\,.\,.\,.\,.\,.\,.\;||$ $'O\mu\text{-}$
$[\Sigma o\phi]o\kappa\lambda\hat{\eta}s\;\Delta\ulcorner|||$ $\Delta|$
$[.\,.\,.\,.]\;\tau os\;||[\text{---}?]$ $\Xi\text{-}$
$['A\rho\iota\sigma\tau\acute{\iota}]as\;[\text{---}]$

The use in English of three or four periods together (*ellipsis points*
or *dots*) as a mark of omission is discussed in pars. 10.31–40.

INTERRUPTIONS AND BREAKS

5.11   Series of periods are used in French, Spanish, Italian, and Russian
to indicate sudden breaks in thought or interruptions in faltering speech (see also par. 5.77). In French, Spanish, and Russian
use three periods with no space between them, but use a 3-to-em
space after them. In Italian use four periods with no space between
or before them. In Italian and Russian any other punctuation
mark is considered to take the place of the first period. (For
examples see chapter 9.)

EXCLAMATION POINT

5.12   An exclamation point is used to mark an outcry or an emphatic
or ironical comment. In order not to detract from its effective-
ness, however, the author should use it sparingly:

Look out!
Your comment was certainly lacking in tact!
How can you say that!

The emperor, it seemed, had forgotten to notify his generals!
Suddenly the ambassador perceived that all was lost!

5.13   The use of an exclamation point as an editorial protest in quoted matter is strongly discouraged. The expression *sic* (in brackets) is preferred (see par. 10.42).

5.14   The exclamation point should be placed inside the quotation marks, parentheses, or brackets when it is part of the quoted or parenthetical matter; otherwise, it should be placed outside:

The woman cried, "Those men are beating that child!"
Her husband replied—calmly—"It is no concern of mine"!
Mrs. Laslow (I could have died!) repeated the whole story.

5.15   In Spanish the exclamation point is used before, as well as after, the clause, but the mark that precedes the clause is inverted:

¡Qué bonita muchacha!

QUESTION MARK

5.16   The question mark, or interrogation point, is used to mark a query or to express an editorial doubt:

Who will represent the poor?
The subject of the final essay was Montezuma II (1480?–1520), the last Aztec emperor of Mexico.

5.17   A question mark should be retained at the end of an interrogative sentence that is included within another sentence:

How can the two men be reconciled? was on everyone's mind.
The question still to be decided was, Which of the two strategies would be less likely to provoke opposition?

5.18   A sentence essentially declarative or imperative in structure may become interrogative by the substitution of a question mark for the period:

This is your reply?   Wait here?

5.19   A request courteously disguised as a question should not be terminated by a question mark:

Will you please rush the manuscript to the publisher.
Will the audience please rise.

5.20   Indirect questions should not be followed by a question mark:

Plimpton was thoughtful enough to ask whether we had eaten.

5.21   In Spanish the question mark is used before, as well as after, the question, but the mark that precedes the clause is inverted:

¿Qué corresponde a cada uno de los siete signos indicados?

107

5.22   The question mark should be placed inside the quotation marks, parentheses, or brackets only when it is part of the quoted or parenthetical matter:

> The ambassador asked, "Then why, sir, are these maneuvers occurring so close to our border?"
>
> Why did he say, "Your bargain is too dear"?
>
> When Crichton was introduced to the agent (had he met him before?), he turned to his host and winked.
>
> If that was the case, why did she delay answering the governor until the morning of his departure (18 March)?

COMMA

5.23   The comma indicates the smallest interruption in continuity of thought or sentence structure. There are a few rules governing its use that have become almost obligatory. Aside from these, the use of the comma is mainly a matter of good judgment, with ease of reading as the end in view.

COMPOUND SENTENCES

5.24   When the clauses of a compound sentence are joined by a conjunction, a comma should be placed before the conjunction unless the clauses are short and closely related:

> The two men quickly bolted the door, but the intruder had already entered through the window.
>
> Everyone present was startled by the news, and several senators who had been standing in the hall rushed into the room to hear the end of the announcement.
>
> Are we really interested in preserving law and order, or are we only interested in preserving our own privileges?
>
> Charles played the guitar and Betty sang.

5.25   In a compound sentence composed of a series of short, independent clauses the last two of which are joined by a conjunction, commas should be placed between the clauses and before the conjunction (see also pars. 5.46, 5.64):

> Harris presented the proposal to the governor, the governor discussed it with the senator, and the senator made an appointment with the president.

5.26   Care should be taken to distinguish between a compound sentence (two or more independent clauses) and a sentence having a compound predicate (two or more verbs having the same subject). Preferably, the comma should not be used between the parts of a compound predicate:

> He had accompanied Sanford on his first expedition and had volunteered to remain alone at Port Royal.
>
> Mrs. Chapuis has been living in the building for over thirty years and is distraught over the possibility of now having to move.
>
> On Thursday morning Kelleher tried to see the mayor but was told the mayor was out of town.

ADVERBIAL CLAUSES OR PHRASES

5.27   If a dependent clause following a main clause is restrictive—that is, if it cannot be omitted without altering the meaning of the main clause—it should not be set off by a comma. If it is nonrestrictive, it should be set off by a comma:

> We shall agree to the proposal if you accept our conditions.
>
> Paul was astonished when he heard the terms.
>
> Paul voted for the proposal, although he would have preferred to abstain.

5.28   A dependent clause that precedes the main clause should usually be set off by a comma whether it is restrictive or nonrestrictive:

> If you accept our conditions, we shall agree to the proposal.
>
> Although he would have preferred to abstain, Paul voted for the proposal.

5.29   An adverbial phrase at the beginning of a sentence is frequently followed by a comma:

> After reading the note, Henrietta turned pale.
>
> Because of the unusual circumstances, the king sent his personal representative.

5.30   The comma is sometimes omitted after short introductory adverbial phrases:

> On Tuesday he tried to see the mayor.
>
> After breakfast the count mounted his horse.
>
> For thirty years the widow had refused to move.

5.31   A comma should not be used after an introductory adverbial phrase that immediately precedes the verb it modifies:

> Out of the automobile stepped a short man in a blue suit.
>
> In the doorway stood a man with a summons.

5.32   An adverbial phrase or clause located between the subject and the verb should usually be set off by commas:

> Wolinski, after receiving his instructions, left immediately for Algiers.
>
> Morgenstern, in a manner that surprised us all, escorted the reporter to the door.

ADJECTIVAL PHRASES OR CLAUSES

5.33   An adjectival phrase or clause that follows a noun and restricts or limits the reference of the noun in a way that is essential to the meaning of the sentence should not be set off by commas; but an adjectival phrase or clause that is nonrestrictive or is purely descriptive, which could be dropped without changing the reference of the noun, is set off by commas:

> The report that the committee submitted was well documented.
>
> The report, which was well documented, was discussed with considerable emotion.
>
> McFetridge, sitting comfortably before the fire, slowly and ceremoniously opened his mail.
>
> The elderly woman sitting beside McFetridge was his nurse.

INTRODUCTORY PARTICIPIAL PHRASES

5.34   An introductory participial phrase should be set off by a comma unless it immediately precedes (and forms part of) the verb:

> Having forgotten to notify his generals, the king arrived on the battlefield alone.
>
> Exhausted by the morning's work, the archaeologists napped in the shade of the ancient wall.
>
> Judging from the correspondence, we may conclude that the two men never reached accord.
>
> Running along behind the wagon was the archduke himself!

PARENTHETICAL ELEMENTS

5.35   Parenthetical elements that retain a close logical relationship to the rest of the sentence should be set off by commas. Parenthetical elements whose logical relationship to the rest of the sentence is more remote should be set off by dashes or parentheses (see pars. 5.77–80, 5.94–96):

> Wilcox, it was believed, had turned the entire affair over to his partner.

110

The Hooligan Report was, to say the least, a bombshell.

The members of the commission were, generally speaking, disposed to reject innovative measures.

Bardston—he is to be remembered for his outspokenness in the Wainscot affair—had asked for permission to address the assembly.

The Wintermitten theory (it had already been dropped by some of its staunchest early supporters) was dealt a decisive blow by the Kringelmeyer experiments.

INTERJECTIONS, TRANSITIONAL ADVERBS, AND SIMILAR ELEMENTS

5.36 Commas should be used to set off interjections, transitional adverbs, and similar elements that effect a distinct break in the continuity of thought (see also par. 5.35):

Well, I'm afraid I was unprepared to find Virginia there.
Yes, I admit that Benson's plan has gained a following.
Indeed, this was exactly what Scali had feared would happen.
That, after all, was more than Farnsworth could bear.
On the other hand, the opposition had been conducted clumsily.
All the test animals, therefore, were reexamined.
Babbington, perhaps, had disclosed more than was necessary.
We shall, however, take the matter up at a later date.
Their credibility, consequently, has been seriously challenged.

When these elements are used in such a way that there is no real break in continuity and no call for any pause in reading, commas should be omitted:

The storehouse was indeed empty.
I therefore urge you all to remain loyal.
Wilcox was perhaps a bit too hasty in his judgment.
Palmerston was in fact the chairman of the committee.

5.37 Use a comma after exclamatory *oh* but not after vocative *O:*

Oh, what a dreadful sight!
O mighty king!

DIRECT ADDRESS

5.38 Use commas to set off words in direct address:

Friends, I am not here to discuss personalities.
The evidence, good people, contradicts my opponent.

111

5.39   Commas should be omitted at the ends of display lines, such as titles, centered headings, signatures, and date lines.

APPOSITIVES

5.40   A word, phrase, or clause that is in apposition to a noun is usually set off by commas (dashes or parentheses might also be used):

> The capital of Rhodesia, Salisbury, was in a state of unrest.
>
> The leader of the opposition, Senator Darkswain, had had an unaccountable change of heart.
>
> We were unable to locate Marsden, the committee member who had written the report.
>
> His second novel, a detective story with psychological and religious overtones, was said to have been influenced by the work of Dostoevski.
>
> My wife, Elizabeth, had written to our congressman.

Sometimes an appositive is disguised by the conjunction *or:*

> The steward, or farm manager, was an important functionary in medieval life.
>
> A "zinc," or line engraving, will be made from the sketch.

5.41   If the appositive has a restrictive function, it is not set off by commas:

> My son Michael was the first one to reply.
>
> Jeanne DeLor dedicated the poems to her sister Margaret.
>
> O'Neill's play *The Hairy Ape* was being revived.
>
> The statement "The poor have much patience" is attributed to Count Précaire.

COORDINATE ADJECTIVES

5.42   Separate two or more adjectives by commas if each modifies the noun alone:

> Shelley had proved a faithful, sincere friend.
>
> Rocco had said that it was going to be a long, hot summer.

If the first adjective modifies the idea expressed by the combination of the second adjective and the noun, no comma should be used:

> He had no patience with the traditional political institutions of his country.
>
> In his path was an angry black panther.

5.43   When two or more complementary or antithetical phrases refer to a single word following, the phrases should be separated from one another and from the following word by commas:

> This harsh, though at the same time logical, conclusion provoked resentment among those affected.
>
> The most provocative, if not the most important, part of the statement was saved until last.
>
> This road leads away from, rather than toward, your destination.
>
> He hopes to, and doubtless will, meet Caspar in Madrid.

5.44   An antithetical phrase or clause beginning with *not* should usually be set off by commas if the phrase or clause is not essential to the meaning of the modified element:

> The delegates had hoped that the mayor himself, not his assistant, would be present.
>
> White, not Thurgood, was the candidate to beat.
>
> Baum attended the lecture, not to hear what Morgan had to say, but to observe the reaction of his audience.
>
> *But:* Baum attended the lecture not so much to hear what Morgan had to say as to observe the reaction of his audience.

5.45   Interdependent antithetical clauses should be separated by a comma:

> The more he read about the incident, the greater became his resolve to get to the bottom of it.
>
> Say what you will, Senator Watson's bill leaves much to be desired.
>
> The higher Fisher climbed, the dizzier he felt.

Short antithetical phrases, however, should not be separated by commas:

> The more the merrier.
>
> The sooner the better.

5.46   In a series consisting of three or more elements, the elements are separated by commas. When a conjunction joins the last two elements in a series, a comma is used before the conjunction (see also par. 5.25):

> Attending the conference were Farmer, Johnson, and Kendrick.
>
> We have a choice of copper, silver, or gold.
>
> The owner, the agent, and the tenant were having an acrimonious discussion.

5.47 When the elements in a series are very simple and are all joined by conjunctions, no commas should be used:

> I cannot remember whether the poem was written by Snodgrass or Shapiro or Brooks.

5.48 When the elements in a series are long and complex or involve internal punctuation, they should be separated by semicolons (see par. 5.64).

5.49 Although the use of *etc.* in running text is to be discouraged, it should, when used, be set off by commas:

> The firm manufactured nuts, bolts, nails, metal wire, etc., in its plant on the Passaic River.

"THAT IS," "NAMELY," AND SIMILAR EXPRESSIONS

5.50 A comma should be used after such expressions as *that is, namely, i.e.,* and *e.g.* The punctuation preceding such expressions should be determined by the magnitude of the break in continuity. If the break is minor, a comma should be used. If the break is greater than that signaled by a comma, a semicolon or an em dash may be used (see pars. 5.66, 5.80), or the expression and the element it introduces may be enclosed in parentheses (see par. 5.96):

> He had put the question to several of his friends, namely, Jones, Burdick, and Fauntleroy.
>
> The committee—that is, several of its more influential members—seemed disposed to reject the Brower Plan.
>
> Keesler maneuvered the speaker into changing the course of the discussion; that is, he introduced a secondary issue about which the speaker had particularly strong feelings.
>
> Several African countries (i.e., Rwanda, Sierra Leone, Mali, and Tanzania) were represented on the committee.

MISTAKEN JUNCTION

5.51 A comma is sometimes necessary to prevent mistaken junction:

> To Anthony, Blake remained an enigma.
>
> Soon after, the conference was interrupted by a strange occurrence.
>
> She recognized the man who entered the room, and gasped.

SEPARATING IDENTICAL OR SIMILAR WORDS

5.52 For ease of reading, it is sometimes desirable to separate two identical or closely similar words with a comma, even though the sense or grammatical construction does not require such separation:

114

> Let us march in, in twos.
> Whatever is, is good.
> *But:* He gave his life that that cause might prevail.

Similarly, a comma should be used to separate unrelated numbers:

> In 1968, 248 editors attended the convention.

Better still, revise the sentence to avoid conjunction of unrelated numbers:

> Attending the convention in 1968 were 248 editors.

TITLES, ADDRESSES, AND DATES

5.53 Although they are not necessary, commas may be used to set off a phrase indicating place of residence immediately following a person's name:

> The first speaker was Andy Porkola, of Toronto.
> Mr. and Mrs. Osaki of Tokyo were also present.

The commas should always be omitted, however, in those cases, historical or political, in which the place name has practically become a part of the person's name or is so closely associated with it as to render the separation by comma artificial or illogical:

> Clement of Alexandria
> Philip of Anjou

5.54 Use commas to set off words identifying a title or position following a person's name (see also pars. 5.40, 14.8–10):

> Merriwether Benson, former president of Acquisition Corporation, had been appointed to the commission.

5.55 Use commas to set off the individual elements in addresses and names of geographical places or political divisions:

> Please send all proofs to the author at 743 Maret Drive, Saint Louis, Missouri.
> During the afternoon the plane landed in Kampala, Uganda.

5.56 In the date style preferred by the University of Chicago Press, no commas are used to mark off the year:

> On 6 October 1966 Longo arrived in Bologna.
> The meetings were held in April 1967.

In the older style, however, commas must be used:

> On October 6, 1966, . . .
> . . . in April, 1967, . . .

5.57   A comma is often used to indicate the omission, for brevity or convenience, of a word or words readily understood from the context:

> In Illinois there are seventeen such institutions; in Ohio, twenty-two; in Indiana, thirteen.
> Thousands rushed to his support in victory; in defeat, none.

5.58   When, in spite of such omissions, the construction is clear enough without the commas (and the consequent semicolons), the simpler punctuation should be used:

> One committee member may be from Ohio, another from Pennsylvania, and a third from West Virginia.
> Ronald adored her and she him.

QUOTATIONS

5.59   A direct quotation, maxim, or similar expression should ordinarily be set off from the rest of the sentence by commas:

> Vera said calmly, "I have no idea what you mean."
> "The driver refused to enter the bus," retorted Eberly.
> "I am afraid," said Kroft, "that I can offer no explanation."
> You know the old saying, Politics makes strange bedfellows.

If the quotation is used as the subject or the predicate nominative of the sentence, however, or if it is a restrictive appositive, it should not be set off by commas:

> "Under no circumstances" was the reply he least expected.
> "Less is more" was that architect's watchword.
> That architect's watchword was "Less is more."
> The watchword "Less is more" aroused considerable controversy.

A colon should be used to introduce a long, formal quotation. (For a detailed discussion of quotations see chapter 10.)

USE WITH OTHER PUNCTUATION

5.60   When the context calls for a comma at the end of material enclosed in quotation marks, parentheses, or brackets, the comma should be placed inside the quotation marks but outside the parentheses or brackets (see also par. 5.59):

> See Brighton's comments on "political expedience," which may be found elsewhere in this volume.

Here he gives a belated, though stilted (and somewhat obscure), exposition of the subject.

Although he rejected the first proposal (he could not have done otherwise without compromising his basic position), he was careful to make it clear that he was open to further negotiations.

Commas should not be used with dashes except when necessary to separate quoted material from the words that identify the speaker (see pars. 5.84–85).

SEMICOLON

5.61 A semicolon is used to mark a more important break in sentence flow than that marked by a comma. Use a semicolon between the two parts of a compound sentence (two independent clauses) when they are not connected by a conjunction:

The controversial portrait was removed from the entrance hall; in its place was hung a realistic landscape.

5.62 The following words are considered adverbs rather than conjunctions and should therefore be preceded by a semicolon when used transitionally between clauses of a compound sentence—*then, however, thus, hence, indeed, yet, so:*

Partridge had heard the argument before; thus, he turned his back on Fenton and reiterated his decision.

Mildred says she intends to go to Europe this summer; yet she makes no definite plans.

Ballard was out of the office when I called; so I left a message.

Or: . . . when I called, and so I left a message.

5.63 If the clauses of a compound sentence are very long or are themselves subdivided by commas, a semicolon may be used between them even if they are joined by a conjunction:

Margaret, who had already decided that she would ask the question at the first opportunity, tried to catch the director's attention as he passed through the anteroom; but the noisy group of people accompanying the director prevented him from noticing her.

5.64 When items in a series are long and complex or involve internal punctuation, they should be separated by semicolons for the sake of clarity:

The membership of the international commission was as follows: France, 4; Germany, 5; Great Britain, 1; Italy, 3; the United States, 7.

The defendant, in an attempt to mitigate his sentence, pleaded that (1) he had been despondent over the death of his wife; (2) he had lost his job under particularly humiliating circumstances; (3) his landlady—whom, incidentally, he had once saved from attack—had threatened to have him evicted; (4) he had not eaten for several days; and (5) he had, in this weakened condition, been unduly affected by an alcoholic beverage.

5.65 Semicolons should be used to separate references when one or more of the references contain internal punctuation:

Gen. 2:3–6; 3:15, 17; 6:5, 9, 14.
MLN 25:18; 26:69; 30:41.

5.66 A semicolon may be used before an expression such as *that is, namely, i.e., e.g.,* if the break in continuity is greater than that signaled by a comma. For comparative examples see par. 5.50.

5.67 The semicolon should be placed outside the quotation marks or parentheses. When the matter quoted ends with a semicolon, the semicolon is dropped:

Curtis assumed that everyone in the room had read "Mr. Prokharchin"; he alluded to it several times during the discussion.

Ambassador Porkola had hoped that the committee would take up the question (several members had assured him privately that they favored such a move); but at the end of August the committee adjourned without having considered it.

COLON

RELATING CLAUSES

5.68 The colon is used to mark a discontinuity of grammatical construction greater than that indicated by the semicolon and less than that indicated by the period. It may thus be used to emphasize a sequence in thought between two clauses that form a single sentence or to separate one clause from a second clause that contains an illustration or amplification of the first:

The officials had been in conference most of the night: this may account for their surly treatment of the reporters the next morning.

Many of the policemen held additional jobs: thirteen of them, for example, doubled as cabdrivers.

In contemporary usage, however, such clauses frequently are separated by a semicolon rather than a colon (see par. 5.61) or are treated as separate sentences:

The officials had been in conference most of the night. This may account for their surly treatment of the reporters the next morning.

5.69   A colon is used to introduce a formal statement, an extract, or a speech in a dialogue:

> The rule may be stated thus: Always . . .
> We quote from the address: "It now seems appropriate . . .
> MICHAEL: The incident has already been reported.
> TIMOTHY: Then, sir, all is lost!

5.70   A colon is commonly used to introduce a list or a series:

> Binghamton's study included the three most critical areas: Mc-Burney Point, Rockland, and Effingham.

If the list or series is introduced by such expressions as *namely, for instance, for example,* or *that is,* a colon should not be used unless the series consists of one or more grammatically complete clauses:

> Binghamton's study included the three most critical areas, namely, McBurney Point, Rockland, and Effingham.
> For example: Morton had raised French poodles for many years; Gilbert disliked French poodles intensely; Gilbert and Morton seldom looked each other in the eye.

5.71   The terms *as follows* or *the following* require a colon if followed directly by the illustrating or enumerated items or if the introducing clause is incomplete without such items:

> The steps are as follows:
> 1. Tie the string to the green pole and . . .

If the introducing statement is complete, however, and is followed by other complete sentences, a period may be used:

> An outline of the procedure follows. Note that care was taken to eliminate the effect of temperature variation.
> 1. Identical amounts of the compound were placed . . .

5.72   A colon should follow a speaker's introductory remark addressed to the chairman or the audience:

> Mr. Chairman, Ladies and Gentlemen:

5.73   A centered (ratio) colon (i.e., with equal space on either side) should be used between chapter and verse in scriptural passages, between hours and minutes in time indications, and between volume and page reference:

> Matt. 2:5–13   4:30 P.M.   *Bot. Gaz.* 109:357.

5.74   A colon is used between the place of publication and the publisher's name in bibliographical references:

> Robert Pinsky, *Landor's Poetry* (Chicago: University of Chicago Press, 1968), p. 95.

USE WITH OTHER PUNCTUATION

5.75   The colon should be placed outside quotation marks or parentheses. When matter ending with a colon is quoted, the colon is dropped:

> Kego had three objections to "Filmore's Summer": it was contrived; the characters were flat; the dialogue was unrealistic.
>
> Herschel was puzzled by one of the changes noted in the behavior of the experimental animals (rhesus monkeys): all the monkeys had become hypersensitive to sound.

DASH

5.76   There are several kinds of dashes, varying from one another according to length. There are en dashes, em dashes, and 2- and 3-em dashes. Each kind of dash has its own uses. The most commonly used dash is the em dash. In the following material, the em dash is referred to simply as "the dash." The other dashes are identified.

SUDDEN BREAKS AND ABRUPT CHANGES

5.77   A dash or a pair of dashes is used to denote a sudden break in thought that causes an abrupt change in sentence structure (see also pars. 5.35, 5.94–96):

> Will he—can he—obtain the necessary signatures?
>
> The Platonic world of the static and the Hegelian world of process—how great the contrast!
>
> Consensus—that was the will-o'-the-wisp he doggedly pursued.
>
> The chancellor—he had been awake half the night waiting in vain for a reply—came down to breakfast in an angry mood.
>
> There came a time—let us say, for convenience, with Herodotus and Thucydides—when this attention to actions was conscious and deliberate.

5.78   Dashes are used to indicate interruptions or breaks in faltering speech:

> I—I—that is, we—yes, *we* have made an awful blunder!
>
> The binoculars—where did you put them?

5.79   An element added to give emphasis or explanation by expanding a phrase occurring in the main clause should be introduced by a dash:

> He had spent several hours carefully explaining the operation—an operation that would, he hoped, put an end to the resistance.
>
> Marsot finally conceded that the plan was bold and unusual—bold and unusual in the sense that . . .

5.80   A defining or enumerating complementary element that is added to or inserted in a sentence may be set off by dashes. Such an element may also, however, be enclosed in parentheses (see par. 5.94) or—at the end of a sentence—be introduced by a colon (see pars. 5.68–71):

> He could forgive every insult but the last—the snub by his former office boy, Tim Warren.
>
> It was to the so-called battered child syndrome—a diverse array of symptoms indicating repeated physical abuse of the child—that he then began to turn his attention.
>
> The influence of three impressionists—Monet, Sisley, and Degas—can clearly be seen in his early development as a painter.

5.81   A dash may be used before an expression such as *that is, namely, i.e., e.g.,* if the break in continuity is greater than that signaled by a comma. For comparative examples see par. 5.50.

5.82   In sentences having several elements as referents of a pronoun that is the subject of a final, summarizing clause, the final clause should be preceded by a dash:

> Ives, Stravinsky, and Bartók—these were the composers he most admired.
>
> Klingston, who first conceived the idea; Barber, who organized the fund-raising campaign; and West, who conducted the investigation—these were the men most responsible for the movement's early success.
>
> Broken promises, petty rivalries, and police harassment—such were the obstacles he encountered.
>
> Winograd, Burton, Kravitz, Johnson—all were astounded by the chairman's resignation.

INTRODUCING A LIST OF PARALLEL COMPLEMENTS

5.83   A word or phrase set on a separate line and succeeded by parallel elements that complete the sentence should be followed by a dash:

> After careful investigation we were convinced—
>   1. that Watson had consulted no one before making the decision;
>   2. that Braun did not know Watson;
>   3. that Braun was as surprised as anyone.

121

5.84   If the context calls for a dash where a comma would ordinarily separate two clauses, the comma should be omitted:

> Because the data had not yet been completely analyzed—the reason for this will be discussed later—the publication of the report was delayed.

5.85   A comma should be used after a dash, however, to separate quoted material from the words that identify the speaker:

> "But—but—," said Tom.

5.86   When a parenthetical element set off by dashes itself requires a question mark or an exclamation point, such punctuation may be retained before the second dash:

> "The ship—oh, my God!—it's sinking!" cried Henrietta.
>
> All at once Cartwright—can he have been out of his mind?—shook his fist in the ambassador's face.
>
> Later that night Alexandra—what an extraordinary woman she was!—rode alone to Bucharest to warn the duke.

QUOTATIONS IN FRENCH, SPANISH, ITALIAN, AND RUSSIAN

5.87   In French, Spanish, Italian, and Russian a dash is used before a speech in direct discourse instead of quotation marks before and after (for examples see chap. 9). When the speech is followed in the same sentence by other matter, a dash is placed after the speech in Spanish, Italian, and Russian, but only ordinary sentence punctuation is used in French. In French and Russian a space appears after a dash that is used to set off a speech but not in Spanish.

INDEXES

5.88   A dash is often used in indexes (without space) before the first words of subentries to save repeating cue words (see par. 18.91).

EN DASH

5.89   The en dash is one-half the length of an em dash and is longer than a hyphen:

> em dash: —   en dash: –   hyphen: -

(In typing, a hyphen is used for an en dash, two hyphens for an em dash; in preparing the manuscript for the printer, the editor will indicate where en dashes are to be set.) The principal use of the en dash is to indicate continuing, or inclusive, numbers—dates, time, or reference numbers:

1968–72	10:00 A.M.–5:00 P.M.
May–June 1967	pp. 38–45
13 May 1965–9 June 1966	John 4:3–6:2

but:

from 1968 to 1972 (*never* from 1968–72)
from May to June 1967
between 1968 and 1970 (*never* between 1968–70)
between 10:00 A.M. and 5:00 P.M.

When the concluding date of an expression denoting a duration of time is in the future, the en dash is still used:

In Professor Lach's magnum opus, *Asia in the Making of Europe* (1965–) . . .
John Doe (1940–); *better:* John Doe (b. 1940)

5.90 Periods or seasons extending over parts of two successive calendar years may be indicated by the use of a solidus (slant line) instead of an en dash:

winter 1970/71	fiscal year 1958/59	362/361 B.C.

5.91 The en dash is also used in place of a hyphen in a compound adjective one element of which consists of two words or of a hyphenated word:

New York–London flight
post–Civil War period
quasi-public–quasi-judicial body
but: non-English-speaking countries

(For hyphenated compounds see pars. 6.9–18 and table 6.1.)

2- AND 3-EM DASHES

5.92 A 2-em dash is used to indicate missing letters (see also par. 5.10). No space appears between the dash and the existing part of the word, but where the dash represents the end of a word, the normal word space follows it:

We ha—— a copy in the library.
H——h [Hirsch?]

5.93 A 3-em dash (with space on each side) is used to denote a whole word omitted or to be supplied; it is also used in bibliographies to indicate the same author as in the preceding item (see par. 16.66).

A vessel which left the ——— in July . . .

PARENTHESES

5.94   Parentheses, like commas and dashes, may be used to set off amplifying, explanatory, or digressive elements. If such parenthetical
elements retain a close logical relationship to the rest of the sentence, commas should be used. If the logical relationship is more
remote, dashes or parentheses should be used (see pars. 5.35,
5.77–79):

> The disagreement between the two men (Westover has discussed
> its origins in considerable detail) ultimately destroyed the organi-
> zation.
>
> The final sample that we collected (under extremely difficult cir-
> cumstances) contained an unexpected impurity.
>
> The Williamsport incident (Martin still turns pale at the mention
> of it) was unquestionably without precedent.
>
> Wexford's analysis (see p. 84) was more to the point.
>
> He had long suspected that the inert gases (helium, neon, argon,
> krypton, xenon, radon) could be used to produce a similar
> effect.

5.95   A combination of parentheses and dashes may be used to distinguish two overlapping parenthetical elements each of which represents a decided break in sentence continuity:

> The Whipplesworth conference—it had already been interrupted
> by three demonstrations (the last bordering on violence)—was
> adjourned without an agreement having been reached.
>
> He meant—I take this to be the (somewhat obscure) sense of his
> speech—that . . .

5.96   An expression such as *that is, namely, i.e., e.g.,* and the element
it introduces, may be enclosed in parentheses if the break in continuity is greater than that signaled by a comma. For comparative examples see par. 5.50.

5.97   Use parentheses to enclose numerals or letters marking divisions
or enumerations run into the text (see also par. 5.7):

> He had, in effect, discovered a remarkable similarity among (1)
> strigiformes, (2) caprimulgiformes, and (3) psittaciformes.
>
> A hyphen is used to show (*a*) the combination of two or more
> words into a single term representing a new idea; (*b*) the division
> of a word at the end of a line; (*c*) a part of a word (prefix, suffix,
> or root); and (*d*) the division of a word into syllables.

5.98   All punctuation except terminal punctuation (periods, question
marks, and exclamation points) should be dropped before a closing parenthesis (see pars. 5.8, 5.14, 5.22). No punctuation should
be used before an opening parenthesis unless the parentheses are

used to mark divisions or enumerations run into the text (see par. 5.97). If required by the context, other nonterminal punctuation should follow the closing parenthesis. For more regarding the use of other punctuation with parentheses, and for examples, see under individual marks. For use of the single parenthesis with figures and letters in outline style, see par. 8.40.

BRACKETS

5.99   Brackets are used to enclose editorial interpolations, corrections, explanations, or comments:

"These [the free-silver Democrats] asserted that the artificial ratio could be maintained indefinitely."

"Despite the damaging evidence that had been brought to light [by Simpson and his supporters], Fernandez continued to believe in his friend's innocence."

"As the Italian [*sic*] Dante Gabriel Ros[s]etti is reported to have said, . . ."

[This was written, it should be remembered, before Zantoni's discovery of the Driscoll manuscript.—EDITOR]

For further discussion of the use of brackets with quoted material see chapter 10.

5.100   Brackets should be used as parentheses within parentheses (but see also par. 5.95):

This thesis has been denied by at least one recognized authority (see William B. Davis, *The Second Irrawaddy Discoveries* [New York: Babbington Press, 1961], pp. 74–82).

During a prolonged visit to Australia, Glueck and an assistant (James Green, who was later to make his own study of a flightless bird [the kiwi] in New Zealand) spent several difficult months observing the survival behavior of cassowaries and emus.

For their use in mathematics see par. 13.19.

5.101   Brackets may also be used to enclose the phonetic transcript of a word:

He attributed the light to the phenomenon called gegenschein [gā'-gən-shīn'].

5.102   Such phrases as *To be continued* and *Continued from* . . . may be placed within brackets and set in italics and in reduced type:

[*Continued from page 138*]
[*To be concluded*]

5.103   For the use of brackets with other punctuation see under individual marks.

QUOTATION MARKS

5.104   The use of quotation marks to set off direct discourse and quoted matter is discussed in chapter 10, and their use with single words or phrases to signal some special usage is discussed in chapter 6. Foreign quotation marks are discussed in chapter 9.

HYPHEN

5.105   The hyphen, sometimes considered a mark of punctuation, is discussed in chapter 6, especially pars. 6.9–18, 6.19–32, and table 6.1.

FOR FURTHER REFERENCE

5.106   The interested reader will find related information on punctuation in the English language in Perrin's *Writer's Guide*, a full listing for which appears in the Bibliography.

6 *Spelling and Distinctive Treatment of Words*

6.1 For general matters of spelling the University of Chicago Press recommends use of *Webster's Third New International Dictionary* and its chief abridgment, *Webster's Seventh New Collegiate Dictionary.* If two or more spellings of a word are given, the first listed is the one preferred in Press publications. This said, a chapter on spelling in a style manual can disregard most of the dozens or hundreds of questions about spelling which arise in the course of writing or editing a serious book. "Look it up in Webster." But there are still spelling matters that a dictionary does not cover or upon which its guidance is obscure, and it is to these that the present chapter addresses itself.

6.2 The first part of the chapter is concerned with actual questions of spelling; the second part, with related questions about distinctive ways of treating words and phrases, especially the use of italics and quotation marks.

SPELLING

PLURALS

6.3 *Proper names.* Names of persons and other capitalized names form the plural in the usual way, by adding *s* or *es:*

> five Toms, four Dicks, and three Harrys
> the Pericleses of modern times
> keeping up with the Joneses
> six Hail Marys

6.4 *Italicized words.* If names of newspapers, titles of books, foreign words, or other italicized names are used in the plural, the inflectional ending is in roman type:

> He had two *Tribune*s and three *Times*es left.
> FitzGerald actually wrote three *Rubaiyat*s.
> The Egyptian *faddan* is divided into twenty-four *qirat*s.

128

If the foreign plural is used for an italicized word, the entire word, of course, is then set in italics:

> *kolkhoz, kolkhozy*   *parashâh, perashiyôth*

6.5   *Letters, noun coinages, numbers.* So far as it can be done without confusion, single or multiple letters used as words, hyphenated coinages used as nouns, and numbers (whether spelled out or in figures) form the plural by adding *s* alone (see also par. 6.55):

the three Rs	several YMCAs and AYHs
thank-you-ma'ams	the early 1920s
in twos and threes	

Abbreviations with periods, lowercase letters used as nouns, and capital letters that would be confusing if *s* alone were added form the plural with an apostrophe and an *s:*

> M.A.'s and Ph.D.'s   *x*'s and *y*'s   *S*'s, *A*'s, *I*'s

6.6   *Choice of plurals.* When Webster gives two different plurals for the same word, the first is the one generally preferred by the University of Chicago Press:

> memorandums (*not* memoranda)   appendixes (*not* appendices)
> *but:*
> symposia (*not* symposiums)   millennia (*not* millenniums)

Note, however, that different senses of the same word may have different plurals. Thus a book may have two *indexes* and a mathematical expression two *indices.*

POSSESSIVES

6.7   The possessive case of singular nouns is formed by the addition of an apostrophe and an *s*, and the possessive of plural nouns (except for a few irregular plurals) by the addition of an apostrophe only. This general rule is well understood and for common nouns needs no examples to illustrate its application. There is only one notable exception to the rule for common nouns, a case wherein tradition and euphony dictate the use of the apostrophe only:

> for appearance' (conscience', righteousness', etc.) sake

6.8   *Proper nouns.* The general rule covers proper nouns as well as common, including most names of any length ending in sibilants:

> Burns's poems
> Marx's theories

Czar Nicholas's assassination
Berlioz's opera
General Noguès's troops
Jefferson Davis's home
Fraser and Squair's French grammar
James Hargreaves's invention
Dickens's novels
plural: the Rosses' and the Williamses' lands

Exceptions are the names *Jesus* and *Moses* and Greek (or helle-nized) names of more than one syllable ending in *es:*

Jesus' nativity	Demosthenes' orations
Moses' leadership	Rameses' tomb
Euripides' plays	Xerxes' army

Even when a proper name is in italic type, its possessive ending is in roman:

the *Saturday Review*'s forty-fifth year of publication

COMPOUND WORDS

6.9 Of ten spelling questions that arise in writing or editing, nine are probably concerned with compound words. Should it be *selfseeking* or *self-seeking?* Is the word spelled *taxpayer, tax-payer,* or *tax payer?*—solid, hyphenated, or open?

6.10 Most such questions are readily answered by the dictionary. If the compound is used as a noun, the chances are good that it will ap-pear in the columns of the unabridged Webster, in one of the three possible spellings. If it is used as an adjective, the chances of find-ing it are still fair. But there will yet be some noun forms and a great many adjective forms for which no "authoritative" spelling can be found. It is then that general principles must be applied. Before these are outlined, however, some definitions are in order.

6.11 *Definitions.* By *open compound* is meant a combination of words so closely associated that they constitute a single concept but are spelled as separate words. *Examples:* settlement house, lowest common denominator, stool pigeon.

6.12 By *hyphenated compound* is meant a combination of words joined by a hyphen or hyphens. *Examples:* kilowatt-hour, mass-produce, ill-favored, love-in-a-mist.

6.13 By *solid* (or *close*) *compound* is meant a combination of two or more elements, originally separate words but now spelled as one word. *Examples:* henhouse, typesetting, makeup, notebook.

6.14   Not strictly compounds but often discussed with them are the many coined words consisting of a word-forming prefix (such as *non-* or *re-* or *pseudo-*) and another word.

6.15   In addition to such classification by form, compounds are also classified by function as *permanent* or *temporary*. A permanent compound is one that has been accepted into the general vocabulary of English and can (or should) be found in dictionaries. A temporary compound is a joining of words, or words and particles, for some specific purpose. A writer may employ the word *quasi-realistic*, for example, assigning some specific meaning to it consonant with his purposes. (One could think of dozens of contexts in which such a term might be useful.) The word *quasi-realistic* is not to be found in Webster, and probably not in other dictionaries either, and so would be considered a temporary compound. Having made its appearance, however, if it were picked up and used by other writers, it could acquire the currency and status of a permanent compound.

6.16   *General principles.* For some years now, the trend in spelling compound words has been away from the use of hyphens; that is, there seems to be a preference to spell compounds solid as soon as acceptance warrants their being considered permanent compounds, and otherwise to spell them open. It should be emphasized that this is a trend, not a rule, but it is sometimes helpful, when deciding how to spell some new combination, to remember that the trend exists.

6.17   A second helpful principle to remember is this: When a temporary compound is used as an adjective before a noun, it is often hyphenated to avoid misleading the reader. *A fast sailing ship*, for example, is ambiguous. Does the phrase mean a sailing ship with the general characteristic of fleetness or a ship that at the moment is sailing fast? Since the latter construction is intended, we write *a fast-sailing ship*, and our reader does not have to pause over it. So, too, not *a free form sculpture* but *a free-form sculpture*. Even though *form sculpture* has no rational meaning (as *sailing ship* does), it could cause a moment's hesitation for the reader: after an adjective like *free* we almost instinctively expect a noun, and there is indeed one there—*form*—but it is intended to hook up with *free* as a kind of adjective to modify *sculpture*, the real noun in the phrase. So to bypass this confusion we insert a hyphen between *free* and *form* and thus make its adjectival function clear:

A free-form sculpture stood on the terrace.

Note that this device is appropriate only before the noun. If the compound adjective occurs after the noun, the relationships are sufficiently clear, and the hyphen is not needed:

A piece of sculpture, free form, stood on the terrace.
The sculpture on the terrace was free form.

6.18 There are, quite literally, scores if not hundreds of other rules for the spelling of compound words. Many of them are nearly useless because of the great numbers of exceptions. To give authors and editors a few firm stepping-stones through the slough of compound-word spelling, table 6.1 has been prepared in an attempt to reduce a few of the dependable rules to systematic form.

WORD DIVISION

6.19 When type is set in justified lines, it is inevitable that words be *divided* (*broken*, or *hyphenated*) at the ends of lines. Such divisions are made between syllables, which should be determined in doubtful cases by consulting Webster.[1] Not all syllable breaks, however, are acceptable end-of-line breaks. The paragraphs that follow are intended to offer editors and proofreaders a brief guide to conservative modern practice in word division. For word division in foreign languages see pars. 9.34–63.

6.20 *General principles.* Most words should be divided according to pronunciation (the American system, reflected in Webster), not according to derivation (the British system):

democ-racy (*not* demo-cracy)   knowl-edge (*not* know-ledge)
aurif-erous (*not* auri-ferous)
antip-odes (*still better* antipo-des; *not* anti-podes)

Consequently, words such as the following, in which the second "syllable" contains only a silent *e*, are never divided:

| aimed | helped | spelled |
| climbed | passed | vexed |

Nor are word endings such as the following, which despite occasional use in verse as disyllables are for all practical purposes monosyllables:

-ceous	-geous	-sion
-cial	-gion	-tial
-cion	-gious	-tion
-cious	-sial	-tious

1. In response to a letter pointing out discrepancies in word division between the *Third International* and the *Seventh Collegiate*, the Webster editors told the University of Chicago Press that the *Collegiate* should be followed wherever possible, as it represented their latest thinking on the subject of word division.

TYPE COMPOUND	SIMILAR COMPOUNDS	REMARKS
	Noun Forms	
master builder	master artist, master wheel *but:* mastermind, masterpiece, mastersinger, masterstroke	Spell temporary compounds with *master* open.
fellow employee	brother officer, mother church, father figure, foster child, parent organization	*Type:* word of relationship +noun. Spell all such compounds open.
decision making	problem solving, coal mining	*Type:* object + gerund. Spell temporary compounds open. See also under Adjective Forms below.
quasi corporation	quasi contract, quasi scholar	Spell *quasi* noun compounds open. But see under Adjective Forms below.
attorney general	postmaster general, surgeon general	Safe to spell all similar compounds open.
vice-president	vice-chancellor, vice-consul *but:* viceroy, vicegerent, vice admiral	Temporary compounds with *vice-* are best hyphenated: *vice-manager, vice-chief.*
scholar-poet	author-critic, city-state, soldier-statesman	*Type:* noun+noun, representing different and equally important functions. Hyphenate.
brother-in-law	mother-in-law, sisters-in-law	Hyphenate all *in-laws.*
great-grandfather	great-great-grandmother	Hyphenate all *great-* relatives.
self-restraint	self-knowledge, self-consciousness	Hyphenate all *self-* compounds. See also under Adjective Forms below.
Johnny-on-the-spot	light-o'-love, Alice-sit-by-the-fire, stay-at-home, ball-of-fire, stick-in-the-mud	*Type:* combination of words including a prepositional phrase describing a character. Hyphenate.
one-half	two-thirds, four and five-sevenths *but:* thirty-one hundredths	*Type:* spelled out fractional number. Connect numerator and denominator with a hyphen unless either already contains a hyphen.

TABLE 6.1—*Continued*

Type Compound	Similar Compounds	Remarks
Noun Forms—Continued		
president-elect	senator-elect, mayor-elect *but:* county assessor elect	Hyphenate -*elect* compounds unless the name of the office is in two or more words.
headache	toothache, stomachache	Spell compounds with -*ache* solid.
checkbook	notebook, textbook, pocketbook, storybook *but:* reference book	Permanent compounds with -*book* are solid except for a few unwieldy ones. Temporary compounds should be spelled open: *pattern book, recipe book.*
boardinghouse	boathouse, clubhouse, greenhouse, clearinghouse *but:* rest house, business house	Permanent compounds with -*house* are solid; temporary ones, mainly open.
Adjective Forms		
highly developed species	poorly seen, barely living, wholly invented, highly complex	*Type:* adverb ending in -*ly*+ participle or adjective. Always open.
Central European countries	Old English, Scotch Presbyterian, New Testament, Civil War, Latin American	*Type:* compound formed from unhyphenated proper names. Always open. (Do not confuse with such forms as *Scotch-Irish, Austro-Hungarian*.)
sodium chloride solution	sulfuric acid, calcium carbonate	*Type:* chemical terms. Leave open.
laissez faire policy	a priori, post mortem, Sturm und Drang	*Type:* foreign phrase used as an adjective. Leave open.
bluish green paint	gray blue, emerald green, coal black, reddish orange	There should be no misunderstanding if all compound adjectives expressing color are spelled open.
self-reliant boy	self-sustaining, self-righteous, self-confident, self-effacing *but:* selfless, selfsame	Hyphenate *self-* compounds, whether they precede or follow the noun. See also under Noun Forms above.

134

TABLE 6.1—*Continued*

Type Compound	Similar Compounds	Remarks
Adjective Forms—*Continued*		
interest-bearing note	curiosity-evoking, dust-catching, thirst-quenching, dissension-producing	*Type:* object+present participle. Hyphenate all before the noun and a few permanent compounds (e.g., *thought-provoking*) after the noun.
twenty-odd performances	sixty-odd, fifteen-hundred-odd, 360-odd	*Type:* cardinal numeral+*odd*. Hyphenate before or after the noun.
ten-foot pole	three-mile limit, 100-yard dash, one-inch margin, 10-meter band, four-year-old boy *but:* 10 percent increase	*Type:* cardinal number+unit of measurement. Hyphenate compound if it precedes noun.
well-known man	ill-favored girl, well-intentioned person *but:* very well known man; he is well known	Compounds with *well-, ill-, better-, best-, little-, lesser-,* etc., are hyphenated when they precede the noun unless the expression carries a modifier.
how-to-do-it book	devil-may-care attitude, matter-of-fact approach, up-to-date equipment, *but:* it is up to date	*Type:* Phrase used as adjective. Hyphenate before noun.
quasi-public corporation	quasi-judicial, quasi-legislative, quasi-stellar	Hyphenate adjectival *quasi-* compounds whether they precede or follow the noun. But see under Noun Forms above.
half-baked plan	half-asleep, half-blooded, half-cocked, half-timbered *but:* halfhearted, halfway	Hyphenate adjectival *half-* compounds, whether they precede or follow the noun.
cross-eyed person	cross-country, cross-fertile, cross-grained *but:* crossbred, crosscut, crosshatched, crosswise	Any temporary adjectival *cross-* compounds can be safely hyphenated.
all-inclusive study	all-around, all-powerful, all-out	Hyphenate *all-* compounds, whether they precede or follow the noun.

135

TABLE 6.1—*Continued*

Type Compound	Similar Compounds	Remarks
Adjective Forms—Continued		
coarse-grained wood	able-bodied, pink-faced, straight-sided, cloud-topped	*Type:* adjective+past participle derived from a noun. Hyphenate such compounds when they precede the noun. After the noun they can generally be left open.
catlike movements	saillike, fencelike, cathedrallike, floorlike *but:* Tokyo-like, gull-like, vacuum-bottle-like	The suffix *-like* is used freely to form new compounds, all of which are spelled solid except those formed from proper names, words ending in *ll*, and word combinations.
a **tenfold** increase	twofold, multifold *but:* 25-fold	Adjectival compounds with *-fold* are spelled solid, unless they are formed with figures.
Words Formed with Prefixes		
pre-, post- **over-, under-** **intra-, extra-** **infra-, ultra-** **sub-, super-** **pro-, anti-** **re-; un-; non-; semi-;** **pseudo-; supra-; co-**	prewar, postwar overstaffed, understaffed intramural, extramural infrared, ultraviolet subjacent, superjacent prowar, antiwar reinduce; unconciliatory; nonviolent; semiactive; pseudosophisticated; supranational; coauthor	Except in the following special situations all words formed with the prefixes in the first column are spelled solid. *Second element capitalized or a figure:* anti-Semitic, un-American, pre-1914, post-1945. *To distinguish homonyms:* re-cover, re-create, un-ionized. *Second element more than one word (N.B., use en dash after prefix with open compound):* pre-latency-period therapy, non-English-speaking people, pre–Civil War.

136

And by a similar principle final syllables in which the liquid *l* sound is the only audible vowel should not be carried over to the next line:

convert-ible (*not* converti-ble)	pos-sible (*not* possi-ble)
en-titled (*not* enti-tled)	prin-ciples (*not* princi-ples)
people (*not* peo-ple)	read-able (*not* reada-ble)

6.21 Division should be made after a vowel unless, by so doing, the division is not according to pronunciation. Where a vowel alone forms a syllable in the middle of a word, run it into the first line. Diphthongs are treated as single vowels:

aneu-rysm (*not* an-eurysm)
criti-cism (*not* crit-icism)
particu-lar (*not* partic-ular)
physi-cal (*not* phys-ical *or* physic-al)
sepa-rate (*not* sep-arate)

6.22 Two consonants standing between vowels are usually separated if the pronunciation warrants:

ad-van-tage	foun-dation	moun-tain
ex-ces-sive	im-por-tant	profes-sor
finan-cier	In-dian	struc-ture
fin-ger		

6.23 Words that have a misleading appearance when divided should be left unbroken if at all possible:

women   often   prayer   water   noisy

6.24 One-letter divisions are not permissible. Such words as the following must not be divided:

acre	enough	item
again	even	oboe
amen	event	onus
among	idol	unite

6.25 Two-letter divisions are permissible at the end of a line, but two-letter word endings should not be carried over to the next line if this can be avoided:

en-chant   di-pole   as-phalt
but:
losses (*not* loss-es)   stricken (*not* strick-en)
money (*not* mon-ey)   fully (*not* ful-ly)

137

6.26   *Compound words.* Hyphenated compounds should not be broken except at the hyphen if this is possible:

> court-martial (*not* court-mar-tial)
> poverty-stricken (*not* pov-erty-stricken; *much less* pover-ty-stricken)

Words originally compounded of other words but now spelled solid should be divided at the natural breaks whenever possible:

> school-master *is better than* schoolmas-ter
> clearing-house *is better than* clear-inghouse
> handle-bar *is better than* han-dlebar
> *never:* passo-ver, une-ven, etc.

6.27   *Words with prefixes.* By the same principle, division after a prefix is preferred to division at any other point in the word:

> dis-pleasure *is better than* displea-sure
> pseudo-scientific *is better than* pseu-doscientific *or* pseudoscien-tific

6.28   *The ending "-ing."* Most gerunds and present participles permit division before the -*ing:*

certify-ing	giv-ing	pranc-ing
chang-ing	improvis-ing	revok-ing
dwell-ing	intrigu-ing	tempt-ing
enter-ing	learn-ing	twin-ing
entranc-ing	picnick-ing	whirl-ing

When the ending consonant is doubled before the addition of -*ing*, however, the added consonant is carried over:

abhor-ring	dab-bing	run-ning
bid-ding	pin-ning	trip-ping
control-ling	occur-ring	twin-ning

And when the original verb ends in an -*le* syllable in which the only audible vowel is the liquid *l* (for example, *startle, fizzle*), one or more of the preceding consonants are carried over with -*ing:*

bris-tling	gig-gling	ruf-fling
chuck-ling	han-dling	siz-zling
dwin-dling	ram-bling	twin-kling

6.29   *Proper names.* Proper nouns, especially given names or surnames of persons, ought not to be divided if possible. When initials are used in place of given names, it is permissible (though undesirable) to break after the initials, but bad practice to break between them:

> *best:* A. E. Housman
> *permissible:* A. E. / Housman
> *never:* A. / E. Housman

138

6.30   *Figures.* When large numbers are expressed in figures, they should be kept intact if possible; but if not, they may be broken after the commas:

$1,365,-000,000

Sums of money in pounds, shillings, and pence should not be broken if this can be avoided:

£6 4s. 6d.

6.31   *Abbreviations.* Abbreviations used with figures should not be separated from the figures:

345 mi.   24 kg   55 B.C.   A.D. 1066   6:35 P.M.

6.32   *Divisional marks.* A divisional mark, such as (*a*) or (1), even when it occurs in the middle of a sentence, preferably should not be separated from what follows it. When such a mark occurs at the end of a line, carry it over to the next line if possible.

O AND OH

6.33   The vocative *O* is capitalized, but not the interjection *oh* unless it begins a sentence or stands alone:

Why, O Lord, did you not help him?
I don't know, oh, truly I don't know why I did it.
Oh! What have I done?

"A HOTEL"

6.34   Such forms as "an historical study" or "an union" are not idiomatic in American English. Before a pronounced *h*, long *u* (or *eu*), and such a word as *one*, the indefinite article should be *a:*

a hotel   a euphonious word
a historical study   such a one
but: an honor, an heir   a union

USE OF LIGATURES

6.35   The ligatures *æ* and *œ* should not be used either in Latin or Greek words or in words adopted into English from these languages:

aes   aetatis   poena
Encyclopaedia Britannica   *Oedipus tyrannus*

139

For most English words derived from Latin or Greek words containing *ae* or *oe*, the preferred spelling is now *e:*

coeval	ecumenical	maneuver
economy	enology	medieval
but: aesthetics, archaeology		

The digraph *æ* is needed for spelling Old English words (along with other special characters) in an Old English context:

Ælfric   Ælfred   wes hæl

And the ligature *œ* is needed for spelling modern French in a French context (but not for French words in an English context):

Œuvres complètes de Racine
le nœud gordien
un coup d'œil
    but:
a tray of hors d'oeuvres
a circular window, or *oeil-de-boeuf*

DISTINCTIVE TREATMENT OF WORDS

6.36   Writers have probably always felt the need for devices to give special expression—emphasis, irony, or whatever—to the written word, to achieve what gesture and vocal intonation achieve for the spoken word. One old device, the use of capital letters to lend importance to certain words, is now totally outmoded and a vehicle of satire:

When John came to the throne he lost his temper and flung himself on the floor, foaming at the mouth and biting the rushes. He was thus a Bad King.[2]

6.37   Other devices, notably the use of italics and quotation marks to achieve special effects, are not outmoded but are used less and less as time goes on, especially by mature writers who prefer to obtain their effects structurally:

The damaging evidence was offered not by the arresting officer, not by the injured plaintiff, but by the boy's own mother.

In the sentence above, for example, there is no need to set the words *boy's own mother* in italics: the structure of the sentence gives them all the emphasis they need. Obviously, an effect of emphasis cannot always be achieved so easily. But the writer who

2. Walter C. Sellar and Robert J. Yeatman, *1066 and All That: A Memorable History of England* (New York: E. P. Dutton, 1931), p. 24.

finds himself underlining frequently for emphasis might consider (1) whether many of his italics are not superfluous, the emphasis being apparent from the context, or (2) if the emphasis is not apparent, whether it cannot be achieved more gracefully by recasting the sentence. The same reservations apply to frequent use of quotation marks to suggest irony or special usage (see par. 6.51). Often the quotation marks offend an intelligent reader who is quite capable of detecting the irony or the oddness of the expression without having it pointed out to him. (Apart from these stylistic uses, of course, italics and quotation marks find purely technical uses, discussed later in the chapter, which are not to be called in question.)

EMPHASIS

6.38   A word or phrase may be set in italic type to emphasize it if the emphasis might otherwise be lost:

> Let us dwell for a moment upon the idea of *conscious* participation.
>
> The artist . . . is one of the few whom society *asks* to be himself.[3]

Seldom should as much as a sentence be set in italics for emphasis and never a whole passage.

FOREIGN WORDS

6.39   Isolated words and phrases in a foreign language may be set in italics if they are likely to be unfamiliar to readers:

> The *grève de zèle* is not a true strike but a nitpicking obeying of work rules.
>
> *Honi soit qui mal y pense* is the motto of the Order of the Garter.
>
> a deed of endowment (*vakfiye*)

As with matter italicized for emphasis, a full sentence in a foreign language (as the second example above) is only occasionally set in italics, and a passage of two or more sentences should never be italicized but should be treated as a quotation (par. 10.5).

6.40   *Translation appended.* If a definition follows a foreign word or phrase, the definition is usually enclosed in quotation marks:

> The word she used was not *une poêle* ("frying pan") but *un poêle* ("stove").
>
> Volition is expressed by the infix *-ainu-*, as in the phrase *ena tuainubo*, "I would like to eat," or *ena tuainu-iai*, "I wanted to eat."

3. Stephen Koch, "Cocteau," *Midway*, Winter 1968, p. 115.

6.41   In linguistic and phonetic studies a word under discussion is often set in italics (as above) and the definition enclosed in single quotation marks, with no intervening punctuation:

> French *le cheval* 'the horse' represents a replacement for Latin *equus*.
>
> The gap is narrow between *mead* 'a beverage' and *mead* 'a meadow'.

6.42   *Familiar words.* Familiar words and phrases in a foreign language should be set in roman type:

effendi	mea culpa
pasha	fazenda
élan	favelas
ménage	barranca
weltschmerz	remuda
kapellmeister	trattoria
a priori	dolce far niente

Since the latest editions of Webster no longer signal whether a foreign word has been sufficiently well accepted into the English vocabulary to merit roman type, the author or editor has to make up his own mind about this. In doubtful cases the decision should always be for roman.

6.43   *Scholarly abbreviations.* It is now the custom at the University of Chicago Press to use roman type also for scholarly Latin words and abbreviations such as:

> ibid.   et al.   ca.   passim

But because of its peculiar use in quoted matter, it seems wise to retain italics for *sic:*

> They are furnished "seperate [*sic*] but equal facilities."

SPECIAL TERMINOLOGY

6.44   Key terms in a discussion, terms with special meaning, and, in general, terms to which the reader's attention is directed are often italicized on first use. Thereafter they are best set in roman:

> As will appear in the following pages, *obstructionism* and *delaying tactics* have been the chief weapons of this group.
>
> What is meant by *random selection?*

In the last example note the italic question mark. This illustrates the printer's rule that punctuation is set in the style of the immediately preceding word.

6.45   *Technical terms.* A technical term, especially when it is accompanied by its definition, is usually set in italics the first time it appears in a discussion:

> *Tabular matter* is copy, usually consisting of figures, that is set in columns.
>
> Ground and polished *thin sections* permit microscopic examination of the cellular structure of some fossils.

6.46   *Technical terms in special senses.* Often it is better to apply a standard technical term in a nonstandard way than to invent a new term. In such instances the term is often enclosed in quotation marks:

> In offset printing "proofs" of illustrations come from the darkroom, not the proof press.
>
> the "Levalloisian" culture complex of Tanzania [application of a European term to an African site]

6.47   *Philosophical terms.* By convention in works of philosophy and theology, terms having special philosophical or theological meaning are often enclosed in single quotation marks. Following punctuation is placed outside the quotation marks:

> If such procedure is justifiable, 'agrees with' must carry the sense of 'is consistent with'.
>
> 'being'   'nonbeing'   'the divine'

QUOTED PHRASES

6.48   Words and phrases quoted from another context, of course, are usually set in quotation marks:

> The "pursuit of happiness" is an end more often mentioned with approbation than defined with precision.

Such uses are discussed in chapter 10.

6.49   Often, however, an author wishes to single out a word or phrase, not quoting it from a specific document as in the example just given but referring it to a general background that will be recognized by his reader. Here quotation marks are also appropriate:

> Myths of "paradise lost" are common in folklore.
>
> In Tate's "alteration" the ending of *Lear* is changed so that Cordelia survives and marries Edgar.

WORDS USED AS WORDS

6.50   References to words as words are italicized, as are terms singled out as terms:

> The distinction between *farther* and *further* should be preserved.
> Use of the word *desuetude* when the word *disuse* will serve is often pretentious.
> The term *gothic* means different things to typographers and paleographers.

IRONY

6.51   Words used in an ironic sense may be enclosed in quotation marks:

> Five villages were subjected to "pacification."
> The "debate" resulted in three cracked heads and two broken noses.

Such use of quotation marks should always be regarded as a last resort, to be used when the irony might otherwise be lost. Skillfully prepared for, an ironic meaning seldom eludes the reader even though quotation marks are not used.

SLANG

6.52   Words classed as slang or argot may be enclosed in quotation marks if they are foreign to the normal vocabulary of the speaker:

> Alfie was accompanied by his "trouble and strife" as he strolled down the Strand.
> Had it not been for Bryce, the "copper's nark," Collins would have made his escape.

USE OF "SO-CALLED"

6.53   When the expression *so-called* is used with a word or phrase, implying that something is popularly or (sometimes) mistakenly given such-and-such designation, the designation itself should not be enclosed in quotation marks or set in italics. *So-called* is sufficient to mark off the usage as a special one:

> The so-called shadow cabinet was thought to be responsible for some of the president's more injudicious decisions.
> A so-called right of sanctuary was offered in justification of the minister's failure to surrender the escaped felon.

LETTERS USED AS WORDS

6.54   Letters used as words demand varied treatments depending upon the kind of letter and its context.

6.55   *Letters as letters.* Individual letters of the Latin (English) alphabet and combinations of letters are italicized:

> the letter *q*   a lowercase *n*   a capital *W*
> The normal sign of the plural in English is a terminal *s* or *es*.
> He signed the document with an *X*.

In some proverbial expressions the distinction is ignored:

> Mind your p's and q's.

6.56   *Named letters.* The name of a letter, as distinct from the letter itself, is usually set in roman type:

> from alpha to omega
> daleth, the fourth letter of the Hebrew alphabet
> an ell   a tee   a vee

6.57   *Letters as musical notes.* Letters standing for musical tones are usually set as roman capitals:

> middle C   440 A
> the key of G major   the key of F-sharp minor
> the D-major triad   an E string

In works on musical subjects where many keys are mentioned, it is common practice to use capital letters for major keys and lowercase for minor. If this practice is followed, the words *major* and *minor* are omitted:

> the key of G
> the e triad: E–G-natural–B
> The second movement of Beethoven's Sonata in c (op. 13) is in the key of A-flat.

In analyzing harmony, chords are designated by capital roman numerals indicating the note in the scale upon which the chord is based:

> V [a chord based on the fifth, or dominant, note of the scale]
> V⁷ [dominant seventh chord]

Step progressions are indicated, for example: IV–I$_4^6$–V–I.

6.58   *Letters as names.* A letter used in place of a name in a hypothetical statement and an initial used alone or with a dash to stand for a name are set as roman capitals:

> If A sues B for breach of contract . . .
> Admiral N—— and Lady R—— were guests.
> Mr. D. is the one to whom to address your request.

6.59   *Letters as shapes.* To indicate shape, gothic letters should be used if possible:

> A V-shaped valley becomes U-shaped by glaciation.
> a T intersection   in the form of an L

6.60   *Letters indicating rhyme schemes.* Lowercase, spaced italic letters are used to indicate rhyme patterns:

> The Italian sonnet consists of an octave and a sestet:
> *a b b a a b b a, c d c d c d.*
> The English, or Shakespearean, sonnet: *a b a b, c d c d, e f e f, g g.*

7 *Names and Terms*

INTRODUCTION

7.1　The purpose of this chapter is to establish a pattern in the use of names and terms associated with names: names of persons and places, of events and movements, of governmental bodies and their actions, of certain things and classifications, as well as titles of literary and artistic works. Which of these should always be capitalized and what titles are commonly set in italics are questions that must be resolved before any reasonable editorial consistency can be attained in a book or journal.

CAPITALIZATION

7.2　Modern publishers of works in the English language, American perhaps more than British, usually discourage excessive use of capital letters in text matter. Proper nouns are still conventionally capitalized,[1] but many words derived from or associated with them may be lowercased with no loss of clarity or significance. Questions and differences of opinion arise over just what is a proper noun, other than the name of a person or a place. It is with this realm

---

1. To *capitalize* a word means to capitalize only the initial letter. A word or phrase to be printed all in capital letters, LIKE THIS, is set in *full caps*.

of uncertainty that the following rules attempt to deal. They reflect the tendency toward the use of fewer capitals, toward what is called a *down* (lowercase) style as opposed to an *up* (uppercase, i.e., capital letter) style.

7.3 Although the pattern of capitalization in the various categories listed is preferred by the University of Chicago Press and is adaptable to most publications, it may require modification in some specialized works. Intelligent editors realize that no one set of rules in the area of capitalization can be universally applicable. And particular authors may have particular and valid reasons for capitalizing 'certain terms normally lowercased in other works. When an author does have reason to depart from the usual pattern, however, he should so inform his editor by providing a list of the terms involved. If the editor can find no valid reason for the author's departure from convention, there should be a consultation between editor and author, and agreement or compromise reached, before the editor undertakes to prepare the manuscript for publication.

7.4 Most authors do not feel strongly about capitalization, however, and many are oblivious to inconsistencies in their manuscripts. The manuscript editor must therefore establish a logical and acceptable style and root out any inconsistencies of capitalization (see par. 2.72). The following categories and lists will, it is hoped, provide a helpful pattern for editors to follow. Rules for capitalizing or lowercasing specific names or terms can never be final. The editor, understanding the nature of the work, must use discretion, judgment, and intuition in deciding when to follow the pattern and when to depart from it.

ITALICS AND QUOTATION MARKS WITH NAMES

7.5 Some names of things and titles of works are conventionally set in italic type. Others, usually shorter works or parts of larger works, are set in roman type and enclosed in quotation marks. Still others are capitalized but neither italicized nor quoted. Like the conventions of capitalization these may also be altered in certain situations. For example, the author of a critical study in literature or music containing many references to short stories or essays as well as book-length works or to both long and short poems or musical compositions is well advised to give *all* titles in italics.

150

PERSONAL NAMES

7.6   Names and initials of persons are capitalized:

Thomas Jefferson   Martha Custis Washington
W. Theodore Watts-Dunton   Margaret Mead
John F. Kennedy   LBJ

Since family and individual preference in the spelling of names varies widely (*Catherine*, for example, has at least five other forms in English: *Katherine, Katharine, Catharine, Kathryn, Cathryn*), it is not only a matter of courtesy but also of accuracy to spell an individual's name as he prefers. If there is any doubt about the spelling of a personal name, consult one of the references listed in the Bibliography. For most names, the Press uses the spelling in *Webster's Biographical Dictionary* (or the Biographical Names section of *Webster's Seventh New Collegiate Dictionary*), *Who's Who*, and *Who's Who in America*.

ENGLISH NAMES WITH PARTICLES

7.7   Many names of French, Spanish, Portuguese, Italian, German, and Dutch derivation include particles: *de, du, la, l', della, von, van, van der, ten*, etc. For names of this type borne by people in English-speaking countries, practice with regard to capitalizing the particles varies widely, and competent authority should be consulted in doubtful cases.[2] Generally the surname retains the particle when used alone:

Eugen D'Albert; D'Albert
Lee De Forest; De Forest
Walter de la Mare; de la Mare
George du Maurier; du Maurier
Richard Le Gallienne; Le Gallienne
Abraham Ten Broeck; Ten Broeck
Martin Van Buren; Van Buren
Wernher Von Braun; Von Braun
Alexander de Seversky; de Seversky
Eamon de Valera; de Valera

FOREIGN NAMES

7.8   *French names.* In French practice, the articles *le, la*, and *les*, as well as the contractions *du* and *des*, are capitalized whether or not a first name or title precedes (in many family names, of course, they are run in—Desmoulins, Lafayette):

François, duc de La Rochefoucauld; La Rochefoucauld
Philippe Du Puy de Clinchamps; Du Puy de Clinchamps

2. For alphabetizing names with particles see par. 18.56.

The preposition *de* (or *d'*) is always lowercased and is often dropped when the surname is used alone:

Alexis de Tocqueville; Tocqueville
Alfred de Musset; Musset
but:
Charles de Gaulle; de Gaulle
Jean d'Alembert; d'Alembert
Comte de Grasse; Admiral de Grasse; de Grasse

7.9 *Spanish, Portuguese, Italian, German, Dutch names.* For other names with particles, romance or germanic, the particles are lower-cased and are usually dropped when the surname is used alone in the original language. In English, writers have shown little consistency in their treatment of such names. The frequent older practice was to retain and capitalize the particle when the surname was used alone. Consequently, for many names the form with the particle is the only familiar one and must necessarily be used. As with French names Press style follows native practice as far as possible.

Giovanni da Verrazano; Verrazano
Luca della Robbia; *in English contexts,* della Robbia
Tomás de Torquemada; Torquemada
Manuel de Falla; *in English contexts,* de Falla
Vasco da Gama; *in English contexts,* da Gama
Heinrich Friedrich Karl von und zum Stein; Stein
Alexander von Humboldt; Humboldt
Maximilian von Spee; Spee
Friedrich von Steuben; *in English contexts often* von (*or* Von) Steuben
Ludwig van Beethoven; Beethoven
Vincent van Gogh; *in English usually* van Gogh
Bernard ter Haar; ter Haar

7.10 Spanish surnames are often composed of both the father's and mother's names, sometimes joined by *y* ("and"). Such names are often shortened to a single name (which is not always the first of the two). It is never incorrect to use both names, but if the person's own preference is known it is appropriate to use only one:

José Ortega y Gasset; Ortega y Gasset *or* Ortega
Pascual Ortiz Rubio; Ortiz Rubio *or* Ortiz

7.11 *Arabic names.* Surnames of Arabic origin often are prefixed by such elements as *Abu, Abd* (*Abdul, Abdel*), *ibn, al,* or *el.* These are

152

part of the surname and should not be dropped when the surname is used alone (for alphabetizing Arabic names see par. 18.61):

> Syed Abu Zafar Navdi; Abu Zafar Navdi
> Aziz ibn-Saud; ibn-Saud

Names of rulers of older times, however, are often shortened to the first name rather than the last:

> Harun al-Rashid; Harun

7.12 *Chinese names.* In Chinese practice, the family name comes before the given name, which is usually of two elements. As romanized, the family name and the first element of the given name are capitalized, and the given name is hyphenated: Chiang Kai-shek, Pai Ch'ung-hsi. Chinese may be referred to by family name alone: Chiang; Pai. Ancient Chinese names are often of only two elements, which may not be separated: Li Po, Fu Tu, Lao-tsu. A few modern names are also of only two elements: Hu Shih.

7.13 *Russian names.* Russian family names, as well as middle names (patronymics), sometimes but not always take different endings for male and female members of the family. For example, Lenin's real name was Vladimir Ilyich Ulyanov; his sister was Maria Ilyinichna Ulyanova. Often in text matter only the given name and patronymic are used; in the index, of course, the name should be listed under the family name, whether this appears in the text or not.

7.14 *Hungarian names.* In Hungarian practice the family name precedes the given name—Molnár Ferenc—but (as with this playwright) the names are often inverted to normal English order when used in a non-Hungarian context: Ferenc Molnár.

TITLES AND OFFICES

7.15 Civil, military, religious, and professional titles and titles of nobility are capitalized when they immediately precede a personal name, as part of the name:

> President Johnson
> General Eisenhower
> John Cardinal Cody
> Emperor Maximilian[3]

3. *But:* the emperor Maximilian. Here the name is in apposition to the title—*the* emperor (who was) Maximilian—and therefore the title is lowercased as not part of the name.

153

7.16   In formal usage, such as acknowledgments and lists of contributors, titles following a personal name are also usually capitalized. A title used alone, in place of a personal name, is capitalized only in such contexts as toasts or in formal introductions:

> The translators wish to acknowledge their indebtedness to C. R. Dodwell, Fellow and Librarian of Trinity College, Cambridge.
>
> Ladies and gentlemen, the President of the United States.

7.17   In text matter, titles following a personal name or used alone in place of a name are, with few exceptions, lowercased.[4] The following lists show various titles and words related to them as they might appear in text sentences.

7.18   *Civil titles and offices*

> Abraham Lincoln, president of the United States; President Lincoln; the president of the United States; the president; the presidency; presidential
>
> William Henry Seward, secretary of state; Secretary (of State) Seward; the secretary of state; the secretary
>
> Everett M. Dirksen, senator from Illinois; Senator Dirksen; the senator from Illinois; the senator
>
> John W. McCormack, Speaker of the House of Representatives; Congressman[5] McCormack; the Speaker[6] of the House; the congressman; the representative from Massachusetts
>
> John V. Lindsay, mayor of New York; Mayor Lindsay; the mayor of New York; the mayor
>
> Earl Warren, chief justice of the United States; Chief Justice Warren; the chief justice
>
> Felix Frankfurter, associate justice of the Supreme Court; Mr. Justice Frankfurter; Justice Frankfurter; the justice
>
> David K. E. Bruce, ambassador to the Court of St. James's *or* ambassador to Great Britain; the ambassador to Great Britain; the American ambassador; the ambassador; the American embassy
>
> Otto Kerner, governor of the state of Illinois; the governor of Illinois
>
> Frederick Lord North, prime minister of England; Lord North; the prime minister of England; the North ministry

4. Named professorships and fellowships are usually capitalized wherever they appear, especially if they include a personal name: Ferdinand Schevill Distinguished Service Professor. *But:* Fulbright scholar.

5. *Congressman*, not *Representative*, is commonly used with names to designate members of the U.S. House of Representatives.

6. Usually capitalized even when used alone, to avoid ambiguity.

Geoffrey Windermere, member of Parliament *or* M.P.; a member of Parliament

George Canning, foreign minister of Great Britain; the British foreign minister

Emperor William (*or* Wilhelm) II of Germany; William II, emperor of Germany; Kaiser Wilhelm; the kaiser

Chancellor Adolf Hitler; the chancellor; the führer

7.19   *Military titles and offices*

General Ulysses S. Grant, commander in chief of the Union army; General Grant; the commander in chief; the general

Omar N. Bradley, General of the Army;[7] General Bradley, chairman of the Joint Chiefs of Staff; the general

Chester W. Nimitz, Fleet Admiral; Admiral Nimitz, commander of the Pacific Fleet; the admiral

Sergeant John Doe; a noncommissioned officer (NCO); the sergeant

General Sir Guy Carleton, British commander in New York City; Sir Guy; the general

7.20   *Religious titles and offices*

Pope John XXIII; the pope; papacy

Francis Cardinal Spellman, *or, less formal and more up to date*, Cardinal Francis Spellman; Cardinal Spellman; the cardinal; the sacred college of cardinals

Archbishop Makarios III; the archbishop

Frederick Temple, archbishop of Canterbury; the archbishop of Canterbury; the archbishop

Rabbi Stephen Wise; the rabbi

the Reverend James Neal, minister of Third Presbyterian Church; Mr. (*or* Dr.) Neal; the minister

the Right Reverend Gerald Francis Burrill, bishop of Chicago [Anglican]; Bishop Burrill; the bishop of Chicago; the bishop; bishopric; diocese

the Reverend George Smith, rector of Saint David's Church [Anglican]; Father Smith *or* Mr. Smith *or* the Reverend Mr. Smith (*not* Reverend Smith); the rector

the Most Reverend John A. Donovan, bishop of Toledo [Roman Catholic]; Bishop Donovan; the bishop of Toledo

the Reverend John Dunn, pastor of Saint Thomas Aquinas Church [Roman Catholic]; Father Dunn; the pastor

the Catholic bishop of New Orleans

the mother superior of the Ursuline convent

---

7. The formal titles *General of the Army* and *Fleet Admiral* are capitalized to avoid ambiguity.

7.21   *Professional titles*

Edward H. Levi, president of the University of Chicago; Mr. Levi; the president; the president's office

William T. Hutchinson, Preston and Sterling Morton Professor of History Emeritus; Professor Hutchinson; the professor of history; a professor emeritus

Bruce A. Morrissette, chairman of the Department of Romance Languages and Literatures; Professor Morrissette; the chairman of the department

Edward Smith, president of Smith Corporation; Mr. Smith; the president of the corporation

7.22   *Titles of nobility*

George VI, king of England; King George; the king of England; the king

Emperor Charles V; the emperor Charles V; the emperor

Anthony Ashley Cooper, third earl of Shaftesbury; the earl of Shaftesbury; the earl

Sir Humphrey Blimp, Bart.; Sir Humphrey; the baronet

Prince Philip, duke[8] of Edinburgh; the duke

Dowager Queen Mary; the dowager queen

Count (*or* Graf) Helmuth von Moltke; Count von Moltke; the count

François de Lorraine, duc de Guise; the second duc de Guise; the duke

7.23   For the sake of clarity, or perhaps unbreakable tradition, some British titles are capitalized when used without a personal name:

Prince of Wales	Princess Royal
Queen Mother	Dame of Sark

And in material intended for a largely British readership a more liberal use of capitals for titles than that recommended above may be desirable.

7.24   In newspaper and magazine writing, epithets denoting roles, such as *citizen, schoolboy, housewife, defendant, historian,* are sometimes capitalized preceding a name. This practice should usually be avoided in book publishing:

the historian Arthur Schlesinger, Sr. (*not* Historian Schlesinger)

7.25   Terms designating academic years are lowercased:

freshman	junior
sophomore	senior

8. Often capitalized in this honorary title.

156

ACADEMIC DEGREES AND HONORS

7.26   The names of academic degrees and honors should be capitalized when following a personal name, whether abbreviated or written in full:

> Clyde M. Haverstick, Doctor of Law
> John K. Follett, M.D.
> Lee Wallek, Fellow of the Royal Academy

But when academic degrees are referred to in such general terms as *doctorate, doctor's, bachelor's, master's,* they are not capitalized.

HONORIFIC TITLES

7.27   Honorific titles and forms of address should be capitalized in any context:

> His Majesty   Your Grace   Excellency
> Her Royal Highness   His Eminence   Your Honor
>   *but:*
> my lord   sir

EPITHETS

7.28   A characterizing word or phrase used as part of, or a substitute for, a personal name is capitalized and not quoted:

> the Great Emancipator   the Sun King
> the Wizard of Menlo Park   the Young Pretender
> Stonewall Jackson   the Great Commoner
> the Autocrat of the Breakfast Table   the Iron Duke
> Babe Ruth   the Swedish Nightingale

When an epithet is used in addition to a full name, it is usually enclosed in quotation marks:

> George Herman ("Babe") Ruth
> Jenny Lind, "the Swedish Nightingale"
> Huey Long, "the Kingfish"

FICTITIOUS NAMES

7.29   The names of fictitious or anonymous persons and names used as personifications are capitalized—

> John Doe   John Barleycorn   Johnny Reb
> Jane Doe   John Bull   Uncle Sam

—except when used in slang expressions:

> real george   merry ned
> by harry!   every man jack

157

KINSHIP NAMES

7.30   A kinship name is lowercased when not followed by a given name, even in direct address or when the term used is substituted for the personal name:

> His father died at the age of ninety-three.
> My brothers and sisters live in California.
> "Happy birthday, Uncle Ed."
> "Thanks, nephew."
> I know that mother's middle name is Marie.
> the Grimké sisters

PERSONIFICATION

7.31   The personification of abstractions—giving them the attributes of persons—is not a common device in today's prose writing. When it is used, the personified noun is usually capitalized:

> When Nature designed her masterpiece, she never dreamed he'd turn out thus.
> In the springtime nature is at its best.
> Then Spring—with her warm showers—arrived.
> The icy blasts of winter had departed.
> Like Milton, he bade Melancholy begone.
> He had suffered from melancholy all his life.

Where there is doubt, the word should be lowercased:

> It was a battle between head and heart; reason finally won.

NATIONALITIES, TRIBES, AND OTHER GROUPS OF PEOPLE

7.32   The names of racial, linguistic, tribal, religious, and other groupings of mankind are capitalized:

Aryan	Magyar
Asian	Malay
Bushman	Mongol (mongoloid)
Caucasian (caucasoid)	Mormon
Frenchman	Negro (negroid)
Hottentot	Nordic
Indian	Oriental
Indo-European	Protestant
Kaffir	Pygmy

7.33   Designations based on mere color, size, or local usage are lowercased:

aborigine	colored	red man
black	highlander	redneck
bushman	pygmy	white

158

PLACE NAMES

7.34   Certain nouns and some adjectives designating parts of the world or regions of a continent or a country are generally capitalized. Descriptive adjectives not part of an accepted appellation are lowercased:

> Antarctica; Antarctic Circle
>
> East; Orient; Far East(ern); Near East(ern); Middle East(ern); Eastern customs; oriental (adj.); the East (U.S.); eastern (direction or locality)
>
> West; Occident; Western world; occidental (adj.); the West, Far West, Middle West, Midwest (U.S.); western, far western, middle western, midwestern(er)
>
> Central America; central Europe, Asia, United States, etc.
>
> the Continent (Europe); continental Europe; the European continent; Continental customs
>
> North Pole; North Polar ice cap; polar regions
>
> North American continent
>
> North Atlantic; northern Atlantic
>
> North Africa; northern, southern, central Africa
>
> Northern Hemisphere
>
> South Pacific
>
> the South, the Southwest (U.S.); the south of France; southern; southwestern
>
> South Temperate Zone
>
> Tropic of Capricorn; the tropics
>
> the equator
>
> Southeast Asia; southeastern, southern, central Asia
>
> Upper Michigan; northern Michigan

7.35   In works dealing with the period since World War II it is customary to capitalize *Western Europe* and *Eastern Europe* when referring to the political rather than simply geographical divisions of the Continent. Similarly, *Central Europe* is capitalized when referring to the political division of World War I. In American Civil War contexts, *Southern(er)* and *Northern(er)* are capitalized.

7.36   *Popular names.* Popular and legendary names of places are usually capitalized and not enclosed in quotation marks:

> Albion
> Back Bay (Boston)
> Badlands (North Dakota)
> Bay Area (San Francisco)

159

> the Badger State
> Benelux countries
> Cathay
> the Channel (English Channel)
> City of Brotherly Love
> Deep South (U.S.); Old South; antebellum South
> Eastern Shore (of Chesapeake Bay)
> Eternal City
> Foggy Bottom
> Lake District
> Land of the Rising Sun
> Left Bank (Paris)
> the Levant
> the Loop (Chicago)
> Near North (Chicago)
> New World; Old World
> Old Dominion (Virginia)
> Promised Land
> Panhandle
> the Piedmont
> South Seas
> South Side (Chicago)
> the States (U.S.)
> Tenderloin (San Francisco)
> Twin Cities
> the Village (New York)
> Wild West
> > *but:*
> iron curtain countries

As a generic name for an idealized state *utopia* is lowercased.

POLITICAL DIVISIONS

7.37   In general, words designating political divisions of the world, a country, state, city, and so forth are capitalized when following the name and an accepted part of it: *empire, state, county, city, kingdom, colony, territory*, etc. They are usually, though not always, lowercased when they precede the name or stand alone:

> Roman Empire; the empire under Augustus; the empire
> Washington State; the state of Washington
> New England states; Middle Atlantic states
> Hennepin County; the county of Hennepin[9]

9. Irish usage: county Kildare.

New York City; the city of New York[10]
Massachusetts Bay Colony; the colony at Massachusetts Bay
the British colonies; the thirteen colonies
United Kingdom; the kingdom of Great Britain
the Province of Ontario; the province
the Union of Soviet Socialist Republics; the Soviet Union; the USSR
the Union of South Africa; the Union
the Union (U.S.)
Northwest Territory
Indiana Territory; the territory of Indiana
Evanston Township; the town of Evanston
Eleventh Congressional District; his congressional district
Fifth Ward; the ward; ward politics
Sixth Precinct; the precinct
the Dominion of Canada; the dominion *or* the Dominion
the Republic of France; the French republic; the republic *or* the Republic; the Fifth Republic
the Republic (U.S.)

TOPOGRAPHICAL NAMES

7.38   Names of mountains, rivers, oceans, islands, and so forth are capitalized. A generic term—such as *lake, mountain, river, valley*— used as part of a name is also capitalized, whether or not it is capitalized in the gazetteer or atlas, where all doubtful spellings should be checked by author or editor:

Bering Strait
Black Forest
Cape Sable
Great Barrier Reef
Himalaya Mountains; the Himalayas
Indian Ocean
Kaskaskia River (*but* the river Elbe)
Mozambique Channel
Nile Delta
Silver Lake
the Sea of Azov
South China Sea
Walden Pond
Windward Islands; the Windwards

10. The City, meaning the business district, the old city, of London, is always capitalized.

7.39   When a generic term is used in the plural following more than one name, it is lowercased:

> between the Hudson and the Mississippi rivers
> the Adirondack and Catskill mountains

7.40   When a generic term precedes more than one name, it is usually capitalized:

> Lakes Michigan and Huron
> Mounts Everest and Rainier

7.41   When a generic term is used descriptively rather than as part of the name, or when used alone, it is lowercased:

> the valley of the Mississippi
> the Hudson River valley
> the French coast (*but* the West Coast [U.S.])
> the California desert
> the Kansas prairie
> the Indian peninsula (*but* the Malay Peninsula)
> along the Pacific coast (*but* Pacific Coast *if the region is meant*)
> the delta

7.42   When a foreign term forms part of a geographic name in English, the meaning of the foreign term should be carefully observed when citing:

> Rio Grande (*not* Rio Grande River)
> Sierra Nevada (*not* Sierra Nevada Mountains *or* the Sierras)
> Mauna Loa (*not* Mount Mauna Loa *or* Mauna Loa Mountain)
> Fujiyama *or* Mount Fuji (*not* Mount Fujiyama *or* Fujiyama Mountain)

STRUCTURES AND PUBLIC PLACES

7.43   Names of buildings, thoroughfares, monuments, and the like are capitalized:

> the White House
> the Capitol (national; distinguish between *capital*, a city, and *capitol*, a building)
> the Mall (Washington, D.C.; London)
> Statue of Liberty[11]

---

11. Regarded as a monument, not a piece of sculpture, and therefore not italicized. For names of statues, etc., see par. 7.145.

the Midway (Chicago)
the Pyramids (*but* the Egyptian pyramids)
the Sphinx
Leaning Tower of Pisa
Stone of Scone

7.44 Such terms as *avenue, boulevard, bridge, building, church, fountain, hotel, park, room, square, street, theater,* are capitalized when part of a specific official or formal name. When they stand alone or are used collectively following two or more proper names, they are lowercased:

Adler Planetarium; the planetarium
Empire State Building; the Empire State
the Empire State and Federal buildings
Fifth Avenue (*by New Yorkers sometimes called* the Avenue)
Fifty-seventh Street
First Congregational Church; the church
Golden Gate Bridge
4146 Grand Avenue
Lincoln Park; the park
the Outer Drive; the drive
the Persian Room (*of a hotel; but* room 16)
Philharmonic Hall in Lincoln Center for the Performing Arts; the hall; the center
Phoenix Theatre (*in this case not* Theater); the theater
Piccadilly Circus
U.S. Route 66
Spassky Gate
Times Square
Madison and State streets

7.45 Titles of foreign structures, streets, etc., given in the original language are not italicized (see also par. 9.17):

Bibliothèque nationale
Bois de Boulogne
Champs-Elysées
Palacio nacional
Palais royal
Piazza delle Terme
Puente de Segovia
18, rue de Provence
Via Nazionale

WORDS DERIVED FROM PROPER NAMES

7.46   Nouns, adjectives, and verbs derived from personal or geographical names are lowercased when used with a specialized meaning:

anglicize	macadam road
arabic figures	manila envelope
arctic boots	mecca
bohemian	morocco (leather)
brussels sprouts	paris green
china (ceramic ware)	pasteurize
diesel engine	pharisaic
dutch oven	philistine
frankfurter	plaster of paris
french (fries, dressing, windows)	quixotic
herculean	roman type
homeric	roman numerals
india ink	russian dressing
italicize	scotch whisky
japan (varnish)	sienna (pigment)
jeremiad	venetian blinds
lombardy poplar	vulcanize

NAMES OF ORGANIZATIONS

GOVERNMENTAL AND JUDICIAL BODIES

7.47   Full names of legislative, deliberative, administrative, and judicial bodies, departments, bureaus, and offices are usually capitalized. Adjectives derived from them are lowercased, as are paraphrastic or incomplete designations, except abbreviations.

7.48   *Legislative and deliberative*

United Nations Security Council; the Security Council; the council

United States Congress; the Seventy-first Congress; Congress; congressional

Senate (U.S.); the upper house of Congress

House of Representatives; the House; the lower house of Congress

Committee on Foreign Affairs; Foreign Affairs Committee; Fulbright committee; the committee

General Assembly of Illinois; Illinois legislature; assembly; state legislature; state senate

Chicago City Council; city council; council

Parliament; parliamentary; an early parliament; the Houses of Parliament

House of Commons; the Commons

Cortes (Spain)
Curia Regis; the great council (England)
Duma (Russia)
States General *or* Estates General (France)
Reichstag (Germany)

7.49   *Administrative*

Department of State; State Department; the department
National Labor Relations Board; the board
Bureau of the Census; Census Bureau; the bureau; the census of 1960
Agency for International Development; AID; the agency
Peace Corps
Chicago Board of Education; the board

7.50   *Judicial*

United States Supreme Court; the Supreme Court; the Court[12]
Arizona Supreme Court; state supreme court
United States Court of Appeals for the Second Circuit; court of appeals; circuit court; the court
Circuit Court of Cook County; county court; circuit court
Municipal Court of Chicago; municipal court
District Court for the Southern District of New York; district court
Juvenile Division of the County Department of the Circuit Court of Cook County
Court of King's Bench; the court
Star Chamber

7.51   Generic terms designating courts are frequently used in place of a full name. They are lowercased, even when they refer to a specific court:

traffic court   family court   juvenile court

7.52   Each state has its own system for denominating its courts. Sometimes capitalization other than the foregoing suggestions is desirable for clarity. For example, in New York and Maryland the highest state court is not the supreme court but the court of appeals:

New York Court of Appeals; the Court of Appeals (capitalized to distinguish it from the U.S. court); the court

12. The word *court* when used alone is capitalized only in references to the U.S. Supreme Court.

165

7.53   Not usually capitalized are:

> administration
> brain trust
> cabinet (*but* Kitchen Cabinet in the Jackson administration)
> court (roÿal)
> crown
> electoral college
> executive, legislative, or judicial branch
> federal (government, agency, court, powers, etc.)
> government
> ministry
> parlement (*but* Parlement of Paris)
> state (powers, laws, etc.; state's attorney)
> witenagemot

POLITICAL AND ECONOMIC ORGANIZATIONS AND ALLIANCES

7.54   Names of national and international organizations, movements, and alliances and of members of political parties are capitalized, but not the words *party*,[13] *movement*, *platform*, and so forth (see also par. 7.56):

> Bolshevik(i); Bolshevist(s)
> Communist party; Communist(s); Communist bloc
> Common Market
> Entente Cordiale; the Entente
> Fascist party; Fascist(s); Fascista (*pl.* Fascisti)
> Federalist party; Federalist(s) (U.S. history)
> Free-Soil party; Free-Soiler(s)
> Hanseatic League; Hansa
> Holy Alliance
> Know-Nothing party; Know-Nothing(s)
> Labour party; Labourites favor the interests of labor[14]
> Loyalist(s) (American Revolution; Spanish civil war; etc.)
> Nazi party; Nazi(s)
> North Atlantic Treaty Organization; NATO
> Progressive party, movement; Progressive(s)
> Quadruple Alliance
> Republican party, platform; Republican(s)
> Tammany Hall; Tammany

13. In certain contexts—for example, a work on the Communist party—where *party* is used in place of the full name and other parties may also be mentioned, the word *party* may be capitalized in references to the Communist party to avoid ambiguity.

14. In capitalized British names, British spelling is retained. If *Labourite* (meaning a person who votes for the Labour party) is lowercased, as it sometimes is, American spelling should be used in a work published in the United States: *laborite*.

7.55 Appellations of political groups other than parties are usually lowercased:

> independent(s)
> labor bloc
> mugwump(s)
> opposition[15]
> right wing; right-winger; leftist (*but usually* the Right; the Left)

7.56 Nouns and adjectives designating political and economic systems of thought and their proponents are lowercased, unless derived from a proper noun:

> bolshevism
> communism
> democracy (*but* Jacksonian Democracy)
> fascism
> Marxism-Leninism
> nazism
> progressivism
> socialism
> utilitarianism

INSTITUTIONS AND COMPANIES

7.57 Full titles of institutions and companies and of their departments and divisions are capitalized, but such words as *school* or *company* are lowercased when used alone:

> the University of Chicago;[16] the Law School; the Department of History; the university; the history department
> Iowa Falls High School; the high school
> the Library of Congress (*not* Congressional Library); the Manuscripts Division; the library
> Smithsonian Institution (*not* Institute); the Smithsonian
> Hudson's Bay Company; the company
> General Foods Corporation; the corporation
> Illinois Central Railroad; the Illinois Central; the railroad
> the Board of Regents of the University of California; the board of regents; the board; the regents
> New York Philharmonic
> Washington National Symphony
> Chicago Curled Hair Division of General Felt Industries

15. Often capitalized in British contexts, meaning the party out of power.

16. The word *the* at the beginning of such titles is capitalized only in formal usage: © 1969 by The University of Chicago.

7.58   Full official names of associations, societies, unions, meetings, and conferences are capitalized. A *the* preceding a name is lowercased in textual matter, even when it is part of the official title. Such words as *society, union, conference,* are lowercased when used alone:

> Boy Scouts of America; a Boy Scout; a Scout
> Congress of Industrial Organizations; CIO
> Fifty-second Annual Meeting of the American Historical Association; the annual meeting of the association
> Green Bay Packers; the Packers; the team
> Independent Order of Odd Fellows; IOOF; an Odd Fellow
> International Workers of the World; IWW; Wobblies
> Ku Klux Klan; KKK; the Klan
> League of Women Voters; the league
> New-York Historical Society; the society
> Republican National Convention; the national convention; the convention
> Textile Workers Union of America; the union
> Union League Club; the club
> Young Men's Christian Association; YMCA

7.59   A substantive title given to a conference is enclosed in quotation marks:

> "Systematic Investigation of the African Later Tertiary and Quaternary," a symposium held at Burg Wartenstein, Austria, July–August 1965
> > *but:*
> the 1965 International Conference on Family Planning Programs

HISTORICAL AND CULTURAL TERMS

PERIODS

7.60   A numerical designation of a period is lowercased unless it is part of a proper name:

> eighteenth century
> the twenties
> quattrocento (fifteenth century)
> Eighteenth Dynasty (*but* Sung dynasty)
> the period of the Fourth Republic

7.61   Some names applied to historical or cultural periods are capitalized, either by tradition or to avoid ambiguity. Such appellations are not enclosed in quotation marks:

168

Christian Era
Middle Ages; High Middle Ages; late Middle Ages
Restoration
Old Regime; *l'ancien régime*
Age of Louis XIV
Era of Good Feelings
Gilded Age
Mauve Decade
Roaring Twenties
Dark Ages
Renaissance; High Renaissance
Enlightenment
Age of Reason
Augustan Age

7.62 Most period designations, however, are lowercased (except for proper nouns and adjectives, of course):

antiquity; ancient Greece; ancient Rome
colonial period (U.S.)
Victorian era
baroque period
romantic period
fin de siècle

7.63 Names of cultural periods recognized by archaeologists and anthropologists and based upon characteristic technology are capitalized:

Stone Age; Old Stone Age   Bronze Age
Neolithic, Paleolithic times   Iron Age

(For geological periods see pars. 7.108–9.)

7.64 Analogous latter-day designations, often capitalized in popular writing, are best lowercased:

age of steam   nuclear age   space age

EVENTS

7.65 Appellations of historical, quasi-historical, political, economic, and cultural events, plans, and so forth are generally capitalized:

Fall of Rome
Reign of Terror
South Sea Bubble
Battle of the Books
Boston Tea Party
Industrial Revolution (often lowercased)
Reconstruction (U.S.)
Prohibition
Great Depression; the depression
New Deal

Kentucky Derby
New York World's Fair
but:
cold war
gold rush; California gold rush
westward movement
panic of 1837
XYZ affair
Dreyfus affair

(For wars, battles, conquests, see par. 7.94; for religious events, par. 7.89; for treaties, acts, par. 7.67.)

CULTURAL MOVEMENTS AND STYLES

7.66   Nouns and adjectives designating philosophical, literary, musical, and artistic movements, styles, and schools and their adherents are capitalized when they are derived from proper nouns. Others are usually lowercased unless, in certain contexts, capitalization is needed to distinguish the name of a movement or group from the same word in its general sense. This classification of names and terms is one most dependent on editorial discretion. In any given work a particular term must be consistently treated. The following list illustrates commonly acceptable style; terms lowercased here may sometimes require capitalization:

Aristotelian	naturalism
baroque	neoclassic(ism)
camp	Neoplatonism
Cartesian	New Criticism
Chicago school of architecture	nominalism
classical	Peripatetic
concrete poetry	philosophe
cubism	Physiocrat
Cynic(ism)	pop art
Doric	Pre-Raphaelite
Epicurean	realism
existentialism	rococo
Gothic	Romanesque
Gregorian chant; plainsong	romantic(ism)
Hudson River school	Scholastics; Schoolmen
humanism	scientific rationalism
idealism	Sophist(s)
imagism	Stoic(ism)
impressionism	surrealism
jazz	Sturm und Drang
miracle plays	symbolism
morality plays	theater of the absurd
mystic(ism)	transcendentalism

(For religious movements and schools of thought see par. 7.81.)

ACTS AND TREATIES

7.67   Full formal or accepted titles of pacts, plans, policies, treaties, acts, laws, and similar documents or agreements are usually capitalized and set in roman type without quotation marks. Incomplete names are usually lowercased:

> Mayflower Compact; the compact
> Constitution of the United States; United States (*or* U.S.) Constitution; the Constitution (usually capitalized when referring to the U.S. Constitution)
> Illinois Constitution; the state constitution; the constitution
> Fifteenth Amendment (to the U.S. Constitution); the amendment
> Bill of Rights (first ten amendments to the U.S. Constitution; also England, 1689)
> due process clause (*sometimes* Due Process Clause)
> Articles of Confederation
> Declaration of Independence
> Wilmot Proviso
> Monroe Doctrine; the doctrine
> Open Door policy (*sometimes* open door policy)
> Peace of Utrecht
> Treaty of Versailles; the Versailles treaty; the treaty at Versailles
> Pact of Paris (*or, less correctly but frequently,* Kellogg-Briand Pact); the pact
> Hawley-Smoot Tariff Act; the tariff act; the act
> Atomic Energy Act *or* McMahon Act; the act
> Marshall Plan; the plan
> Magna Charta
> Reform Bills; Reform Bill of 1832 (England)
> Corn Laws (England) (*sometimes* corn laws)
> New Economic Policy (USSR); NEP
> Second Five-Year Plan; five-year plans

7.68   References to pending legislation are lowercased:

> The anti-injunction bill was introduced on Tuesday.
> A gun-control law is being considered.

LEGAL CASES

7.69   The names of legal cases (plaintiff and defendant) are usually italicized, except *v.* (versus):

> *Miranda* v. *Arizona*
> *Green* v. *Department of Public Welfare*
> *West Coast Hotel Co.* v. *Parrish*

171

In works dealing primarily with law, case names are not italicized in footnote citations:[17]

> Thompson v. Shapiro, 270 F. Supp. 331 (D. Conn. 1967)

In a discussion a case name may be shortened:

> the *Miranda* case
> *Miranda*

Where the person rather than the case is meant, the name should of course be in roman type:

> Escobedo's case, trial

AWARDS

7.70   Names of awards and prizes are capitalized:

> Nobel Prize in physics; Nobel Peace Prize; Nobel Prize winners
> Pulitzer Prize in fiction
> Academy Award; Oscar
> International Music Scholarship
> Heywood Broun Memorial Award
> Laetare Medal
> Guggenheim Fellowship (*but* Guggenheim grant)
> National Merit scholarships

CALENDAR AND TIME DESIGNATIONS

SEASONS AND DAYS OF THE WEEK

7.71   Names of days of the week and months of the year are capitalized. The four seasons are lowercased (unless personified; see par. 7.31).

Tuesday	spring	the vernal (spring) equinox
November	fall	winter solstice

(For *centuries* and *decades* see par. 7.60.)

HOLIDAYS AND HOLY DAYS

7.72   The names of religious holidays and seasons are capitalized:

Ash Wednesday	Lent
Christmas Eve	Maundy Thursday
Easter Day	Passover
Feast of Saint Michael and All Angels	Pentecost
Good Friday	Ramadan
Halloween; All Hallows' Eve	Twelfth Day
Hanukkah	Yom Kippur
Holy Week	Yuletide

17. For more information on acceptable legal style, see *A Uniform System of Citation*, published by the Harvard Law Review Association.

So too are most secular holidays and other specially designated days:

All Fools' Day, April Fools' Day	New Year's Day
Arbor Day	National Book Week
Fourth of July; the Fourth; Independence Day	Thanksgiving Day
	V-E Day
Labor Day	Veterans Day
Mother's Day	*but:* D day

Mere descriptive appellations like *election day* or *inauguration day* are lowercased.

TIME AND TIME ZONES

7.73   When spelled out, designations of time and time zones are lowercased. Abbreviations are capitalized:

Greenwich mean time (GMT)	central daylight time (CDT)
daylight saving time (DST)	eastern standard time (EST)

RELIGIOUS NAMES AND TERMS

7.74   In few areas is an author more tempted to overcapitalize or an editor more loath to urge a lowercase style than in that of religion. That this is probably due to unanalyzed acceptance of the pious customs of an earlier age, to an unconscious feeling about words as in themselves numinous, or to fear of offending religious persons is suggested by the fact that overcapitalization is seldom seen in texts on the religions of antiquity or latter-day primitive religions. It is in the contexts of Christianity, Judaism, Islam, Buddhism, and Hinduism that we are tempted and fall. The editors of the University of Chicago Press urge a spare, *down* style in this field as in others: capitalize what are clearly proper nouns and adjectives, and lowercase all else except to avoid ambiguity. The following paragraphs attempt to be an empirical guide to the present state of capitalization in religious contexts.

GOD, DEITIES, AND REVERED PERSONS

7.75   Like all proper nouns the names of the one supreme God (as Allah, El, God, Jehovah, Yahweh) as well as the names of other deities (Astarte, Dagon, Diana, Pan, Shiva) are capitalized.

173

7.76   *The one God.* Other references to deity as the one supreme God, including references to the persons of the Christian Trinity, are capitalized:

Adonai	Most High
the Almighty	the Omnipotent
Christ	the Paraclete
the Father	Prince of Peace
the First Cause	Providence
Holy Ghost; Holy Spirit	the Savior (Jesus Christ)
the Holy One	Son of God
King of Kings	Son of man
Lamb of God	the Supreme Being
the Logos	the Third Person (of the Trinity)
the Lord, our Lord	the Word
Messiah (Jesus Christ)	

7.77   Pronouns referring to the foregoing are today seldom capitalized except in instances where capitalization offers a simple way to avoid ambiguity:

Trust in Him.
God gives man what He wills.
> *but:*

God in his mercy
Jesus and his disciples

Nor are most derivatives, whether adjectives or nouns, capitalized:

(God's) fatherhood, kingship, omnipotence
(Jesus') sonship
messianic hope
godlike; godly
christological
> *but:*

Christology; Christlike; Christian

7.78   *Revered persons.* Appellations of revered persons such as prophets, apostles, and saints are often capitalized:

the Apostle to the Gentiles	Messiah (Jewish)
the Baptist	Mother of God
the Beloved Apostle	our Lady
the Blessed Virgin	the Prophet (Muhammad)
Buddha	Queen of Heaven
the Divine Doctor	the Twelve
the Fathers; church fathers	the Virgin (Mary)
the Lawgiver	

7.79   *Platonic ideas.* Words for transcendent ideas in the Platonic sense, especially when used in a religious context, are often capitalized:

Good; Beauty; Truth; One

174

RELIGIOUS BODIES

7.80   *Broad groups.* Names of religions, churches, and communions and of their members, as well as derived adjectives, are capitalized:

> Anglicanism; an Anglican; the Anglican church; the Anglican communion
> Buddhism; a Buddhist; Buddhist ideas
> Catholicism; the Church Catholic; the Catholic church
> the Church of England, of Scotland, of Sweden, etc.
> Islam; Islamic; Muslim
> Judaism; Orthodox Judaism; Reform Judaism; an Orthodox Jew
> Orthodoxy; the Orthodox church; the (Greek, Russian, Serbian, etc.) Orthodox churches
> the Reformed Church in America; the Reformed church
> Roman Catholicism; a Roman Catholic; the Roman Catholic church; the Roman communion
> Shinto
> Vedanta

7.81   *Denominations and other groups and movements.* Treat similarly Christian denominations, sects, and orders; non-Christian sects; and most religious movements:[18]

> Arianism; the Arian heresy
> the Baptist church
> Christian Brothers
> Christian Science; a Christian Scientist
> Dissenter
> Essene; the Essenes
> a Gentile; gentile laws
> Gnosticism; a Gnostic; the Gnostic heresy, gospels
> High Church (*or* high church) movement, party
> Hussite
> Jehovah's Witnesses
> Methodism; Methodist; the Methodist church
> Monophysitism; Monophysite; Monophysite *or* Monophysitic churches
> Mormonism; Mormon; the Mormon church; Latter-Day Saints
> Nonconformist
> Order of Preachers; the Dominican order; the order; a Dominican

18. Many of these terms are used either specifically or generically and capitalized or lowercased accordingly—e.g., Puritan and puritan, Fundamentalism and fundamentalism.

175

Society of Jesus; a Jesuit; Jesuit teaching; jesuit, jesuitical (*derogatory*)

Sufi; Sufism

Theosophy; Theosophist

Zen; Zen Buddhism

Related terms formed with prefixes are variously treated:

Anabaptist; anti-Semite; antinomian

7.82   *Local groups.* The names of smaller organized religious bodies and the buildings in which they meet are usually capitalized:

Abbey of Mont Saint-Michel
Bethany Evangelical Lutheran Church
Church of the Redeemer
Congregation Anshe Mizrach
Grace Presbyterian Church
Midwest Baptist Conference
Our Lady of Sorrows Basilica
Saint Andrew's Greek Orthodox Church
Saint Leonard's House
Saint Mary's Cathedral, Salisbury (*but* Salisbury cathedral)
Sinai Temple

Note that in the foregoing examples, *church* is capitalized when it is part of the official name of an organized body of Christians or of a building (the Church of England, Saint Matthew's Church) but lowercased when merely descriptive (the Presbyterian church). When standing alone, *Church* is often capitalized when it refers to the whole body of Christians, worldwide or throughout time, but lowercased when it refers to a division of the universal Church or to a denomination. Terms like *cathedral, congregation, meeting* (Quaker), *mosque, synagogue,* and *temple* likewise are capitalized only when part of an official name.

7.83   *Councils, synods, and meetings.* The accepted names of historic councils and synods and the official names of modern counterparts are capitalized:

Council of Chalcedon; Fourth General Council
Council of Nicaea
General Convention (Episcopal church)
Second Vatican Council; Vatican II
Synod of Whitby

RELIGIOUS WRITINGS

7.84   *The Bible.* Capitalize names—and use roman type—for the Judeo-Christian Bible and its versions and editions:

Authorized, or King James (*not* Saint James) Version
Breeches Bible

Codex Sinaiticus
Complutensian Polyglot Bible
Douay (Rheims-Douay) Version
Holy Writ
Jerusalem Bible
New English Bible
Peshitta
Revised Standard Version
Scripture(s) (i.e., the Bible)
Septuagint
Vinegar Bible
Vulgate

Also the books of the Bible (but note exceptions):

Genesis
Chronicles
Job; Book of Job
Psalms; Psalm 22 (*but* a psalm, the penitential psalms)
Ezekiel (Ezechiel)
2 Esdras (4 Kings)
the Rest of Esther
John; the Gospel of John; the Fourth Gospel
Acts; the Acts; Acts of the Apostles
Romans; the Epistle to the Romans
3 John
Revelation; the Revelation of Saint John the Divine; the Apocalypse

(For abbreviations of the books of the Bible see par. 14.38.)

And various divisions and sections of the Bible:

Old Testament; New Testament
Apocrypha
the Law; the Prophets; the Writings
Pentateuch
Hagiographa
the Gospels; the Epistles
the synoptic Gospels
the pastoral Epistles

7.85 *Other works.* Other sacred or highly revered works are similarly treated:

Book of the Dead	Talmud
Dead Sea Scrolls	Tripitaka
Koran	Upanishads
Mishnah	Vedas

7.86 *Adjectives.* Adjectives derived from the names of sacred books are generally lowercased (apocryphal, biblical, scriptural, talmudic), but a few retain the initial capital (Koranic, Mishnaic, Vedic).

177

7.87   *Shorter religious writings and utterances.* Various scriptural selections of special importance bear names that are usually capitalized:

> the Decalogue, Ten Commandments
> the Beatitudes
> Sermon on the Mount
> the Miserere
> the Shema
> *but:*
> the parable of the unjust steward

So also many special prayers and canticles (mostly of scriptural origin) used devotionally:

Gloria Patri (*but* doxology)	the Litany of the Saints
Hail Mary, Ave Maria	the Lord's Prayer; the Our Father
Kaddish (*or* kaddish)	Nunc Dimittis
the Litany (Anglican)	Te Deum

7.88   *Creeds and confessions.* Names of particular creeds and confessions are also capitalized:

Apostles' Creed	Nicene Creed
Augsburg Confession	the Thirty-nine Articles
Luther's Ninety-five Theses	Westminster Confession

EVENTS AND CONCEPTS

7.89   Biblical and other religious events and religious concepts of major theological importance are often capitalized:

the Atonement	Hegira (Muhammad's)
the Creation	Inquisition
the Crucifixion	Original Sin
Crusades; Crusaders	Pilgrimage of Grace
the Deluge; the Flood	Redemption
Diaspora (of the Jews)	Resurrection
the Exodus (from Egypt)	the Second Coming (of Christ)
the Fall (of Man)	the Second Covenant

RELIGIOUS SERVICES

7.90   *Eucharistic rite.* In referring to the eucharistic sacrament, the expression *the Mass* is always capitalized, as are equivalent expressions:

the Divine Liturgy	the Liturgy of the Lord's Supper
Holy Communion	

The terms *High Mass* and *Low Mass* are sometimes capitalized when used generically. In reference to individual celebrations, however, lowercase style is used:

> There is a high mass at noon.
> Three masses are said daily.

Terms for the elements of the Holy Communion are capitalized in contexts where the doctrine of the real presence is assumed:

> Body and Blood of Christ   Precious Blood
> the Divine Species   the Sacrament

7.91   *Other services.* Names of other rites and services are not capitalized in run of text:

> prime, terce, sext, etc.   seder
> morning prayer; matins (mattins)   confirmation
> evening prayer; evensong   vesper service
> bar mitzvah   worship service
> baptism

OBJECTS OF RELIGIOUS USE OR SIGNIFICANCE

7.92   Objects of religious use or significance are preferably given lowercase treatment:

> ark   relic of the true cross
> chalice and paten   rosary
> holy water   sanctuary
> mezuzah   shofar
> phylacteries   stations of the cross

MILITARY TERMS

FORCES AND GROUPS OF PARTICIPANTS

7.93   Full titles of armies, navies, air forces, fleets, regiments, battalions, companies, corps, and so forth are capitalized. The words *army*, *navy*, etc., are lowercased when standing alone or used collectively in the plural or when they are not part of an official title:

> Afrika Korps (German, World War II)
> Allied armies
> Allied Expeditionary Force; the AEF
> the Allies (World Wars I and II); Allied forces
> Army of Northern Virginia
> Army of the Potomac; the army
> Axis powers (World War II)
> Central Powers (World War I)

Combined Chiefs of Staff (World War II)
Continental navy (American Revolution)
Eighth Air Force
Fifth Army; the Fifth; the army
First Battalion, 178th Infantry; the battalion; the 178th
French foreign legion
Highland Light Infantry
Joint Chiefs of Staff (U.S.)
King's Own Yorkshire Light Infantry
Luftwaffe
National Guard; the guard
Pacific Fleet (U.S.; World War II)
Red Army; Russian army
Rough Riders
Royal Air Force; British air force
Royal Army Educational Corps
Royal Artillery; the British army
Royal Horse Guards
Royal Navy; the British navy
Royal Scots Fusiliers; the fusiliers
Seventh Fleet; the fleet
Task Force Fifty-eight; the task force
Thirty-third Infantry Division; the division; the infantry
Union army (American Civil War)
United States Army; the army; the American army; the armed forces
United States Coast Guard; the Coast Guard
United States Marine Corps; the Marine Corps; the U.S. Marines; the marines
United States Signal Corps; the Signal Corps

WARS, BATTLES, CAMPAIGNS, AND THEATERS OF WAR

7.94 Full titles of wars are capitalized. The words *war* and *battle* are lowercased when used alone (*battle* is often lowercased also when used with the name of the spot where the battle took place).

American Civil War;[19] the Civil War; the war

American Revolution; American War of Independence; the Revolution; the revolutionary war; the American and French revolutions

19. "The earlier official title, War of the Rebellion, has been dropped, out of deference to Southern wishes; and the cumbrous title 'The War Between the States' is grossly inaccurate. 'The War for Southern Independence' suggested by the historian Channing is well enough; but why change 'The Ameri-

> Battle of Bunker Hill *or* battle of Bunker Hill; the battle at Bunker Hill
> Battle of the Bulge
> Conquest of Mexico; the conquest
> European theater of operations (World War II); ETO
> French Revolution; the Revolution; revolutionary France
> Korean War
> Maginot line
> Mexican border campaign
> Norman Conquest; the conquest of England; the conquest
> Operation Overlord
> revolution(s) of 1848
> Seven Years' War
> Shays's Rebellion
> Spanish-American War
> Spanish civil war
> Third Battle of Ypres *or* third battle of Ypres
> Vicksburg campaign
> War of Jenkins' Ear
> western front (World War I)
> western theater of war (American Civil War)
> Whisky Rebellion
> World War I; the First World War; the Great War; the war; the two world wars

MILITARY AWARDS AND CITATIONS

7.95 Specific names of medals and awards are capitalized:

> Medal of Honor; congressional medal
> Distinguished Flying Cross
> Distinguished Service Cross
> Purple Heart
> *but:* croix de guerre

SHIPS, AIRCRAFT, AND SPACECRAFT

7.96 Names of specific ships, submarines, airplanes, and spacecraft are italicized, but not such abbreviations as *S.S.* or *H.M.S.*[20] preceding them:

---

can Civil War,' which it was? During the war it was generally called 'The Second American Revolution' or 'The War for Separation' in the South." (Samuel Eliot Morison, *The Oxford History of the American People* [New York: Oxford University Press, 1965], p. 614 n.)

20. Do not use *ship, schooner, frigate, aircraft carrier,* or other such designations with these abbreviations.

Bonhomme Richard	*Graf Zeppelin*
H.M.S. *Frolic*	Lindbergh's *Spirit of St. Louis*
C.S.S. *Shenandoah*	*Sputnik II*
S.S. *United States*	*Gemini VI*
U.S.S. *SC-530*	*Mariner IV*

7.97   Designations of class or make, names of trains, and names of space programs are capitalized but not italicized:

U-boat	ICBM
DC-3	Nike
Boeing 707	Project Apollo
Broadway Limited	

SCIENTIFIC TERMINOLOGY

SCIENTIFIC NAMES OF PLANTS AND ANIMALS

7.98   The rules for the naming (taxonomy) of plants and animals are complex, and the style conventions are not as immutable as they sometimes appear to laymen. (The rule, cited below, on lowercasing the species name, for example, is not universally observed.) The discussion and examples here, however, should help the inexperienced copy editor avoid the most dangerous pitfalls in this field.

7.99   *Genus and species.* Whether in lists or in run of text, the scientific (Latin) names of plants and animals are set in italic type. The genus name is capitalized, the species name lowercased (even though it may be a proper adjective):

> Many specific names, such as *Rosa caroliniana* and *Styrax californica*, reflect the locale of the first specimens described.
>
> The Pleistocene saber-toothed cats all belonged to the genus *Smilodon*.
>
> In Europe the pike, *Esox lucius*, is valued for food as well as sport.

After the first use the genus name may be abbreviated:

> The "quaking" of the aspen, *Populus tremuloides*, is due to the construction of the petiole. An analogous phenomenon noted in the cottonwood, *P. deltoides*, is similarly effected.

7.100   Subspecies names, when used, follow the specific name and are also set in italic type:

> *Trogon collaris puella*
> *Noctilio labialis labialis* (also written *Noctilio l. labialis*)

In systematic work the name of the person (or persons) who proposed a specific or subspecific name is added in roman type, the name often being abbreviated:

Molossus coibensis J. A. Allen
Diaemus youngii cypselinus Thomas
Felis leo Scop.
Quercus alba L.
Euchistenes hartii (Thomas)

Use of parentheses in the last example means that Thomas described the species *hartii* but referred it to a different genus.

7.101 Other designations following generic, specific, or subspecific names are also set in roman type:

Viola sp.
Rosa rugosa var.

7.102 *Larger divisions.* Divisions larger than genus—phylum, class, order, and family—are capitalized and set in roman type:

Chordata [phylum]	Monotremata [order]
Chondrichthyes [class]	Hominidae [family]

So also are intermediate groupings:

Ruminantia [a suborder]
Felinae [a subfamily]
Selachii [a term used of various groups of cartilaginous fishes]

7.103 *English derivatives.* English derivatives of scientific names are lowercased:

amoeba, amoebas [from *Amoeba*]
mastodon [like the foregoing, identical with the generic name]
carnivores [from the order Carnivora]
felids [from the family Felidae]

VERNACULAR NAMES OF PLANTS AND ANIMALS

7.104 Common names of plants and animals are capitalized in a bewildering variety of ways, even in lists and catalogs having professional status. It is often appropriate to follow the style of an "official" list, and if the author wishes to do so, he should let his editor know what list he is following.

7.105 In the absence of such a list the University of Chicago Press prefers a *down* style for names of wild plants and animals, capitalizing only proper nouns and adjectives used with their original reference:

dutchman's breeches	Cooper's hawk
mayapple	Canada thistle
black-eyed susan	Virginia creeper
New England aster	jack-in-the-pulpit
Michaelmas daisy	Rocky Mountain sheep
rhesus monkey	black bass

183

7.106   The same principles may usually be followed for breeds of domestic animals and horticultural varieties of plants, especially the older ones:

white leghorn fowl	golden retriever
Rhode Island red	King Charles spaniel
Hereford cattle	brahma fowl (*but* Brahman or
Poland China swine	Brahma cattle)
Dandy Dinmont	boysenberry
English setter	rambler rose

7.107   Many domestic breeds and varieties, however, have been given special names, sometimes fanciful, that must be respected. This is particularly true of horticultural varieties of plants that may be patented or may possess names registered as trademarks:

Queen of the Market aster	Golden Bantam corn
Peace rose	Hale Haven peach

GEOLOGICAL TERMS

7.108   Names of geological eras, periods, epochs, series, and episodes are capitalized (but not the words *era*, *period*, etc.):

Cenozoic era
Tertiary period
Pliocene epoch
Lower Jurassic period
Pennsylvanian (or Upper Carboniferous) period

Modifiers such as *early*, *middle*, or *late*, used merely descriptively, are usually lowercased:

the early Pliocene
late Pleistocene times

7.109   The term *Ice Age* is capitalized in reference to the Recent or Pleistocene glacial epochs but lowercased when used in a general sense. Glacial and interglacial stages are lowercased:

Illinoian (*European:* Riss) stage
second interglacial stage *or* II interglacial

ASTRONOMICAL TERMS

7.110   The names of asteroids, planets and their satellites, stars, and constellations are capitalized:

Big Dipper	85 Pegasi
North Star	Scorpio

Cassiopeia's Chair   Saturn
Aldebaran   Ursa Major
α Centauri (*or* Alpha Centauri)   Phobos

7.111   Names of other unique celestial objects are capitalized except for generic words forming part of the name:

the Milky Way   the Magellanic clouds
the Crab nebula   the Coalsack
the Galaxy (*but* a galaxy, our   Halley's comet
galaxy)

7.112   Objects listed in well-known catalogs are designated by the catalog name, usually abbreviated, and a number:

NGC 6165   Bond 619   Lalande 5761

7.113   The names *sun* and *moon* are lowercased, as is *earth* except when used (without the definite article) in connection with the names of other planets:

The planets Venus and Earth, respectively second and third in order outward from the sun, resemble each other closely.

7.114   Terms merely descriptive in nature applied to unique celestial objects or phenomena are not capitalized:

the gegenschein   the rings of Saturn

Nor are terms applied to meteorological phenomena:

aurora borealis   sun dog

MEDICAL TERMS

7.115   *Diseases and syndromes.* The names of diseases, syndromes, signs, symptoms, tests, and the like should be lowercased, except for proper names forming part of the term:

Hodgkin's disease   dumping syndrome
infectious granuloma   syndrome of Weber
Ménière's syndrome   finger-nose test

7.116   Names of infectious organisms are treated like other taxonomic terms (see pars. 7.98–103), but the names of diseases or pathological conditions based upon such names are lowercased and set in roman type:

In streptococcemia, or streptococcus infection, microorganisms of the genus *Streptococcus* are present in the blood.

The disease condition trichinosis is characterized by infestation by trichinae, small parasitic nematodes. It is commonly caused by eating underdone pork containing *Trichinella spiralis*.

185

7.117   *Drugs.* Generic names of drugs should be used so far as possible and given lowercase treatment. Proprietary names (trade names or brands), if used at all, should be capitalized and enclosed within parentheses after the first use of the generic term:

> The patient was kept tranquilized with meprobamate (Miltown).

PHYSICAL AND CHEMICAL TERMS

7.118   *Laws, principles, etc.* Only proper names attached to the names of laws, theorems, principles, etc., are capitalized:

> Boyle's law
> Avogadro's theorem
> Planck's constant
> (Einstein's) general theory of relativity
> the second law of thermodynamics
> Newton's first law

7.119   *Chemical symbols and names.* Names of chemical elements and compounds are lowercased when written out; the chemical symbols, however, are capitalized and set without periods (for a complete list see par. 14.51):

> sulfuric acid; H_2SO_4 tungsten carbide; WC
> sodium chloride; NaCl   ozone; O_3

The figure giving the number of atoms in a molecule is placed in the inferior position after the symbol for the element, as in the examples above.

7.120   The *mass number*, formerly placed in the superior position to the right of the element symbol, is now according to international agreement placed in the superior position to the left of the symbol: ^{238}U, ^{14}C. In work intended for a nonprofessional audience, however, the mass number is still often placed in the old position (U^{238}, C^{14}). Such locutions as

> uranium 238; U-238   carbon 14; C-14

are also seen in popular writing and need not be changed.

TRADEMARKS

7.121   Dictionaries indicate registered trademark names. A reasonable effort should be made to capitalize such names:

> Coca-Cola (*but* soft drink)
> Gold Medal flour
> Levi's

Anacin, Bufferin, Excedrin (*but* aspirin)
Frigidaire (*but* refrigerator)
Kleenex (*but* tissue)
Ping-Pong (*but* table tennis)
Pyrex dishes
Vaseline (*but* petroleum jelly)
Orlon
Dacron
but: nylon

TITLES OF WORKS

GENERAL RULES

7.122   The following rules concerning capitalization, spelling, punctuation, italics, and quotation marks apply to titles mentioned in textual matter.[21] (For various styles of capitalization in bibliographies see chapter 16; for titles in footnotes see chapter 15; for capitalization in foreign titles see chapter 9.) The rules govern titles of all publications (books, journals, newspapers, magazines, pamphlets, reports, etc.); of short works (poems, stories, articles); of divisions of long works (parts, chapters, sections); of unpublished lectures, papers, documents; of plays and radio and television programs; and of musical and graphic works.

7.123   *Capitalization.* Capitalize the first and last words and all nouns, pronouns, adjectives, verbs, adverbs, and subordinate conjunctions. Lowercase articles, coordinate conjunctions, and prepositions, regardless of length, unless they are the first or last words of the title or subtitle. Lowercase the *to* in infinitives. Long titles of works published in earlier centuries may retain the original capitalization, except that any word in full capitals should carry only an initial capital. No word in a quoted title should ever be set in full capitals, regardless of how it appears on the title page of the book itself. Small capitals cannot be used in italic titles because there is no such thing in most typefaces as *italic* small caps. When the abbreviations A.D. or B.C. (set in small capitals in running text) appear in italic titles, they are set as full capitals: *A.D., B.C.*

21. In many publishing houses there is a custom of typing book titles in full caps instead of underlining (which takes twice as long). This is a useful, time-saving device, but typists should remember that its use should be reserved for reports, interdepartmental memorandums, letters to authors or other publishers, and the like. Never should titles in copy intended for publication be so typed.

7.124 How to capitalize hyphenated compounds in titles is a frequent puzzle. A rule of thumb that usually proves satisfactory is (1) always capitalize the first element and (2) capitalize the second element if it is a noun or proper adjective or if it has equal force with the first element:

> Twentieth-Century Literature
> Tool-Maker
> Non-Christian
> Blue-Green

Do not capitalize the second element if (*a*) it modifies the first element or (*b*) both elements constitute a single word:

> English-speaking People
> Medium-sized Library
> E-flat Minor
> Re-establish
> Self-sustaining Reaction

Note that although modern practice tends toward deleting traditional hyphens (*reestablish, tool maker*) they should be retained where they occur in titles being cited because they are part of the original spelling. Only capitalization and punctuation may be altered.

7.125 *Spelling.* Retain the spelling of the original title. But change & to *and*, and spell out names of centuries (*12th Century* becomes *Twelfth Century*) and other numbers usually spelled out in text.

7.126 *Punctuation.* Add punctuation if necessary. (Title pages are usually designed to require a minimum of punctuation; elements of a title may be set on separate lines or in different type sizes. When such titles are cited and run in one line, they must be punctuated for clarity.) Insert a colon (not a semicolon or a dash) between the main title and the subtitle (be sure it *is* a subtitle and not a part of the main title requiring only a comma before it). If there is a dash in the original title, retain it. Add commas in series, including one before the *and* preceding the final word in a series. Set off, with commas, dates not grammatically related to the rest of the title.

7.127 Old-fashioned titles connected by *or* are usually treated so:

> *England's Monitor; or, The History of the Separation*

7.128 Some examples of titles showing modern capitalization and punctuation:

> *Disease, Pain, and Sacrifice: Toward a Psychology of Suffering*
> *Melodrama Unveiled: American Theater and Culture, 1800–1850*
> *Browning's Roman Murder Story: A Reading of "The Ring and the Book"*
> *The Labour Party in Perspective—and Twelve Years Later*
> *Thought and Letters in Western Europe, A.D. 500–900*
> *Foreign Aid Re-examined*
> "The Take-off into Self-sustained Growth"
> Sonata in B-flat Major
> "Digression concerning Madness"
> *Learning to Look*
> *Noble-Gas Compounds*
> "What to Listen For"

BOOKS AND PERIODICALS

7.129   As in footnotes, titles and subtitles of published books, pamphlets, proceedings and collections, periodicals, and newspapers and sections of newspapers published separately (*New York Times Book Review*) are set in italics when they are mentioned in the text. Such titles issued in microfilm are also italicized. In scientific and legal works, where titles are otherwise treated in references and footnotes (see pars. 16.52, 15.140), titles mentioned in the text are nevertheless italicized and usually capitalized according to the rule outlined above (par. 7.123).

7.130   Obviously, a title mentioned in the text need not be complete there when it is cited in full in a footnote. Also, as part of an expository sentence, it may be adjusted to fit the syntax of the sentence. Thus an initial article, *A* or *The*, following a possessive noun or pronoun is awkward and should be omitted:

> Had he read Faulkner's *Fable?* (*But:* Faulkner's novel *A Fable* was first on the list of required readings.)
> His *Rise of the West* won the National Book Award.

An initial article should also be omitted if another article precedes it:

> The dreadful *Old Curiosity Shop* character, Quilp . . .
> An *Oxford Universal Dictionary* definition . . .

Where an initial article does not offend the syntax, it should be retained as part of the title (except in newspaper titles):

> In *The Old Curiosity Shop*, Dickens . . .

189

7.131   When newspapers and periodicals are mentioned in the text, an initial *The*, omitted in footnote citations (see par. 15.65), is set in roman type and, unless it begins a sentence, is lowercased:

> She reads the *Sun-Times* every morning.
> The *New York Times* and the *Christian Science Monitor* are among the most widely respected newspapers.
> His book is reviewed in the *American Historical Review*.

7.132   A title as the object of a preposition such as *on* or *about* is a locution avoided by many careful writers.

Questionable:

> In his well-known book on *Modern English Usage* Fowler provides an excellent article on the use and abuse of italics for emphasis.

Better:

> In his well-known book on English usage Fowler . . .
> > *or:*
> In his well-known *Dictionary of Modern English Usage* . . .

7.133   A title is a singular noun and must therefore take a singular verb:

> *The Counterfeiters* is perhaps Gide's best-known work.
> *Ends and Means* marks a new turn in Aldous Huxley's thought.

7.134   *Articles and parts of a book.* Titles of articles and features in periodicals and newspapers, chapter titles and part titles, titles of short stories, essays, and individual selections in books are set in roman type and enclosed in quotation marks:

> "A Defense of Shelley's Poetry," by Kathleen Raine in the *Southern Review*
> Caldwell's "Country Full of Swedes"
> "Talk of the Town" in last week's *New Yorker*
> "Wordsworth in the Tropics," from Huxley's *Collected Essays*
> "Maternal Behavior and Attitudes," chapter 14 of *Human Development*

7.135   Such common titles as *foreword, preface, introduction, contents, appendix, glossary, bibliography, index,* are lowercased in passing references:

> In his preface to . . .
> The editor's preface gives an excellent summary.
> Allan Nevins wrote the foreword to . . .
> The table of contents lists all the subheadings.
> The bibliographical essay is incomplete.

The book contains a glossary as well as a subject index and an index of names.

These titles are capitalized (no quotation marks) when cross-reference is made from one part to another of the same book:

> Full citations are listed in the Bibliography.
> Further examples will be found in the Appendix.

7.136 The word *chapter* is lowercased and spelled out in text; it may be abbreviated in parenthetical references: (chap. 3). Chapter numbers in text references are given in arabic figures, or spelled out, even when the actual chapter numbers are in roman numerals.

7.137 *Series and editions.* Titles of book series and editions are capitalized and set in roman type without quotation marks. The words *series* and *edition* are lowercased when they are not part of the title:

> Chicago History of American Civilization series
> Modern Library edition
> Phoenix Books

POEMS AND PLAYS

7.138 Titles of collections of poetry and of long poems published separately are italicized. Titles of short poems are in roman type and quoted:

> *Paradise Lost*
>
> "The Love Song of J. Alfred Prufrock," from *Prufrock and Other Observations*

In literary studies where many poems are mentioned it is better—and easier for editor and reader—to set all the titles alike, in italics.

7.139 When a poem is referred to by its first line rather than a title, capitalization should follow the poem, not the rules for capitalizing titles:

> "Shall I compare thee to a Summer's day?"

7.140 Titles of plays are italicized, regardless of the length of the play or whether it is published separately or in a collection:

> Shaw's *Arms and the Man*, in volume 2 of his *Plays: Pleasant and Unpleasant*

7.141 Words denoting parts of poems and plays are usually lowercased and set in roman type:

> canto 2   act 3
> stanza 4   scene 5

UNPUBLISHED WORKS

7.142   Titles of dissertations and theses, manuscripts in collections, lectures and papers read at meetings, machine copies of typescripts (mimeograph, Xerox, etc.), are set in roman type and quoted. Names of depositories, archives, and the like, and names of manuscript collections are capitalized and set in roman type without quotation marks. Such words as *diary*, *journal*, *memorandum*, are set in roman type, not quoted, and usually lowercased in text references:

> In a master's thesis, "Charles Valentin Alkan and His Pianoforte Works"
>
> "A Canal Boat Journey, 1857," an anonymous manuscript in the Library of Congress Manuscripts Division
>
> Papers of the Continental Congress in the National Archives

MOTION PICTURES AND TELEVISION AND RADIO PROGRAMS

7.143   Titles of motion pictures are italicized. Titles of television and radio programs are in roman type and quoted.

> the movie *Blow-up*
> *A Man for All Seasons*
> NBC's "Bonanza"
> Harry Bouras's "Critic's Choice" on WFMT

MUSICAL COMPOSITIONS

7.144   Titles of operas, oratorios, motets, tone poems, and other long musical compositions are italicized. Titles of songs and short compositions are usually set in roman type and quoted. As with other such arbitrary distinctions (e.g., poems), where many titles of musical compositions are mentioned in a critical study, all may be italicized regardless of individual length. Many musical compositions, because of the nature of the art, do not have descriptive titles but are identified by the name of a musical form in which they are written plus a number or a key or both. Such designations are capitalized but not italicized or quoted. Some of these also have descriptive titles, given them either by the composer or, more often, by a later critic or performer; these appellations are italicized if the work is long, quoted if it is short:

> Air with Variations ("The Harmonious Blacksmith") from Handel's Suite no. 5 in E
> Bach's Prelude and Fugue in E-flat ("St. Anne")

Beethoven's Fifth Symphony
Brahms's Ballade op. (*or* opus) 118 no. 3
Death and Transfiguration
Don Giovanni
Harold in Italy
Hungarian Rhapsody no. 12
"Jesu Joy of Man's Desiring"
the *Messiah* (not *The Messiah*)
"Ode to Billie Joe"
Piano Sonata no. 2 (*Concord, Mass., 1840–60*), or the *Concord* Sonata, by Charles Ives
Piano Concerto no. 5 (*Emperor*), or the *Emperor* Concerto, by Beethoven
String Quartet in D Minor (*Death and the Maiden*), or *Death and the Maiden* Quartet (but the song: "Death and the Maiden")
Symphony no. 41 (*Jupiter*), or the *Jupiter* Symphony
William Tell Overture
"Wohin" from *Die schöne Müllerin*

PAINTINGS AND SCULPTURE

7.145 Titles of paintings, drawings, statues, and other works of art are italicized:

Grant Wood's *American Gothic*
El Greco's *View of Toledo*
Hogarth's series of drawings *The Rake's Progress*
Rembrandt's etching *Christ Presented to the People*
Rodin's *The Thinker*

Traditional or descriptive titles of works of art are given in roman:

Victory of Samothrace
Apollo Belvedere
Mona Lisa

NOTICES

7.146 Specific wording of short signs or notices run in textual matter should be capitalized like titles but neither italicized nor quoted:

He has a No Smoking sign in his car.
The door was marked Authorized Personnel Only.

MOTTOES

7.147 Mottoes and inscriptions may well be treated the same way:

The flag bore the motto Dont Tread on Me.

FOR FURTHER REFERENCE

7.148   The most readily available and generally accurate sources for the spelling and capitalization of personal names are *Webster's Biographical Dictionary*, *Who's Who*, *Who's Who in America*, *Dictionary of National Biography* (British), and *Dictionary of American Biography*. For geographical names: *Webster's Geographical Dictionary* and *The Columbia Lippincott Gazetteer of the World*.

8 *Numbers*

8.1 There is no simple, consistent system of style for the use of numbers in textual matter. The following suggestions are an attempt to give an empirical guide to current good usage. They provide a sketch of proper use of various forms of numbers and should answer the commonest, if not all the most vexatious, questions of when to use figures and when to spell out numbers. See chapter 7, "Names and Terms"; chapter 11, "Illustrations, Captions, and Legends"; and chapter 16, "Bibliographies," for detailed information on the use of numbers in these respective subjects.

FIGURES OR WORDS?—GENERAL PRINCIPLES

8.2 *Exact numbers.* In nonscientific text matter exact numbers of less than one hundred should be spelled out, and numbers of one hundred or more should be expressed in figures (University of Chicago Press style):

> Thirty leading Republicans from eleven states urged the governor to declare his candidacy.
> The property is held on a ninety-nine-year lease.
> His son is twenty-four years old.
> The first edition ran to 2,670 pages in three volumes, with 160 copperplate engravings.
> The entire length of 4,066 feet is divided into twelve spans of paired parabolic ribs.
> The three new parking lots will provide space for 540 more cars.

Two important exceptions to this rule are year numbers and numbers referring to parts of a book, which, except in rare circumstances, are expressed in figures:

> The assassination of Julius Caesar in 44 B.C. marked the end of the Roman republic.
> You will find three examples of good usage on page 6.
> For further data refer to figure 34 and table 8.

Numbers applicable to the same category should be treated alike throughout a paragraph; do not use figures for some and spell out others. If the largest contains three or more digits, use figures for all:

196

There are 25 graduate students in the philosophy department, 56 in the classics department, and 117 in the romance languages department, making a total of 198 students in the three departments.

In the past ten years fifteen new buildings have been erected. In one block a 103-story office building rises between two old apartment houses only 3 and 4 stories high.

8.3   *Round numbers.* Approximate figures in hundreds or thousands or millions should be spelled out. Note that *thousand* is used only with even thousands; a number such as 2,500 is spelled *twenty-five hundred:*

Government officials estimated that forty thousand Viet Cong were killed during the *Tet* offensive.

He wrote a fifteen-hundred-word essay in response to the question.

Very large round numbers may be expressed in figures and units of millions or billions:

At the time, the earth's population was estimated as 2.3 billion.

A figure of about 4.5 billion years is often given as the age of the solar system.

8.4   *Initial numbers.* At the beginning of a sentence any number that would ordinarily be written in figures is spelled out:

One hundred ten men and 103 women will receive advanced degrees this quarter.

Twenty-seven percent of the cost was guaranteed.

Nineteen sixty-eight marked the sesquicentennial of the state of Illinois.

If this is impracticable or cumbersome, the sentence should be reconstructed so that it does not begin with a number.

FIGURES OR WORDS?—SPECIAL CASES

PHYSICAL QUANTITIES

8.5   *Scientific usage.* In mathematical, statistical, technical, or scientific text, physical quantities, such as distances, lengths, areas, volumes, pressures, and so on, are expressed in figures:

45 miles	$10°$ C, $10.5°$ C
3 cubic feet	$10°$ (of arc), $10°.5$ *or* $10°30'$
240 volts	6 meters
45 pounds	30 cubic centimeters
21 hectares	an 8-point table with 6-point
10 picas	boxheads

8.6 *Nonscientific usage.* In ordinary text matter such quantities should be treated according to the rules governing the spelling out of numbers:

> The temperature dropped twenty degrees in less than an hour.
> The train approached at a speed of seventy-five miles an hour.
> Some students live more than fifteen kilometers from the school.
> Type the entries on three-by-five-inch index cards.

Fractional quantities, however, are cumbersome to write out and should be expressed in figures:

> Manuscripts should be typed on 8½-by-11-inch paper.

8.7 *Abbreviations.* If an abbreviation is used for the unit of measure, the quantity should always be expressed by a figure (for the use of periods with abbreviations see pars. 14.2, 14.45):

3 mi.	12 v.	50 lb.	35-mm film
350° F.	7 hr.	13 g	137 mm

8.8 *Symbols.* If a symbol is used instead of an abbreviation, the quantity is again expressed by a figure:

$3\frac{1}{2}''$ $36°30'N$ $9'$

And for two or more quantities, the symbol should usually be repeated:

$3'' \times 5''$ $30°–50°$

DECIMALS AND PERCENTAGES

8.9 Decimal fractions and percentages (including academic grades) are normally set in figures. In scientific and statistical copy use the symbol "%"; in humanistic copy, in general, use the word *percent:*

> The five-year credit will carry interest of 3 percent.
> College graduates averaged 2.3 children per couple.
> Of the cultures tested, fewer than 25% yielded positive results.
> For these purposes pi will be considered equal to 3.14159.
> Grades of 3.8 and 95 are identical.

Note that in British practice a decimal point is usually a raised dot (3·14159) and in Continental practice, a comma (3,14159).

MONEY

8.10 *United States currency.* Isolated references to amounts of money in United States currency are spelled out or expressed in figures in accord with the general rule (par. 8.2). If the number is spelled out, so is the unit of currency, and if figures are used, the symbol "$" precedes them:

> Hundreds of teen-agers paid five dollars each to hear the Beatles in person.
>
> The fare has been raised to twenty-five cents.
>
> The committee raised a total of $325.

Fractional amounts over one dollar are set in figures like other decimal fractions. Whole-dollar amounts are set with ciphers after the decimal point when they appear in the same context with fractional amounts—and only then:

> Articles bought for $6.00 were sold for $6.75.
>
> The agent received $5.50, $33.75, and $175.00 for the three sales.

Like other very large round numbers, sums of money that would be cumbersome to express in figures or to spell out in full may be expressed in units of millions or billions, accompanied by figures and a dollar sign:

> A price of $3 million was agreed upon by both firms.
>
> Teen-age consumers account for an annual market of some $15 billion.
>
> The $10.4 billion deficit results from increased military expenditures.

8.11 *British currency.* Sums of money in pounds, shillings, and pence are handled similarly to sums in dollars:

> threepence   nineteen shillings   four pounds
>
> two shillings and sixpence (*colloquially* two and six *or* half a crown)
>
> £14 19s. 6d. *or* £14.19.6   £52 million   £1,346 million

The term *billion* should be avoided, since in British usage a billion is the equivalent of the American trillion.

8.12 In some connections sums of money may be expressed in terms of guineas (the guinea is a unit of value equal to twenty-one shillings):

> thirty guineas   342 guineas (gns.)

8.13 *Other currencies.* Most other currencies of the world employ a system like that of the United States, with a unit symbol preceding the number. Conventions of expressing large numbers and decimals vary, however (see pars. 8.9, 8.35). If an author or editor has to deal with exact amounts of money in currencies other than American or British, he should consult the table "Foreign Money" in the United States Government Printing Office *Style Manual*.

DATES

8.14   *The day of the month.* The University of Chicago Press prefers that in all text the day, month, and year be written without internal punctuation in this form:[1]

> *Saturday Review,* 5 October 1968, p. 26
> On 22 November 1963 the president was assassinated.

Other acceptable forms are:

> On November 22, 1963, the president was assassinated.
> The course of events on the twenty-second of November, 1963, remains a source of controversy.

After an exact date has been used, an elliptical reference to another date in the same month is spelled out:

> On 5 November the national elections took place. By the morning of the sixth, returns for all but a few precincts were in.

Do not use *st, d,* and *th* after figures in dates to indicate ordinals: April 15, *not* April 15th.

8.15   *Centuries and decades.* Spell out (in lowercase letters) references to particular centuries and decades:

> twentieth century   during the sixties and seventies
> *but:* the 1930s

8.16   *The year abbreviated.* In informal contexts the full number of a particular year is sometimes abbreviated:

> the class of '68   the spirit of '76
> He told them he was born in '07.

8.17   *Eras.* Figures are used for year numbers followed or preceded by era designations, and words are used for centuries. The abbreviations for eras are conventionally set in small caps. Note that the abbreviations beginning with *A* (for *anno,* "the year") properly precede the year number, whereas others follow it. Among the most frequently used era designations are A.D. (*anno Domini,* "in the year of the Lord"); A.H. (*anno Hegirae,* "in the year of [Muhammad's] Hegira," or *anno Hebraico,* "in the Hebrew year"); A.U.C. (*anno urbis conditae,* "in the year of the building of the city" [i.e., Rome, in 753 B.C.]); B.C. ("before Christ"); C.E. and B.C.E. ("of the common era" and "before the common era"— equivalent to A.D. and B.C.); and B.P. ("before the present").

1. When use of an all-digit style is desirable (in dating memorandums, for example), the unambiguous European form with lowercase roman numeral for the month is recommended: *10 xi 68* for *10 November 1968.*

Greek philosophy reached its highest development in the fourth century B.C.
Britain was invaded successfully in 55 B.C. and A.D. 1066.
Mubarak published his survey at Cairo in A.H. 1306 (A.D. 1888).
After 621 B.C.E. worship was permitted only at Jerusalem.
Radiocarbon dating indicates that the campsite was in use by about 13,500 B.P.

In the last example note the use of the comma in a year number of more than four digits (see par. 8.34).

8.18   Because of the literal meaning of A.D., conservative usage long rejected such an expression as "the second century A.D." in favor of "the second century of the Christian Era" or "the second century after Christ." Recognizing, however, that A.D. has taken on a purely conventional significance and that many careful writers no longer avoid the locution, this press accepts with (relative) cheerfulness such a sentence as

Timbuktu was founded in the ninth century A.D.

TIME OF DAY

8.19   Times of day are usually spelled out in text matter:

The directors expected the meeting to continue until half-past three.
Freshman girls must be in their rooms by midnight on weekdays.
He left the office at four.
The family always ate dinner at seven o'clock.

But figures are used (with ciphers for even hours) when the exact moment of time is to be emphasized:

The program is televised at 2:30 in the afternoon.
If we don't eat dinner, we can catch the 6:20 train.
The county will return to standard time tomorrow morning at 2:00.

8.20   Figures are used in designations of time with A.M. or P.M. Never use A.M. with *morning* or P.M. with *evening*, and never use *o'clock* with either A.M. or P.M. or figures:

at 4:00 P.M.	12:00 M. (noon)
at 10:45 in the morning	12:00 P.M. (midnight)
11:30 A.M.	eight o'clock

Note that small caps are used for abbreviations A.M. and P.M. (*ante* and *post meridiem*). These should be set without space between.

8.21   In the military twenty-four-hour system of expressing time, no punctuation is used between the hours and minutes:

> General quarters sounded at 0415.
> Visiting hours are from 0930 to 1100 and from 1800 to 2030.

NAMES

8.22   *Monarchs, etc.* Kings, emperors, and popes with the same names are differentiated by numerals, traditionally roman:

George VI	Louis XIV	Charles V
Napoleon III	Boniface VIII	John XXIII

In Continental practice the numeral is sometimes followed by a period or a superscript abbreviation, indicating that the number is an ordinal (Wilhelm II., François Ier). These should be edited out in an English context.

8.23   *Vehicles, etc.* Sometimes similarly treated are yachts, racing automobiles, and spacecraft (but not warships):

America IV	*Bluebird III*	*Mariner IV*

8.24   *Family names.* Roman numerals are also used to differentiate male members of a family with identical names. The American custom is this. If Robert Allen Smith's son or grandson is given the same name, the latter adds "Jr." to his name (a nephew or grand-nephew would use "II"). If later a third member of the family is given the name, he adds "III"; a fourth, "IV"; and so on. On the death of the eldest of the name, Robert Allen Smith, Jr., drops the "Jr.," Robert Allen Smith III (if a grandson) becomes Robert Allen Smith, Jr., and so on. If the original or a subsequent bearer of the name was a famous person, however, a younger namesake often keeps the suffix:

> Douglas Fairbanks, Jr.
> Adlai E. Stevenson III

GOVERNMENTAL DESIGNATIONS

8.25   *Governments.* Particular dynasties, governments, and governing bodies in a succession are usually designated by an ordinal number spelled out preceding the noun:

Eighteenth Dynasty	Third Reich
Fifth Republic	Second International
Second Continental Congress	Ninetieth Congress

8.26 *Political divisions.* Spell out in ordinal form numerals less than one hundred designating political divisions:

Fifth Ward	Fourteenth Precinct
Court of Appeals for the Tenth Circuit	Second Congressional District
	Ninth Naval District

8.27 *Military units.* Similarly, spell out in ordinal form numerals less than one hundred designating military subdivisions:

Fifth Army	Seventy-seventh Regiment
Second Infantry Division	323d Fighter Wing
Third Battalion, 122d Artillery	

ORGANIZATIONS

8.28 *Churches, etc.* Numerals designating a religious organization or house of worship are generally spelled out in ordinal form before the name:

First Baptist Church	Seventh-day Adventists

but: Muhammad's Mosque of Islam No. 2

8.29 *Unions and lodges.* Numerals designating local branches of labor unions and of fraternal lodges are usually expressed in arabic figures after the name:

> Typographical Union No. 16
>
> American Legion, Department of Illinois, Crispus Attucks Post No. 1268
>
> Amalgamated Meat Cutters and Butcher Workmen of North America, Local No. 15

ADDRESSES AND THOROUGHFARES

8.30 *Highways.* State, federal, and interstate highways are designated by arabic numerals:

U.S. Route 41 (U.S. 41)	Interstate 90 (I-90)	Illinois 12

8.31 *Numbered streets.* It is preferable, except where space is at a premium, to spell out the names of numbered streets under one hundred:

Fifth Avenue	Twenty-third Street

The address "1212 Fifth Street" is easier to read than "1212—5th St.," a device sometimes employed in typing addresses.

8.32   *Building numbers.* Address numbers are usually written in arabic numerals before the name of the street, in English and American addresses:

> 5750 Ellis Avenue, Chicago, Illinois 60637
> 70 Great Russell Street, London, W.C. 1, England

According to local custom and preferences of building owners, however, address numbers that can be expressed in one or two words are often spelled out:

> Four Hundred East Randolph   One Park Avenue
> One Thousand Lake Shore Drive   Thirty West Adams Street

FORMS AND USES OF NUMBERS

PLURALS OF NUMBERS

8.33   The plurals of spelled-out numbers are formed like the plurals of other nouns:

> The contestants were in their twenties and thirties.
> The family was at sixes and sevens.

The plurals of figures are formed by the addition of *s* alone:

> Among the scores were two 240s and three 238s.
> The bonds being offered are convertible $4\frac{1}{2}$s.
> Jazz forms developed in the 1920s became popular in the 1930s.

USE OF THE COMMA

8.34   In most figures of one thousand or more, commas should be used between every group of three digits, counting from the right:

> 32,987   1,512   1,000,000

Exceptions to this rule are page numbers, addresses, numbers of chapters of fraternal organizations and the like, decimal fractions of less than one, and year numbers of four digits, which are written in figures without commas. (Year numbers of five or more digits use the comma.)

8.35   British practice is similar to American in marking off groups of three digits with commas. In Continental practice, however, periods or spaces are often used: 93.000.000; 93 000 000. Except in quoted matter, these should be edited to conform to American practice.

INCLUSIVE NUMBERS

8.36   Inclusive numbers (continued numbers) are separated by an en dash. The University of Chicago Press abbreviates inclusive numbers according to the following principles:

First Number	Second Number	Examples
Less than 100	Use all digits	3–10; 71–72
100 or multiple	Use all digits	100–104; 600–613
More than 100 but less than 110 (in multiples of 100)	Use changed part only (i.e., omit 0)	107–8; 1002–3
More than 109 (in multiples of 100)	Use last two digits (or three if needed)	321–25; 415–532; 1536–38

Note the following instances of continued numbers other than pages:

the war of 1914–18   the winter of 1900–1901 (*or* 1900/1901)
A.D. 325–27   A.D. 300–325   *but:* 327–325 B.C.

(For the use of an en dash between numbers see par. 5.89.)

ROMAN NUMERALS

8.37   Table 8.1 shows the formation of roman numerals with their arabic equivalents. The general principle is that a smaller letter before a larger one subtracts from its value, and a small letter after a larger one adds to it; a bar over a letter multiplies its value by one thousand. Roman numerals may also be written in lowercase letters (i, ii, iii, iv, etc.), and in older practice a final *i* was

TABLE 8.1: Roman and Arabic Numerals

Arabic	Roman	Arabic	Roman	Arabic	Roman
1	I	16	XVI	90	XC
2	II	17	XVII	100	C
3	III	18	XVIII	200	CC
4	IV	19	XIX	300	CCC
5	V	20	XX	400	CD
6	VI	21	XXI	500	D
7	VII	22	XXII	600	DC
8	VIII	23	XXIII	700	DCC
9	IX	24	XXIV	800	DCCC
10	X	30	XXX	900	CM
11	XI	40	XL	1,000	M
12	XII	50	L	2,000	MM
13	XIII	60	LX	3,000	MMM
14	XIV	70	LXX	4,000	$\overline{\text{MV}}$
15	XV	80	LXXX	5,000	$\overline{\text{V}}$ (*or* ꟻ)

often made like a *j* (vij, viij). Also, in early printed works, IƆ is sometimes seen for D and CIƆ for M. The University of Chicago Press now uses arabic numerals in many situations where roman numerals were formerly more common, such as references to volume and chapter numbers.

ENUMERATIONS

8.38   Enumerations that are run into the text may be indicated by figures or italic letters between parentheses. In a simple series with little or no punctuation within each item, separation by commas is sufficient. Otherwise, semicolons are used:

> This was determined by a chi-square test using as observed frequencies (*a*) the occurrence of one class and (*b*) the total occurrence of all classes among the neighbors of the subject classes.

> Data are available on three different groups of counsel: (1) the Public Defender of Cook County, (2) the member attorneys of the Chicago Bar Association's Defense of Prisoners Committee, and (3) all other attorneys.

> Specifically, the committee set down fundamental principles, which in its opinion were so well established that they were no longer open to controversy: (1) the commerce power was complete, except as constitutionally limited; (2) the power included the authority absolutely to prohibit specified persons and things from interstate transit; (3) the only limitation upon this authority, as far as the Keating-Owen bill was concerned, was the Fifth Amendment, which protected against arbitrary interference with private rights; and (4) this authority might be exercised in the interest of the public welfare as well as in the direct interest of commerce.

8.39   *Outline style.* For long enumerations it is usually best to set each item on a line by itself. The numerals may be set flush with the margin of the text in which the enumeration occurs, or they may be given paragraph indention. In either case runover lines are best aligned with the first word following the numeral (University of Chicago Press preference, where this is known as *outline*, or *syllabus*, *style*):

> The inadequacy of the methods proposed for the solution of both histological and mounting problems is emphasized by the number and variety of the published procedures, which fall into the following groups:
>
> 1. Slightly modified classical histological techniques with fluid fixation, wax embedding, and aqueous mounting of the section or the emulsion

206

2. Sandwich technique with separate processing of tissue and photographic film after exposure
3. Protective coating of tissue to prevent leaching during application of stripping film or liquid emulsion
4. Freeze substitution of tissue with or without embedding followed by film application
5. Vacuum freeze-drying of tissue blocks followed by embedding
6. Mounting of frozen sections on emulsion, using heat or adhesive liquids

8.40 For an enumeration in which items are subdivided, a more elaborate form of outline style is called for. The following example illustrates the form favored by the University of Chicago Press. Note that the divisional numerals or letters for the top three levels are set off by periods and those for the lower levels by single or double parentheses:

    I. Historical introduction
    II. Dentition in various groups of vertebrates
        A. Reptilia
            1. Histology and development of reptile teeth
            2. Survey of forms
        B. Mammalia
            1. Histology and development of mammalian teeth
            2. Survey of forms
                a) Primates
                    (1) Lemuroidea
                    (2) Anthropoidea
                        (*a*) Platyrrhini
                        (*b*) Catarrhini
                            i) Circopithecidae
                            ii) Pongidae
                b) Carnivora
                    (1) Creodonta
                    (2) Fissipedia
                        (*a*) Aeluroidea
                        (*b*) Arctoidea
                    (3) Pinnipedia
                c) Etc. . . .

In the foregoing example, note that roman numerals, since they vary in width, are aligned on the following period or parenthesis. Any runover lines would be aligned as in the preceding example.

FOR FURTHER REFERENCE

8.41 For special uses of numbers not covered in this chapter, the reader is referred to the United States Government Printing Office *Style Manual.*

9 *Foreign Languages in Type*

9.1   This chapter is intended as an aid to authors and editors in solving some of the problems that arise in preparing foreign language copy for setting in type. Some of the suggestions are addressed primarily to authors (such as the recommendations on choice of transliteration systems), others primarily to manuscript editors (such as the hints on what kinds of capitalization one is likely to encounter in various languages). It should be emphasized that the chapter does not pretend to constitute a style manual for any of the languages treated. Nor does it pretend to be comprehensive: only the languages that editors are likely to meet in the course of general bookwork are covered at all, and of these some are covered more completely than others, depending partly upon the relative importance of the languages in scholarly work and partly upon the complexity of the problems they raise.

9.2   The kinds of problems one encounters with foreign language copy differ according to whether the copy was originally written with the same alphabet as English, whether it has been transliterated or romanized, or whether it is to be set in the alphabet of the original (Greek being the only common example of the last). The organization of the chapter reflects these three categories.

LANGUAGES USING THE LATIN ALPHABET

9.3   With languages using an alphabet basically similar to that of English (the *Latin* alphabet), editorial questions arise mainly from differing systems of capitalization, punctuation, and syllabification (word division). But since some of these languages supplement the basic Latin alphabet with additional letters or use a variety of accents and diacritics on the familiar letters, there is the additional, mechanical problem of assuring that the typesetter has sorts for these special characters.

GENERAL PRINCIPLES

9.4   *Capitalization.* The chief problem concerning capitalization is what to do with titles of books and articles in bibliographies, footnotes, and run of text. Here the University of Chicago Press recommends following a simple rule: In any language but English capitalize only the words that would be capitalized in normal prose. For all the languages in question this means capitalizing the first word of the title and any proper nouns that occur in it.[1] For German it means capitalizing common nouns also. For Dutch it means capitalizing proper adjectives also, but not common nouns. (This rule is already followed in scientific style for all languages, including English [see par. 16.52].) The rule can easily

1. The rule for French titles followed by the *French Review, PMLA,* and *Romanic Review,* and commended by the University of Chicago Department of Romance Languages and Literatures, is as follows. Always capitalize the first word and any proper nouns in the title; if the first word is an article, capitalize the substantive and any intervening adjective(s); if the first word is neither an article nor an adjective, lowercase all following words. Thus: *Le Rouge et le noir; L'Illusion comique; Les Fausses Vérités; A la recherche du temps perdu; Dans le labyrinthe.* The Press accepts this rule for studies in French literature but for general use (especially when books and articles in several languages are cited) prefers the simpler rule stated in the text.

211

be extended to the names of foreign journals and even of learned societies without offending the sensibilities of native speakers of these languages.

9.5 In English, capitalization is applied to more classes of words than in any other European language. Consequently, it is always surprising to an English-speaking person learning his first foreign language—say, French—to discover that the equivalents of *I* and *American* and *Tuesday* are spelled with no capitals. The remarks under "Capitalization" in the sections that follow are an attempt to mitigate some of the manuscript editor's surprises—to suggest some of the more obvious ways in which various languages differ from English in their use of capitals.

9.6 Except where it is stated to the contrary, the language in question is assumed to use lowercase type for all adjectives (except adjectives used as proper nouns), all pronouns, the names of the months, and the days of the week. In addition, it can be assumed that capitals are used much more sparingly than in English for names of offices, institutions, places, organizations, and so on. (For the capitalization of foreign personal names, see pars. 7.6–14.)

9.7 *Punctuation.* Continental punctuation is in some ways even more "foreign" to the English-speaking editor than Continental capitalization. The remarks under "Punctuation" in the sections below are an attempt to point out some of the more obvious departures from what is familiar to us. Further information on foreign punctuation can be found in chapter 6.

9.8 Note too that the remarks apply to foreign punctuation in a foreign language context, that is, in an article or book in that language or a verbatim quotation from such a work. A bit of foreign language dialogue or a sentence or two quoted in a foreign language introduced into an English context would be punctuated in English fashion, especially with regard to quotation marks:

"L'état," said the Sun King modestly, "c'est moi."

9.9 *Word division.* Anyone who has ever read a book in English that was composed and printed in a non-English-speaking country knows how easy it is to err in word division when working with a language not one's own. Condensed rules for dividing words in the Latin-alphabet foreign languages most frequently met in book and journal work are given below. Although the rules are not entirely comprehensive, they will be found to cover most contingencies.

212

9.10   *Special characters.* English is one of very few languages that can be set without accents, diacritics, or special alphabetic characters for native words. (An Italian typesetter might consider our *k* and *w* special characters, since these letters do not occur in Italian words, but they are nonetheless included in Italian type fonts.) Whenever passages in a foreign language occur in a book, the manuscript editor should scan them carefully for special characters, especially unusual ones. The ordinary umlauted (as in German) and accented (as in French) lowercase vowels can be disregarded, but anything more unusual, including accented capital letters, should be listed for the information of the typesetter (see par. 2.111).

9.11   In the case of an entire book or article in a foreign language, the chances are good that all the special characters employed by that language will turn up in the copy. Consequently, the typesetter should be instructed (if possible, about three months before copy deadline) to obtain the special characters for that language, in the sizes and faces needed.[2]

DANISH

9.12   *Capitalization.* The polite personal pronouns *De, Dem, Deres,* and the familiar *I* are capitalized. Formerly, common nouns were capitalized as in German.

9.13   *Special characters.* Danish has three additional alphabetic letters, and special characters are required for these:

Å å, Æ æ, Ø ø

DUTCH

9.14   *Capitalization.* The pronouns *U, Uw,* and *Gij* when they appear in personal correspondence are capitalized. Proper adjectives are capitalized as in English. When a word beginning with the diphthong *ij* is capitalized, both letters are capitals: *IJsland.* When a single letter begins a sentence, it is not capitalized, but the next word is: *'k Heb niet.* . . . (For the capitalization of particles with personal names see par. 7.9.)

9.15   *Special characters.* Dutch requires no special characters outside the ordinary Latin alphabet.

2. The lists of special characters given below are based on the United States Government Printing Office *Style Manual.*

FINNISH

9.16   *Special characters.* Finnish requires two umlauted vowels:

Ä ä, Ö ö

FRENCH

9.17   *Capitalization.* Names denoting roadways, squares, etc., are lowercased, whether part of an address or used alone:

le boulevard Saint-Germain   13, rue des Beaux-Arts
la place de l'Opéra   le carrefour de Buci

In names of political, military, religious, or other institutions, the first substantive only is capitalized:

l'Académie française   le Conservatoire de musique
l'Assemblée nationale   la Légion d'honneur
l'Eglise catholique (*but* l'église de Saint-Eustache)

If such names are hyphenated (and French makes frequent use of hyphens), both elements are capitalized:

la Comédie-Française

Names of buildings are generally capitalized:

l'Hôtel des Invalides   le Palais du Louvre

Names of members of religious groups are lowercased:

un chrétien   des juifs   une carmélite   un protestant

In most geographical names, the substantive is lowercased and the modifying word capitalized:

la mer Rouge   le pic du Midi   le massif Central

9.18   *Punctuation.* Small angle marks called *guillemets* (« ») are used for quotation marks and are placed on the lower part of the type body. A small amount of space is added between the guillemets and the quoted material:

A vrai dire, Abélard n'avoue pas un tel rationalisme: « je ne veux pas être si philosophe, écrit-il, que je résiste à Paul, ni si aristotélicien que je me sépare du Christ », ou encore: « Vois combien il est présomptueux de discuter par la raison ce qui dépasse l'homme et de ne pas s'arrêter avant d'avoir éclairé toutes ses paroles par le sens ou la raison humaine. »[3]

3. Emile Bréhier, *Histoire de la philosophie*, vol. 1, fasc. 3 (Paris: Presses universitaires de France, 1931), p. 517.

9.19   Punctuation belonging to the quoted matter is placed inside the closing guillemets:

« Va-t'en! » m'a-t-il dit.

Punctuation belonging to the including sentence is placed outside, and a period belonging to the quotation is dropped:

D'où vient l'expression « sur le tapis »?
Est-ce Louis XV qui a dit: « Après moi, le déluge »?

When the end punctuation of the simultaneously terminating quotation and including sentence is identical, the mark outside the closing guillemets is dropped:

Qui a dit: « Où sont les neiges d'antan? »

9.20   If a quotation in text (that is, not a block quotation) is more than one paragraph long, guillemets are placed at the beginning of each additional paragraph and closing guillemets at the end of the last.

9.21   Guillemets are also used for quotations within quotations. When the second quotation runs over to additional lines, each runover line begins with opening guillemets. If the two quotations end simultaneously, however, only one pair of terminating guillemets is used:

Raoul suggéra à sa sœur: « Tu connais sans doute la parole « De « l'abondance du cœur la bouche parle. »

9.22   In quoted conversation, the guillemets are frequently replaced by dashes. The dash is used before each successive speech but is not repeated at the end of the speech. A space is added after the dash:

— Vous viendrez aussitôt que possible? a-t-il demandé.
— Tout de suite.
— Bien. Bonne chance!

If a quotation is used in dialogue, guillemets are employed to set off the quotation.

9.23   A series of three closely spaced periods is frequently used to indicate interruptions or sudden breaks in thought. A space is used after, but not before, such points of suspension:

« Ce n'est pas que je n'aime plus l'Algérie... mon Dieu! un ciel! des arbres!... et le reste!... Toutefois, sept ans de discipline.... »

9.24   *Word division.* The fundamental principle of French word division is to divide as far as possible on a vowel, avoiding consonantal ending of syllables except where *n* nasalizes a preceding vowel:

a-che-ter   ba-lan-cer (*not* bal-anc-er)
in-di-vi-si-bi-li-té   ta-bleau (*not* tab-leau)

215

9.25   Two adjacent and different consonants of which the second is *l* or *r* (but not the combinations *rl* and *lr*) are both carried over to the following syllable. Otherwise, different consonants are divided:

é-cri-vain	par-ler	plas-tic
qua-tre	Mal-raux	ob-jet

9.26   In groups of three adjacent consonants the first goes with the preceding syllable; the others are carried over:

es-prit   res-plendir

9.27   There are as many syllables as there are vowels or diphthongs, even if some vowels are not sounded:

fui-te   guer-re   pro-prié-tai-re

9.28   A mute *e* following a vowel, however, does not form a syllable:

é-taient   joue-rai

9.29   When preceding other vowels and sounded as consonants, *i, y, o, ou,* and *u* do not form syllables:

bien	é-tions	loin
é-cuel-le	fouet-ter	yeux

9.30   Division should not be made after an apostrophe:

jus-qu'à demain

9.31   *Special characters.* French as sometimes set employs the following special characters:

À à, Â â, Ç ç, É é, È è, Ê ê, Ë ë, Î î, Ï ï, Ô ô, Œ œ, Ù ù, Û û

Note, however, that French may be set without accents on capital letters (University of Chicago Press preference),[4] and if necessary the digraph *Œ œ* may be set as separate characters (*OE oe*). This leaves as the essential minimum the *C* with cedilla and the lowercase accented vowels, sorts that are found in many English and American fonts.

GERMAN

9.32   *Capitalization.* The most striking feature of German capitalization is that all nouns and words used as nouns are capitalized:

ein Haus   Weltanschauung   das Sein

Although proper adjectives are generally lowercased, those derived from personal names, and used with their original signification, are capitalized:

die deutsche Literatur   die Platonischen Dialoge

---

4. French printers vary in practice, some retaining accents on all capitals (except the word *à*, which never carries the accent when capitalized), some retaining accents only on *E*, some omitting them altogether. English and American publishers reflect all these practices.

The pronouns *Sie, Ihr,* and *Ihnen,* as polite second-person forms, are capitalized. As third-person pronouns they are lowercased. Also, in correspondence such forms as *Du, Dein, Ihr, Euch,* etc., are capitalized.

9.33   *Punctuation.* The apostrophe is used to note the colloquial omission of *e:*

> wie geht's   was gibt's   hab' ich

The apostrophe is also used to note the omission of the genitive ending, *s,* after proper names ending in *s, ß, x, z:*

> Jaspers' Philosophie   Leibniz' Meinung

9.34   In German, quotations take pairs of primes („ "), double, inverted quotation marks (,, "), or (sometimes inverted) guillemets:

> Adam Smith hat sehr wohl gesehen, daß in ,,Wirklichkeit die Verschiedenheit der natürlichen Anlagen zwischen den Individuen weit geringer ist als wir glauben."

Punctuation is placed inside or outside closing quotation marks according to whether it belongs to the quotation or the including sentence.

9.35   *Word division.* The fundamental principle of German word division is to divide on a vowel as far as possible:

> Fa-brik   hü-ten   Bu-ße

9.36   If two or more consonants stand between vowels, usually only the last is carried over:

> Karp-fen   klir-ren   Ver-wand-te
> Klemp-ner   Rit-ter   Was-ser

9.37   The consonantal groups *ch, sch, ph, st,* and *th* are separated only when the letters belong to different syllables:

> Hä-scher   Philoso-phie   Morgen-stern
> (*but* Häus-chen)   (*but* Klapp-hut)   (*but* Reichs-tag)

9.38   If *ck* must be divided, it is separated into *k-k:*

> Deckel—Dek-kel

9.39   In non-German words combinations of *b, d, g, k, p,* and *t* with *l* or *r* are carried over:

> Hy-drant   Me-trum   Pu-bli-kum

9.40   Compound words are separated first into their component elements, and within each element the foregoing rules apply:

> Für-sten-schloß   In-ter-esse   Tür-an-gel

9.41 *Special characters.* German is almost never set in the old *Fraktur* type nowadays. For setting in roman type, one special character, the double *s*, is needed, plus the umlauted vowels:

ß, Ä ä, Ö ö, Ü ü

It is acceptable to set ß as *ss* and umlauted capitals as *Ae, Oe,* and *Ue,* but seldom should lowercase umlauted letters be so set.

HUNGARIAN

9.42 *Special characters.* Hungarian requires several varieties of accented vowels:

Á á, É é, Í í, Ó ó, Ö ö, Ő ő, Ú ú, Ü ü, Ű ű

ITALIAN

9.43 *Capitalization.* In Italian, titles preceding a proper name are normally lowercased:

il commendatore Ugo Emiliano   la signora Rossi

The formal second-person pronouns *Ella, Lei, Loro* are capitalized.

9.44 *Punctuation.* A series of closely spaced dots is used to indicate a sudden break in thought or an interruption in faltering speech. If other punctuation precedes the series, three periods are used; otherwise, four periods are used:

« Piano!... Ho sentito muovere di là.... C'è qualcuno.... Dev'essere la.... cosa dell'ingegnere.... »

9.45 The apostrophe is used to indicate the omission of a letter. Space should be added after an apostrophe that follows a vowel. No space is used after an apostrophe that follows a consonant:

po' duro   de' malevoli   l'onda   all'aura

9.46 Quotation marks in Italian are the same as French guillemets:

Anche il primo incontro di Henry James con l'Italia, nel 1869, riflette il tradizionale atteggiamento americano del tempo. Le lettere che scrive a casa mentre dal Gottardo, attraverso Milano, Verona, Padova, Venezia, Mantova, Firenze, scende a Roma, parlano con insistenza della « meraviglia profonda », dell' « estasi e della passione » che lo invadono via ch'egli viene a contatto con « l'atmosfera italiana », « la melodiosa lingua d'Italia », lo « Spirito del Sud », finché la sera della sua prima giornata romana, trascorsa « vagando come ubriaco per le strade, preda a una gioia delirante », scrive al fratello William: « Finalmente — per la prima volta — io vivo! »[5]

5. Franca Piazza, trans., *Città e paesaggi di Toscana visti da Henry James* (Florence: G. Barbèra, 1961), pp. 7–8.

218

In dialogue, however, dashes are used instead of guillemets. Each successive speech is introduced by a dash, and if other matter follows the speech in the same paragraph, another dash is used at the end of the speech.

—Avremo la neve— annunziò la vecchia.

9.47 *Word division.* The fundamental principle of Italian word division is to divide after the vowel, letting each syllable begin with a consonant as far as possible. Where there is only one consonant in intervocalic position, place it with the following vowel:

a-cro-po-li   mi-se-ra-bi-le   ta-vo-li-no

9.48 Certain consonantal groups must also be placed with the following vowel. These are *ch, gh, qu, gli, sc,* and *r* or *l* preceded by any consonant other than themselves:

a-qua-rio	na-sce	rau-che
fi-glio	pa-dre	ri-flet-te-re
la-ghi	pe-sta	u-sci-re

9.49 Consonants, however, must be divided when (1) double, (2) in the group *cqu,* and (3) in a group beginning with *l, m, n,* or *r:*

ac-qua	cam-po	par-te
af-fre-schi	com-pra	poz-zo
cal-do	den-tro	sen-to

9.50 Vowel combinations are not divided:

miei   pia-ga   pie-no   tuo

9.51 No division occurs immediately after an apostrophe:

dal-l'accusa	quel-l'uomo
del-l'or-ga-no	un'ar-te

9.52 *Special characters.* Italian makes very limited use of the grave accent. In the following list the lowercase vowels are necessary, but the capitals can easily be dispensed with:

À à, È è, Ì ì, Ò ò, Ù ù

LATIN

9.53 *Capitalization.* The tendency of editors around the world is to capitalize Latin according to the principles of their own languages. In English-speaking countries, however, titles of ancient and medieval books and shorter pieces are capitalized not as English titles but as English prose; that is, only the first word, proper nouns, and proper adjectives are capitalized:

De bello Gallico	*Sic et non*
Cur Deus homo?	*De viris illustribus*

Modern works with Latin titles are usually capitalized in the English fashion:

Novum Organum   *Religio Medici*

9.54   *Word division.* A Latin word has as many syllables as it has vowels or diphthongs (*ae, au, ei, eu, oe, ui*):

o-pe-re   gra-ti-a   na-tu-ra

9.55   When a single consonant occurs between two vowels, divide before the consonant:

Cae-sar   me-ri-di-es

9.56   In the case of two or more consonants, divide before the last consonant except in the combinations: mute (*p, ph, b, t, th, d, c, ch, g*) + liquid (*l, r*), and *qu* or *gu:*

cunc-tus   scrip-tus
om-nis   (*but* pa-tris, e-quus, lin-gua, ex-em-pla)

9.57   Compound words are separated first into their component elements; within each element the foregoing rules apply:

ab-rum-po   ad-est   red-e-o   trans-i-go

9.58   *Special characters.* Latin requires no special characters for setting ordinary copy. Elementary texts, however, usually mark the long vowels, and so all five vowels with the macron would be needed for setting such works. Also, authors occasionally like to mark short quantities, and so vowels with the breve may be useful as well. The entire series for elementary Latin thus is:

Ā ā, Ă ă, Ē ē, Ĕ ĕ, Ī ī, Ĭ ĭ, Ō ō, Ŏ ŏ, Ū ū, Ŭ ŭ

NORWEGIAN

9.59   *Capitalization.* As in Danish, the polite personal pronouns *De, Dem, Deres* and the familiar *I* are capitalized. Formerly, common nouns were capitalized as in German.

9.60   *Special characters.* Norwegian requires the same special characters as Danish:

Å å, Æ æ, Ø ø

POLISH

9.61   *Capitalization.* Names of the days (but not of the months) are capitalized in Polish.

9.62   *Special characters.* Polish requires the following special characters:

Ą ą, Ć ć, Ę ę, Ł ł, Ń ń, Ó ó, Ś ś, Ź ź, Ż ż

PORTUGUESE

9.63   *Special characters.* Portuguese employs three special characters:
Ã ã, Ç ç, Õ õ

In addition, however, Portuguese makes extensive use of accents: all five vowels with both the acute and the grave are needed, plus *a*, *e*, and *o* with the circumflex. The vowels *i* and *u* sometimes appear with the diaeresis (*ï*, *ü*), but the same letters with the grave may be substituted for them. If display lines are to be set in full or small capitals, accented sorts must be available, but for text work they may be dispensed with.

SPANISH

9.64   *Capitalization.* Titles preceding names are lowercased in Spanish: *el señor Jaime López.* When a question or an exclamation occurs within a sentence, its first word is lowercased (see example in par. 9.67).

9.65   *Punctuation.* Guillemets are used for quotation marks, and in a quotation enclosed by guillemets, dashes may be used to set off words identifying the speaker:

> El demonio, el activo demonio cuyo poder había quebrantado Hernán Cortés con espada y con lanza, gozaba utilizando al hijo como instrumento de sus infernales designios. « Vino el negocio a tanto —comenta Suárez—, que ya andaban muchos tomados por el diablo ». Los frailes, desde los púlpitos, lanzaban catilinarias y aconsejaban a los padres sobre la forma en que debían salvaguardar el honor de sus familiares.[6]

In dialogue, dashes are used to introduce each successive speech. If other matter follows the quoted speech in the same paragraph, a dash should be added at the end of the speech.

> —Esto es el arca de Noé— afirmó el estanciero.

9.66   A series of three periods is used to indicate a sudden break in thought or an interruption in faltering speech:

> Hemos comenzado la vida juntos... quizá la terminaremos juntos tambien...

9.67   In Spanish, the question mark and the exclamation point are repeated, in inverted form, at the beginning of a question or an exclamation:

> ¿Qué pasa, amigo?
>
> Por favor, señor ¿donde está la biblioteca municipal?
>
> Alguien viene. ¡Vamonos!

6. Fernando Benítez, *Los primeros Mexicanos: La vida criolla en el siglo XVI*, 3d ed. (Mexico, D.F.: Ediciones ERA, 1962), p. 181.

9.68   *Word division.* The fundamental principle of Spanish word division is to divide on a vowel or group of vowels. Two or more adjacent vowels may not be divided:

au-tor	fue-go	re-cla-mo
bue-no	mu-jer	se-ño-ri-ta
cam-biáis	ne-ga-ti-va	tie-ne
ca-ra-co-les	pre-fe-rir	viu-da

9.69   A single vowel may not stand alone at the end of a line:

acei-te (*not* a-ceite)	ene-ro (*not* e-nero)
ati-co (*not* a-tico)	uni-dad (*not* u-nidad)

9.70   Some two- and three-syllable words may be divided, while others may not:

aho-ra	cie-go	leer
ao-jo	creer	lí-nea
aún	ellos	oa-sis
au-to	eo-lio	oí-do
baúl	ideas	oír

9.71   A single intervocalic consonant goes with the following vowel, except that compound words are usually divided according to derivation:

ave-ri-güéis	mal-es-tar	semi-es-fe-ra
des-igual	nos-otros	sub-or-di-nar
fle-xi-bi-li-dad	re-ba-ño	(*but* bien-aven-tu-
in-útil	re-unión	ra-do)

9.72   Spanish *ch*, *ll*, and *rr* are considered single characters:

ci-ga-rri-llo	mu-cha-cho

9.73   Two adjacent consonants may be separated:

ac-cio-nis-ta	al-cal-de	efec-to
ad-ver-ten-cia	an-cho	is-la

The following pairs, however, containing *l* or *r*, except rarely in compounds, are inseparable: *bl, cl, fl, gl, pl,* and *br, cr, dr, fr, gr, pr, tr:*

ci-fra	ma-dre	re-gla
co-pla	ne-gro	se-cre-to
im-po-si-ble	no-ble	te-cla
le-pra	pa-tria	(*but* sub-lu-nar,
li-bro	re-fle-jo	sub-ra-yar)

9.74   Groups of three consonants not ending with one of the inseparable pairs listed always have an *s* in the middle. They are divided after the second consonant, since an *s* is always disjoined from a following consonant:

cons-pi-rar	ins-tan-te	obs-cu-ro
cons-ta	in-ters-ti-cio	obs-tan-te

9.75   *Special characters.* Spanish employs one special character:

       Ñ ñ

In addition, however, all five vowels with the acute accent are needed, plus *u* with the diaeresis (*ü*). As with Portuguese, accented capitals can probably be safely dispensed with for ordinary text work.

SWEDISH

9.76   *Capitalization.* In Swedish the second-person pronouns *Ni, Eder,* and *Er* are capitalized in correspondence.

9.77   *Special characters.* Swedish requires the following special characters:

       Å å, Ä ä, Ö ö

TURKISH

9.78   *Capitalization.* In Turkish the names of months and days of the week are capitalized.

9.79   *Special characters.* Turkish requires the following special characters:

       Â â, Ç ç, Ğ ğ (*or* Ğ ğ), İ ı, Ö ö, Ş ş, Û û, Ü ü

Note that there are dotted and undotted varieties of both the capital and the lowercase *i*. A dotted lowercase *i* retains its dot when capitalized.

TRANSLITERATED AND ROMANIZED LANGUAGES

9.80   In general work it is usual to transliterate Russian and Arabic from their original alphabets to the Latin alphabet and to transcribe the spoken forms of Chinese and Japanese into Latin characters, that is, to *romanize* these languages.

RUSSIAN

9.81   There are many systems for transliterating Russian, the most important of which are summarized in table 9.1. Journals of Slavic studies generally prefer a "linguistic" system making free use of diacritics, since such a system more nearly reflects the one-symbol-to-one-sound nature of the Cyrillic alphabet. But for a book or article reaching a more general audience, a system without diacritics or ligatures is desirable. The preference of the University of Chicago Press, for general use, is the system of the United States Board on Geographic Names. Regardless of the system of transliteration, however, well-known Russian names should be given in the form in which they have become familiar to English-speaking readers: that is, the spellings of *Webster's Biographical Dictionary* and the *Columbia Lippincott Gazetteer* or *Webster's Geographical Dictionary* should prevail:

> Tchaikovsky   Chekhov   Catherine the Great
> Moscow   Nizhni Novgorod (Gorki)   Dnieper

TABLE 9.1: TRANSLITERATION OF RUSSIAN

CYRILLIC ALPHABET		U.S. BOARD ON GEOGRAPHIC NAMES	LIBRARY OF CONGRESS	"LINGUISTIC" SYSTEM
Upright	Cursive			
А а	*А а*	a		
Б б	*Б б*	b		
В в	*В в*	v		
Г г	*Г г*	g		
Д д	*Д д*	d		
Е е	*Е е*	ye,[1] e	e	e
Ё ё[2]	*Ё ё*	yë,[1] ë	ë	e, ë
Ж ж	*Ж ж*	zh		ž
З з	*З з*	z		
И и	*И и*	i		
Й й	*Й й*	y	ĭ	j
К к	*К к*	k		
Л л	*Л л*	l		
М м	*М м*	m		
Н н	*Н н*	n		
О о	*О о*	o		
П п	*П п*	p		
Р р	*Р р*	r		
С с	*С с*	s		
Т т	*Т т*	t		
У у	*У у*	u		
Ф ф	*Ф ф*	f		
Х х	*Х х*	kh		x, ch
Ц ц	*Ц ц*	ts	t͡s	c
Ч ч	*Ч ч*	ch		č
Ш ш	*Ш ш*	sh		š
Щ щ	*Щ щ*	shch		šč
Ъ ъ[3]	*Ъ ъ*	''	''	''
Ы ы[3]	*Ы ы*	y		
Ь ь[3]	*Ь ь*	'	'	'
Э э	*Э э*	e	ė	è
Ю ю	*Ю ю*	yu	i͡u	ju
Я я	*Я я*	ya	i͡a	ja

NOTE: The Library of Congress and "linguistic" systems employ the same characters as the U.S. Board system except where noted.

1. Initially and after a vowel or ъ or ь.

2. Not considered a separate letter.

3. Does not occur initially.

9.82 *Capitalization.* Conventions of capitalization in the Cyrillic original are about the same as those of French and should be preserved in transliteration. Pronouns, days of the week, months, and most proper adjectives are lowercased. Geographical designations are capitalized when they apply to formal political units or formal institutions but otherwise are lowercased:

Tverskaya guberniya	Moskovskiy universitet
tverskoe zemstvo	russkiy kompozitor

9.83 Titles of books and articles and the names of periodicals are lowercased except for the first word and proper nouns:

N. A. Kuryakin. *Lenin i Trotskiy.*

O. I. Skorokhodova. *Kak ya vosprinimayu i predstavlyayu okruzhayushchiy mir* [How I perceive and imagine the external world]. Moscow: Izd. Akad. Pedag. Nauk, 1954.

9.84 In the Cyrillic originals of these citations the author's name and the title are both set in ordinary type (called in Russian *pryamoy*, "upright"); the author's name, however, is letterspaced. The Cyrillic *kursiv* is more sparingly used than our italic—never for book titles.

9.85 *Punctuation.* Russian resembles French in its use of guillemets for quotations and of dashes for dialogue:

« Bozhe, bozhe, bozhe! » govorit Boris.
— S kem ya rabotayu?
— S tovarishchem.
— Kak my rabotaem?
— S interesom.

Quotation marks of the German type (see par. 9.34) are sometimes used instead.

9.86 Suspension points are also used in Russian as in French:

Ya... vy... my tol'ko chto priyekhali.

An exclamation mark or question mark, however, in Russian takes the place of one dot:

Mitya!.. Gde vy byli?..

9.87 A dash is sometimes used between subject and complement when the equivalent of *is* or *are* is omitted:

Moskva — stolitsa Rossii.

A dash is also used in place of a verb omitted because it would be identical to the preceding verb:

Ivan i Sonya poyedut v Moskvu poyezdom, Lëv i Lyuba — avtobusom.

9.88   *Word division.* Transliterated Russian should be divided according to the rules governing word division in the Cyrillic original. In the rules and examples that follow, the transliteration system of the United States Board on Geographic Names is the one used.

9.89   Combinations representing single Cyrillic letters should never be divided:

ye, yë, zh, kh, ts, ch, sh, shch, yu, ya

9.90   Combinations of a vowel plus short *i* (transliterated *y*) should never be divided:

ay, ey, yey, *etc.*

9.91   The following consonantal combinations may not be broken in dividing:

b *or* p ⎱
g *or* k ⎬ *plus* l *or* r, *namely:* ⎰ bl, pl   br, pr
f *or* v ⎰   ⎨ gl, kl   gr, kr
                                                 ⎱ fl, vl   fr, vr

also:

dv, dr   tv, tr   sk, skv, skr   st, stv, str   zhd   ml

9.92   Words may be divided after prefixes, but generally the prefixes themselves should not be divided:

bes-poryadok   za-dat'   na-zhat'   obo-gnat'
pere-vod   pred-lozhit'   pro-vesti

9.93   Words may be divided after a vowel or diphthong before a single (Cyrillic) consonant:

Si-bir'   ry-ba   voy-na   Khru-shchëv   da-zhe

or before a consonantal combination (see par. 9.91):

puteshe-stvennik   khi-trit'   pro-stak   ru-brika

9.94   Division may be made between single consonants or between consonants and consonantal combinations:

ubor-ku   mol-cha   mor-skoy   chudes-nym   sred-stvo

9.95   Division may be made between single vowels or between a single vowel and a diphthong:

ma-yak   nochna-ya   oke-an   ori-entirovat'   svo-yëm

9.96   Compound words are preferably divided between parts:

radio-priyëmnik   gor-sovet   kino-teatr

ARABIC

9.97   In transcribing from Arabic—or Aramaic, Hebrew, Persian, etc.—the author should use a system employing as few diacritics as possible, except in linguistic or highly specialized studies. If the *hamza*

226

(ʾ) and the ʿ*ain* (ʿ) are used, they may be represented in typescript by an apostrophe and a raised *c*.

9.98 *Transliteration.* For the editor and for the author who is not a specialist, the preliminary information in any Baedeker for Egypt is helpful in answering transliteration questions. For the transliteration system used in North Africa a French Baedeker may be consulted. The system used by the United States Board on Geographic Names is complicated, and a simpler system, without diacritics, is to be preferred.

9.99 *Special characters.* For Arabic materials to be set in type, sorts for the hamza and ʿain should be obtained in the appropriate sizes. If necessary, a Greek smooth breathing (ʾ) may be used for the hamza and a rough breathing (ʿ) for the ʿain. Sometimes an apostrophe (ʾ) and a turned comma (ʿ) are used for these two signs.

9.100 *Spelling.* Having selected a system of transliteration, the author should stick to it with as few exceptions as possible. Of course, isolated references in text to well-known persons or places should employ the forms familiar to English-speaking readers: *Avicenna*, not *ibn-Sina; Mecca*, not *Makka; Faiyum*, not *Madinat al-Fayyum* or some other variant.

9.101 In particular, the definite article, *al*, should always be joined to the noun with a hyphen: *al-Islam*. And although the sounds *t*, *d*, *r*, *z*, *s*, *sh*, and *n* are elided with the article in speech, the preferred scholarly usage is to write the article-noun combination without indication of the elision:

al-Nafud (*not* an-Nafud)   Bahr al-Safi (*not* Bahr as-Safi)

Preferably, also, the *h* so often appended to Arabic words ending in *a* should be omitted:

Adiwaya (*not* Adiwayah)   al-mudda (*not* al-muddah)

9.102 *Capitalization.* Problems of Arabic capitalization occur only in transliterations, since the Arabic alphabet does not distinguish between capital and lowercase letter forms, as the Latin and Cyrillic alphabets do. Hence practice in capitalizing transliterated Arabic varies widely. For transliterated titles of books and articles in Arabic the preference of the University of Chicago Press is to capitalize only the first word and proper nouns:[7]

ʿAbd al-Rahman al-Sabarti, ʿ*Ajaib al-athar fi al-tarajim wa al-akhbar* [The marvelous remains in biography and history] (Cairo, A.H. 1297 [A.D. 1879]).

7. The Library of Congress preference, it should be stated, is to capitalize *all* nouns.

9.103   The same system may appropriately be used for the names of journals and organizations. Note that the article in Arabic is never capitalized except at the beginning of a sentence or at the beginning of a book or article title.

9.104   *Personal names.* In alphabetizing Arabic personal names the article is ignored and the person is listed under the capital letter of his last name. Thus in University of Chicago Press usage, an Ishaq al-Husayni is listed as Husayni, Ishaq al-. (For other Press preferences in citing Arabic names, see par. 7.11.)

CHINESE AND JAPANESE

9.105   *Romanization.* The accepted way to romanize Chinese is the modified Wade-Giles system to be found in the "List of Syllabic Headings" in the American edition of Mathews's *Chinese-English Dictionary* (pp. xviii–xxi), omitting the circumflex and the breve but retaining the umlaut *ü*. In general, hyphens should be used to indicate meaningful elements: *shih-hsüeh yen-chiu.*[8] The final authority for the spelling of Chinese place names is the *Postal Atlas of China;* where this widely accepted guide is not available, the spelling of well-known place names may be checked in *Webster's Geographical Dictionary* or the *Columbia Lippincott Gazetteer of the World* or other authoritative geographical reference works in the English language. (For alphabetizing Chinese and Japanese names and terms see pars. 18.62–63.)

9.106   Japanese is usually romanized following the system used in Kenkyusha's *New Japanese-English Dictionary.* (Some systems place an apostrophe after *n* at the end of a syllable when followed by a vowel or *y: Gen'e, San'yo.*) A macron is used over a long vowel in all Japanese words except well-known place names (Kyoto, Hokkaido) and words that have entered the English language and are thus not italicized (shogun, daimyo). Hyphens should be used sparingly: *Meiji jidai shi no shinkenkyū.*

9.107   *Capitalization and italics.* Since there are neither capital letters nor italic type in Chinese and Japanese, writers in these languages show little concern about what English-speaking editors do with their words when they are romanized. Rules applicable to other languages are therefore generally used for romanized Oriental languages. Proper nouns (personal and place names) are capitalized (see par. 7.12) and set in roman type. Common nouns and

8. The Library of Congress restricts hyphenation to proper names.

228

other words used as words in an English sentence are lowercased and set in italics as foreign words (see par. 6.39). Names of institutions, schools of thought, religions, and so forth are usually in roman type if they are capitalized, in italics if they are lowercased:

> Tung-lin Academy; Tung-lin movement
>
> Buddhism, Taoism, *feng-shui* and other forms of magic . . .
>
> Under the Ming dynasty the postal service was administered by the Board of War (*ping-pu*) through a central office in Peking (*hui-t'ung kuan*).
>
> The heirs of the Seiyukai and Minseito are the Liberal and Progressive parties of Japan.
>
> It was Genro Saionji (the *genro* were the elder statesmen of Japan) who said . . . [note that *genro* is both singular and plural]

9.108   Titles of books and periodicals are set in italics, and titles of articles are set in roman and enclosed in quotation marks:

> Ch'en Shih-ch'i, *Ming-tai kuan shou-kung-yeh ti yen-chiu* [Studies on government-operated handicrafts during the Ming dynasty]
>
> Fang Hao, "Liu-lo yü hsi p'u ti chung-kuo wen-hsien" [The lost Chinese historical literature in Spain and Portugal], *Hsüeh-shu chi-k'an* [Academy Review Quarterly]
>
> Okamoto Yoshitomo, *Jūrokuseiki Nichi-O kotsuchi no kenkyu* [Study of the intercourse between Japan and Europe during the sixteenth century]
>
> Akiyama Kenzō, "Goresu wa Ryukyujin de aru" [The Gores are the Ryukyuans], *Shigaku-Zasshi* 39 (1928): 268–85.

The first word of a romanized title is always capitalized, and proper names (especially in Japanese) often are.

9.109   Chinese and Japanese characters, while difficult for the printer, are necessary in references to works that can be found, even in Western libraries, only if the ideographs for the author's name and the title of the work are known. In general, their use should be confined to notes, bibliographies, and indexes; in running text they disrupt the type line and should be avoided. When ideographs are used in a bibliography, they are placed in brackets following the romanized version of the item they represent (asterisks here show where the ideographs should be placed):

> Fang Hao [* *]. "Liu-lo yü hsi p'u ti chung-kuo wen-hsien" [* * * * * * * *] [The lost Chinese historical literature in Spain and Portugal], *Hsüeh-shu chi-k'an* [* * * *] (Academy Review Quarterly) 1 (1953): 161–79.

EDITING AND COMPOSING CLASSICAL GREEK

9.110   Long quotations in classical Greek are perhaps not so common in scholarly writing now as they once were, but they occur often enough that an editor ought to be able to face them without panic. The information that follows is intended to arm an editor (who does not read Greek) well enough to handle such isolated quotations—preparing the Greek copy for setting, answering proofreaders' queries, and checking end-of-line word division. The information given may even be sufficient for the prospective editor of an entire book in Greek, but for one who does not know Greek such work is so time-consuming and the chances for error are so numerous that if possible it should be turned over to a specialist.

9.111   The first thing necessary for setting Greek is a font of Greek type. If a book contains any Greek at all, the publisher should make certain well ahead of copy deadline that his typesetter has Greek type in the required sizes. If he does not, (1) the publisher or typesetter will have to have the passages set elsewhere and inserted in the English pages, (2) the Greek copy will have to be killed or translated into English, or (3) it will have to be transliterated into the Latin alphabet—something that should be done only if the Greek consists of isolated words and phrases or of short passages. Table 9.2 shows the usual way of transliterating Greek.

BREATHING

9.112   Every vowel or diphthong, and the letter ρ, beginning a word takes a breathing. The rough breathing (‘) carries the sound of *h* (ἐν); the smooth breathing (’) has no sound (ἐν). The breathing is placed over the second vowel of a diphthong: αἰ, εἰ, εὐ, αὐ, οὐ, οἰ. All words beginning with ρ or υ take the rough breathing.

ACCENTS

9.113   There are three accents used in Greek: acute (´), grave (`), circumflex (^). The accent belongs over the lowercase vowel and over the second vowel of a diphthong but is placed before the capital (Ἕλλην, τοῖς, τούς).

9.114   The circumflex accent may be used only on one of the *last two* syllables; the grave may be used on the last syllable only. The acute accent on the last syllable is changed to grave when preceding

230

another accented word in the same clause. There is practically no other occasion for the grave accent, except on the indefinite enclitic τὶς used alone.

9.115 A few monosyllables which are closely connected with the word following are called *proclitics* and take no accent. The proclitics are: the forms of the article ὁ, ἡ, οἱ, αἱ; the prepositions εἰς, ἐν, ἐκ (ἐξ); the conjunctions εἰ, ὡς; the adverb οὐ (οὐκ, οὐχ).

TABLE 9.2: GREEK ALPHABET AND TRANSLITERATION

Name of Letter	Greek Alphabet		Transliteration
Alpha	A	α α¹	a
Beta	B	β	b
Gamma	Γ	γ	g
Delta	Δ	δ ∂¹	d
Epsilon	E	ε	e
Zeta	Z	ζ	z
Eta	H	η	ē
Theta	Θ	θ ϑ¹	th
Iota	I	ι	i
Kappa	K	κ	k
Lambda	Λ	λ	l
Mu	M	μ	m
Nu	N	ν	n
Xi	Ξ	ξ	x
Omicron	O	ο	o
Pi	Π	π	p
Rho	P	ρ	r; *initially,* rh
Sigma	Σ	σ s²	s
Tau	T	τ	t
Upsilon	Υ	υ	u; *exc. after* a, e, ē, i, *often* y
Phi	Φ	φ φ¹	ph
Chi	X	χ	kh
Psi	Ψ	ψ	ps
Omega	Ω	ω	ō

NOTE: In transliterated Greek, the rough breathing is represented by an *h*, which precedes the vowel or diphthong and follows the letter rho (*r*); the smooth breathing is ignored. Accents and other diacritical marks are usually omitted.

1. Old style character.
2. Final letter.

9.116   An *enclitic* is a short word pronounced as if part of the preceding word. It loses its accent ('Ἀρταξέρξης τε) except in case of a dissyllabic enclitic after a word with acute accent on next to the last syllable, as 'Ἀρταξέρξης ἐστί. Some of the common enclitics: τὶς; εἰμί, ἐστί, ἐσμέν, εἰσί; φημί, φησί, φατόν, φατέ, φασί (ἐστί becomes ἔστι at the beginning of a sentence and following οὐκ, μή, ὡς, ἀλλά, τοῦτο). The word before an enclitic receives an added acute accent on the last syllable if it had originally the circumflex accent on the next to the last, or the acute on the third from the last, syllable. The circumflex on the last syllable is not changed by the addition of an enclitic.

PUNCTUATION

9.117   In Greek, the period and comma are the same as in English; the colon and semicolon are both represented by an inverted period (·); the Greek interrogation point is the same as the English semicolon (;). When a final vowel is elided before a second word beginning with the same vowel, the apostrophe (') is used in its place, especially if the initial vowel of the second word has a rough breathing. The apostrophe should never be used in place of a breathing.

NUMBERS

9.118   Numbers, when not written out, are represented in ordinary Greek text by the letters of the alphabet, supplemented by three special characters, ς' = 6, ϟ' = 90, and ϡ' = 900. The diacritical mark resembling an acute accent distinguishes the letters as numerals, and is added to a sign standing alone or to the last sign in a series, 111 = ρια'. For thousands, the foregoing signs are used with a different diacritical mark: ͵α = 1,000, ͵αρια' = 1,111, ͵βσκβ' = 2,222. The entire series of Greek numerals is shown in table 9.3.

WORD DIVISION

9.119   In Greek, word division follows rules that are straightforward and fairly easy to apply.

9.120   When a single consonant occurs between two vowels, divide before the consonant:

ἔ-χω   ἐ-γώ   ἐ-σπέ-ρα

232

9.121   If a consonant is doubled, or if a mute is followed by its corresponding aspirate, divide after the first consonant:

ἀπ-φύς   Ἀτ-θίς   Βακ-χίς   ἔγ-χος

9.122   If the combination of two or more consonants begins with a liquid (λ, ρ) or a nasal (μ, ν), divide after the liquid or nasal:

ἄλ-σος   ἀρ-γός   ἄμ-φω   ἄν-θος
(*But, before* μν: μέ-μνημαι)

TABLE 9.3: GREEK NUMERALS

1	α′	24	κδ′
2	β′	30	λ′
3	γ′	40	μ′
4	δ′	50	ν′
5	ε′	60	ξ′
6	ς′	70	ο′
7	ϛ′	80	π′
8	η′	90	ϙ′
9	θ′	100	ρ′
10	ι′	200	σ′
11	ια′	300	τ′
12	ιβ′	400	υ′
13	ιγ′	500	φ′
14	ιδ′	600	χ′
15	ιε′	700	ψ′
16	ις′	800	ω′
17	ιϛ′	900	ϡ′
18	ιη′	1,000	,α
19	ιθ′	2,000	,β
20	κ′	3,000	,γ
21	κα′	4,000	,δ
22	κβ′	5,000	,ε
23	κγ′		

9.123   The division comes before all other combinations of two or more consonants:

πρᾶ-γμα   ἀ-κμή   ἄ-φνω   ἔ-τνος   ἄ-στρον

9.124   Compound words are divided into their original parts; within each part the foregoing rules apply. The most common type of compound word begins with a preposition:

ἀμφ-   ἀν-   ἀπ-   ὑπ-   ἐξ-έβαλον
ἀφ-   ἐφ-   ὑφ-   κατ-   καθ-ίστημι

233

FOR FURTHER REFERENCE

9.125 The United States Government Printing Office *Style Manual* answers a good many questions about setting foreign language copy not considered in this manual. Hart's *Rules for Compositors* is also useful. (See the Bibliography.)

10 *Quotations*

INTRODUCTION

10.1   Almost every serious study depends in part on works that have preceded it. The temptation to use apt quotations gathered during research may lead, in extreme cases, to the self-effacement of the author and the irritation of the reader. Ideally, the author of a work of original scholarship should present his argument in his own words, illustrating and amplifying his text by judicious choice of quotations from the works of others. In selecting quotations, the author is well advised to consider his future readers. Is direct quotation desirable, or would a paraphrase be more effective? Will the reader who, for lack of time or inclination, chooses to skip over long or frequent direct quotations miss any significant point? This is not to denigrate the use of quotations, however, but only to caution against their overuse or misuse. "Quoting other writers and citing the places where their words are to be found are by now such common practices that it is pardonable to look upon the habit as natural, not to say instinctive. It is of course nothing of the kind, but a very sophisticated act, peculiar to a civilization that uses printed books, believes in evidence, and makes a point of assigning credit or blame in a detailed, verifiable way."[1]

10.2   Whether an author paraphrases or quotes his source directly, he should give credit to words and ideas taken from another. In most instances a footnote or a parenthetical reference to the bibliography is sufficient acknowledgment. If an author quotes at length, or uses many short passages, from a copyrighted work or from certain manuscript materials, he must have written permission from the holder of the copyright or of the literary rights (see chap. 4). Commonly known facts, available in numerous sources, should not be documented, or quoted.[2]

ACCURACY

10.3   Direct quotations must reproduce *exactly* not only the wording but the spelling, capitalization, and the punctuation of the original. The initial letter, however, may be changed to a capital or a lowercase letter (see pars. 10.9–11), and a final punctuation mark may be changed to make the quotation fit in the syntax of

1. Jacques Barzun and Henry F. Graff, *The Modern Researcher* (New York: Harcourt, Brace & Co., 1957), p. 288.

2. This chapter takes up rules and suggestions for incorporating quoted matter in text. The use of quotation marks for purposes other than direct quotation is described in chapters 5 and 6. Rules for citing, in footnotes, the sources of quotations are to be found in chapter 15. How to type block quotations in preparing a manuscript for publication is explained in chapter 2 (par. 2.22), as well as the manuscript editor's responsibilities regarding quoted material (par. 2.78).

the text. In a passage from a modern book, journal, or newspaper an obvious typographical error may be silently corrected, but in a passage from an older work or from a manuscript source any idiosyncrasy of spelling should be observed. In quoting from older works an author may consider it desirable to modernize spelling and punctuation for the sake of clarity. When he does this, he should so inform the reader, either in a footnote or, in a book containing many such quotations, by a general statement in the preface or elsewhere.

10.4 It is impossible to overemphasize the importance of meticulous accuracy in quoting from the works of others. An author should check every direct quotation against the original if possible or against his first, careful transcription of the passage. (An author who takes notes carelessly is in for trouble later, if he no longer has access to his sources.) Checking quotations is an operation to be performed on the *final typescript*, not left until type has been set. Resetting type to rectify an author's sins of transcription discovered in galley proofs or in page proofs is an extremely costly process, and is chargeable to the author. Thus, rigorous attention to accuracy in the typescript saves time at the proof stage, avoids excessive alteration costs, and lessens the chance of further errors being introduced as type is reset.

RELATION TO TEXT

10.5 Quotations may be incorporated in the text in two ways: (1) run in, that is, in the same type size as the text and enclosed in quotation marks (see example in par. 10.8); or (2) set off from the text, without quotation marks and printed in a smaller (reduced) type size or indented or both (see example in par. 10.10). Quotations set off from the text are called *block* quotations; sometimes, usually by printers, they are referred to as *extracts* or *excerpts*.

RUN IN OR SET OFF

10.6 Whether to run in or set off a quotation is commonly determined by its length. In general, quoted matter that runs to eight or ten typed lines is set off from the text; shorter quotations are run into the text. Before arbitrarily following this rule, however, the author (and the editor) should consider the nature of the material, the number of quotations, and the appearance of the printed page. Many quotations of varying lengths—some over ten typed lines— skillfully integrated with the text in which they appear are less

237

distracting to the reader if they are all run in, regardless of length. On the other hand, in material where the quotations are being compared or otherwise used as entities in themselves it is best to set them all off from the text, even quotations of one or two lines. In other words, comparable quotations in the text should be typographically comparable.

10.7   Quotations of two or more lines of poetry are usually set off from the text (see par. 10.18). If more than one line is run into the text, the end of a line of poetry is marked by a solidus (/), with a thin space on either side:

> Andrew Marvell's praise of John Milton, "Thou hast not missed one thought that could be fit, / And all that was improper dost omit" ("On *Paradise Lost*"), might well serve as our motto.

SYNTAX

10.8   The skill with which an author incorporates fragmentary quotations into his own text reflects his awareness of syntax, verb tenses, personal pronouns, and so forth. He will quote only as much of the source as he needs and will phrase his sentence in such a way that the quoted words fit logically, as grammatical parts of the sentence. Ronald S. Crane, master of the felicitous quotation, provides many illustrations in his two-volume *The Idea of the Humanities* (Chicago: University of Chicago Press, 1967). Among them (1:281):

> In short, there has been "almost a continual improvement" in all branches of human knowledge; and since this improvement has taken place not merely in the speculative sciences but likewise in those other forms of learning, such as politics, morality, and religion, "which apparently have a more immediate influence upon the welfare of civil life, and man's comfortable subsistence in it," it seems to follow, "as a corollary, plainly deducible from a proposition already demonstrated," that human happiness has also increased.

INITIAL CAPITAL OR LOWERCASE

10.9   When a quotation, either run into or set off from the text, is used as a syntactical part of the author's sentence, it begins with a lowercase letter, even though the original is a complete sentence beginning with a capital:[3]

> Benjamin Franklin admonishes us to "plough deep while sluggards sleep."

3. For altering capitalization other than the initial letter of a quotation see par. 10.36.

With another aphorism, he reminded his readers that "experience keeps a dear school, but fools will learn in no other"—an observation as true today as then.

but:

As Franklin advised, "Plough deep while sluggards sleep."

With another aphorism, "Experience keeps a dear school, but fools will learn in no other," he puts his finger on a common weakness of mankind.

His aphorism "Experience keeps a dear school, but fools will learn in no other" is a cogent warning to men of all ages.

10.10 The initial letter of a block quotation may also be lowercased if the syntax demands it. The following quotation from Aristotle is a complete paragraph in the original:

> In discussing the reasons for political disturbances Aristotle observes that
>> revolutions also break out when opposite parties, e.g. the rich and the people, are equally balanced, and there is little or no middle class; for, if either party were manifestly superior, the other would not risk an attack upon them. And, for this reason, those who are eminent in virtue usually do not stir up insurrections, always a minority. Such are the beginnings and causes of the disturbances and revolutions to which every form of government is liable. [*Politics* 5.4]

10.11 Similarly, if a quotation is a complete sentence, even though it forms part of a sentence in the original, a lowercase letter may be changed to a capital where the construction of the text suggests it. To use the second sentence in the preceding quotation from Aristotle:

> As Aristotle remarked, "Those who are eminent in virtue usually do not stir up insurrections, always a minority."

but:

> Aristotle's observation that "those who are eminent in virtue usually do not stir up insurrection, always a minority" might serve as a subject for debate.

10.12 In legal works any change in capitalization is indicated by brackets:

> [r]evolutions . . .
> [T]hose . . .

INTRODUCTORY PHRASES AND PUNCTUATION

10.13 A formal introductory phrase, such as *thus* or *the following*, is usually followed by a colon:

> The role of the author has been variously described. Henry Fielding, at the beginning of his *History of Tom Jones*, defines it thus:

239

"An author ought to consider himself, not as a gentleman who gives a private or eleemosynary treat, but rather as one who keeps a public ordinary, at which all persons are welcome for their money."

Of the Ten Commandments he had already broken the following:
Thou shalt not take the name of the Lord thy God in vain.
Honor thy father and thy mother.
Thou shalt not bear false witness against thy neighbor.

10.14 Such introductory phrases as

Professor Jones writes:
He said (stated, observed, etc.):

are awkward and usually redundant. A sensitive writer will avoid them.

10.15 A quotation consisting of more than one complete sentence is usually introduced by a colon if the text preceding the quotation is not a complete sentence but a phrase like

As the chairman of the committee suggested:
And again:

If the quotation is only one sentence, a comma follows such a phrase instead of a colon. A colon is usually not used if the introductory text is a complete sentence:

The chairman of the committee suggested an alternative.
What, you might ask, are the alternatives?

PARAGRAPHING BLOCK QUOTATIONS

10.16 When a block quotation begins with a complete sentence, it may take a paragraph indention or it may begin flush, no paragraph. The usual practice is to follow the original; if the quoted matter does not begin a paragraph in the source from which it is taken, the block quotation begins flush, with no ellipsis points (see par. 10.39). (If ellipsis points *are* used to indicate the omission of the first part of a paragraph, the ellipsis points begin after a paragraph indention.) An author may wish, however, to paragraph his quotations as if they were part of his text, taking into account the sense of his discussion, and the editor should respect his practice in the matter. Internal paragraphing—in quotations of more than one paragraph—should be retained. Note that only the first paragraph of a continuous prose quotation set off from the text may be printed with no paragraph indention. When several paragraphs, or items with runover lines, must be set flush, extra space should be inserted between them.

10.17   A long quotation may begin with a few words, or a sentence, quoted in the text and continue as a block quotation. This device should be used only if a few words of text intervene between the quoted matter in the text and its continuation:

> "There is no safe trusting to dictionaries and definitions," in Charles Lamb's opinion.
>
>> We should more willingly fall in with this popular language, if we did not find *brutality* sometimes awkwardly coupled with *valour* in the same vocabulary. The comic writers . . . have contributed not a little to mislead us upon this point. To see a hectoring fellow exposed and beaten upon the stage, has something in it wonderfully diverting. ["Popular Fallacies," *Essays of Elia*]
>
> "In short," says Crane, summarizing Gordon's philosophy,
>
>> there has been "almost a continual improvement" in all branches of human knowledge; . . .

Less felicitous, but permissible in most instances, is to set off the entire quotation, putting the intervening words of text in brackets as an interpolation:

> In short [says Crane, summarizing Gordon's philosophy], there has been . . .

10.18   Quotations from poetry are usually centered on the page and set line for line.[4] Alignment of the original should be reproduced as closely as possible:

> Sure there was wine
> Before my sighs did drie it: there was corn
> Before my tears did drown it.
> Is the yeare onely lost to me?
> Have I no bayes to crown it?
> No flowers, no garlands gay? all blasted?
> All wasted?
>
> George Herbert, "The Collar"

In a work containing quotations from poems with lines too long to be centered on the page, such as Walt Whitman's "Song of Myself," all poetic quotations may be set with a uniform indention—for example, two or three picas from the left, any runover lines being further indented:

> My tongue, every atom of my blood, form'd from this soil, this air,

4. For lines of poetry run into the text see par. 10.7.

241

> Born here of parents born here from parents the same, and their
> parents the same,
> I, now thirty-seven years old in perfect health begin,
> Hoping to cease not till death.

10.19   Quotation marks at the beginning of a line of poetry, in older
practice, were usually *cleared*, that is, placed outside the alignment of the poem:

> He holds him with his skinny hand,
> "There was a ship," quoth he.
> "Hold off! unhand me, grey-beard loon!"
> Eftsoons his hand dropt he.
>
> Coleridge, *The Ancient Mariner*

In modern practice such quotation marks are commonly aligned
with the first letter of the line above:

> He holds him with his skinny hand,
> "There was a ship," quoth he.

QUOTATION MARKS

DOUBLE AND SINGLE

10.20   Quoted words, phrases, and sentences run into the text are enclosed
in double quotation marks. (Note that in the fields of linguistics
and philosophy single marks are used in certain contexts to enclose individual words or letters; see pars. 6.41, 6.47.) Single quotation marks enclose quotations within quotations; double marks,
quotations within these; and so on. (British practice is often,
though not always, the reverse: single marks are used first, then
double, and so on.)

> "Don't be absurd!" said Henry. "To say 'I mean what I say' is
> the same as 'I say what I mean' is to be as confused as Alice at
> the Mad Hatter's tea party. 'Not the same thing a bit!' said the
> Hatter. 'Why you might just as well say that "I see what I eat" is
> the same thing as "I eat what I see"!' "

WITH MORE THAN ONE PARAGRAPH

10.21   If a passage of more than one paragraph from the same source is
quoted and is not to be set as an excerpt, quotation marks are
used at the beginning of each paragraph and at the end of the
last paragraph. That is, quotation marks are not used at the *end* of
any paragraph in the quotation except the last one.

10.22   Poetry quotations, when not treated as excerpts, take quotation
marks at the beginning of the quotation, at the beginning of each
stanza, and at the end of the quotation.

10.23   A quotation of a letter carries quotation marks before the first line (usually the salutation) and after the last line (usually the signature), as well as at the beginning of each new paragraph within the letter.

10.24   Note that the usual practice of setting these kinds of material as block quotations obviates the use of quotation marks.

WITH DIRECT DISCOURSE

10.25   Direct discourse, whether run into or set off from the text, should always be enclosed in quotation marks. Note that a change in speaker is usually indicated by a new paragraph. If one speech occupies more than a paragraph, the rule for quoting more than one paragraph applies (see par. 10.21).

> "Ransomed? What's that?"
> "I don't know. But that's what they do. I've seen it in books; and so of course that's what we've got to do."
> "But how can we do it if we don't know what it is?"
> "Why, blame it all, we've *got* to do it. Don't I tell you it's in the books? Do you want to go to doing different from what's in the books, and get things all muddled up?"
>
> Mark Twain, *The Adventures of Huckleberry Finn*

10.26   Where the name of the speaker introduces the speech, as in a play or a discussion, no quotation marks are used:

> DR. LEVENE: Mr. Chairman, we have heard the revolutionary notion today, first of all, that the smooth muscle cell can behave like the fibroblast to synthesize collagen, and, second, that it does the job of a macrophage: it takes up fat. . . .
>
> DR. TAYLOR: I wish to inquire as to how those proposing the smooth muscle theory reconcile their thoughts with the concept that was given considerable support by the late Dr. Lyman Guff and also by Dr. McMillan; . . .

IN BLOCK QUOTATIONS

10.27   Material set off from the text as a block quotation should not be enclosed in quotation marks. Any quoted matter within a block quotation should be enclosed in double quotation marks, even if the source quoted uses single marks. Therefore, when a quotation run into the text in the typescript is converted into a block quotation by author or editor, the initial and final quotation marks must be deleted and the internal marks changed. If, for example, the Mad Hatter's retort to Alice quoted in the example (par. 10.20) became a block quotation, the quotation marks would be changed:

"Not the same thing a bit!" said the Hatter. "Why you might just as well say that 'I see what I eat' is the same thing as 'I eat what I see'!"

Similarly, if a quotation set off from the text in the typescript is run into the text by the author or the editor, initial and final quotation marks must be added and any internal marks changed accordingly.

WHEN NOT TO USE QUOTATION MARKS

10.28 *With display type.* Quotation marks are not used with display quotations (quotations used as ornaments to the text rather than as part of the text itself) or before a display initial letter beginning a chapter or section:

> *Oh, what a tangled web we weave,*
> *When first we practice to deceive!*
>
> Sir Walter Scott

O F THE MAKING OF MANY BOOKS there is no end," declared an ancient Hebrew sage, who had himself magnificently aggravated the situation he was decrying.

10.29 *Figures of speech.* Proverbial, biblical, and well-known literary expressions used figuratively in the author's text should not be quoted:

> No one could convince him that practice makes perfect.
> If reading maketh a full man, he is half empty.

10.30 *Yes and no.* The words *yes* and *no* should not be quoted, except in direct discourse:

> Ezra always answered yes; he could not bring himself to say no.

ELLIPSES

10.31 Any omission of a word or phrase, line or paragraph, from a quoted passage must be indicated by ellipsis points (dots), never by asterisks (stars). The ellipsis points are printed on the line like periods, not above it like multiplication dots in mathematics. They are separated from each other and from the text and any contiguous punctuation by 3-to-em spaces. The number of dots and the spacing between them and the preceding and following words are important and should be checked carefully by the manuscript editor.

10.32 Three dots indicate an omission within a sentence or between the first and last words of a quoted fragment of a sentence. Thus an omission in the sentence

> The glottal stop, which is common in this family of languages, is marked by an apostrophe

could be shortened as

> The glottal stop . . . is marked by an apostrophe.

(For ellipsis points indicating missing letters in mutilated manuscripts, see par. 5.10.)

10.33 Other punctuation may be used on either side of the three ellipsis dots if it helps the sense or better shows what has been omitted. Consider the following passage (Dan. 3:4–6) in original and cut versions:

> Then an herald cried aloud, To you it is commanded, O people, nations, and languages, that at what time ye hear the sound of the cornet, flute, harp, sackbut, psaltery, dulcimer, and all kinds of musick, ye fall down and worship the golden image that Nebuchadnezzar the king hath set up: and whoso falleth not down and worshippeth shall the same hour be cast into the midst of a burning fiery furnace.

> To you it is commanded . . . that at what time ye hear the sound of the cornet, flute, . . . and all kinds of musick, ye fall down and worship the golden image . . . : and whoso falleth not down and worshippeth shall . . . be cast into . . . a burning fiery furnace.

Here the comma after "flute" and the colon after "image . . ." are optional rather than required.

10.34 Four dots—a period, followed by three spaced dots—indicate the omission of (1) the last part of the quoted sentence, (2) the first part of the next sentence, (3) a whole sentence or more, or (4) a whole paragraph or more. When there is a question mark or an exclamation point in place of the period in the original, this mark is retained and three dots used for the ellipsis:

> Let such Imps of Ill-nature . . . rail on. . . . But to my gentle Readers of another Cast, I would willingly apologize, and endeavour to rescue my Heroine from sharing too much of their Censure. . . . Pray imagine yourselves in her Situation.

> Why is it that they array themselves against me? . . . Where were they during the rebellion?

245

When a sentence in the text ends with a quotation that is itself a deliberately incomplete sentence, three dots only need be used:

> Everyone knows that the Declaration of Independence begins with the words "When, in the course of human events . . ." But how many people can recite more than the first few lines of the document?

10.35   When four dots indicate the omission of the *end of a sentence*, the first dot is the period—that is, there is no space between it and the preceding word. Although it might be pedantically accurate to consider the fourth dot the period, the three preceding dots representing the omission and therefore spaced, the distinction is not readily apparent to a reader and indeed may serve to distract him from the sense of the quotation. What precedes an ellipsis indicated by four dots should be a grammatically complete sentence, either as it is quoted or in combination with the text preceding it. Similarly, what follows four dots should also be a sentence. In other words, unless the reader is to be hopelessly muddled, every succession of words preceding or following *four* ellipsis points should be functionally a sentence. The careful writer should quote enough from his source and so arrange his text that the reader will be able to grasp the sense without tripping over the syntax. A complete passage from Emerson's essay "Politics" reads:

> The spirit of our American radicalism is destructive and aimless: it is not loving, it has no ulterior and divine ends; but is destructive only out of hatred and selfishness. On the other side, the conservative party, composed of the most moderate, able, and cultivated part of the population, is timid, and merely defensive of property. It vindicates no right, it aspires to no real good, it brands no crime, it proposes no generous policy, it does not build, nor write, nor cherish the arts, nor foster religion, nor establish schools, nor encourage science, nor emancipate the slave, nor befriend the poor, or the Indian, or the immigrant. From neither party, when in power, has the world any benefit to expect in science, art, or humanity, at all commensurate with the resources of the nation.

With judicious use of ellipsis points, the passage might be shortened as follows:

> The spirit of our American radicalism is destructive and aimless. . . . the conservative party . . . is timid, and merely defensive of property. It vindicates no right, it aspires to no real good. . . . From neither party . . . has the world any benefit to expect in science, art, or humanity, at all commensurate with the resources of the nation.

246

The first and third sentences in the shortened quotation are grammatically complete, although the original ends of both sentences have been omitted, and therefore each is concluded with a period followed by three points indicating ellipsis. To retain the original internal punctuation—a colon following "aimless" and a comma following "good"—would here only confuse the reader. The second sentence, also grammatically complete although missing its introductory phrase and the nonrestrictive clause in the middle, illustrates the point discussed in the following paragraph.

CAPITALIZATION FOLLOWING ELLIPSES

10.36   Most authors will readily change the *first* letter of a quoted passage from a capital to lowercase or from a lowercase letter to a capital to fit the context in which they use it (see pars. 10.9–11). To do so in the middle of a quoted passage is questionable. Readers who understand the significance of ellipsis points and see a period followed by three of them will automatically expect a new sentence to follow; if it begins with a lowercase letter, they will know that the beginning of the original sentence has been omitted and will be better able to find the passage in the source, should they care to look it up. It is not entirely improper, however, to capitalize the initial letter of a sentence, such as the second sentence in the above extract from Emerson's "Politics":

> . . . aimless. . . . The conservative party . . .

What is done about this matter in any given work is the responsibility of the author who is doing the quoting. He will follow his scholarly predilections, also keeping his potential readers in mind. The editor should not arbitrarily capitalize a lowercase letter beginning a sentence following ellipsis points but may suggest it to the author.

OMISSION OF LINES OR PARAGRAPHS

10.37   A full line of ellipsis points is in general used only in quotations from poetry, to indicate the omission of one or more full lines. The dots are spaced and the length of the line approximates that of the line of poetry immediately above it.

10.38   Occasionally a full line of dots may be used to indicate omission of a number of paragraphs or pages in a prose quotation consisting of widely scattered bits from the original. Usually, however, in a quotation of several paragraphs, the omission of an intervening paragraph or paragraphs is adequately indicated by a period and three ellipsis points at the end of the paragraph preceding the omitted part. And if a paragraph in the quotation, other than the first paragraph, begins with a sentence that does not open a paragraph in the original, it should be preceded by three dots following the usual paragraph indention. It is thus possible on occasion to use ellipsis points at the end of one paragraph *and* at the beginning of the next.

WHEN NOT TO USE ELLIPSIS POINTS

10.39 In general, no ellipsis points should be used (1) before or after an obviously incomplete sentence, (2) before or after run-in quotations of a complete sentence, (3) before a block quotation beginning with a complete sentence (see par. 10.16), (4) after a block quotation ending with a complete sentence. If ellipsis points are considered necessary before or after a quoted passage—and sometimes it is desirable to include them—three should precede and four, including the period, should follow the quoted matter if it ends with a complete sentence or if it ends the sentence in the text. But ellipsis points are seldom used at the beginning or end of a quoted passage. After all, unless it is the opening or closing sentence in a work that is being quoted, something precedes and follows the passage, and it is not necessary to emphasize the fact.

10.40 Note that a 2-em dash, rather than ellipsis points, is used to indicate illegible or missing letters in manuscript material (see par. 5.92).

INTERPOLATIONS AND ALTERATIONS

10.41 An author may make his own insertions in quoted material (1) to clarify an ambiguity, (2) to provide a missing word or letters, (3) to give the original foreign word or phrase where an English translation does not convey the exact sense. Any such interpolations are enclosed in brackets (not parentheses). When an interpolated word takes the place of a word in the original, ellipsis points are omitted:

> In disbelief he, like Horatio, asked scornfully, "What, has this thing [the ghost of Hamlet's father] appear'd again tonight?"
>
> "Well," said she, "if Mr. L[owel]l won't go, then neither will I."
>
> James "preferred to subvert the religion and laws of his people" rather than to "follow the character and reasons of his state [*indolis rationesque sui Regni*]."

Even in its romantic origins, Jebb tells us, satire "is the only [form] which has a continuous development extending from the vigorous age of the Commonwealth into the second century of the Empire."

Contempt, scorn, or doubt may sometimes be expressed by [!] or [?], although such interpolations are usually best left unmade.

"SIC"

10.42 *Sic* ("so," "thus," "in this manner") may be inserted in brackets, following a word misspelled or wrongly used in the original. (Note that *sic* is a complete word, not an abbreviation, and therefore takes no period.) Overuse of this device, however, is to be discouraged. In most books it is wholly unnecessary to call attention to every variant spelling, every oddity of expression, in quoted material. An exclamation point should never be used after *sic;* the insertion of *sic* alone is enough to call attention to the error in the source. While not really necessary, it would be permissible to use *sic* in the following sentence from Thoreau's *Walden:*

> Or on a Sunday afternoon, if I chanced to be at home, I heard the cronching [*sic*] of the snow made by the step of a long-headed farmer, who from far through the woods sought my house, to have a social "crack."

ITALICS ADDED

10.43 When an author wishes to emphasize or call attention to a certain word or words in material he is quoting, he may underline them so that they will be printed in italics. The reader must be told that he has done so, either in the footnote giving the source of the quotation, in parentheses directly following the quotation, or in brackets following the italicized passage in the quotation; one or the other system should be used throughout a book. "Italics mine," "italics added," "emphasis added," are all acceptable phrases, but, again, choose one and stick with it.[5]

10.44 Occasionally it may be desirable to point out that italics in a quotation were *not* the author's doing but were indeed in the original. Here, the usual phrase is "italics in original" or, better, the name of the quoted author, "Tocqueville's italics."

5. Note that an explanation such as "Underlined words do not appear in the second edition" makes sense in the manuscript but not in print, where the words in question are set in italics, not underlined. Hence in a manuscript intended for publication the explanation should read, "Words in italics do not appear in the second edition."

CITING SOURCES IN TEXT

10.45   The source of a direct quotation is usually given in a note or footnote (see chap. 15), or, in scientific works, in a parenthetical reference to the bibliography (see chap. 16). Sometimes, however, it is desirable, or more practicable, to give the source in the text.

10.46   In a work containing no footnotes or bibliography and only a few quoted passages the source of a quotation may be given, in full, in parentheses following the quotation, or it may be worked into the text:

> The programs of today reflect the demands of a musically more sophisticated audience. "The age is fortunately nearly past when eighteenth-century composers were subject in concert programs to a kind of 'type-casting' in which a few Scarlatti pieces, or a little Couperin on the part of the more adventurous, a Mozart sonata or a Bach organ fugue were served up as well-styled appetizers to be unregretted by late-comers and to act as finger warmers and curtain raisers to the 'really expressive' music of the nineteenth century" (Ralph Kirkpatrick, *Domenico Scarlatti* [Princeton: Princeton University Press, 1953], p. 280).

> At the beginning of the introduction to her well-known book *Mythology* (Boston: Little, Brown & Co., 1942) Edith Hamilton observes that "the real interest of the myths is that they lead us back to a time when the world was young and people had a connection with the earth, with trees and seas and flowers and hills, unlike anything we ourselves can feel."

If another passage is quoted from the same source in the next page or two of text, and there is no intervening quotation from another source, "ibid." may be used in the parenthetical reference: (ibid., p. 282).

10.47   In works, particularly literary studies, where there are frequent quotations from a single source it is usually preferable to put the identifying page or line numbers, act and scene, book, part, or the like in parentheses following each quotation. This practice is not only a convenience to the reader but keeps the bottoms of the pages from being strewn with short footnotes, each beginning with "ibid."

10.48   The full citation to the source is given in a footnote the first time it is mentioned with, if desirable, the explanation that all subsequent quotations from the source are to the edition cited. (If there is a reason to use more than one edition of a work, this fact must of course be mentioned and the edition specified each time.)

10.49   If part designations are explained in the footnote, it is unnecessary to include their abbreviations in the text references. For example, if the footnote explains:

References are to act, scene, and line,

the text reference following a passage may read simply:

1. 2. 14–15 (meaning act 1, scene 2, lines 14–15)[6]

Or, similarly, following appropriate explanation in a footnote:

3:22–23 (meaning volume 3, pages 22–23)
12. 45–50, *or* 12:45–50 (meaning book 12, lines 45–50)
2. 8. 14 (meaning book 2, canto 8, stanza 14)

"Ibid." should not be used for subsequent text references to act, scene, etc., because to repeat the part numbers generally takes less space.

10.50   When such shortened source citations follow quotations in the text, they present certain problems for the copy editor. No one solution to these seems to fit every case or to meet the approval of every experienced editor and every discerning author. The suggestions that follow, however, may help in achieving a logical and consistent style.

PUNCTUATION IN RUNNING TEXT

10.51   If the quotation is short and comes in the middle of the text sentence, there is no problem; the source is given after the closing quotation mark and the rest of the text sentence follows:

With his "Nothing will come of nothing; speak again" (act 1, scene 1) Lear, exasperated, tries to draw from his youngest daughter a verbal expression of filial devotion.

10.52   When the quoted passage falls at the end of a sentence and is not itself a question or an exclamation, the source follows the final quotation mark, and the period or other terminal punctuation is given outside the final parenthesis:

Lear, trying to draw from his youngest daughter an expression of filial devotion, says with some exasperation, "Nothing will come of nothing; speak again" (act 1, scene 1).

10.53   But what to do when the quotation comes at the end of the sentence and is itself a question or an exclamation, demanding its own final punctuation?

6. If roman numerals are preferred for act numbers, the citation would read: I, 2,14–15.

> And finally, in the frenzy of grief that kills him, Lear rails, "Why should a dog, a horse, a rat, have life, / And thou no breath at all?" (act 5, scene 3).

Some authors argue that there should be no punctuation following a source citation in such a case, or that the citation stands by itself and the period here should precede the closing parenthesis. If, however, this quotation did not end the sentence, there would be no punctuation problem:

> "Why should a dog, a horse, a rat, have life, / And thou no breath at all?" (act 5, scene 3) cries Lear in the frenzy of grief that kills him.

By analogy, it seems reasonable to regard the question mark as part of the quotation itself also when it comes at the end of the text sentence and the source citation as the final element in the whole sentence. A period therefore concludes the sentence, *after* the parenthesis.

FOLLOWING A BLOCK QUOTATION

10.54 The editorial problem here is twofold. Should the source citation be given in brackets, indicating that it has been added by the author, or should it appear in parentheses to match source citations given in the text? And how should it be punctuated? It is difficult to be dogmatic on either point.

10.55 The University of Chicago Press prefers to enclose such source citations in brackets but will settle for parentheses in works containing many quotations from a single literary work, some run into the text and some set off from it. This is a matter for the editor to decide, and sometimes for the author to stipulate. Both should aim for consistency: *all* source citations following block quotations must be enclosed either in brackets or in parentheses throughout a book. Brackets are *never* used to enclose citations in the running text, unless, of course, the source is for some reason set *within* the quotation marks.

10.56 The source citation for a *prose* excerpt follows the last line of the quotation. Since a prose quotation, to be set off from the text, is commonly more than one sentence and is frequently more than one paragraph, it seems logical to bring it to an end before giving its source, that is, to give the source *after* the terminal punctuation of the last sentence. A period is unnecessary after such source citations, but if a period is used, it goes within the brackets, since the citation is not included in the preceding sentence but stands alone. Note that any word or abbreviation beginning such a citation must have an initial capital. As observed above, however, part designations may usually be omitted.

From Joseph Addison in *The Spectator:*

> I shall endeavour to enliven morality with wit, and to temper wit with morality. . . . The mind that lies fallow but a single day sprouts up in follies that are only to be killed by a constant and assiduous culture. [No. 10, 12 March 1710/11]

From W[illiam] D[ean] Howells, *Literary Friends and Acquaintance* (New York: Harper & Bros., 1900):

> Then and always he [Walt Whitman] gave me the sense of a sweet and true soul. . . . The apostle of the rough, the uncouth, was the gentlest person; his barbaric yawp, translated into the terms of social encounter, was an address of singular quiet, delivered in a voice of winning and endearing friendliness. [P. 75]

10.57 The source citation for a *poetry* excerpt is not set on the same line as the last line of the quoted matter but on the line below it, either flush right or indented 1 em from the right. The same strictures and suggested alternatives for citations following prose excerpts apply here: brackets are preferable; parentheses are acceptable; no period need follow the citation; any first word or abbreviation carries an initial capital.

From Milton's *Paradise Lost;* reference is to book and lines:

> So glistered the dire Snake, and into fraud
> Led Eve, our credulous mother, to the Tree
> Of Prohibition, root of all our woe.
>
> [9.643–45]

From Alexander Pope, *The Rape of the Lock;* reference is to canto and lines:

> The meeting points the sacred hair dissever
> From the fair head, forever, and forever!
>
> [3.153–54]

From Shakespeare's *Love's Labour's Lost;* reference is to act, scene, and lines:

> For wisdom's sake, a word that all men love;
> Or for love's sake, a word that loves all men.
>
> [4.3.354–55]

From Edmund Spenser, *The Faerie Queene;* reference is to book, canto, and stanza:

> Who will not mercie unto others shew,
> How can he mercy ever hope to have?
>
> [6.1.42]

FOREIGN LANGUAGE QUOTATIONS

10.58   Quotations in a foreign language that are incorporated into an English text are treated like quotations in English. They are not italicized. Quotation marks and ellipsis points follow English style. Foreign styles of punctuating quoted matter vary widely and are used only when an entire work is in a foreign language (see chap. 9).

TRANSLATING QUOTATIONS

10.59   Since the author wishes to communicate with his readers, he will be considerate of them when he quotes from a foreign language source. In a study of, say, Racine he will quote from Racine's plays in the original French only. In a work to be read by classicists he may similarly quote freely from Latin or Greek sources.[7] In a book for a wider audience, however, it is usually best to provide English translations of all such quoted matter.

10.60   The author should translate foreign quotations himself only if no English translation of his source has been published, or if the published translations are unacceptable to him. If the footnote identifying his source gives only a foreign language title, he should add "my translation" to it. If he uses a published translation, the footnote must give the title of the translation and the translator's name, as well as the bibliographical details and the relevant page number of the translation. No careful writer will *re*translate from a foreign language a passage from a book originally published in English!

---

7. Most printers make extra charges for setting Greek, Cyrillic, or other non-Latin alphabets. The author who quotes from works in these languages, and does not wish to transliterate the passages, should so advise his publisher.

11 *Illustrations, Captions, and Legends*

ILLUSTRATIONS

DEFINITIONS

11.1   The term *illustration* refers to a variety of materials such as line drawings, paintings, photographs, charts, graphs, and maps. Tables, since they are set in type rather than reproduced from artwork, are not considered illustrations. In a book in which tables occur they are separately listed in the preliminary pages and are separately numbered—and in this manual they are dis-

255

cussed separately in a chapter of their own. Although each type of illustration requires slightly different treatment, peculiar to its own kind, some general remarks can be made about the preparation of all these materials for reproduction. At this point, however, a few definitions and distinctions are in order.

11.2 *Line and continuous-tone copy.* First, artwork containing only blacks and whites, with no shading—a pen-and-ink drawing, for instance, or a bar chart—is known as *line copy*. Artwork that does contain shading—such as a painting, wash drawing, or photograph—is known as *continuous-tone copy* or, less accurately, *halftone copy*. Mechanically the two kinds of copy are handled differently for reproduction, and authors and editors should endeavor to keep the distinction in mind.

11.3 *Letterpress and offset.* Second, most scholarly or trade books containing illustrations are printed either by the *letterpress* process or the *offset* process, and the methods for handling art copy differ accordingly. (We are not speaking here of art books containing fine-quality reproductions of paintings, which are often printed by a third process, *gravure*.)

11.4 Of the two, letterpress is the more restrictive. A line illustration is photographed directly, and from the negative is made a metal plate known as a *line engraving*, *line cut*, or *zinc*, which prints along with the parts of the book that are set in type. Continuous-tone copy is also photographed, but through a screen that breaks up the image into dots of varying size, and from that negative is made another kind of metal plate called a *halftone engraving*, or *halftone cut*. Halftone cuts do not print well on ordinary book paper, and so they are usually grouped together and printed separately on special coated paper that permits sharp reproduction. In such instance they are known as *plates*. The pages of plates are then joined to the text at appropriate places in one of various ways. A single leaf (two pages), such as a frontispiece, may be glued to the next page at the inner margin; this is called a *tip-in*. An entire section of plates, seldom fewer than sixteen pages and preferably thirty-two, may be stitched and bound in as a separate signature. Smaller numbers of pages, in multiples of four, are likely to appear either as an *insert*, laid inside the center fold of a signature before stitching, or a *wraparound*, folded around the outside of a signature (like the cover of a pamphlet) before stitching. Whatever method is used, it is seldom possible to have every page of plates at exactly the best spot for it in the text. As an alternative to printing sepa-

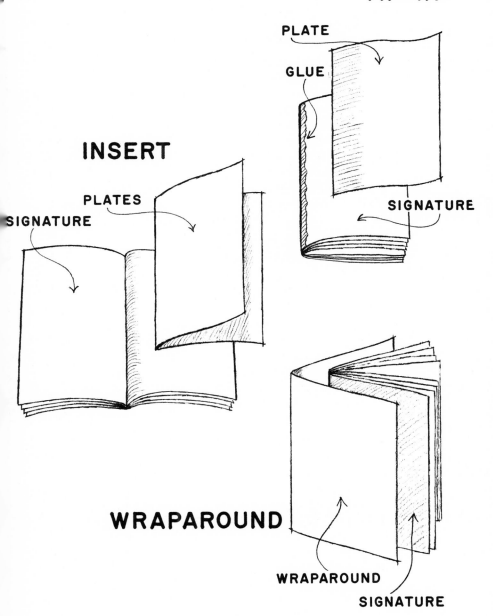

Fig. 11.1. Three ways in which plates and text signatures of a book may be joined

rate plates, the whole book may be printed on paper that will take the halftones; they may then be placed wherever the author wants them, on pages by themselves or mixed with type matter.

11.5   Offset printing permits greater freedom, since metal cuts and metal type are not used in the actual printing of the book. Line and continuous-tone copy are both photographed for reproduction in much the same way as in letterpress, but no cuts are made. Instead, proofs of the madeup pages (minus illustrations) are also photographed, and the images of the illustrations and of the type pages are combined to make the plates from which the book is actually printed. By the offset process, halftones of good quality can be printed on the same paper as typeset matter, and so they need not be gathered in special sections but may be scattered through the book wherever they are needed.

ARTWORK FOR OFFSET REPRODUCTION

11.6   Because in offset reproduction halftones and line work normally print together, editorial preparation of the copy is simpler and will be described first.

11.7   *Placement and numbering.* An illustration should be placed as close as possible to the first text reference to it, or after that point—but not before it. To show placement the author or editor writes (for example) "fig. 1 here" or simply "fig. 1" in the margin of the manuscript at the best place for the illustration, encircling the words so they will not be set by mistake. The editor must later see that these directions are transferred to the galley proof, as a guide to the printer in making up the pages.

11.8   If there are many illustrations, they should be numbered, and text references to them should be by the numbers: "figure 1 shows . . . ," "see figure 2," "(fig. 3)." *Never* should a figure be referred to as "the figure opposite" or "the photograph reproduced on this page." The exigencies of page makeup may well be such as to rule out that placement—and then the reference will have to be rewritten in page proof. The examples given illustrate some of the conventions observed at this press: "figure" (or "plate"—see the later discussion) is set in roman lowercase type and the number is an arabic numeral. The word "figure" is spelled out unless the reference is a simple parenthetical one.

11.9   In a book in which line and halftone illustrations are mixed and distributed through the text, they should be numbered continuously throughout, beginning with figure 1. There are exceptions, of course. Maps, unless they are used to illustrate specific points, are usually separately numbered (map 1, map 2, etc.) or not numbered at all. (Tables, we have seen, are always numbered separately, not being considered illustrations.) Also, in a book in which the chapters are by different authors—a book of conference papers or a symposium—numeration of figures customarily starts over with each chapter. This is true also of a book (such as this style manual) employing *double numeration* throughout. Here a figure is given a number consisting of the number of the chapter in which it appears plus the number of the figure within that chapter. For example, figure 9.3 is the third figure in chapter 9.

11.10   *Physical handling of the copy.* The first thing an editor receiving a package of illustrations should do is to turn each one over to make sure it is completely identified on the back by (at least) the name of the author, title of the book, and number of the figure. In a symposium the author of the chapter should be noted too. The subject should also be identified either on the back or in a separate list of illustrations. "Top" should be written on any illustrations that might accidentally be reproduced wrong side up. Anything written on the back of a photograph or a piece of artwork should be written *lightly* in soft pencil, using as little pressure as possible; an indentation of the surface may show up in the finished reproduction as a shadow. Any legend or caption on a photograph or drawing must be transcribed to copy paper. It cannot be set from copy on the back of the artwork or on a flap pasted to it. Staples, of course, should never be used on any illustration copy, nor should paper clips unless they are well padded with several thicknesses of paper to prevent scratching and indentation.

11.11   *Markup.* In a large publishing house editors seldom have occasion to mark illustration copy for reproduction, but in a house too small to boast a production department, art and photo markup is a normal editorial task. What follows is only a sketch of what is typically involved in simple markup, not a set of directions. Unless an editor is thoroughly conversant with art and photo markup for the particular process and materials being used, he should seek advice from a trained production person or from his supplier before doing any markup.

11.12   For black-and-white copy (and this is all we are considering in this chapter) the chief things to tell the offset cameraman are (1) whether or not the negative he makes is to be screened (for halftone reproduction) and if so what grade of screen is to be used, and (2) what the dimensions of the finished reproduction should be.

11.13 For (1) the editor might write "Make halftone, 133-line screen, crop as shown" or "Make line neg, size as shown." Such directions are best written in the margin of any piece of illustration copy, but for a photograph they may be written on the back, where there is more room.

11.14 For (2) the editor must decide how much of the illustration is to be used (photographs, particularly, are commonly *cropped* in reproduction—that is, only part of the image appears on the printed page). He places small *crop marks* in the margin to show just what area the cameraman is to include, whether all or part of the area of the copy. Ordinary soft pencil is best for marking on artwork, black grease pencil on photographs. Then he writes one of the dimensions of the finished reproduction, usually the width, between the appropriate crop marks. (This is recommended for the nonprofessional in preference to the direction "reduce 2:1" or "reduce 50%" or whatever.)

11.15 When a photograph or piece of artwork is to be reduced to fit a particular space, it must be *scaled;* that is, finished dimensions must be computed from original dimensions. There are many ways of doing this, all of them based on the fact that when a piece of artwork is reduced in the engraving process, all dimensions shrink in the same proportion. That is, when the long side of an eight-by-ten-inch photograph is reduced to five inches, the short side automatically reduces to four inches. We will describe two common methods of scaling, one mechanical (or better, visual), the other arithmetical.

11.16 First method: When the photograph has been cropped, lay a piece of tracing paper over it and draw—lightly!—a rectangle the size of the usable area of the photograph (*A*). Next (*B*), mark on the top line the width you want the finished cut to be, and draw a diagonal line across the rectangle. Then (*C*) drop a vertical line from the mark you made to the diagonal line, using a draftsman's triangle or a rectangular piece of cardboard, such as a tablet back. Finally (*D*), run another line, parallel to the top and bottom of the rectangle, from the point where your vertical line hits the diagonal to the left side of the rectangle. You now have a small rectangle inside the large one, and this represents the actual size of the finished engraving.

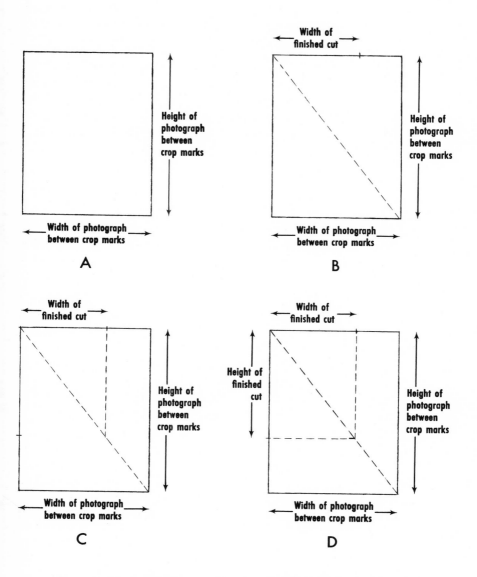

Fig. 11.2. Scaling photographs and artwork by means of a diagonal

11.17   Second method: After the photograph has been cropped, measure the width and height *in picas* to the nearest half pica. (Why picas? The type area of a printed page is always measured in picas, and since picas are so much smaller than inches, fractions give less trouble in computation.) From the page specifications determine how wide or how high the finished reproduction should be, and set down one of these dimensions (which will probably be the width), again in picas. To determine the other dimension of the finished piece, substitute in one of the following equations:

$$\text{reduced height} = \frac{\text{original height} \times \text{reduced width}}{\text{original width}}$$

$$\text{reduced width} = \frac{\text{original width} \times \text{reduced height}}{\text{original height}}$$

For example: The original photograph measures (between crop marks) 45 picas wide and 27 picas high. The reproduction is to drop into a type column that is 15 picas wide. So the reduced height will be

$$\frac{27 \times 15}{45} = 9 \text{ picas.}$$

ARTWORK FOR LETTERPRESS REPRODUCTION

11.18   Preparing copy for reproduction by letterpress is very similar to what has been described for offset. The chief differences exist when a distinction must be made in the book between text figures, printed from zincs, and plates, printed from halftone engravings on special paper.

11.19   The two types of art copy should be kept separate and appropriately marked "figure 1," "figure 2," etc., and "plate 1," "plate 2," etc. Both are scaled according to the editor's favorite method, and the engraver will be told to "make zinc" for the text figures and to "make halftone on copper" with such-and-such—perhaps 133-line—screen for the plates.

CORRECTIONS ON ART COPY

11.20   Unless drawings have been made especially for reproduction after consultation between author, editor, and production man, they often require changes, major or minor, before they can be reproduced. Changes are of two sorts: (1) those necessary to ready the artwork physically for reproduction—strengthening weak lines, redrawing fuzzy line copy, whiting out unwanted marks in the background, and so on, and (2) editorial changes—bringing spelling and capitalization of labels into conformity with other drawings and with the text, attaining consistency in the use of symbols and wording, improving clarity, and so on. All names on a map that is to be redrawn and any words appearing in other kinds of illustrations must be typed as a separate list for typesetting. In a publishing house with a production department, a production man is responsible for seeing that artwork corrections are made, an editor for editorial changes. In a small house, the editor is responsible for all.

11.21   Corrections on artwork, unless they are so gross and simple that an editor's unskilled and shaky hand is not likely to spoil the drawing, should be left to an artist. The directions to the artist are not written on the drawing or photograph itself, but on a flap of tracing paper (*overlay*) taped to the back of the piece and folded down over the face. On this the editor marks what is to be done (writing with the least possible pressure), and when the corrections have been made, he removes the overlay before sending the copy to the engraver or platemaker.

CAPTIONS AND LEGENDS

11.22   Most text figures and plates require some sort of explanatory material to make them understandable to the reader. This is supplied by the *caption* and *legend*—two terms often confused or considered synonymous, but at the University of Chicago Press distinguished elegantly the one from the other. A caption is a title or headline, traditionally set above the illustration in caps and small caps, but now placed almost anywhere and set in whatever type the designer specifies, or omitted entirely. A legend is an explanation, sometimes (like a caption) in title form but more commonly in the form of a statement and consisting of one or more sentences. (On a map, of course, the legend is the key to the symbols used—something quite different from what we are describing here.) The following is an example of a traditional caption and legend—for a halftone plate, as are the two following examples:

> COLINTON PARISH CHURCH AS IT APPEARED IN WALKER'S TIME
>
> This photograph shows the church as it appeared before 1908, when it was extensively enlarged and reconstructed. It had changed little from the time of Walker's ministry until then. The coffin-shaped object in the foreground is an eighteenth-century

263

mortsafe, a block of cast iron placed over a newly made grave to discourage "resurrectionists" from digging up the body for sale to anatomists. (Courtesy of the Reverend W. B. Johnston, B.D., minister of Colinton.)

Less traditionally, caption and legend may be run on. Note the period after the caption:

PLATE 1

A GROUP OF ARTIFACTS FROM SITE 3. In all these objects the high degree of finish and the aesthetic appeal are notable. *A*, *C*, *E*, flint points, and *B*, obsidian bird point, all approximately natural size; *D*, grain-storage jar of grayish clay decorated in black ($\times 1/20$); *F*, votive figure of red clay, undecorated ($\times 1/5$).

When the identifying copy for a plate is a mere tag, and especially if real captions and legends are used for other plates in the book, it should be set as a caption:

PLATE 2. WALL DRAWING OF HUNTSMEN

11.23 Text figures nowadays frequently carry legends only, captions being omitted, especially in scientific writing, where such figures are used in profusion:

Fig. 1. Clearly visible here are the giant transparent vacuole *V* and its septa *S* wrapped around the end of the resorbing bone.

An identifying tag, functionally a caption, is often used but set as if it were part of the legend:

Fig. 2. Photomicrographs of mouse-radius rudiments. *A*, left radius cultivated for 3 days in PTE; *B*, right radius similarly cultivated; *C*, left radius cultivated for 2 days in PTE.

Fig. 3. Idealized random distribution curve

EDITORIAL CONVENTIONS AND TYPOGRAPHY

11.24 The University of Chicago Press is far less doctrinaire about editorial style than it was when earlier editions of this manual were published, and this is particularly true of captions and legends. There are a few held-over conventions, however, that represent matters of preference.

11.25 *Punctuation.* A period is not used after a caption set on a line by itself but is used if the caption and legend are run together. Similarly, the period is not used after a one-line legend that is a mere title (see examples above).

264

11.26   *Numeration.* Press preference is for the use of arabic numerals with plates as well as text figures. Further, if halftone illustrations print with the text, preference is to number them with the text figures, not separately as if they were plates. In a book containing numbered figures, each figure should bear its own number. Even though figures are printed side by side and are to be compared, it is preferred that they be numbered separately—figures 37 and 38, for example, not figures 37a and 37b. Especially painful to a careful editor is a figure stuck in at the last moment and given a designation such as figure 43A. If the figure *must* be included and no other nearby figure can be killed, and if it is too late or too expensive to renumber the rest of the figures, of course this must be done. And if it is done, the example given illustrates the typographical preference of the Press in handling the makeshift (the sequence would then be 43, 43A, 44, etc.).

11.27   If a book is illustrated wholly with photographs, reproduced either as plates or as text illustrations, the author and editor might consider whether they need to be numbered at all. The criterion is text reference. If the illustrations are not referred to in the text or are referred to in such a way that they can easily be identified without numbers, numbers are useless and should be eliminated. In such case, however, illustrations and legends must still be assigned temporary numbers (not to be used in the printed book) to identify them and to make sure they will be matched up properly in printing. The number should be written on the back of the art copy and transferred to the engraver's proof when it comes in. The same number should be written on the typed legend copy (encircled so that it will not be set) and transferred to the galley proof when it comes in.

11.28   *Identifying parts of an illustration.* Such words as *top, bottom, left, right, above, below, left to right, clockwise from left,* and the like, are frequently used in legends to identify individual subjects in an illustration or parts of a composite. These are set in italics, and Press preference is that they precede rather than follow the phrase identifying the object or person:

>   Fig. 4. *Above left,* William Livingston; *right,* Henry Brockholst Livingston; *below left,* John Jay; *right,* Sarah Livingston Jay.

If a list follows the introductory tag, a colon rather than a comma is preferred:

>   *Left to right:* Dean Rusk, Hubert H. Humphrey, President Johnson, Robert S. McNamara.

265

11.29 Letters of the Latin alphabet, abbreviations, and symbols are all used as keys for identifying parts of a figure. When such a key is referred to in a legend, the form used in the legend should reflect as closely as possible the form used in the figure itself. If capital letters are used in the figure, capitals should be used in the legend, and so on. The typeface used in the legend for the key should, however, always be italic, whatever is employed in the figure.

> Fig. 5. Four types of Hawaiian fishhooks: *a*, barbed hook of tortoise shell; *b*, trolling hook with pearl shell lure and point of human bone; *c*, octopus lure with cowrie shell, stone sinker, and large bone hook; *d*, barbed hook of human thigh bone.

> Fig. 6. Facial traits of (*A*) *Propithecus verreauxi verreauxi* and (*B*) *Lemur catta*, which vary from one individual to the next: *ea*, ear; *ca*, cap; *cpl*, capline; *br*, brow.

When symbols are used in a figure, use of the same symbols in the legend requires the least effort of the reader:

> Fig. 7. Dependence of half-life on atomic weight for elements in the radium-uranium region: $\bigcirc$ = even α-emitters; $\bullet$ = odd α-emitters; $\square$ = isotopes capable of K-capture or β-decay.

If the symbols are not available in type or in the appropriate size of type, they must then be described:

> Fig. 8. Dependence of half-life on atomic weight for elements in the radium-uranium region: *open circles*, even alpha-emitters; *solid circles*, odd alpha-emitters; *open squares*, isotopes capable of K-capture or beta-decay.

In the last example, note also that in a scientific context the names of the Greek letters may usually be substituted for the letters themselves.

CREDIT LINES

11.30 In connection with most illustrative matter used in a book or a journal article a *credit line*—a brief statement of the source of the illustration—is either necessary or appropriate. The only significant exception is an illustration (chart, graph, drawing, photograph, etc.) by the author himself.

11.31 *Permissions.* Illustrative material in copyright, whether unpublished work protected by common-law copyright or published work protected by statutory copyright, requires permission of the copyright holder before it can be reproduced. It is the author's re-

266

sponsibility, not the publisher's, to make sure what is in copyright and to obtain permission to reproduce it. If the author is working with a publisher at the time, however, he ought to consult him about the form in which to request permission (see chap. 4).

11.32 *Placement.* The credit line may appear in any one of several locations and in various forms. Set in very small type, a short credit line may run parallel to the lower edge of the illustration or even to one of the vertical edges, especially if the illustration is a photograph. It may run at the end of the legend, usually in parentheses and sometimes in a different style of type, or the pertinent facts may be worked into the legend copy. Again, if most or all of the illustrations are from a single source, that fact may be stated in the preface or acknowledgments or on the copyright page. Finally, in a heavily illustrated book, especially one in which it is desirable to keep the illustrated pages uncluttered, what are called *box credits* may be resorted to. This is a lumping together of all the picture credits for a volume on one page or a series of pages in the front or the back of the book. Picture agencies, incidentally, may demand a higher fee for the use of an illustration if box credits are employed.

11.33 *Form.* The form of the credit line itself varies according to its placement and according to the type and copyright status of the illustration. For material in copyright, the copyright holder may demand a certain form of credit line, but, apart from this contingency, credit lines of a given type (say, those for charts reproduced from published works) should follow a consistent pattern. If the credit appears on a line by itself, end punctuation is omitted. In the discussion and examples that follow, we attempt to suggest some simple and workable patterns for credit lines of various types. In all, the assumption is that the credit line will run under the illustration or at the end of the legend.

11.34 *Previously published material.* An illustration reproduced from a source protected by copyright always requires formal permission from the copyright holder. There is no fixed style for such credit lines, but they should be consistent and for a work of book length should include a page number, figure number, or the like. A short form is appropriate if the work from which the illustration has been taken is listed in the bibliography. The person who grants permission to reproduce the illustration may, however, specify a certain form of credit line including the full facts of publication and even a copyright notice.

[*a kinship diagram*] Reprinted, by permission, from Wagner, *Curse of Souw*, p. 82.

[*a portrait engraving*] From a drawing by J. Webber for Cook's *Voyage to the Pacific Ocean, 1776–1780*, reprinted, by permission of the author, from Edwin H. Bryan, Jr., *Ancient Hawaiian Life* (Honolulu, 1938), p. 10.

[*a photograph of a lemur*] Reprinted, by permission, from Alison Jolly, *Lemur Behavior*, pl. 6. Photograph by C. H. Fraser Rowell. © 1966 by The University of Chicago.

11.35   Illustrations may be reproduced from published works without seeking permission if the work is in the public domain. A work is in the public domain if it was never copyrighted (as is true of most publications of the United States government) or if the copyright has run full term and lapsed. Even though permission is not required, it is good policy to use a credit line, however—out of deference to the reader if not the creator of the material.

Illustration by Joseph Pennell for Henry James, *English Hours* (Boston, 1905), facing p. 82.

Reprinted from John D. Shortridge, *Italian Harpsichord Building in the Sixteenth and Seventeenth Centuries*, U.S. National Museum Bulletin 225 (Washington, n.d.).

11.36   *Original material.* It was mentioned above that any illustrations that are by the author himself do not need credit lines. This is not to say that credit lines should *not* be used, however, if there is some reason for the inclusion. And there are often reasons apart from vanity for appending a credit line to an illustration of the author's own creation. If, for example, all but a few of the illustrations in a book are from one source and this source is acknowledged in the preliminaries, it would be appropriate to place under a photograph taken by the author a line reading:

Photograph by the author, *or*, Photo by author

Somewhat different is the case of material commissioned by the author for his book, usually maps, photographs, or drawings. Ordinarily such material is purchased outright, and so no credit is legally owed the supplier. But professional courtesy dictates mention of the creator of the material either in the preliminaries or below each piece, where the credit line might read:

Map by Gerald F. Pyle
Photograph by James L. Ballard
Drawing by Joseph E. Alderfer

If a map or drawing is signed and the signature is reproduced, nothing further is needed, of course.

11.37   For material that the author has obtained free, a credit line is again seldom legally required but usually appended nonetheless. It is in such credit lines only that the word *courtesy* is used:

> Photograph courtesy of Ford Motor Company
> *or:* Courtesy of Ford Motor Co.

If the name of the photographer is well known or if the supplier of the print requests it, the photographer's name may be given also:

> Photograph by Henri Cartier-Bresson, courtesy of the Museum of Modern Art.

11.38   Agency material—photographs and reproductions of prints, drawings, paintings, and the like, obtained from a commercial agency—usually requires a credit line. The contract or bill of sale will specify what is expected. Typical credits might be:

> Photograph from Black Star
> Woodcut from the Bettmann Archive

Sometimes an author does not pick up and reproduce material from another author directly but nonetheless is indebted to him. He may, for example, use data from a table in another book to construct a chart for his own, or he may revise another's graph with fresh data, or he may redraw a figure with or without significant changes. In such situations, although the author's material is technically original, a credit line is in order. Again there is no set form, and the full citation need not be given if it appears in the bibliography. Thus for a chart based on a table in another book the credit line might read:

> Data from Ronald Andersen and Odin W. Anderson, *A Decade of Health Services* (Chicago: University of Chicago Press, 1967), table 51.

If the book is fully listed elsewhere, the citation could be:

> Data from Andersen and Anderson, *A Decade of Health Services*, table 51.
> *or:* Data from Andersen and Anderson 1967, table 51

Other typical credit lines are:

> [*a graph*] Adapted from Simms 1946
> [*a drawing*] Redrawn from Yates, *Art of Memory*, p. 337

THE LIST OF ILLUSTRATIONS

11.39   A task often falling to the manuscript editor (but more properly done by the author) is preparing the list of illustrations. Not every illustrated book requires such a list, of course. The criterion is: Are the illustrations of interest apart from the text they illustrate? For a scientific monograph on interstellar particles, illustrated

---

ILLUSTRATIONS

Plates

Hermetic Silence, from Achilles Bocchius's *Symbolicarum quaestionum* . . . (1555)	*frontispiece*	
The Wisdom of Thomas Aquinas, fresco by Andrea da Firenze	*facing page*	50
Justice and Peace, fresco by Ambrogio Lorenzetti (detail)		81
The Zodiac, from Robert Fludd's *Ars memoriae*		336
The De Witt Sketch of the Swan Theater		337

Figures

1. The Human Image on a Memory *Locus*	*page*	111
2. The Ladder of Ascent and Descent, from Ramon Lull's *Liber de ascensu et descensu intellectus* (Valencia, 1512)		180
3. Memory Theater, or Repository, from J. Willis's *Mnemonica* (1618)		209
4. Suggested Plan of the Globe Theater		358

Fig. 11.3. A typical list of illustrations

largely by graphs, the answer is obviously no. For a book on Roman architecture, illustrated by photographs of ancient buildings, the answer is obviously yes. For some other illustrated books, the answer may not be so easy to give, and the author and editor must decide whether the list of illustrations is worth the space it will take.

11.40   *Preparing the list.* The list of illustrations follows the table of contents, normally on a new recto page, and is headed simply Illustrations. (The list of tables, if there is one, follows on another recto page.) *Headline style* (important words capitalized) is usually employed for the identifying titles. If illustrations are of more than one type, they are listed by category, as Plates, Figures, Maps, etc., and by number if numbers are used in the text (see par. 11.27). For figures and maps that print with the text (and hence have folios assigned to them, whether or not the folios are actually expressed on the page) page numbers are given (*000* in the copy as first prepared). For plates and for maps printed separately, another type of location is given. If plates are to be inserted in groups of four or more pages at one location, each group is listed under the tag *Following page 000* when copy is prepared. If they are to be inserted in the text two pages at a time (each page of plates accordingly lying opposite a text page), the location is given as *facing page 000*. Needless to say, each *000* is changed to a real number once page proofs are out and page numbers are known.

11.41   *Editing captions.* It should be remembered that the list of illustrations is a *list*, not a reprinting of the captions and legends. If the captions are very short and if they adequately identify the subjects of the pictures, they may do double duty in the list of illustrations. But remember that the reader does not have the illustration in front of him as he reads the list, and so a cryptic, allusive caption is of little use there as identification for the picture. If the captions and legends are long, they must be pared down for use in the list of illustrations, which should do no more than identify each illustration.

CHECKING ILLUSTRATIONS IN PROOFS

11.42   Among the various tasks often performed after a book is in proof is the preparation of the list of illustrations, just discussed. For that reason the editor should see to it that he has an extra copy of the captions and legends before they are sent out for typesetting. Proofs for captions and legends often do not come back with the galley proofs of the text, and thus he may find himself without anything from which to prepare the list.

11.43   Captions, legends, illustrations, and text all conjoin at some particular stage in the production of a letterpress book, usually in page proofs. At this stage the author and editor should make sure that the illustrations are (1) in correct sequence, (2) in appropriate places, (3) right side up (sometimes hard to see in a photomicrograph), (4) accompanied by the correct captions and legends, and (5) correctly listed in the preliminaries.

11.44 For an offset book, checking these things is trickier: since engravings are not made, we never see proof (in the normal sense) of the illustrations. Page proofs of an offset book include only type matter, blank spaces being left where illustrations are to go. It is then up to the offset platemaker, guided by adequate instructions from the author and editor, to drop the illustrations in the right holes, and the next stage the editor sees is printed sheets or even bound books. For many editors this requires too arduous an act of faith, and so they demand a further stage of "proof"—photographic prints made from the negatives from which plates will be made—for all pages or for those with illustrations. Various kinds of prints are made—among them, *blueprints* ("blues"), *silver prints*, and *vandykes*—but all have the same function. At the University of Chicago Press such prints are mandatory for any illustrated book printed by the offset process.

FOR FURTHER REFERENCE

11.45 The reader who wants to know more about the mechanical processes involved in the reproduction of illustrations may consult the lucidly written and beautifully illustrated book *Bookmaking*, by Marshall Lee. Frances W. Zweifel's *Handbook of Biological Illustration* discusses preparation of various kinds of illustrative materials, not only biological. Both books are fully listed in the Bibliography.

12 Tables

12.1 Tables offer authors and editors a useful means of presenting large amounts of detailed information in small space. A simple table like table 12.1 or 12.2 can often give information that would require several paragraphs to present textually and can do so with greater clarity. Tabular presentation is not simply the best but usually the only way that large quantities of individual, similar facts can be arranged. Whenever the bulk of information to be conveyed threatens to bog down a textual presentation, the author should give serious consideration to possible use of a table.

12.2 In planning a table, the author should give attention to its physical dimensions, making sure that it does not exceed the limits imposed by the size of the page. A useful rule of thumb is that a table typed in elite type, single-spaced, on $8\frac{1}{2}$-by-11-inch paper, with normal margins, will just about fill the type area of a 6-by-9-inch printed page when set in 8-point type. In other words, a full-page table typed in the usual way is roughly equivalent to a full-page table set in the usual size of type for an average-sized book. This is true whether the table is designed for the columns to run parallel to the long dimension of the page (a *vertical* table) or parallel to the short dimension (a *broadside* table) (see table 12.3).

12.3 The width of the table, controlled by the number of columns and the width of the material in them, is the significant factor. A table too long for one page may continue on a second page or subsequent pages if necessary, but the remedies for a table that is too wide are limited. The first remedy, already alluded to, is to set the table broadside, and a further or alternate remedy (and a distasteful one) is to set the table in smaller type, perhaps 6-point. Further than this, it may be possible to set the table vertically across two full pages. But this is the limit. If a table cannot be accommodated by these means, it must be printed separately on a large sheet of paper and bound in the book as a foldout insert. Because of the high cost of such an operation and the consequent

TABLE 12.1

FACTOR LOADINGS OF THE FOUR
MECHANICAL TASKS

Tasks	Factor I	Factor II
1.............	40	10
2.............	10	30
3.............	10	50
4.............	40	10

TABLE 12.2

ROLE-STYLE DIFFERENTIAE IN THE LEWIN, LIPPITT, AND
WHITE "GROUP ATMOSPHERE" STUDIES

Authoritarian	Democratic	Laissez faire
1. All determination of policy by leader	All policies a matter of group discussion and decision, encouraged and assisted by the leader	Complete freedom for group or individual decision, with a minimum of leader participation
2. Techniques and activity steps dictated by the authority, one at a time, so that future steps were uncertain to a large degree	Activity perspective gained during discussion period. General steps to group goal sketched, and when technical advice was needed the leader suggested two or more alternative procedures from which choice could be made	Various materials supplied by leader, who made it clear that he would supply information when asked. He took no other part in work discussion
3. Leader usually dictated the task and companion of each member	Members were free to work with whomever they chose, and division of tasks was left to the group	Complete nonparticipation of the leader
4. Leader tended to be "personal" in his praise and criticism of each member's work; remained aloof from active group participation except when demonstrating	Leader was "objective" in his praise and criticism, and tried to be a regular group member in spirit without doing too much work	Leader did not comment on member activities unless questioned, did not attempt to appraise or regulate the course of events

TABLE 12.3

STATISTICAL SIGNIFICANCE OF MODAL ERRORS IN ANALYSTS' INITIAL DIAGNOSES

ACTUAL DISEASE	MALE CASES		FEMALE CASES		ALL CASES	
	Modal Error	p	Modal Error	p	Modal Error	p*
Bronchial asthma.........	Ulcerative colitis	.70	Neurodermatitis	.70	Neurodermatitis	.20
Neurodermatitis.........	Rheumatoid arthritis	.20	Bronchial asthma	.50	Rheumatoid arthritis[1] Bronchial asthma	.05 .70
Rheumatoid arthritis.......	Hypertension	.20	Hypertension	.10	Hypertension	.10
Hypertension...........	Ulcerative colitis	.05	Rheumatoid arthritis	.01	Rheumatoid arthritis	.20
Ulcerative colitis........	Bronchial asthma	.01	Neurodermatitis	.05	Neurodermatitis[2] Bronchial asthma	.10 .10
Peptic ulcer...........	Ulcerative colitis	.01	Thyrotoxicosis	.70	Ulcerative colitis	.02
Thyrotoxicosis..........	Ulcerative colitis	.20	Bronchial asthma	.02	Bronchial asthma	.01

NOTE: Each numerical entry is the obtained level of statistical significance, the probability of obtaining the given result by chance.
[1] For all cases, arthritis and asthma were tied for the largest error. (The difference between the p values for arthritis and asthma is a consequence of the identical number of errors was distributed over cases. For example, one case of neurodermatitis was diagnosed as arthritis by five analysts. There was no such unusual concentration among the asthma errors.)
[2] For all cases, neurodermatitis and asthma were tied for the largest error.

need to increase the price of the book, this is something no publisher is likely to do except for a very important table in a very important book.

ARRANGEMENT OF ELEMENTS

12.4   The directions and recommendations that follow reflect the current practices of the University of Chicago Press. As is true of the other chapters of this book, the reader should realize that these ways of doing things are not necessarily the only or even the best ways: they are simply the preferences of this press. Ruled tables, for example, are usual in the publications of this press, in part because Monotype composition has always been readily available. For a publisher who is restricted to Linotype, open tables or tables with horizontal rules alone may be the only practical way tabular matter can be arranged.

TABLE NUMBER

12.5   Every table should be given a number and should be cited in the text by that number, either directly or parenthetically:

> Table 14 shows the results of the past three elections in Calcutta. The Congress party has not failed to achieve a majority in any of the past three elections in Calcutta (see table 14).

In no circumstances should a table be referred to in such terms as "the table opposite," "the table above/below," or the like. Page makeup often prevents placing a table on the same page with, or opposite, its discussion.

12.6   Tables are numbered in the order in which they are to appear in the text—which should also be the order in which they are first mentioned. Arabic numerals are used, and each table is given a number, even though there are only a few tables in the book. Tables intended to be compared should be given separate numbers (14, 15, 16, *not* 14a, 14b, 14c).

12.7   Numeration of tables normally continues straight through the book. One exception is the symposium or book of conference papers, in which the numeration starts over with each chapter or paper. Another is a book, often a text or reference work like this manual, in which text sections, figures, and tables are given double numbers reflecting their locations in the book (see par. 1.55).

12.8 The title, or caption, set above the body of the table, should identify the table briefly. It should not furnish background information or describe the results illustrated by the table. For example,

EFFECT OF DMSO ON ARTHRITIC RATS AND NONARTHRITIC
RATS AFTER 20, 60, AND 90 DAYS OF TREATMENT

should be edited to:

EFFECT OF DMSO ON RATS

The column headings 20, 60, and 90 days and the cross rows for arthritic and nonarthritic rats will give the results. Again, the kind of editorial comment implied by a title like

HIGH DEGREE OF RECIDIVISM AMONG
REFORM SCHOOL PAROLEES

should be eliminated.

RECIDIVISM AMONG REFORM SCHOOL PAROLEES

is sufficient. A table should give merely facts—discussion and comment being reserved for the text.

12.9 Grammatically, the caption should be substantival in form. Relative clauses should be avoided, in favor of participles. Not

NUMBER OF FAMILIES THAT SUBSCRIBE TO
WEEKLY NEWS MAGAZINES

but rather:

FAMILIES SUBSCRIBING TO WEEKLY NEWS MAGAZINES

12.10 The table caption may carry a subheading, usually enclosed in parentheses and sometimes set in a different style of type from the caption:

INVESTMENT IN AUTOMOTIVE VEHICLES SINCE 1900
(In Thousands of Dollars)

EFFECT OF AGE ON ACCUMULATION OF PAH
BY KIDNEY SLICES OF FEMALE RATS
($M = 200\ \mu\mathrm{g\ PAH/cc}; t = 15\ \mathrm{min}$)

Indication of the number of individuals in the group under consideration (for example: N = 253) may be treated as a subheading if it applies to the entire table. (If it does not, it may be given wherever appropriate: as a subheading to a column heading, as a series of values in a column of their own, or as a footnote to any particular value in the table.) If possible, N should be set as a small cap whenever it is used in this way.

12.11   A minor grammatical point: in conservative practice, *percent* is still not considered a noun, although colloquially it is commonly so used. Accordingly, copy for a title reading

PERCENT OF CASES DIAGNOSED CORRECTLY

preferably should be edited to read

PERCENTAGE [*or* PROPORTION] OF CASES DIAGNOSED CORRECTLY

COLUMN HEADINGS

12.12   A table always has at least two columns and usually has more. Except for the very simplest of tables, the columns carry headings at the top, brief identifications of the nature of the material in the columns. These are often called *boxheads* or *boxheadings*, from the fact that in a fully ruled table they are enclosed within rectangles of rules, or *boxes*. The style of the boxheads reflects that of the table title with regard to capitalization and whether they are set centered or flush. They are usually set in smaller type than the title and the table proper—for instance, 6-point heads with an 8-point table.

12.13   The nature of tabular matter sometimes demands two or more levels of boxheads (see table 12.4). *Decked heads*, as they are called, are most practical in fully ruled tables; in unruled tables they tend to be hard to follow down the columns. A practical working maximum might be considered two levels in unruled tables and three in ruled. Excessive decking of the heads can sometimes be avoided by the use of a *cut-in head*—a head that cuts across the body of the table and applies to the tabular matter lying below it (see table 12.5).

12.14   Like the table title, the boxheads are substantival in form, and the same grammatical strictures apply to them. If the first column of the table (the *stub*—discussed below) carries a boxhead, it should be singular in number. The other boxheads may be singular or plural according to sense.

12.15   The boxheads may carry subheadings if they are needed, usually to indicate the unit of measurement used in the column below. Subheadings are normally enclosed in parentheses, and abbreviations, if employed consistently throughout a series of tables, are acceptable: ($), (lb.), (%), (mi.), (×100 km), and so on. If the columns of a table must be numbered for purposes of text reference, arabic numerals are set in parentheses as subheadings to the lowest level of boxheads (see table 4).

12.16   The boxheads must often be adapted to fit special conditions of length or form. If the heads are long and the columns narrow, it may be best to set them vertically (see table 12.6). In such instance they should read from bottom to top (so that they read correctly when the book is rotated 90° clockwise). If a long table

TABLE 12.4

EFFECT OF NITROGLYCERIN ON EXTRACTION AND CLEARANCE OF RB[86] BY THE HEART

	DOSE[a] (µg) (1)	PERCENTAGE E-RB[86]			C-RB[86]			BLOOD FLOW (Q)		
		Control (2)	Drug (3)	Δ (4)	Control (5)	Drug (6)	Δ (7)	Control (8)	Drug (9)	Δ (10)
Constant flow[b]	1	74.8	76.3	2.5↑	26.9	27.5	0.7↑	36	36	.....
	2	71.2	74.8	3.6↑	25.6	27.0	1.4↑	36	36	.....
	4	72.6	78.3	4.7↑	26.1	28.2	2.1↑	36	36	.....
Constant pressure[c]	1	79.5	75.3	4.2↓	26.2	31.6	5.4↑	33	42	9↑
	2	78.3	74.1	4.2↓	28.2	35.6	7.4↑	36	48	12↑
	4	76.6	72.8	3.8↓	29.9	39.3	9.4↑	39	54	15↑

[a] Intracoronary injection.
[b] Left coronary arteries perfused by pump.
[c] Left coronary arteries autoperfused from carotid artery.

TABLE 12.5

CONGRESS PARTY VOTE IN FIVE DISTRICTS

	1952			1957			1962		
	% of Vote	Seats Won	Total Seats	% of Vote	Seats Won	Total Seats	% of Vote	Seats Won	Total Seats
	Parliamentary Elections								
Belgaum.............	55.6	2	2	50.3	1	2	56.7	1	2
Calcutta (entire city)..	36.8	1	4	40.3	1	4	46.3	1	4
Guntur...............	31.6	1	2	56.5	3	3	43.5	1	3
Kaira................	61.1	2	2	50.6	1	2	45.6	0	2
Madurai town........	52.6	2	2	34.5	1	1	39.6	1	1
	Legislative Assembly Elections								
Belgaum.............	54.3	12	15	47.4	7	17	54.1	10	16
Calcutta (entire city)..	39.7	17	26	42.6	8	26	47.2	14	26
Guntur...............	25.2	3	18	39.3	16	25	41.5	12	25
Kaira................	52.6	13	13	50.0	8	13	43.8	4	13
Madurai town........	38.6	1	2	48.6	2	2	51.0	2	2

is very narrow, columns and heads may be *doubled up*, the two halves of the table running side by side, with boxheads repeated over the second half (see table 12.7). When this is done with an unruled table, a single vertical rule must be inserted between the two parts of the table; and with a ruled table, a double vertical rule.

TABLE 12.6

PLACE OF OFFENSE AND RESIDENCE OF OFFENDER

TYPE OF OFFENSE	NUMBER OF OFFENDERS	NUMBER OF SEPARATE OFFENSES	DISTANCE TO RESIDENCE OF NEAREST OFFENDER							
			Less than 1 Block	1.1–2 Blocks	2.1–3 Blocks	3.1–4 Blocks	4.1–5 Blocks	6 or More Blocks	Offense Committed outside Addams Area	Unknown
Trespassing..........	.02 (6)	.03 (5)	.....	.40 (2)	.20 (1)	.....	.....	.....	.40 (2)	.....
Carrying weapons....	.04 (14)	.04 (7)	.29 (2)	.....	.....	.14 (1)	.....	.....	.57 (4)	.....
Drinking, disorderly conduct, glue-sniffing, creating disturbance..........	.07 (24)	.07 (13)	.23 (3)	.08 (1)	.16 (2)	.....	.....	.46 (6)	.....	.08 (1)
Lewd fondling, attempted rape, intercourse...........	.02 (8)	.03 (6)	.50 (3)	.....	.17 (1)	.....	.....	.....	.17 (1)	.17 (1)
Curfew-breaking, loitering............	.07 (24)	.08 (16)	.19 (3)	.13 (2)	.07 (1)	.....	.....	.....	.56 (9)	.07 (1)
Shooting firecrackers, opening hydrant, pulling fire alarm...	.05 (16)	.05 (10)	.40 (4)	.60 (6)	.....	.....	.....	.....	.....	.....
Malicious mischief, property damage...	.09 (31)	.09 (17)	.41 (7)	.23 (4)	.06 (1)	.06 (1)	.12 (2)	.06 (1)	.06 (1)	.....
Fighting, assault, affray	.11 (36)	.14 (26)	.39 (10)	.23 (6)	.12 (3)	.....	.04 (1)	.....	.15 (4)	.08 (2)
Theft, burglary, purse-snatching, strong-arming...........	.54 (184)	.48 (92)	.29 (27)	.13 (12)	.05 (5)	.07 (6)	.....	.01 (1)	.37 (34)	.08 (7)
Subtotal........	..... (343)	..... (192)	.31 (59)	.17 (33)	.07 (14)	.04 (8)	.02 (3)	.04 (8)	.29 (55)	.06 (12)
Total.........	(343)	(192)	.65 (125)						.29 (55)	.06 (12)

NOTE: Decimal fraction = fraction of total; number in parentheses = absolute number.

12.17 Sometimes a very long table must be run on successive pages. If so, the table number is repeated at the head of each page, with a *continued* line; for example:

TABLE 1—*Continued*

The boxheads are also repeated but the title is not. Headings are usually handled the same way in long tables whether the table is vertical or broadside. An exception is the broadside table beginning on a left-hand page. Here it is permissible and appropriate to omit the head matter on the facing page. The effect is then that of a table continuing uninterrupted across the two pages. Often, however, the editor cannot know in advance whether a long table will begin on a left- or a right-hand page, and so it may be best to

TABLE 12.7

RELATIVE CONTENTS OF ODD ISOTOPES
FOR HEAVY ELEMENTS

Element	Z	γ	Element	Z	γ
Sm	62	1.48	W	74	0.505
Gd	64	0.691	Os	76	0.811
Dy	66	0.930	Pt	78	1.16
Eb	68	0.759	Hg	80	0.500
Yb	70	0.601	Pb	82	0.550
Hf	72	0.440			

repeat the head matter for every page. In marking up a long table for typesetting, the editor should circle repeated boxheads on all manuscript pages but the first (meaning "do not set"), as the page breaks in the printed book will probably not come at those points. A note should explain to the typesetter what headings are wanted on the runover parts of the table.

THE STUB

12.18 The left-hand column of a table is known as the *stub* (like the stub of one kind of checkbook). It is a vertical listing of the items about which information is given in the columns of the table body, and it carries a boxheading only if identification is necessary. The listing may be a straight sequential one (as all the states of the United States listed alphabetically) or a classified one (as the states listed by geographic sections). In the latter instance, the categories are set as subheadings within the stub, usually in italic type and either centered (table 12.8) or flush left (table 12.9). Items in the stub should not ordinarily be numbered, and ditto marks should never be used. Runover (or *turnover*) lines are usually indented one

281

em, and the word *Total*, if it occurs at the foot of the stub, is indented one em more than the greatest indention above (see table 12.6). In many tables, *leaders* (a row of spaced periods) are set after each stub item to lead the eye to the appropriate entry in the next column.

12.19 The author and editor should take pains to achieve consistency in the stub. Items that are logically similar should be treated similarly: Authors, Publishers, Printers, *not* Authors, Publishing concerns, Operates printshop. In a series of tables, the same item should always bear the same name in the stub: the Union of Soviet Socialist Republics, for instance, should not appear as USSR in one table and Soviet Union in another.

TABLE 12.8

WEST NILE VIRUS-NEUTRALIZATION TESTS ON SERA
FROM MAMMALS AND BIRDS

SPECIES	NUMBER TESTED	POSITIVE	
		Number	Percentage
Mammals			
Camel	9	7	78
Cow	36	6	17
Donkey	15	7	47
Gamoose (water buffalo)	188	135	72
Goat	49	1	2
Horse	14	12	86
Sheep	64	15	23
Rat	43	0	....
Bat	48	4	8
Total mammals	466	187	40
Birds			
Chicken (domestic)	24	4	16
Rebleedings on previous negatives	15	2	13
Crow (*Corvus corone sardonius*)	163	102	65
Duck (domestic)	14	2	14
Dove (*Streptopelia senegalensis senegalensis*)	8	2	25
Goose (domestic)	29	6	27
Heron (*Bubulcus ibis ibis*)	65	18	28
Hoopoe (*Upupa epops major*)	5	0	....
Kestrel (*Falco tinnunculus*)	3	3	....
Kite (*Milvus migrans aegyptius*)	1	1	....
Pigeon (domestic)	59	15	25
Sparrow (*Passer domesticus*)	26	11	42
Quail (*Coturnix c. coturnix*)	8	0	....
Total birds	420	170	40
Grand total	886	357	40

SOURCE: Data from Taylor et al., 1956.

12.20   Stub items employ sentence-style capitalization, not headline-style. That is, only the first word and proper nouns and adjectives are capitalized. Periods at the ends of lines are omitted.

THE BODY

12.21   By the *body* of the table is meant the vertical columns, typically consisting of figures, to the right of the stub and below the box-heads. These columns are the real substance of the table, the array of information which the rest of the table merely supports and clarifies. They should accordingly be arranged in as clear and orderly a fashion as possible.

TABLE 12.9

PUERTO RICANS IN THE CONTINENTAL UNITED STATES
AND IN NEW YORK CITY, 1910–50

CENSUS YEAR AND GENERATION	CONTINENTAL UNITED STATES		NEW YORK CITY	
	Number	Percent Increase	Number	Percentage of Total
By birth:				
1910...........	1,513	.....	554	36.6
1920...........	11,811	680.6	7,364	62.4
1930...........	52,774	346.8	.....	.....
1940...........	69,967	32.6	61,463	87.8
1950...........	226,110	223.2	187,420	82.9
By parentage:				
1950...........	75,265	.....	58,460	77.7

SOURCE: "Puerto Ricans in Continental United States," Census of Population, 1950, Special Report, P-E, No. 30 (U.S. Bureau of the Census, 1953), p. 3D-4. Statistics for 1950 are for April of that year and are based on a 20 percent sample area. Puerto Ricans "by parentage" were born in the continental United States.

12.22   Whenever possible, mixing of different kinds of information in one column is to be avoided. For instance, place dollar amounts in one column, percentages in another, and information expressed in words in another. If a boxheading does not apply to one of the items in the stub, that *cell* (as the intersection is called) should be left blank: it is unnecessary to insert *not applicable* or *n.a.* If there are no data for a particular cell, leaders—three or more in number—should be inserted to lead the eye to the next occupied cell; leaders may run all the way across the column (table 12.8) or occupy the same horizontal space as the widest entry in the column (table 12.9). If the quantity in a given cell is zero, however, 0 should be set (table 12.8).

12.23   Attention should be given to alignment of the information in the columns both horizontally and vertically. Horizontally, each cell aligns with the item in the stub to which it applies. If the stub item occupies more than one line and the column entry one line, align on the last line of the stub item. If both contain more than one line, align first lines. Vertically, in a column of figures align on the decimal points and commas (every figure of 1,000 or more

TABLE 12.10

U.S. AUTOMOBILE PRODUCTION, 1900–1963

CALEN- DAR YEAR	PASSENGER CARS		MOTOR TRUCKS AND BUSES		TOTAL	
	Number	Value (×1,000)	Number	Value (×1,000)	Number	Value (×1,000)
1900	4,192	$ 4,899	....	....	4,192	$ 4,899
1905	24,250	38,670	750	$ 1,330	25,000	40,000
1910	181,000	215,340	6,000	9,660	987,000	225,000
1915	895,930	575,978	74,000	125,800	969,930	701,778
1920	1,905,560	1,809,171	321,789	423,249	2,227,349	2,232,420
1925	3,735,171	2,458,370	530,659	458,400	4,265,830	2,916,770
1930	2,787,456	1,644,083	575,364	390,752	3,362,820	2,034,835
1935	3,273,874	1,707,836	697,367	380,997	3,971,241	2,088,834
1940	3,717,385	2,370,654	754,901	567,820	4,472,286	2,938,474
1945	69,532	57,255	655,683	1,181,956	725,215	1,239,210
1950	6,665,863	8,468,137	1,337,193	1,707,748	8,003,056	10,175,885
1955	7,920,186	12,452,871	1,249,106	2,020,973	9,169,292	14,473,844
1960	6,674,796	12,164,234	1,194,475	2,350,680	7,869,271	14,514,914
1963	7,637,728	14,427,077	1,462,708	8,076,184	9,100,436	17,503,261

SOURCE: Automobile Manufacturers Association.
NOTE: A substantial proportion of the trucks and buses consists of chassis only; therefore the value of the bodies for these chassis is not included. Value is based on vehicles with standard equipment. Federal excise taxes are excluded.

must have commas) (tables 12.7, 12.9). Dollar signs and percentage signs are aligned, and in a column containing all the same kinds of figures they are used only at the top and after any horizontal rule that cuts across the column (table 12.10). (Of course, if it is apparent from title or boxhead what the figures in a particular column are, the signs need not be used at all.) Plus, minus, and equals signs are also aligned; in a column of figures that all begin with a single zero to the left of the decimal point, zeros may be omitted on all but the first and last figures of the column (table 12.11). If possible, all decimal fractions in a column should be carried to the same number of places. In a column consisting of information expressed in words, alignment may be more complicated: if entries are predominantly short, it is best to center them, but if they are long it may be preferable to set them flush left.

12.24 In a Monotype table or one that will be reproduced by offset, braces may be used to show relationship of groups (see table 12.12). In a Linotype table, braces are better avoided altogether. In the example, note that the braces could be eliminated by merging the stub and the first column, the present stub items being set as subheads between the groups of chemical formulas.

12.25 In a table that includes totals at the feet of the columns, a horizontal rule is placed above the totals, cutting across the body columns, but not the stub. Subtotals, averages, and means are simi-

TABLE 12.11

OBSERVED MAGNITUDES AND RESIDUALS

Phase (Days)	m_v	No. Obs.	O−C (Mag.)	Phase (Days)	m_v	No. Obs.	O−C (Mag.)
−0.2894...	9.41	6	−0.009	+0.0560...	11.76	7	+0.016
− .2637...	9.49	5	+ .004	+0.0659...	11.58	8	+ .027
− .2458...	9.58	5	+ .023	+0.0753...	11.33	7	− .031
− .2306...	9.59	4	− .035	+0.0859...	11.14	5	− .024
− .2200...	9.67	5	− .007	+0.0937...	10.97	5	− .040
− .2106...	9.73	8	− .009	+0.1036...	10.88	8	+ .040
− .2007...	9.79	10	− .016	+0.1147...	10.73	8	+ .052
− .1911...	9.88	12	+ .004	+0.1246...	10.56	12	+ .030
− .1817...	9.95	10	+ .002	+0.1351...	10.39	14	+ .001
− .1718...	10.02	8	− .010	+0.1445...	10.31	11	+ .033
− .1615...	10.16	17	+ .036	+0.1546...	10.13	10	− .032
− .1506...	10.23	14	− .017	+0.1641...	10.10	11	+ .032
− .1396...	10.37	14	.00	+0.1744...	9.97	10	− .016
− .1311...	10.44	16	− .039	+0.1847...	9.90	9	+ .003
− .1212...	10.59	17	− .027	+0.1941...	9.79	9	− .041
− .1121...	10.78	14	+ .015	+0.2050...	9.71	8	− .046
− .1013...	10.91	17	− .018	+0.2157...	9.71	6	+ .025
− .0906...	11.12	14	− .002	+0.2242...	9.63	8	− .015
− .0809...	11.30	10	− .003	+0.2345...	9.57	7	− .022
− .0715...	11.51	12	+ .018	+0.2507...	9.50	7	− .021
− .0617...	11.69	10	+ .002	+0.2708...	9.48	7	+ .020
− .0509...	11.88	7	+ .004	+0.2811...	9.43	4	− .003
− .0313...	12.05	5	− .023	+0.94.....	9.42	5	+ .025
− .0169...	12.08	4	− .010	+1.90.....	9.35	5	− .045
− .0082...	12.07	7	− .020	+2.04.....	9.41	7	+ .015
+ .0060...	12.16	5	+ .070	+2.67.....	9.38	5	− .015
+ .0139...	12.09	4	.00	+3.04.....	9.42	3	+ .025
+ .0261...	12.03	5	− .058	+4.04.....	9.44	6	+ .045
+ .0356...	12.02	6	.00	+4.48.....	9.36	7	−0.035
+0.0460...	11.87	6	−0.038				

larly treated, and if the table continues below these figures, another rule separates them from the continuation. In a table that exceeds one page in length and in which dollar totals appear at the end, it is usual to strike a subtotal at the foot of the first page. These figures appear opposite a stub entry *Carried forward* and below a rule. At the head of the next page they are repeated opposite a stub entry *Brought forward*.

TABLE 12.12

MOLECULAR HEATS OF GASES AT 20° C

Number of Atoms	Substance	C_p (cal/mole ° C)	C_v (cal/mole ° C)	γ
Monatomic............	A	4.97	2.98	1.666
	He	4.97	2.98	1.666
Diatomic.............	N_2	6.96	4.955	1.402
	O_2	7.03	5.03	1.396
	H_2	6.865	4.88	1.408
	CO	6.97	4.98	1.40
	NO	7.10	5.10	1.39
	HCl	7.04	5.00	1.41
	Cl_2	8.29	6.15	1.35
Three, 4, or 5 atoms per molecule...........	H_2O	8.20	6.20	1.32
	NH_3	8.80	6.65	1.31
	CO_2	8.83	6.80	1.299
	SO_2	9.65	7.50	1.20
	CH_4	8.50	6.50	1.31
Polyatomic (5–26 atoms per molecule)........	$CHCl_3$	15.2	12.20	1.25
	C_2H_6	12.35	10.30	1.20
	C_2H_5OH	20.9	18.5	1.13
	$C_4H_{10}O$	32.5	31	1.05
	$C_{10}H_{16}$	55	54	1.03

FOOTNOTES

12.26   Footnotes are generally set in smaller type than the body and often match the boxheads. They are set on the same measure as the table itself, and short notes may be set two or three to the line.

12.27   Footnotes are of three general kinds and should appear in this order: (1) source notes, (2) other general notes, and (3) notes on specific parts of the table. In a table of two or more pages, (1) and (2) are placed at the foot of the first page; notes of type (3) may be placed on the pages to which they apply or gathered at the end of the whole table.

12.28   If data for the table are not the author's own but are taken from another source, the author will wish to include a source note, in troduced by the word *Source(s)*, often set in caps and small caps and followed by a colon:

> SOURCE: Paul C. Standley and Louis O. Williams, *Flora of Guatemala*, Fieldiana: Botany, vol. 24, pt. 8, nos. 1 and 2 (Chicago: Museum of Natural History, 1966).

12.29 Other unnumbered notes, applying to the table as a whole, follow and are introduced by the word *Note(s)*. These might include remarks on reliability of the data presented or how they were gathered or handled; if the entire table is reproduced without change from another source, credit is best given in a general note such as that illustrated in the second of the following examples:

> NOTES: Since data were not available for all items on all individuals, there is some disparity in the totals.
>
> This table may be compared with table 14, which presents similar data for Cincinnati, Ohio.
>
> NOTE: Reprinted by permission of the publisher from *Aging and Levels of Biological Organization*, ed. Austin M. Brues and George A. Sacher (Chicago: University of Chicago Press, 1965), p. 135. © 1965 by The University of Chicago.

12.30 Notes on specific parts of the table employ superior reference marks, as note numbers in text. In a table consisting entirely of information in words, these may indeed be numerals (table 12.3), but when a table consists entirely or partly of figures, it is better to use letters (table 12.4) or symbols. Superior letters give the cleaner appearance to a table and should always be used in statistical matter. If mathematical or chemical formulas appear as part of the data, however, superior letters and figures are better avoided because of the possibility of mistaking them for exponents (table 12.13). In such tables the following series is used:

> * (asterisk or star), † (dagger), ‡ (double dagger), § (section mark), ‖ (parallels), # (number sign)

When more symbols are needed, these may be doubled and tripled in the same sequence:

> **, ††, ‡‡, §§, ‖‖, ##, ***, †††, ‡‡‡, §§§, ‖‖‖, ###

One warning: in statistical material, * and ** are often used to indicate probabilities of .05 and .01, respectively. If this is the case in tables in which the arbitrary symbols must be employed as reference marks, asterisks should be omitted from the series.

12.31 Reference marks should be used only on the boxheadings, the body, and the stub of a table, never on the number or title. Any note that might be attached to the number or title would be a general note and should be so treated. The indexes should be placed on the table in whatever order the reader will find easiest to follow, normally beginning at the upper left and extending across the table and downward, row by row.

TABLE 12.13

PURINE AND PYRIMIDINE SUBSTRATES OF
THIOPURINE TRANSMETHYLASE

Purine	Methylation Product (mμmole)	Pyrimidine	Methylation Product (mμmole)
6-SH, 2-NH$_2$, 7-CH$_3$	7.34	2-SH, 4-OH, 6-NH$_2$*	2.16
6-SH, 7-CH$_3$	6.82	2-SH, 4-OH*, †	1.51
6-SH*, †	3.98	2-SH, 4-OH, 5-CH$_3$†	1.16
6-SH, 2-NH$_2$*, †	2.75‡	2,4-(SH)$_2$	0.79
6-SH, 2-OH	1.36	2-SH, 4,6-(OH)$_2$	0.69
6-SH, 2,8-(OH)$_2$†	(+)§	2-SH, 4,6-(NH$_2$)$_2$*	0.47
		2,4-(SH)$_2$, 5-CH$_3$	0.31
2-SH	5.28	2-SH, 4-NH$_2$	0.25
2-SH, 6-OH*	4.80	2-SH, 4-NH$_2$, 5-CH$_3$	0.10
2-SH, 6-CH$_3$	4.59		
2-SH, 6-NH$_2$	3.32	4-SH, 6-NH$_2$	2.09
2,8-(SH)$_2$	1.47	4-SH, 2,6-(NH$_2$)$_2$	1.51
2,6-(SH)$_2$	0.69		
		5-SH, 2,4-(OH)$_2$	1.37
8-SH, 6-NH$_2$	4.59		
8-SH	3.05		

SOURCE: Shapiro and Schlenk 1965.
NOTE: The incubation mixture, containing 0.043 mM S-adenosylmethionine-C^{14}H$_3$ (26.1 μc per μmole), 86 mM phosphate, pH 7.4, 0.29 mM methyl acceptor, and 100,000 x g supernatant fraction of mouse kidney in a total volume of 0.35 ml, was incubated for 30 min at 37° C.
* Authentic samples were employed to verify the synthesis of the corresponding methylthio derivative.
† Reaction products of C^{14}- and S^{35}-labeled bases have been isolated and identified.
‡ Due to poor solubility of the substrate, only minimum values were obtained.
§ Previously shown to be a substrate (14) but not assayed in this series.

SPECIAL TYPES OF TABLES

12.32   Sometimes in writing a book an author has to deal with material that is not strictly tabular (as is the material considered thus far) but does not belong in an appendix and cannot be incorporated in the run of text. In such an instance a figure, drawn by an artist, may be called for, but if the material lends itself to being set in type, a table of some special sort is probably the answer (tables 12.14–18).

TABLE 12.14

The Family of Galla Placidia Augusta

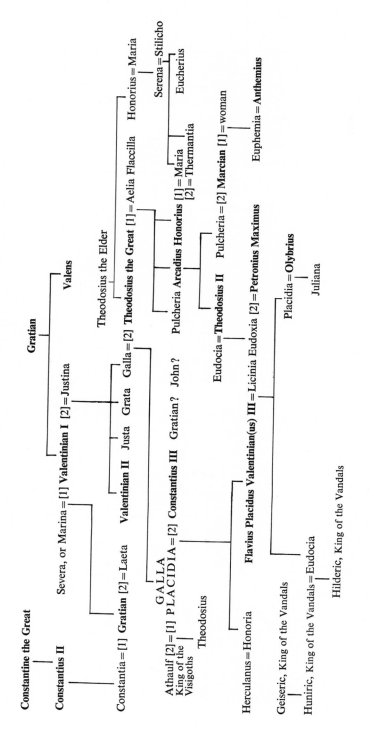

NOTE: Stemma are simplified. Emperors are shown in boldface type.

12.33   The ancestry of a human being, for example, or the pedigree of an animal calls for a genealogical table. Such a table can be set by Linotype if it is fairly simple, but a complicated one like table 12.14 requires hand-setting or a combination of Monotype and hand-setting.

12.34   Cross relationships of various kinds are depicted easily in another special type of table (see table 12.19). Here, strictly speaking, there

TABLE 12.15

OUTLINE OF MECHANISMS CONSIDERED FOR
THE METHIONINE-ACTIVATING ENZYME

(E = enzyme; X = a component of the reaction
mixture other than ATP or enzyme)

I. β-γ bond broken before $C^{5'}$-O bond
  A. ADP an intermediate
    1. $ATP \rightleftharpoons ADP + P_i$
    2. $ATP + X \rightleftharpoons ADP + P\text{-}X$
    3. $ATP + E \rightleftharpoons ADP + P \cdot \cdot E$
  B. ADP not an intermediate
    1. Phospho-adenosine diphosphate:
        2′-phospho-ADP; 3′-phospho-ADP;
        N^6-phospho-ADP; other forms of N-phospho-
        ADP
    2. ADP-sulfonium or other ADP-methionine com-
       pounds
    3. ADP-enzyme
      a. Irreversible: $ATP + E \rightarrow ADP \cdot \cdot E + P_i$
                   $ATP + E + X \rightarrow ADP \cdot \cdot E + P\text{-}X$
      b. Reversible: $ATP \rightleftharpoons ADP \cdot \cdot E + P_i$
      $ATP + E + X \rightleftharpoons ADP \cdot \cdot E + P\text{-}X$
      $ATP + E \rightleftharpoons ADP \cdot \cdot E \cdot \cdot P_i$
II. $C^{5'}$-O bond broken before β-γ bond
  A. Either adenosine or *cyclo*-adenosine an intermediate
    1. $ATP \rightarrow$ adenosine (or *cyclo*-adenosine) $+ PPP_i$
    2. $ATP + X \rightarrow$ adenosine (or *cyclo*-adenosine) $+ PPP\text{-}X$
    3. $ATP + E \rightarrow$ adenosine (or *cyclo*-adenosine) $+ PPP \cdot \cdot E$
  B. Neither adenosine nor *cyclo*-adenosine an intermediate
    1. $ATP \rightarrow$ "tripolyphospho-adenosine"
    2. $ATP + X \rightarrow AX + PPP_i$
    3. a. $ATP + X + E \rightarrow AX + PPP_i \cdot \cdot E \rightarrow AX + PP_i + P_i + E$
       b. $ATP + E \rightarrow A \cdot \cdot E \cdot \cdot PPP_i + X \rightarrow AX + PP_i + P_i + E$

TABLE 12.16

Defect		Above the Common Rate
1 Tenth	⎫	⎧ 3 Tenths
2 Tenths	⎪	⎪ 8 Tenths
3 Tenths	⎬ Raises the price ⎨ 1.6 Tenths
4 Tenths	⎪	⎪ 2.8 Tenths
5 Tenths	⎭	⎩ 4.5 Tenths

290

is no stub, since the items down the left-hand side of the table are identical to the column headings. Hence they are best set in the same style of type. Such a table may be set with both vertical and horizontal rules enclosing the cells, but it is more frequently set open or with the usual kind of ruling.

TABLE 12.17

STRUCTURAL FORMULAS OF COMPOUNDS TESTED FOR S-ADENOSYL DERIVATIVE FORMATION WITH RAT-LIVER OR YEAST METHIONINE-ACTIVATING ENZYME

$$CH_3—S—CH_2—CH_2—\overset{\overset{CH_3}{|}}{\underset{\underset{NH_2}{|}}{C}}—COOH \qquad \alpha\text{-Methylmethionine}$$

$$CH_3—S—CH_2—CH_2—\underset{\underset{NH_2}{|}}{CH}—COOH \qquad \text{Methionine}$$

$$C_2H_5—S—CH_2—CH_2—\underset{\underset{NH_2}{|}}{CH}—COOH \qquad \text{Ethionine}$$

$$CH_3—Se—CH_2—CH_2—\underset{\underset{NH_2}{|}}{CH}—COOH \qquad \text{Selenomethionine}$$

$$C_2H_5—Se—CH_2—CH_2—\underset{\underset{NH_2}{|}}{CH}—COOH \qquad \text{Selenoethionine}$$

$$\overset{\overset{F}{|}}{\underset{\underset{F}{|}}{F—C}}—S—CH_2—CH_2—\underset{\underset{NH_2}{|}}{CH}—COOH \qquad \begin{array}{l}\text{S-Trifluoromethylhomocysteine}\\\text{(Trifluoromethionine)}\end{array}$$

$$CH_3—CH_2—CH_2—S—CH_2—CH_2—\underset{\underset{NH_2}{|}}{CH}—COOH \qquad \text{S-Propylhomocysteine}$$

$$\begin{array}{l}CH_3\\\quad\diagdown\\\quad\quad CH—CH_2—CH_2—S—CH_2—CH_2—\underset{\underset{NH_2}{|}}{CH}—COOH \quad \text{S-Isoamylhomocysteine}\\CH_3\diagup\end{array}$$

TABLE 12.18

MENDELIAN CROSS: COCKER SPANIEL AND BASENJI

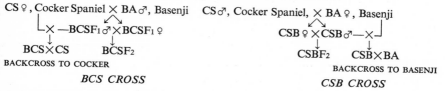

NOTE: The basic plan was to repeat each of the two crosses with four matings and obtain two litters from each mating. Because of deaths among the cocker spaniel females, replication was completed only three times in the BCS cross.

TYPOGRAPHICAL CONSIDERATIONS

12.35 The examples thus far in this chapter have been of ruled Monotype tables of "classic" design, representing the norm for many years at the University of Chicago Press. The specifications for these tables are as follows:

Typeface:	Times Roman No. 327
Table number:	8-point caps, centered
Title:	8-point caps and small caps, centered
Boxheads:	7-point caps and lowercase, centered; if two or more levels, top level in caps and small caps
Body:	8-point solid with italic as needed
Notes:	7-point solid, flush style, additional space between notes
Ruling:	Half-point rules: double at top of table, single at foot; vertical rules between columns

TABLE 12.19

OBSERVATIONS OF MUTUAL GROOMING BY
AGE AND SEX CLASSES

Animals Grooming \ Animals Groomed	Silver-backed male	Black-backed male	Female	Juvenile	Infant	Total
Silverbacked male......	0	0	0	0	3	3
Blackbacked male......	0	0	0	0	0	0
Female...............	0	1	5	13	76	95
Juvenile.............	1	1	9	10	12	33
Infant...............	0	0	2	0	1	3
Total............	1	2	16	23	92	134

12.36 Table 12.20 was designed for a scientific book that included a large number of tables that cut into the text, many of them small, as this one is. It is a Linotype table, but one requiring a certain amount of handwork. The specifications are:

Typeface:	Old Style No. 7
Table number:	9-on-10-point caps, flush left
Title:	9-on-10-point italic caps and lowercase, flush left
Boxheads:	6-on-8-point, centered
Body:	8-point solid
Ruling:	Hairline rules top and bottom and vertically between columns; 3-point rule width of table above heading and below entire table

12.37   Table 12.21 was produced by typewriter composition in a very simple, clean style. Vertical ruling was deliberately restricted to the boxheads, although with little or no increase in cost the rules could have been extended downward between the columns. Ten- and 8-point type was used, but the effect is of smaller faces because the table was reduced photographically before printing. Specifications are:

Typeface:	Univers
Table number:	10-point caps, flush left
Title:	10-point caps and lowercase (only first word and proper nouns and adjectives capitalized), flush left
Boxheads:	Top level, 8-point caps; lower level, 8-point caps and lowercase, capitalized as title
Body:	10-point solid
Notes:	8-point caps and lowercase
Ruling:	Half-point rules: single above and below boxheads and body, double above and below entire table; vertical rules between boxheads only

TABLE 12.20

Effects of Ovariectomy on Ratio of $C^{14}O_2$ from Glucose-6-C^{14} and Glucose-1-C^{14}

Experimental Group	Non-ovariectomized	Ovariectomized
Control	0.66	0.73
Precancerous	1.05	.64
Tumor-bearing	1.15	0.71

12.38   Table 12.22 is a straight Linotype table with no vertical ruling, the most economical mode of arranging tabular matter if metal type is to be used. Specifications are:

Typeface:	News Gothic
Table number:	8-point caps, centered
Title:	8-point caps and lowercase, centered
Column heads:	8-point italic caps and lowercase
Body:	8-point solid
Notes:	7-point solid, additional space between notes
Ruling:	Hairline rules: double at top of table, single above and below the body and between levels of column heads; no vertical rules

TABLE 12.21

Mean expenditure for selected physician services per individual by age and sex: 1963

AGE AND SEX	MEAN EXPENDITURE				N
	In-hospital surgery	Hospital	Home	Office	
Age					
0-5	$ 2	$1	$2	$15	969
6-17	3	1	1	9	1969
18-34	8	3	a	16	1798
35-54	11	5	1	25	1736
55-64	8	9	2	24	606
65 and over	11	7	6	25	725
Sex					
Male	6	3	1	16	3807
Female	8	4	1	19	3996
Total	7	4	1	18	7803

[a] Less than 50 cents.

TABLE 12.22

Median Incomes of Civilian Male Labor Force, 1964

Age	Years of Education Completed				
	0-8	9-11	12	13-15	16+
17-19	2010	2926	3196	3147	—
20-21[a]	2391	3314	3924	4668	5280
22-24[b]	3160	4026	4789	5168	6213
25-29[c]	3673	4500	5366	5502	8353
30-34	4296	5339	6167	6910	9853
35-44	4710	5860	6528	7389	10846
45-54	4717	5636	6549	7855	9883
55 and over	4229	4944	6135	6642	

[a] Incomes for males 21 years of age and under estimated from DOD Survey of civilian non-veterans, 16-21 years of age. Adjusted for unemployment.

[b] Incomes interpolated from data for ages "20-21" and "25-29."

[c] Median total incomes taken from *Statistical Abstract of the United States, 1966*, Table 157, p. 115. Figures were adjusted for unemployment rates of 2.8 per cent for males 25 and older and with more than 8 years of education, and 4.7 per cent unemployment for males with less than 8 years of education.

FOR FURTHER REFERENCE

12.39   Readers seeking further theoretical and technical help with the construction of tables may consult James A. Davis and Ann M. Jacobs, "Tabular Presentation," in the *International Encyclopaedia of the Social Sciences* (1968). Also helpful are Hans Zeisel, *Say It with Figures*, and the *Publication Manual* of the American Psychological Association.

13 *Mathematics in Type*

13.1   Mathematics is known in the trade as *difficult*, or *penalty, copy* because it is slower, more difficult, and more expensive to set in type than any other kind of copy normally occurring in books and journals. The uninformed author can, by exercising poor judgment in selecting notation and by ignoring the elements of good manuscript preparation, add enormously to the cost of typesetting his material. The book or journal editor must continually face this problem; in a borderline case, a manuscript may be rejected because of such nonmathematical considerations.

13.2   This chapter will be devoted to explaining some of the problems in setting technical material and to suggesting ways of minimizing those problems. It is intended for authors, who frequently are unfamiliar with techniques of composition, and for copy editors, who usually do not have mathematical backgrounds.

COMPOSITION

13.3   Type can be set by hand, cast by hot-metal machines (Monotype or, for some work, Linotype), or "set" on light-sensitive film or paper by phototypesetting machines. Hand composition, the oldest and most versatile way to set type, is the slowest and most expensive method of setting mathematical copy because of the many pieces of printing type and nonprinting lead required to make up a page of mathematics. To keep the cost of mathematical composition as low as possible, as much of the composition as is practical is generally done by machine. Nevertheless, some handwork is nearly always required in setting mathematical copy. For happy results the author and editor must be fully aware of the possibilities and limitations of mechanical typesetting. For most mathematical books and journals today, this still means Monotype setting. Accordingly, use of this method is assumed in the present chapter.

SIGNS AND SYMBOLS, THE FIRST PROBLEM

13.4   Mathematical signs and symbols represent a major problem for the compositor, one that the author and editor should face and solve as early as possible. All compositors who do typesetting of mathematical copy have a supply of matrices of most of the common and some of the special signs and symbols. Certain characters, such as standard operation signs, are common and widely available. But no one compositor will have all the signs and symbols available. The number of special signs and symbols is almost limitless, with new ones being introduced all the time. There is an understandable reluctance on the part of compositors to order every special sign or symbol available; the matrices are expensive, and some may be used only rarely.

LIST OF SYMBOLS AND SPECIAL CHARACTERS

13.5   The author should submit with the manuscript a list of the symbols and special characters used. Ideally, this list, or one prepared

296

by the editor, should show all the symbols and special characters in the manuscript, the first and last pages on which each appears, and an estimate of how often each is used.

13.6 Before or during the manuscript editing, the list should be submitted to the production department, which can check with the compositor to whom the manuscript will be sent to determine if all the needed signs and symbols are available. If the compositor does not have all the signs and symbols needed, it is advisable either to have the compositor order the needed matrices or to have the author select substitutions from those that are available.

SUBSTITUTIONS FOR FACILITATING COMPOSITION

13.7 It may also be advisable for the editor to consider, and perhaps suggest to the author, other substitutions that can facilitate composition. Symbols or letters with accents or other marks placed above or below them usually must be set by hand. Therefore, equivalents avoiding this notation should be substituted whenever possible. For example, a′, a″, ′a, ″a, a*, a#, a† can be set easily from the standard keyboard and matrices, whereas ã, ā, â, $\overline{\overline{a}}$, a̦, ä, á, à, require either special symbols or extra work to "make up" the symbols. Again, it is easier to set $\langle mv \rangle_{av}$ than $\overline{mv}$, especially in the text line, since overbars must either be set from special-symbol matrices or made up by handwork. If the number of required special symbols greatly exceeds the limits of the keyboard or matrix case, it may be necessary to leave blank spaces (pieces of lead) where these symbols can be inserted later by hand. Substitutions that make it possible to set copy with the least amount of handwork can help to reduce the time and cost of composition.

13.8 Waiting until the manuscript is edited and ready for composition before asking the compositor if he has the needed symbols may result in frustrating production delays. It may take the compositor twelve weeks or longer to obtain the needed matrices.

UNUSUAL TYPE SIZES

13.9 Most mathematics books are set in 10-point type, the type size in which the greatest number of mathematical symbols are available. If a book is planned for a type size other than 10-point, or if it has extract (reduced) matter or footnotes containing mathematical expressions to be set in a smaller-sized type, it is even more important to check early on the availability of special symbols. The author can avoid the problem as far as footnotes are concerned by the simple expedient of incorporating footnoted material in the text, either parenthetically or as a "Remark." This is now a widely accepted custom and one warmly approved by editors. Bibliographic footnotes can be eliminated by citing the author and date (see par. 16.47 for the style recommended by this press) in the text and including a reference list at the end of the book or chapter.

MANUSCRIPT PREPARATION

13.10 The author who is preparing a manuscript for a specific publisher should obtain from the publisher either a style sheet or, perhaps, another book that can be followed generally for style. The more care and attention given to manuscript preparation, the fewer problems there will be in processing the manuscript.

13.11 In general, the more of the manuscript that can be done on the typewriter the better. It may not be possible, however, for the author to type all the copy, even on a "math" typewriter with special keys. Some signs and symbols, especially the Greek, German, script, and sans serif characters and the newer or more esoteric symbols, may have to be drawn by hand. Neatness is very important here, for a poorly prepared manuscript with special characters drawn in an illegible hand can become, after the addition of editorial changes and typographical instructions, a nightmare for compositor, proofreader, and editor; and, in checking proofs, the author will be faced with a great many errors to correct.

13.12 The standard advice on manuscript preparation applies: the copy should be typed double space on $8\frac{1}{2}$-by-11-inch white paper, with margins at least $1\frac{1}{4}$ inches wide. If equations or symbols are to be handwritten, generous space in the typescript should be allowed for them. Since marginal notes to the operator may have to be added by the editor, ample margins are particularly important.

STYLE AND GENERAL USAGE

13.13 Obviously the author and editor will give careful attention to matters of style, usage, sense, meaning, clarity, accuracy, and consistency. For example, 0.2×10^5 should not be used in one place and 0.02×10^6 in another unless there is a reason. Decimal fractions should always be preceded by a zero: 0.25, not .25.

13.14 All the copy, including the equations, should be in good sentence form and should "read" as clearly and grammatically as any other kind of copy. The signs are substitutes for words: $A + B = C$ reads "*A* plus *B* equals *C*."

13.15 *Punctuation.* Although it is not a universal practice to punctuate mathematical copy, including *displayed* expressions (expressions set on separate lines, usually centered), the use of punctuation may be regarded as an aid to clarity. Without punctuation, it can be difficult to tell where one sentence ends and another begins, especially in places where there is a heavy use of signs and symbols.

13.16 In elisions, if commas or operational signs are required, they should come after each term and after the three ellipsis dots if a final term follows them. For example:

$$x_1, x_2, \ldots, x_n \qquad \text{not} \qquad x_1, x_2, \ldots x_n$$

$$x_1 + x_2 + \ldots + x_n \qquad \text{not} \qquad x_1 + x_2 + \ldots x_n$$

$$y = 0, 1, 2, \ldots \qquad \text{not} \qquad y = 0, 1, 2 \ldots$$

In mathematical expressions some compositors raise the dots slightly above line; others set them on line. In ordinary text, of course, the ellipsis dots are always on line.

13.17 *Numeration.* Sections, theorems, and equations may be numbered, and, if the numeration system is not too cumbersome, this offers a convenient and space-saving method of cross-referring. The system preferred by most mathematicians is double numeration; that is, chapter number followed by equation number, starting with number 1 in each chapter.

13.18 There is little point in numbering all displayed equations. Usually only those that are referred to elsewhere should be numbered. All numbered equations should be displayed. For example:

Wrong:
Hence it is apparent that $abc = xyz$. (1.1)

Right:
Hence it is apparent that

$$abc = xyz\,. \tag{1.1}$$

The displayed equation is either centered on the line or given a standard indention from the left margin (as in this chapter). The equation number is usually placed flush right, but it is not uncommon to see it placed flush left.

299

13.19   *Signs of aggregation.* The preferred order for enclosures, beginning inside with parentheses, is:

$$\left\{\left[\left(\{[(\qquad)]\}\right)\right]\right\}.$$

These may be supplemented for special kinds of work as follows:

$$\left[\!\left[\left\{\left[\left(\left[\!\left[\{[(\qquad)]\}\right]\!\right]\right)\right]\right\}\right]\!\right].$$

Exception to either sequence is made where conventional notation requires the use of particular signs.

DIFFICULT EXPRESSIONS

13.20   *Difficult* terms and equations may occur both in displayed form and in text. Such terms and equations in the text (*in line*) require handwork to *lead in* above or below, or both. To avoid this handwork, it is advisable to display difficult terms and equations. Or, if the terms and equations cannot be displayed, it may be possible to write them in a form that allows them to be set in line. For example, the expressions $\displaystyle\sum_{n=0}^{\infty}$ and $\displaystyle\prod_{n=0}^{\infty}$ require leading above and below line, but $\Sigma_{n=0}^{\infty}$ and $\Pi_{n=0}^{\infty}$ can be substituted without any change of meaning.

13.21   Difficult equations and fractions such as the following should generally be displayed:

$$a = \sum_{k=1}^{n} x_k m_k \Big/ \sum_{k=1}^{n} x_m .$$

It is also better to display long expressions to avoid unfortunate line breaks.

13.22   *The radical sign.* For practical reasons it is preferable, especially in in-line text copy, to use the partial rather than the complete radical sign whenever possible: $\sqrt{2}$ can be set in text without handwork, but $\sqrt{2}$ cannot. Although there are expressions that should not, for reasons of clarity, be written without the overbar on the radical sign, many can be *enclosed* (in parentheses or brackets) to show the extent of the material covered without using the radical-sign rule. The following expressions, left and right, are exact equivalents:

$$\sqrt{xy} \qquad \sqrt{(xy)}$$

$$\sqrt{x+y} \qquad \sqrt{(x+y)}$$

$$\sqrt{\dfrac{x}{y}} \qquad \sqrt{(x/y)}$$

$$\sqrt{\dfrac{x+y-z}{a-b+c}} \qquad \sqrt{[(x+y-z)/(a-b+c)]}$$

13.23 *Exponents.* If an exponential expression, particularly in text, is very complex, it may be worthwhile to rewrite it in a simpler form. An exponential function such as

$$e^{\dfrac{2\pi i \Sigma n_j}{\sqrt{(x^2+y^2)}}}$$

can be set in line as $\exp[2\pi i \Sigma n_j / \sqrt{(x^2 + y^2)}]$. For other expressions with complicated exponents, make a simple substitution. For example,

$$A^{\dfrac{2\pi i \Sigma n_j}{\sqrt{(x^2+y^2)}}}$$

can be set in line as "A^α, where $\alpha = 2\pi i \Sigma n_j / \sqrt{(x^2 + y^2)}$."

13.24 *Fractions.* If an equation such as $\dfrac{x}{a} + \dfrac{y}{b} = 1$ occurs in line rather than displayed, it is advisable to set it with a solidus (/): $x/a + y/b = 1$. The use of the solidus can make it much easier for the compositor to set some fractions: for subscripts and superscripts, solidus fractions should always be used.

USE		INSTEAD OF
$\dfrac{x}{a} + \dfrac{y}{4/a}$ or $x/a + ay/4$		$\dfrac{x}{a} + \dfrac{y}{\dfrac{4}{a}}$
$\dfrac{A/B}{(A - B/C)^{1/2}}$ or $(A/B)/(A - B/C)^{1/2}$		$\dfrac{\dfrac{A}{B}}{\sqrt{A - \dfrac{B}{C}}}$

301

USE	INSTEAD OF
$(x^2 + y^2)^{(a^2+b^2)/2ab}$	$(x^2 + y^2)^{\frac{a^2+b^2}{2ab}}$
$\int_0^{a/b}$	$\int_0^{\frac{a}{b}}$
$\prod_{a/b}^{\infty}$	$\prod_{\frac{a}{b}}^{\infty}$

BREAKING DISPLAYED EQUATIONS

13.25   Even in displayed form, some long equations may not fit on one line. An equation that runs over one line to make two lines should, if possible, be broken before an operational sign. The second line may be set either flush right, a standard indention from the right margin (to allow space for an equation number), or aligned on operational signs.

$$\|T_a f - f\| = \sup_s \|T_s^{s+a} f(s + a) - f(s)\|$$
$$- \sup_{s \leqq A} \|T_s^{s+a} f(s + a) - f(s)\| + 2 \sup_{s \geqq A} \|f(s)\| \ .$$

If the equation takes more than two lines, it is common practice to align runover lines on operational or descriptive signs:

$$X, \ Y(s, t) = \int_{-\infty}^{\infty} \ldots \int_{-\infty}^{\infty} e^{i(sx+ty)} \, dF_{x,y}(x, y)$$
$$= \int_{-\infty}^{\infty} e^{ity} \left[\int_{-\infty}^{\infty} e^{isx} \, dF_{x|y}(x) \right] dF_y(y)$$
$$= \int_{-\infty}^{\infty} e^{ity} x \,|\, y(s\,|\,y) \, dF_y(y) \ .$$

Fractions and expressions in parentheses ( ), in brackets [ ], in braces { }, and following radical signs should not be broken unless it is absolutely necessary.

13.26   A determinant or matrix that occupies several lines in the text and that the author feels cannot be cut (one part appearing at the bottom of one page and the second part at the top of the next) without its readability being destroyed should be labeled as a figure and referred to in the text by the figure number. The compositor can then move it to a nearby location to avoid breaking it. Tables, line drawings, and halftone illustrations are handled in this way as a matter of course.

ILLUSTRATIONS

13.27   Most of the illustrations used in mathematics are line drawings (rather than halftones), usually charts and graphs. If the illustrations include letters, signs, or symbols that are to correspond to those in the text, the hand-lettering should approximate the typeface used in the text. It can be confusing, for example, if the points *a*, *b*, and *c* are italic type in the text and the illustration identifies them as script letters.

13.28   Some material is just too difficult, if not outright impossible, to set in type and may have to be produced by either drawings or a combination of type and drawings:

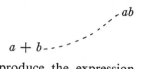

To produce the expression above, type was set, reproduction proofs of the type were pulled, the curved line was drawn on a proof, and a zinc engraving was made. The expression was then printed in the same way as an illustration (text figure).

MARKING MATHEMATICAL COPY

ITALIC TYPE

13.29   The editor may either underline all copy to be set in italic or give general instructions to the compositor to set all letters used as mathematical terms in italic unless they are marked otherwise. Since compositors experienced in setting mathematics understand that mathematical terms, such as $A + B = C$, are set in italic type, it is not usually necessary to mark such expressions, although the editor should prepare general instructions covering even such obvious matters as this. The general instructions to the compositor should also specify italic type for letters used in subscripts and superscripts.

13.30   *Abbreviations.* Abbreviations such as log (logarithm), max (maximum), exp (exponential function), tan (tangent), cos (cosine), cosh (hyperbolic cosine), lim (limit), arg (argument), cov (covariance), diag (diagonal), and var (variance) are set in roman: $\sin x$ (not: *sin x*), $\log_a x$, $\langle mv \rangle_{av}$, y_{min} .

Abbreviations for units of measurement and for chemical elements are also set in roman type.

LETTERS IN NONITALIC TYPE

13.31   Special instructions and marking must be used if letters are to be set in any face other than italic. Although it is rather uncommon, a mathematics book may require the use of some letters in roman, usually to indicate properties different from those expressed by the same letters in italic. Underlining is the standard method of indicating italic, but it can be used instead, with covering instruction to the compositor, to indicate letters that are to be in a roman face. If, however, the editor does not use general instructions but underlines all letters to be set italic, then another method—circling, overscoring, or color coding—may be used to show roman letters. Double underlining is used to indicate small capitals. Wavy underlining is used to indicate boldface type. (Boldface is normally used for vectors. The author should clearly identify all vectors, to distinguish them from their components, which are set in italic. The editor will find it difficult to make the distinction.) Color codes are often used to indicate other type faces. For example, red underlining or circling can be used to indicate German, blue to indicate script, green to indicate sans serif, and so forth. The covering instructions to the compositor must explain clearly the marking and coding system used.

13.32 *Using correct terminology.* The copy editor and printer are often misled by authors who confuse German with script, specifying the latter when they mean the former. Boldface and sans serif are also frequently mislabeled. Examples of each are shown below:

GERMAN	SCRIPT	BOLDFACE	SANS SERIF
𝔄𝔅ℭ𝔇	𝒶ℬ𝒸𝒟	**ABCD**	ABCD

DEFINITIONS, THEOREMS, PROOFS, ETC.

13.33 For definitions, theorems, propositions, corollaries, and lemmas, it is common practice to set the head in caps and small caps and the text in italic, and this material should be underlined properly by the editor. The texts of proofs, examples, remarks, demonstrations, and solutions are usually set in roman, with only the word "proof," for example, set in italic.

> DEFINITION 1.1. *The graph of an equation consists of all the points whose coordinates satisfy the given equation.*
>
> THEOREM 2.2. *Two nonvertical lines are parallel if and only if their slopes are equal.*
>
> LEMMA 3.3. *K is unbounded if and only if $A = B$.*
>
> ASSUMPTION. *A is nonempty and has a nonempty intersection with B.*
>
> RULE 4.4. *The length of a vertical segment joining two points is the ordinate of the upper point minus the ordinate of the lower.*
>
> *Proof.* Let $A = B$. Hence $C = D$.
>
> *Solution.* If $y = 0$, then $x = 5$.

MARKING FOR CLARITY

13.34   What may be perfectly clear to the author can be utterly bewildering to anyone who is not a mathematician. The author must take particular care to clarify ambiguous expressions.

13.35   It is not advisable, however, to mark the copy excessively. Provided that inferior and superior characters have been marked in a few places by the symbols $\vee$ and $\wedge$ (see example below), and new characters or symbols identified when they first appear, a trained compositor will have no difficulty with well-prepared copy. If the spatial relationship of terms is *not* clearly shown in typed or hand-written expressions, they should be marked so that there can be no doubt in the mind of the compositor. For example, in the expression

$$\mathrm{x}^{k}_{t1}$$

it may not be clear in the manuscript whether this means

$$X^{k}_{t1} \quad \text{or} \quad X^{k}_{t^1} \quad \text{or} \quad X^{k}_{t_1} ;$$

it should be marked in one of the following ways for complete clarity:

$$\text{or} \quad \quad \text{or} \quad .$$

13.36   The examples above show the subscripts and superscripts aligned, the setting generally preferred by authors for elegance and clarity. The handwork involved is considerable, however, particularly if double use of suffixes and indices occurs frequently throughout a book. Therefore, with frequent occurrence, it may be advisable to instruct the typesetter to stagger them for ease and economy in setting. (There should be previous agreement between the editor and the author on this point, however, as on any other departure from the form in the typescript.) If they are staggered, the general rule is to set the subscript before the superscript:

$$X_1{}^2 , \quad Y_m{}^n .$$

If the subscript or the superscript is lengthy, however, the two should be set aligned or parentheses should be added for clarity:

$$X^{3}_{2v_{n-1}} \quad \text{or} \quad (X_{2v_{n-1}})^3 ; \quad \text{not} \quad X_{2v_{n-1}}{}^3 .$$

NOTE: A prime (') is always set adjacent to a letter or symbol:

$$X'_{x,y} , \quad \text{not} \quad X_{x,y}{}' .$$

13.37   Figure 13.1 shows a page of manuscript as marked initially by the author and then by the editor before being sent to the typesetters. Figure 13.2 shows the same page set in type. The author's marks

[*Text continued on page 314*]

Opr.: Letter symbols in ital. unless marked

Therefore $F_x{}^n \subset G \cap B_n$ and $F_x{}^n \cap B_m = \emptyset$ for $n \neq m$ since $b \in G$.

(null set) *("element of")*

The temperature function is

$$u(x,\ t) = \frac{2}{L} \sum_1^\infty \exp\left(-\frac{u^2\pi^2 kt}{L^2}\right) \sin\frac{n\pi x}{L} \int_0^L f(x') \sin\frac{n\pi x'}{L}\,dx'. \qquad (3.1)$$

An $m \times n$ matrix $\underset{\sim}{A}$ over a field F is a rectangular array of mn elements $a_j{}^i$ in F, arranged in m rows and n columns:

$$\underset{\sim}{A} = \begin{bmatrix} a_1{}^1 & a_2{}^1 & \cdots & a_n{}^1 \\ a_1{}^2 & a_2{}^2 & \cdots & a_n{}^2 \\ \cdot & \cdot & \cdots & \cdot \\ a_1{}^m & a_2{}^m & \cdots & a_n{}^m \end{bmatrix}.$$

The modulus of the correlation coefficient of X_1 and X_2 is

("greater than")

$$\rho = |\langle x_1,\ x_2 \rangle| / \|x_1\|\ \|x_2\| \quad \text{for} \quad \|x_1\| > 0, \qquad 1 = 1,\ 2.$$

(angle brackets) *(ell)* *(ell)*

Hence

$$\frac{\partial F}{\partial x} = \lim_{\Delta x \to 0} \frac{\Delta F}{\Delta x} = \lim_{\Delta x \to 0} \frac{1}{\Delta x}\left\{ \int_{a,b}^{x+\Delta x, y} P\,dx + Q\,dy \right.$$
$$\left. - \int_{a,b}^{x,y} P\,dx + Q\,dy \right\} + P + Q.$$

From equation (2.4), where $M = [(a + b - 1)/(k + 1)]$, we obtain

$$\alpha_\nu(a + b) = (-1)^\nu {\sum}' \frac{(i_1 + \cdots + i_M)!}{i_1! \cdots i_M!} \prod_{h=1}^M (-1)^{i_h} \binom{a + b - kh - 1}{h}^{i_h},$$

(lc Gr. nu)

the sum being extended over all sets $(i_1, \cdots, i_M)$.

To summarize our findings:

(lc Gr. eta)

$$v^*(z,\ t_n) \gtrless H_\delta{}_1 [v(x) + o(1)] - 2\eta \gtrless v(z) + o(1) + \eta^{1/2}o(1).$$

(lc oh) *(lc oh)* *(cap oh)*

Fig. 13.1. An example of a well-prepared page of mathematical copy with suggested marking for clarity. This page is not intended to make mathematical sense, but merely to illustrate good preparation of mathematical copy.

306

Therefore $F_x{}^n \subset G \cap B_n$ and $F_x{}^n \cap B_m = \emptyset$ for $n \neq m$ since $b \in G$. The temperature function is

$$u(x,\, t) = \frac{2}{L} \sum_1^\infty \exp\left(-\frac{u^2\pi^2 kt}{L^2}\right) \sin \frac{n\pi x}{L}$$

$$\times \int_0^L f(x') \sin \frac{n\pi x'}{L}\, dx' \,.$$

(3.1)

An $m \times n$ matrix $\mathbf{A}$ over a field F is a rectangular array of mn elements $a_j{}^i$ in F, arranged in m rows and n columns:

$$\mathbf{A} = \begin{bmatrix} a_1{}^1 & a_2{}^1 & \cdots & a_n{}^1 \\ a_1{}^2 & a_2{}^2 & \cdots & a_n{}^2 \\ \cdot & \cdot & \cdots & \cdot \\ a_1{}^m & a_2{}^m & \cdots & a_n{}^m \end{bmatrix} \,.$$

The modulus of the correlation coefficient of X_1 and X_2 is

$$\rho = |\langle X_1,\, X_2 \rangle| / \|X_1\|\, \|X_2\| \quad \text{for} \quad \|X_l\| > 0\,, \quad l = 1,\, 2\,.$$

Hence

$$\frac{\partial F}{\partial x} = \lim_{\Delta x \to 0} \frac{\Delta F}{\Delta x} = \lim_{\Delta x \to 0} \frac{1}{\Delta x} \left\{ \int_{a,b}^{x+\Delta x, y} P\, dx + Q\, dy \right.$$

$$\left. - \int_{a,b}^{x,y} P\, dx + Q\, dy \right\} + P + Q \,.$$

From equation (2.4), where $M = [(a + b - 1)/(k + 1)]$, we obtain

$$a_\nu(a + b) = (-1)^\nu \sum{}' \frac{(i_1 + \ldots + i_M)!}{i_1! \ldots i_M!}$$

$$\times \prod_{h=1}^M (-1)^{i_h} \binom{a + b - kh - 1}{h}^{i_h},$$

the sum being extended over all sets $(i_1, \ldots, i_M)$.

To summarize our findings:

$$v^*(z,\, t_n) \geq H_{\delta_i}[v(x) + o(1)] - 2\eta \geq v(z) + o(1) + \eta^{1/2}O(1)$$

Fig. 13.2. The page of manuscript shown in figure 13.1 set in type

307

TABLE 13.1

Ambiguous Mathematical Symbols

Hand-written Symbols and Letters[a]	Symbols Set in Type[b]	Marginal Notation to Operator[c]	Remarks and Suggestions for Manuscript Preparation
a	a	lc "aye"	In typescript, leave single space before
α	a	lc Gr. alpha	and after $\propto$ and all other descrip-
$\propto$	$\propto$	variation	tive signs ($=$, $\leq$, $\in$, $\cap$, $\subset$, etc.)
∞	∞	infinity	
B	B	cap "bee"	
β	β	lc Gr. beta	
χ	χ	lc Gr. chi	Carelessly written χ also easily misread
X	X	cap "ex"	as numeral 4
x	x	lc "ex"	
$\times$	$\times$	"times" or "mult"	Leave single space before and after $\times$ and all other operational signs ($+$, $-$, $\div$, etc.)
δ, ∂	δ	lc Gr. delta	
∂	∂	partial differential	Simpler to use printer's term "round dee"
d	d	lc "dee"	
ϵ	ϵ	lc Gr. epsilon	
$\in$	$\in$	"element of"	
η	η	lc Gr. eta	
n	n	lc "en"	
γ	γ	lc Gr. gamma	
τ	τ	lc Gr. tau	
r	r	lc "are"	
t	t	lc "tee"	
ι	ι	lc Gr. iota	Author should avoid using ι and i to-
i	i	lc "eye"	gether because of similarity in print
κ	κ	lc Gr. kappa	
k	k	lc "kay"	
K	K	cap Gr. kappa	
K	K	cap "kay"	
l	l	lc "ell"	Typed l and 1 identical; note "ell" but
1	1	numeral 1	leave numeral unmarked
ν	ν	lc Gr. nu	Avoid using ν and v together because
v	v	lc "vee"	of similarity in print
O	O	cap "oh"	Zero usually unmarked; degree sign (if
o	o	lc "oh"	typed as lc "oh") and Greek letters
0	0	zero	identified in margin
O	O	cap Gr. omicron	
o	o	lc Gr. omicron	
$\circ$	$\circ$	degree sign	

[a] Symbols and letters commonly mistaken for each other are arranged in groups.

[b] Letters in mathematical expressions will automatically be set in italics unless marked otherwise.

[c] Only if symbols, letters, or numbers are badly written is it necessary to identify them for the compositor.

TABLE 13.1—*Continued*

Hand-written Symbols and Letters[a]	Symbols Set in Type[b]	Marginal Notation to Operator[c]	Remarks and Suggestions for Manuscript Preparation
	Λ	cap Gr. lambda	
	$\wedge$	matrix symbol	
	ϕ, φ	lc Gr. phi	Preference for form φ should be specified by author; ϕ more commonly used
	$\emptyset$	empty set or null set	
	Π	product	
	Π	cap Gr. pi	
	π	lc Gr. pi	
	ρ	lc Gr. rho	
	p	lc "pee"	
	θ, ϑ	lc Gr. theta	Preference for form ϑ should be specified by author; θ more commonly used
	Θ	cap Gr. theta	
	U	cap "you"	
	$\cup, \smile$	union symbol	
	υ	lc Gr. upsilon	
	μ	lc Gr. mu	
	u	lc "you"	
	ω	lc Gr. omega	
	w	lc "doubleyou"	
	Z	cap "zee"	
	z	lc "zee"	
	2	numeral 2	
	$'$	prime	Type apostrophe for prime; raise superscript one-half space above line
	1	superscript 1	In handwritten formulas, take care to distinguish comma from subscript 1 and prime from superscript 1
	$,$	comma	
	1	subscript 1	
	—	em dash	Type two hyphens for em dash; no space on either side
	–	minus sign	To indicate subtraction, leave single space on each side of sign; omit space after sign if negative quantity is represented
	$\cdot$	multiplication dot	Type period one-half space above line for multiplication dot, allowing single space on each side; do *not* show space around a center dot in a chemical formula ($CO_3 \cdot H_2$)

309

TABLE 13.2

FONTS OF TYPE

ROMAN LOWERCASE.   a b c . . . z æ œ ff fi fl ffi ffl

ROMAN SMALL CAPS.   A B C . . . Z Æ Œ &

ROMAN CAPS.   A B C . . . Z Æ Œ &

ROMAN FIGURES AND FRACTIONS.   1 2 3 4 5 6 7 8 9 0
$\frac{1}{2} \ \frac{1}{3} \ \frac{2}{3} \ \frac{1}{4} \ \frac{3}{4} \ \frac{1}{6} \ \frac{1}{8} \ \frac{3}{8} \ \frac{5}{8} \ \frac{7}{8}$

ROMAN PUNCTUATION.   . , ; : - ' ! ? ([

ITALIC LOWERCASE, FIGURES, AND ACCENTS.   Identical with the corresponding roman type.

ITALIC CAPS.   *A B C . . . Z Æ Œ &*

ITALIC FIGURES.   *1 2 3 4 5 6 7 8 9 0*

GERMAN 99.   𝔄 𝔅 ℭ 𝔇 𝔈 𝔉 𝔊 ℌ ℑ 𝔎 𝔏 𝔐 𝔑 𝔒 𝔓 𝔔 ℜ 𝔖 𝔗 𝔘 𝔙 𝔚 𝔛 𝔜 ℨ
abcdefghijflmnopqrſstuvwxyz

GERMAN 100.   𝕬 𝕭 𝕮 𝕯 𝕰 𝕱 𝕲 𝕳 𝕴 𝕵 𝕶 𝕷 𝕸 𝕹 𝕺 𝕻 𝕼 𝕽 𝕾 𝕿 𝖀 𝖁 𝖂 𝖃 𝖄 𝖅
abcdefghijflmnopqrſstuvwxyz

GREEK 155.   Α Β Γ Δ Ε Ζ Η Θ Ι Κ Λ Μ Ν Ξ Ο Ρ Σ Τ Υ Φ Χ Ψ Ω
$\alpha \beta \gamma \delta \epsilon \zeta \eta \theta \iota \kappa \lambda \mu \nu \xi o \pi \rho \sigma \tau \upsilon \varphi \chi \psi \omega$ ϝ ϑ ϐ ς

GREEK 160.   **Α Β Γ Δ Ε Ζ Η Θ Ι Κ Λ Μ Ν Ξ Ο Π Ρ Σ Τ Υ Φ Χ Ψ Ω**
α β γ δ ε ζ η θ ι κ λ μ ν ξ ο π ϱ σ τ υ φ χ ψ ω ϑ

SUPERIOR AND INFERIOR GREEK LOWERCASE. $\mathrm{H}^{\alpha\beta\gamma\delta\epsilon\zeta\eta\theta\iota\kappa\lambda\mu\nu\xi}$
$^{o\pi\rho\sigma\tau\upsilon\phi\chi\psi\omega}$ $^{\digamma\varphi\varsigma}$

$\mathrm{H}_{\alpha\beta\gamma\delta\epsilon\zeta\eta\theta\iota\kappa\lambda\mu\nu\xi o\pi\rho\sigma\tau\upsilon\phi\chi\psi\omega}$ $_{\digamma\vartheta\varphi\varsigma}$

HEBREW 280.   תשרקצפפעסנמלכיטחזוהדגבא

TABLE 13.2—*Continued*

RUSSIAN 308.　А Б В Г Д Е Ж З И І Й К Л М Н О П Р С Т
У Ф Х Ц Ч Ш Щ Ъ Ы Ь Ѣ Э Ю Я Ѵ

CUSHING 25J.　A B C D E F G H I J K L M N O P Q R S
T U V W X Y Z

a b c d e f g h i j k l m n o p q r s t u v w x y z

CUSHING 25K.　*A B C D E F G H I J K L M N O P Q R S T
U V W X Y Z*

a b c d e f g h i j k l m n o p q r s t u v w x y z

GOTHIC.[1]　A B C D E F G H I J K L M N O P Q R S T U V W
X Y Z

SCRIPT.　𝒶 𝐵 𝒞 𝒟 𝒠 𝐹 𝒢 𝒣 𝒥 𝒥 𝒦 𝓛 𝑀 𝒩 𝒪 𝒫 𝒬 𝒬 𝒮 𝒥 𝒰 𝒱 𝒲
𝒳 𝒴 𝒵

SUPERIOR LETTERS.[2]　A^{ABC}　A^{abc}　$A^{\alpha\beta\gamma}$　A^{123}

INFERIOR LETTERS. A stock similar to the superior letters. Examples are: B_{DEF}　B_{def}　$B_{\delta\epsilon\zeta}$　B_{456}

SYMBOLS.　$+\ -\ \times\ \div\ =\ \pm\ \mp\ /\ \|\ <\ >\ \leq\ \geq\ \equiv\ \neq\ \not\equiv\ \doteq\ \sim$
$\simeq\ \rightarrow\ \surd\ (\ )\ \{\ \}\ [\ ]\ \infty\ \propto\ {}^\circ\ {}'\ {}''$

$| |\ (\ )\ \{\ \}\ [\ ]\ /\ \sqrt{}\ \int\ \oint\ [\![\ ]\!]\ \langle\ \rangle$

SUPERIOR SYMBOLS.　$A^{+\ -\ =\ \times\ \div\ \pm\ <\ >\ \leqq\ \geqq\ \surd\ \odot\ \infty\ /\ (\ )\ \{\}\ [\ ]\ 1/2\ 1/4\ \int\ ,\ .}$
$A^{'\ \|\ |\ \perp}$

INFERIOR SYMBOLS.　$B_{+\ -\ =\ \times\ \div\ \pm\ <\ >\ \leqq\ \geqq\ \surd\ \odot\ \infty\ /\ (\ )\ \{\}\ [\ ]\ 1/2\ 1/4\ \int\ \|}$
$B_{.\ ,\ ;\ :\ '\ \|\ \perp}$

SPLIT FRACTIONS.　$\frac{1\ 2\ 3\ 4\ 5\ 6\ 7\ 8\ 9\ 0}{1\ 2\ 3\ 4\ 5\ 6\ 7\ 8\ 9\ 0}$

MISCELLANEOUS.　$\varpi\ \delta\ !\ {}^\circ\ ''\ \%\ @\ \P\ \int\ \supset\ \triangle\ \angle\ \odot\ \circledcirc\ \oplus\ \circledS\ \ominus\ \ominus$
$\circledast\ \rightarrow\ \perp\ \triangle\ ※\ \circ\ {}^*(6\ pt.)\ \dagger(6\ pt.)\ *\ \dagger\ \ddagger\ \S\ \$\ \#\ {}^{d\ h\ s}$
${}^{mg}\ {}^M\ \ngeqq\ \nleqq\ \#\ \prec\ \precsim\ \succsim\ \leftrightarrow\ \leftrightharpoons\ \rightleftarrows\ \rightleftharpoons\ \male\ \female\ \female\ \not\prec$

---

1. Not available for machine composition.

2. A stock of these letters on *small* bodies can serve as superior letters, inferior letters, or limits of summations indifferently.

TABLE 13.3

STANDARD SIGNS AND SYMBOLS

Symbol	Meaning	Symbol	Meaning
$+$	Plus	$\perp$	Perpendicular to
$-$	Minus	$\perp$s	Perpendiculars
$\times$	Multiplied by	$\parallel$	Parallel
$\div$	Divided by	$\parallel$s	Parallels
$=$	Equal to		Not parallels
$\pm$	Plus or minus	$\angle$	Angle
$\mp$	Minus or plus		Angle
	Plus or equal		Angle
	Double plus		Angles
	Difference between		Right angle
$-:$	Difference excess		Equal angles
$\equiv$	Identical with, congruent	$\triangle$	Triangle
	Not identical with		Triangles
$\neq$	Not equal to	$/$	Rising diagonal
$\approx$	Nearly equal to		Falling diagonal
$\cong$	Equals approximately		Parallel rising diagonal
	Equals approximately		Parallel falling diagonal
	Equal to or greater than		Rising parallels
	Equal to or less than		Falling parallels
$<$	Less than		Triple vertical
	Less than	$\equiv$	Quadruple parallels
$>$	Greater than		Arc
	Greater than		Arc
	Greater than or less than		Sector
	Not less than		Segment
	Not greater than	$\bigcirc$	Circle
	Less than or equal to		Circles
	Less than or equal to		Ellipse
$\leq$	Less than or equal to	$\varnothing$	Diameter
	Less than or equal to	$\square$	Square
	Less than or greater than		Squares
	Greater than or equal to		Rectangle
	Greater than or equal to		Rectangles
$\geq$	Greater than or equal to		Cube
	Greater than or equal to		Rhomboid
	Equivalent to		Rhomboids
$\neq$	Not equivalent		Pentagon
	Not equivalent		Hexagon
$\subset$	Included in	$\therefore$	Hence, therefore
$\supset$	Excluded from	$\because$	Because
$\sim$	Difference	$\cdot$	Multiplied by
s	Difference	$:$	Ratio
$\#$	Equal and parallel	$::$	Proportion
	Approaches a limit	$\div$	Geometrical proportion
	Is measured by	$'$	Minute

312

TABLE 13.3—*Continued*

$''$	Second	/	Single bond
$\circ$	Degree	|	Single bond
$\overset{.}{'}$	Dotted minute	\\	Single bond
$\overset{.}{''}$	Dotted second	|	Single bond
$\overset{.}{\circ}$	Dotted degree	|	Single bond (punched to
$\underline{''}$	Canceled second		right)
$'''$	Triple prime	\\\\	Double bond
$\sqrt{}$	Square root	‖	Double bond
$\sqrt[3]{}$	Cube root	//	Double bond
$\sqrt[4]{}$	Fourth root	‖	Double bond
$\sqrt[n]{}$	nth root	⋮	Triple bond
∠	Horizontal radical	↔	Reaction goes both right
Σ	Summation of		and left
Π	Product sign	↕	Reaction goes both up
π	Pi (3.1416)		and down
$\cup$	Union sign	⇋	Equilibrium reaction be-
$\cap$	Intersection sign		ginning at right
!	Factorial sign	⇌	Equilibrium reaction be-
$\emptyset$	Empty set; null set		ginning at left
$\in$	Is an element of	⇌	Reversible reaction begin-
$\notin$	Is not an element of		ning at left
e	Base (2.718) of natural	⇆	Reaction begins at right
	system of logarithms		and is completed to left
e	Charge of the electron	⇆	Reaction begins at right
Δ	Delta		and is completed to right
∇	Nabla; del	⇄	Reaction begins at left
$\propto$	Variation		and is completed to right
∞	Infinity	⇄	Reaction begins at left
ℳ	Mills		and is completed to left
⊢	Assertion sign	⇋	Reversible reaction begin-
h	Planck's Constant		ning at right
$\hbar$	$h/2\pi$	↕	Reversible
k	Boltzmann's Constant	⇑	Elimination
$\bar{c}$	Mean value of c	⇓	Absorption
∂	Partial differential	⇕	Exchange
∂	Partial differential	⚡	Electrolysis
$\int$	Integral	◠	Ring opening
$\oint$	Contour integral	◡	Repositioning
⌐	Horizontal integral	○	Ring cycle
˘	Mathmodifier	↗	Reversible reaction
˓	Mathmodifier	↙	Reversible reaction
$\sim$	Cycle sine		
ꭓ	Quantic		

313

[*Text continued from page 305*]

merely identify ambiguous symbols. The editor's marking was done for a compositor experienced in mathematical setting; for an inexperienced compositor the marking must be more elaborate.

13.38   *Mistaken identity.* In the manuscript certain letters, numbers, and symbols can be easily misread, especially when Greek, German, script, and sans serif letters are handwritten rather than typed. Some of the handwritten and typed characters that cause the most difficulty are shown in table 13.1.

13.39   These and other signs and symbols that can be misread by the compositor should be clearly identified, either by marginal notations or otherwise. Illegible handwriting and unidentifiable signs and symbols can reduce composition speed and result in time-consuming and costly corrections. In the folklore of publishing, the story is told of an author who drowned himself when, on reading proof of his thousand-page manuscript, he found that χ had been set as x throughout. It may be inconceivable to an author that a compositor, even though working on the third shift in a plant a thousand miles away, or in another country, could make such a misinterpretation. Unfortunately, authors are seldom available at the time of composition to answer questions, and decisions or interpretations have to be made. Although experienced typesetters become very skillful at deciphering, they do make mistakes.

FOR FURTHER REFERENCE

13.40   Readers who wish to explore the problems of mathematical type-setting more fully are referred to *Mathematics in Type*, by the William Byrd Press (1954); *Setting Mathematics*, by Arthur Phillips (1956); and "A Manual for Authors of Mathematical Papers," by the American Mathematical Society (1962).

14   *Abbreviations*

INTRODUCTION

14.1 For several centuries the use of abbreviations and symbols in formal, general writing has become less and less frequent, whereas for the past fifty years at least such use has been on the increase in technical writing of all kinds. In the main this chapter is concerned with abbreviations and symbols in general writing; authors and editors of technical material, especially in a fast-changing field, will usually know and follow the fashions of that field as reflected in the journal literature—but the chapter does offer some guidance in technical work, especially to the generalist editor confronted with special-interest copy to prepare for typesetting. Outside the area of science and technology, abbreviations and symbols find their most frequent use in tabular matter, footnotes, bibliographies, and lists of various kinds.

14.2 It is often an open question whether or not periods should be used with particular abbreviations.[1] The trend now is strongly away from the use of periods with all kinds of abbreviations that have carried them in the past. In our view this is to the good: anything that reduces the fussiness of typography, including the elimination of unneeded punctuation, makes for easier reading. In the examples that follow, however, the periods have been left wherever they have traditionally appeared, to make clear which abbreviations in conservative practice have been free of periods. It is simple enough for the user of this manual to omit periods if that is the style he wishes to adopt. One caution: If periods are omitted after abbreviations that spell words (for example, *in., a., no.*), these may be confusing in some contexts—but certainly not in tabular matter. Another caution, if periods are used: In an abbreviation with internal periods (A.M., *N.Y., Litt.D., N.Dak.*), there should be no space after the internal periods.

1. In British practice, a distinction is made between a true abbreviation, in which the end of the word is lopped off (*vol., Inc., diam.*), and a suspension, in which the interior of the word is removed (*Mr., dept., acct.*). It is usual in Britain to spell the latter class without periods. This logical practice shows few signs of catching on in America, however.

316

14.3   Despite the long-continued trend in general writing to get along without abbreviations, some few words are never (*almost* never) spelled out. Among these are *Mr., Mrs., Messrs.,* and *Dr.* before a name, abbreviations for affiliations or scholarly degrees after a name (*Litt.D., M.P., Ph.D.*), and abbreviations such as A.M. and P.M., A.D. and B.C. On the other hand a symbol or figure beginning a sentence is always (*almost* always) spelled out, or if it cannot be, the sentence is recast:

> Alpha particles are . . . (*not* α particles are . . .)
> Eighteen forty-five was . . . (*not* 1845 was . . .)

For other advice on the use of figures in run of text the reader is referred to chapter 8.

NAMES AND TITLES

PERSONAL NAMES

14.4   Normally, abbreviations should not be used for given names:

> Benjamin (*not* Benj.) Harrison   William (*not* Wm.) Warfield

A signature, however, should be given as the person wrote it:

> Benj. Franklin   Geo. D. Fuller   Ch. Virolleaud

Some names contain a middle initial that does not stand for a name, and some given names consist only of initials. A purist would omit the period after these initials. For convenience and consistency—and with the approval of at least one bearer of such a middle initial, Harry S. Truman—it is recommended that all initials given with a name be followed by a period:

> Charles C. Thomas
> P. J. Carter

When persons are referred to by initials only, such as American presidents since FDR or the name of a subject of a biography, no periods are used:

> JFK (John Fitzgerald Kennedy)
> JM (James Madison)

14.5   *Titles before names.* When a civil or military title is used with the surname alone, the title must be spelled out:

> General Washington   Alderman Despres
> Lieutenant Colonel Smith

With full names, most such titles are abbreviated:

> Brig. Gen. Thomas Tilney   Sen. Everett M. Dirksen

317

CIVIL AND MILITARY TITLES

Adj. Gen.	Insp. Gen.	Rep.
Adm.	Judge Adv. Gen.	S1c., seaman, first
Ald.	Lt.	class
A1c., airman, first	Lt. Col.	2d Lt.
class	Lt. Comdr.	Sfc., sergeant, first
Brig. Gen.	Lt. Gen.	class
Bvt., brevet	Lt. Gov.	Sen.
Capt.	Lt. (jg.)	Sgt.
Col.	Maj.	Sp3c., specialist,
Comdr.	Maj. Gen.	third class
Cpl.	M. Sgt.	S. Sgt.
CWO, chief warrant	Pfc., private, first	Supt.
officer	class	T2g., technician,
Ens.	PO, petty officer	second grade
Fr., Father	Prof.	T. Sgt.
1st Lt.	Pvt.	Vice Adm.
1st Sgt.	Q.M. Gen.	WO, warrant officer
Gen.	Q.M. Sgt.	
Gov.	Rear Adm.	

14.6 Always abbreviated, whether with the full name or surname, are the social titles:

Mr.   Mrs.   Messrs.   M.   MM.   Mme   Mlle   Dr.

14.7 The titles *Reverend* and *Honorable* are spelled out if preceded by *the:*

the Reverend Henry L. Brown; the Reverend Mr. (*or* Dr.) Brown (*never* Reverend Brown *or* the Reverend Brown)

the Very Reverend Robert C. Wilson; the Right Reverend David O. Carlson; the Right Reverend Monsignor Thomas L. Bennett

the Honorable Charles H. Percy

In other instances with the full name the title is abbreviated:

Rev. Henry L. Brown; Very Rev. Robert C. Wilson; Rt. Rev. David O. Carlson; Rt. Rev. Msgr. Thomas L. Bennett; Hon. Charles H. Percy

14.8 *Titles, degrees, affiliations, etc., after names.* The abbreviations *Jr., Sr., II, III* (or *2d, 3d*), etc., after a person's name are part of that name and so are used in connection with any titles or honorifics. *Jr.* and *Sr.* are preceded by a comma; the others are not:

Mrs. Nathaniel Jefferson, Sr.   Rev. Oliver C. Jones, Jr.
Dexter Harrison III, LL.D.

Note that these abbreviations are used only with the full name —*never* Mr. Jones, Jr., for example. (See also par. 8.24.)

14.9   The abbreviation *Esq.* is never used when any other title is given, either before or after the name:

> Anthony Wright, Esq. (*not* Mr. Anthony Wright, Esq. *or* Anthony Wright, Esq., M.A.)

14.10   *Mr., Mrs.,* and *Dr.* are also dropped if another title is used:

> Leroy S. Wells, Ph.D.

14.11   The following list includes many frequently used abbreviations:

SCHOLARLY DEGREES AND TITLES OF RESPECT

A.B., Bachelor of Arts
A.M., Artium Magister (Master of Arts)
B.A., Bachelor of Arts
Bart., Baronet
B.D., Bachelor of Divinity
B.S., Bachelor of Science
D.B., Bachelor of Divinity
D.D., Divinitatis Doctor (Doctor of Divinity)
D.D.S., Doctor of Dental Surgery
Esq., Esquire
J.D., Juris Doctor (Doctor of Law)
J.P., justice of the peace
Kt., Knight
L.H.D., Litterarum Humaniorum Doctor (Doctor of Humanities)

Litt.D., Litterarum Doctor (Doctor of Letters)
LL.B., Legum Baccalaureus (Bachelor of Laws)
LL.D., Legum Doctor (Doctor of Laws)
M.D., Medicinae Doctor (Doctor of Medicine)
M.P., Member of Parliament
Ph.B., Philosophiae Baccalaureus (Bachelor of Philosophy)
Ph.D., Philosophiae Doctor (Doctor of Philosophy)
Ph.G., Graduate in Pharmacy
S.B., Bachelor of Science
S.M., Master of Science
S.T.B., Sacrae Theologiae Baccalaureus (Bachelor of Sacred Theology)

COMPANY NAMES

14.12   The following abbreviations are frequently used as parts of firm names:

> Bro., Bros., Co., Corp., Inc., Ltd., &

In straight text it is best to give a firm name in its full form, but *Inc.* or *Ltd.* is usually dropped:

> A. G. Becker and Company   Aldine Publishing Company

14.13   In footnotes, bibliographies, lists, etc., the abbreviations listed above may be freely (but consistently) used:

> Macmillan Co.   Chicago & North Western Railway
> Ginn & Co.   Great Lakes Dredge & Dock Co.

14.14 In closely set tabular matter further abbreviation is often used (*RR, Ry, Assoc., Mfg.*, etc.).

AGENCIES AND ORGANIZATIONS

14.15 Both in run of text (preferably after one spelled-out use) and in tabular matter, notes, etc., the names of government agencies, network broadcasting companies, associations, fraternal and service organizations, unions, and other groups are often abbreviated. Such abbreviations are usually set in full caps with no periods:

FTC	AFL-CIO	IOOF
AMA	NBC	HOLC
UNESCO	YMCA	WAVES
CORE	NATO	USMC

NAMES WITH "SAINT"

14.16 *Saint* is often abbreviated (*St.*, pl. *SS.*) when it stands before the name of a saint. University of Chicago Press preference is to spell this word out in text, abbreviating only in tabular matter, notes, and where space is at a premium:

> Saint Ignatius Loyola wrote . . .
> Saint Michael the Archangel
> the Church of Saints Constantine and Helena
> Saint Paul's Cathedral

It is further Press preference that *Saint* be omitted before the names of apostles, evangelists, and church fathers:

> Matthew, Mark, Luke, Paul, Peter, Bartholomew, Augustine, Ambrose, Jerome, etc.

When *Saint* forms part of a personal name, the bearer's usage is followed:

> Augustus Saint-Gaudens   Ruth St. Denis
> W. E. St. John Brown

GEOGRAPHICAL TERMS

STATES

14.17 The names of states, territories, and possessions of the United States should always be spelled in full when standing alone. When they follow the name of a city or any other geographical term, it is preferable to spell them out except in lists, tabular matter, footnotes, bibliographies, and indexes. In such instances the first of the two forms illustrated is used; the two-letter form is authorized by the U.S. government for use with ZIP code addresses:

Ala.	AL	Ky.	KY	Okla.	OK
Alaska	AK	La.	LA	Oreg.	OR
Ariz.	AZ	Maine	ME	Pa.	PA
Ark.	AR	Md.	MD	P.R.	PR
Calif.	CA	Mass.	MA	R.I.	RI
C.Z.		Mich.	MI	Samoa	
Colo.	CO	Minn.	MN	S.C.	SC
Conn.	CT	Miss.	MS	S.Dak.	SD
Del.	DE	Mo.	MO	Tenn.	TN
D.C.	DC	Mont.	MT	Tex.	TX
Fla.	FL	Nebr.	NB	Utah	UT
Ga.	GA	Nev.	NV	Vt.	VT
Guam	GU	N.H.	NH	Va.	VA
Hawaii	HI	N.J.	NJ	V.I.	VI
Idaho	ID	N.Mex.	NM	Wash.	WA
Ill.	IL	N.Y.	NY	W.Va.	WV
Ind.	IN	N.C.	NC	Wis.	WI
Iowa	IA	N.Dak.	ND	Wyo.	WY
Kans.	KS	Ohio	OH		

NAMES WITH "FORT," "SAINT," ETC.

14.18   Prefixes of geographic names should not be abbreviated in text:

Fort Wayne	Mount Airy	South Orange
Saint Louis	San Diego	Port Arthur

Where space must be saved, such prefixes (except *San*) may be abbreviated (*Ft., St., Pt., Mt., S.* [*South*], etc.).

NAMES OF COUNTRIES

14.19   The names of countries, except for the Soviet Union, which is often abbreviated *USSR*, are spelled out in text. In tabular and other tight matter they may be abbreviated as necessary:

U.S., U.K. (*or* G.B.), Fr., W.Ger., Swed., It., etc.

14.20   As an adjective, *U.S.* is gaining currency in serious prose, although it is still not used in the most formal writing:

U.S. courts   U.S. dollars   U.S. involvement in Asia

ADDRESSES

14.21   In text (or in letter writing, which this manual does not deal with) addresses should be spelled out, including the following words:

> Avenue, Boulevard, Building, Court, Drive, Lane, Parkway, Place, Road, Square, Street, Terrace; North, South, East, West

Exceptions are the abbreviations

> NW, NE, SE, and SW,

used in some city addresses after the street name. State names are spelled out in addresses. (For the use of figures in addresses see pars. 8.31–32.)

14.22   Again, addresses may be abbreviated in close-set matter, especially state names and the words mentioned above as spelled out in text:

> Ave., Blvd., Bldg., Ct., Dr., La. *or* Ln., Pkwy., Pl., Rd., Sq., St., Terr.; N., S., E., W. (*before street name*)

POINTS OF THE COMPASS

14.23   When abbreviation of the points of the compass is called for (seldom in formal text), the following system may be used:

> *Cardinal:* N, E, S, W; *intercardinal:* NE, SE, SW, NW
> *Others:* NNE, ENE, ESE, SSE, etc.; N by E, NE by N, NE by E, E by N, etc.

LATITUDE AND LONGITUDE

14.24   When standing alone, the words *latitude* and *longitude* are never abbreviated:

> the polar latitudes
> the zone from ten to forty degrees north latitude
> from 10°30′ north latitude to 10°30′ south latitude
> longitude 90° west

14.25   In technical work and in tabulations of coordinates, one of the following systems is used:

> lat. 42°15′30″ N   long. 89°17′45″ W
> lat. 42-15-30 N   long. 89-17-45 W
> lat. 42°15.5′ N   long. 89°17.75′ W
> lat. 42°15.́5 N   long. 89°17.́75 W

In any of these systems, periods may be omitted after *lat.* and *long.*

TIME

14.26 Note that *units* of time are treated in a later section of this chapter (see par. 14.44).

YEARS

14.27 Accepted abbreviations for various systems of chronology are used in text or other matter, normally in small caps. The abbreviations beginning with *A* precede the year number; the others follow it. (For further explanation and examples see par. 8.17.)

A.D., *anno Domini* (in the year of [our] Lord)

A.H., *anno Hegirae* (in the year of the Hegira); *anno Hebraico* (in the Hebrew year)

A.M., *anno mundi* (in the year of the world)

A.S., *anno salutis* (in the year of salvation)

A.U.C., *anno urbis conditae* (year from the building of Rome, 753 B.C.)

B.C., before Christ

B.C.E., before the common era (Jewish)

B.P., before the present

C.E., common era (Jewish)

MONTHS

14.28 Names of the months are always spelled out in text, whether alone or in dates. In chronologies, footnotes, tabular matter, etc., they may be abbreviated according to one of the following systems, preferably the first. The second is used mainly in catalogs of periodical literature.

Jan. Feb. Mar. Apr. May June July Aug. Sept. Oct. Nov. Dec.

Ja F Mr Ap My Je Jl Ag S O N D

DAYS OF THE WEEK

14.29 Like the months, the names of the days of the week should be spelled out in text but may be abbreviated in other situations according to one of the following systems. The second is used only in very closely set catalogs and the like.

Sun. Mon. Tues. Wed. Thurs. Fri. Sat.
Su M Tu W Th F Sa

TIME OF DAY

14.30 The abbreviations indicating which half of the day clock time applies to are normally set in small caps and used in regular text as well as tabular and other such matter:

A.M., *ante meridiem* (before noon)
M., *meridies* (noon)
P.M., *post meridiem* (after noon)

(For the use of figures with these abbreviations see par. 8.20.)

SCHOLARSHIP

14.31 It was scholars who thought up abbreviations in the first place, and it is in the realm of scholarship that abbreviations still flower most vigorously. Some general principles concerning their use are widely agreed upon. (1) Abbreviations to the greatest extent possible should be kept out of the running text except in technical matter;[2] this includes such abbreviations as *etc.*, *e.g.*, and *i.e.* (2) Abbreviations such as these should preferably be confined to parenthetical references. (3) Scholarly abbreviations should mainly be used in footnotes, tabular matter, and other technical copy.

PARTS OF A BOOK

14.32 Abbreviations of the various parts of a book, article, or series of books, in University of Chicago Press style, are lowercased. Unless otherwise indicated, the plural is formed by the addition of *s:*

app., appendix	l., line (*pl.* ll.)[4]
art., article	n., note (*pl.* nn.)
bk., book	no., number
chap., chapter	p., page (*pl.* pp.)
col., column	par., paragraph
div., division	pl., plate
eq., equation (*pl.* eqq.)	pt., part
ex., example (*pl.* exx.)	sec., section
f., and following (*pl.* ff.)[3]	ser., series
fasc., fascicle	st., stanza
fig., figure	supp., supplement
fn., footnote (*pl.* fnn.)	v., verse (*pl.* vv.)
fol., folio	vol., volume

2. The editors of this manual consider it to be technical copy!

3. See pars. 15.109, 18.3.   4. See par. 15.107.

GENERAL ABBREVIATIONS

14.33   The following abbreviations are not confined to scholarly work:

abbr., abbreviated, -ion
abr., abridged; abridgment
anon., anonymous
b., born; brother
bibliog., bibliography, -er, -ical
biog., biography, -er, -ical
biol., biology, -ical, -ist
bk., block
c., chapter (*in law citations only*)
Cia, *Compañia*, Company (*no period*)
Cie, *Compagnie*, Company (*no period*)
comp., compiler; compiled by
cont., continued
copr. *or* ©, copyright
cp., compare
d., daughter; died
dept., department
d.h., *das heißt* (namely)
d.i., *das ist* (that is)
dict., dictionary
dist., district
div., division; divorced
do., ditto (the same)
doz., dozen
Dr. u. Vrl., *Druck und Verlag* (printed and published by)
dram. pers., dramatis personae
ed., edition; edited by; editor (*pl.* eds.)
encyc., encyclopedia
engg., engineering
engr., engineer
esp., especially
gen., genus
geog., geography, -er, -ical
geol., geology, -ical, -ist
geom., geometry, -ical

hdqrs., headquarters
hist., history, -ical, -ian
incl., inclusive
inst., institute, -ion
I.Q., intelligence quotient
L., Left (*in stage directions*)
lit., literally
m., married
marg., margin, -al
math., mathematics, -ical
med., median; medical; medieval; medium
memo, memorandum
mgr., manager
misc., miscellaneous
mus., museum; music, -al
nat., national; natural
n.d., no date
n.p., no place; no publisher
N.S., New Style (*after 1752*)
n.s., new series
O.S., Old Style (*before 1752*)
o.s., old series
path., pathology
perf., perforated
perh., perhaps
pub., publication, -lisher
quart., quarterly
R., Right (*in stage directions*)
s., son
S.A., *Société anonyme*
sociol., sociology
theol., theology, -ian, -ical
trans., translated, -or
treas., treasurer
univ., university
usw., *und so weiter* (and so forth)
yr., your; year

GRAMMAR

14.34   In dictionaries and grammatical works the following abbreviations are useful:

abbr., abbreviation	lit., literally
abl., ablative	loc., locative
acc., accusative	m. *or* masc., masculine
act., active	n., noun
adj., adjective	neg., negative
adv., adverb	neut., neuter
art., article	nom., nominative
compar., comparative	p., past
conj., conjunction; conjugation	part., participle
constr., construction	pass., passive
contr., contraction	perf., perfect
dat., dative	pers., person
def., definite	pl., plural
deriv., derivative	p.p., past participle
dial., dialect	prep., preposition
dim., diminutive	pres., present
f. *or* fem., feminine	pron., pronoun
fr., from	refl., reflexive
fut., future	sing., singular
gen., genitive	subj., subject; subjunctive
ger., gerund	subst., substantive
imper., imperative	superl., superlative
indef., indefinite	syn., synonym
indic., indicative	trans., transitive
infin., infinitive	v., vb., verb
instr., instrumental	v.i., verb intransitive
interj., interjection	voc., vocative
intrans., intransitive	v.t., verb transitive
irreg., irregular	

PHILOLOGY

14.35   In philology and linguistics the following abbreviations are standard. Note the lack of periods after many of these:

AFr., Anglo-French	It., Italian
AN, Anglo-Norman	lang., language
AS, Anglo-Saxon	Lat., Latin
colloq., colloquial, -ly, -ism	ME, Middle English
cons., consonant	MHG, Middle High German
EE, Early English	Mod. E., modern English
Eng., English	obs., obsolete
Fr., French	OE, Old English
Gael., Gaelic	OFr., Old French
Ger., German	OHG, Old High German
Gr., Greek	ON, Old Norse
IE, Indo-European	Sp., Spanish

LATIN ABBREVIATIONS

14.36   Latin has always been the language of abbreviation par excellence. Many of the surviving abbreviations are medieval, and some probably go back to ancient Roman times. A good many of the abbreviations in the following list have lost currency but are included as a means of recognizing them when they turn up in older works of scholarship. In Press style all are set in roman type:

ab. init., *ab initio*, from the beginning
aet., *aetatis*, aged
ad inf., *ad infinitum*, to infinity
ad init., *ad initium*, at the beginning
ad int., *ad interim*, in the meantime
ad lib., *ad libitum*, at will
ad loc., *ad locum*, at the place
bibl., *bibliotheca*, library
ca., *circa*, about, approximately
Cantab., *Cantabrigiensis*, of Cambridge
cf., *confer*, compare
con., *contra*, against
D.V., *Deo volente*, God willing
e.g., *exempli gratia*, for example
et al., *et alii*, and others
etc., *et cetera*, and so forth
et seq., *et sequentes*, and the following
fl., *floruit*, flourished
f.v., *folio verso*, on the back of the page
ibid., *ibidem*, in the same place
id., *idem*, the same
i.e., *id est*, that is
inf., *infra*, below
infra dig., *infra dignitatem*, undignified
in pr., *in principio*, in the beginning
loc. cit., *loco citato*, in the place cited
loq., *loquitur*, he (she) speaks
m.m., *mutatis mutandis*, necessary changes being made
MS (*pl.* MSS), *manuscriptum -a*, manuscript(s)
N.B., *nota bene*, take careful note
non obs., *non obstante*, notwithstanding
non seq., *non sequitur*, it does not follow
n., *natus*, born
ob., *obiit*, died
op. cit., *opere citato*, in the work cited
Oxon., *Oxoniensis*, of Oxford
pass., *passim*, throughout
PPS, *post postscriptum*, a later postscript
pro tem., *pro tempore*, for the time being
prox., *proximo*, next month
PS, *postscriptum*, postscript
Q.E.D., *quod erat demonstrandum*, which was to be demonstrated
q.v., *quod vide*, which see

R., *rex*, king; *regina*, queen
R.I.P., *requiescat in pace*, may he (she) rest in peace
s.a., *sine anno*, without year; *sub anno*, under the year
sc., *scilicet*, namely; *sculpsit*, carved by
s.d., *sine die*, without setting a day for reconvening
sec., *secundum*, according to
s.l., *sine loco*, without place
sup., *supra*, above
s.v., *sub verbo, sub voce*, under the word
ult., *ultimo*, last month
ut sup., *ut supra*, as above
v., *vide*, see
vs., v., *versus*, against
viz., *videlicet*, namely

BIBLE

BOOKS

14.37 In text, references to whole books of the Bible or whole chapters are spelled out:

The opening chapters of Ephesians constitute Paul's most compelling sermon on love.

Jeremiah, chapters 42–44, records the flight of the Jews to Egypt when Jerusalem fell in 586 B.C.

14.38 Exact references to scriptural passages, whether used in text, parenthetically, or in notes, use abbreviations for the names of many of the books of the Bible (see also par. 15.126 for the form of such citations).

AUTHORIZED VERSION

Old Testament

Genesis	Gen.	1 Kings	1 Kings
Exodus	Exod.	2 Kings	2 Kings
Leviticus	Lev.	1 Chronicles	1 Chron.
Numbers	Num.	2 Chronicles	2 Chron.
Deuteronomy	Deut.	Ezra	Ezra
Joshua	Josh.	Nehemiah	Neh.
Judges	Judg.	Esther	Esther
Ruth	Ruth	Job	Job
1 Samuel	1 Sam.	Psalms	Ps. (*pl.* Pss.)
2 Samuel	2 Sam.	Proverbs	Prov.

Ecclesiastes	Eccles.	Obadiah	Obad.
Song of Solomon	Song of Sol.	Jonah	Jon.
Isaiah	Isa.	Micah	Mic.
Jeremiah	Jer.	Nahum	Nah.
Lamentations	Lam.	Habakkuk	Hab.
Ezekiel	Ezek.	Zephaniah	Zeph.
Daniel	Dan.	Haggai	Hag.
Hosea	Hos.	Zechariah	Zech.
Joel	Joel	Malachi	Mal.
Amos	Amos		

Apocrypha

1 Esdras	1 Esd.
2 Esdras	2 Esd.
Tobit	Tob.
Judith	Jth.
The Rest of Esther	Rest of Esther
The Wisdom of Solomon	Wisd. of Sol.
Ecclesiasticus	Ecclus.
Baruch	Bar.
The Song of the Three Holy Children	Song of Three Children
Susanna	Sus.
Bel and the Dragon	Bel and Dragon
Prayer of Manasses	Pr. of Man.
1 Maccabees	1 Macc.
2 Maccabees	2 Macc.

New Testament

Matthew	Matt.	1 Timothy	1 Tim.
Mark	Mark	2 Timothy	2 Tim.
Luke	Luke	Titus	Titus
John	John	Philemon	Philem.
Acts of the Apostles	Acts	Hebrews	Heb.
Romans	Rom.	James	James
1 Corinthians	1 Cor.	1 Peter	1 Pet.
2 Corinthians	2 Cor.	2 Peter	2 Pet.
Galatians	Gal.	1 John	1 John
Ephesians	Eph.	2 John	2 John
Philippians	Phil.	3 John	3 John
Colossians	Col.	Jude	Jude
1 Thessalonians	1 Thess.	Revelation	Rev.
2 Thessalonians	2 Thess.		

In the (Roman Catholic) Douay Version of the Bible, the books and fragments of the Apocrypha are inserted in the Old Testament at appropriate points:

DOUAY VERSION

Genesis	Gen.	Canticle of Canticles	Cant.
Exodus	Exod.	Wisdom	Wisd.
Leviticus	Lev.	Ecclesiasticus	Ecclus.
Numbers	Num.	Isaias	Isa.
Deuteronomy	Deut.	Jeremias	Jer.
Josue	Josue	Lamentations	Lam.
Judges	Judges	Baruch	Bar.
Ruth	Ruth	Ezechiel	Ezech.
1 Kings	1 Kings	Daniel	Dan.
2 Kings	2 Kings	Osee	Osee
3 Kings	3 Kings	Joel	Joel
4 Kings	4 Kings	Amos	Amos
1 Paralipomenon	1 Par.	Abdias	Abdias
2 Paralipomenon	2 Par.	Jonas	Jon.
1 Esdras	1 Esdras	Micheas	Mich.
2 Esdras	2 Esdras	Nahum	Nah.
Tobias	Tob.	Habacuc	Hab.
Judith	Jth.	Sophonias	Soph.
Esther	Esther	Aggeus	Aggeus
Job	Job	Zacharias	Zach.
Psalms	Ps.	Malachias	Mal.
Proverbs	Prov.	1 Machabees	1 Mach.
Ecclesiastes	Eccles.	2 Machabees	2 Mach.

The Douay names and abbreviations for the New Testament books are identical to those of the Authorized Version except for the last book, which is called Apocalypse (*abbr.* Apoc.).

THE NONCANONICAL APOCALYPTIC
BOOKS

Book of Enoch	En.
Sibylline Oracles	Sib. Or.
Psalms of Solomon	Ps. Sol.
Book of Jubilees	Bk. Jub.
Testaments of the Twelve Patriarchs	XII P.
Assumption of Moses	Asmp. M.
Apocalypse of Baruch	Apoc. Bar.

VERSIONS AND SECTIONS OF THE BIBLE

14.39   In the field of biblical scholarship, it is customary to refer to various versions and sections of the Bible by abbreviations:

330

Syr.	Syriac
MT	Masoretic text
LXX	Septuagint
Vulg.	Vulgate
AV	Authorized (King James) Version
DV	Douay Version
RV	Revised Version
RV m	Revised Version, margin
ERV	English Revised Version
ERV m	English Revised Version, margin
ARV	American Revised Version
ARV m	American Revised Version, margin
RSV	Revised Standard Version
EV	English version(s)
AT	American Translation
NEB	New English Bible
JB	Jerusalem Bible
OT	Old Testament
Apoc.	Apocrypha
NT	New Testament

MEASURE

14.40 Abbreviations of units of measure are identical in the singular and plural.

ENGLISH MEASURE

14.41 Abbreviations for the English units of measure find very little use in straight text except for technical work. On the rare occasions in which they are used in scientific copy they are usually set without periods. Like other abbreviations these are most useful in tabular work. (For the use of figures with abbreviations, see pars. 8.7–8.)

14.42 *Length, area, and volume*

LENGTH	AREA
in. *or* ″, inch	sq. in. *or* in.², square inch
ft. *or* ′, foot	sq. ft. *or* ft.², square foot
yd., yard	sq. yd. *or* yd.², square yard
rd., rod	sq. rd. *or* rd.², square rod
mi., mile	sq. mi. *or* mi.², square mile
	a., acre

VOLUME

cu. in. *or* in.³, cubic inch
cu. ft. *or* ft.³, cubic foot
cu. yd. *or* yd.³, cubic yard

14.43 *Weight and capacity.* The complicated English system of measures is further complicated in the case of weight by having three systems to deal with: *avoirdupois* (the common system), *troy* (used mainly by jewelers), and *apothecaries'* measure. There is little chance of confusion between systems, however, and the abbreviations are similar. If need be, an abbreviation can be referred to the appropriate system in this way: *lb. av., lb. t., lb. ap.* Also, the systems of capacity measure used in the United States and in the British Commonwealth differ, but the names of the units are the same, and abbreviations seldom have to be distinguished.

WEIGHT	DRY MEASURE	LIQUID MEASURE
gr., grain	pt., pint	min. *or* ♏, minim
s. *or* ℈, scruple	qt., quart	fl. dr. or f. ʒ, fluid dram
dr. *or* ʒ, dram	pk., peck	fl. oz. *or* f. ℥, fluid ounce
dwt., pennyweight	bu., bushel	gi., gill
oz. *or* ℥, ounce		pt., pint
lb. *or* # (*avdp. only*),		qt., quart
pound		gal., gallon
cwt., hundredweight		bbl., barrel
tn. *or* ton		

14.44 *Time.* Abbreviations for the standard units of time (which themselves are not peculiarly English) are given here. (For other abbreviations concerned with time, see pars. 14.26–30.)

sec., second	h., hr., hour	mo., month
min., minute	d. *or* day	yr., year

INTERNATIONAL MEASURE

14.45 The international metric system of measurement employs three basic units: the *meter*, for length; the *gram*, for mass (weight); and the *liter*, for capacity.[5] Multiples or fractions of the basic units are indicated by prefixes (listed here with their abbreviations):

milli- (.001)	m	deca- (*or* deka-) (10)	dk
centi- (.01)	c	hecto- (100)	h
deci- (.1)	d	kilo- (1,000)	k

For some kinds of work additional prefixes are used:

micro- (10^{-6})	μ	myria- (10^4)	my
nano- (10^{-9})	n	mega- (10^6)	M
pico- (10^{-12})	p	giga- (10^9)	G
femto- (10^{-15})	f	tera- (10^{12})	T
atto- (10^{-18})	a		

5. A variant of the metric system used by physical scientists, the *cgs* system, considers the centimeter, gram, and second (of time) as the basic units.

332

The metric abbreviations are always set without periods in scientific copy and are so treated in general copy with increasing frequency. Here they are given with periods to distinguish the few that have never carried them.

14.46   *Length, area, and volume*

LENGTH		AREA	
mym.	myriameter	mya.	myriare
km.	kilometer	km.^{2}	square kilometer
hm.	hectometer	hm.^{2}	square hectometer
dkm.	decameter	dkm.^{2}	square decameter
m.	meter	m.^{2}	square meter
dm.	decimeter	dm.^{2}	square decimeter
cm.	centimeter	cm.^{2}	square centimeter
mm.	millimeter	mm.^{2}	square millimeter
μ	micron (0.001 mm.)	μ^2	square micron
mμ	millimicron		
		ha.	hectare
		a.	are
		ca.	centiare

VOLUME	
km.^{3}	cubic kilometer
hm.^{3}	cubic hectometer
dkm.^{3}	cubic decameter
m.^{3}	cubic meter
dm.^{3}	cubic decimeter
cm.^{3}	cubic centimeter
mm.^{3}	cubic millimeter
μ^3	cubic micron

14.47   *Weight and capacity*

WEIGHT		CAPACITY	
myg.	myriagram	myl.	myrialiter
kg.	kilogram	kl.	kiloliter
hg.	hectogram	hl.	hectoliter
dkg.	decagram	dkl.	decaliter
g.	gram	l.	liter
dg.	decigram	dl.	deciliter
cg.	centigram	cl.	centiliter
mg.	milligram	ml.	milliliter
μg.	microgram		

14.48   *Time.* The international system employs the same basic units of time as the English system (par. 14.44), but to these are added two small units:

msec., millisecond (1/1,000 second)
μsec., microsecond (1/1,000,000 second)

Forms such as the following are used in astronomy and related fields:

$$3^h30^m \; or \; 3^h\!.5 \qquad 14^h21^m7^s$$

14.49 *Extension of system.* The metric prefixes are applied to many other units, and the abbreviations are similar to those above:

c., cycle	f., farad	w., watt	H., hertz
kc., kilocycle	mf., millifarad	kw., kilowatt	kH., kilohertz
Mc., megacycle	µf., microfarad		MH., megahertz
	pf., picofarad		

PHYSICS AND CHEMISTRY

PHYSICS

14.50 Among the abbreviations frequently met with in works on physics are the following:

A, angstrom unit	ft-lb., foot-pound
a.c., alternating current	H., hertz (cycles per second)
AF, audiofrequency	h.p., horsepower
a-h., ampere-hour	K., Kelvin
amp., ampere	kph, km/hr, kilometers per hour
at. wt., atomic weight	kw., kilowatt
atm., atmosphere	kwh., kilowatt hour
avdp., avoirdupois	mc, millicurie
bar., barometer	mev., Mev., million electron volts
Bé., Baumé	m.p., melting point
bev., Gev., billion electron volts	mph, miles per hour
b.h.p., brake horsepower	neg., negative
b.p., boiling point	psi, pounds per square inch
Btu., British thermal unit	r, roentgen
C., Celsius (centigrade)	R., Réaumur
cc., cubic centimeter	RF, radiofrequency
c.p., candle power	rpm, revolutions per minute
cu., cubic	sp. gr., specific gravity
db., decibel	std., standard
d.c., direct current	temp., temperature
emf, electromotive force	v., volt
ev., electron volt	w., watt
F., Fahrenheit	wt., weight
FM, frequency modulation	

CHEMICAL ELEMENTS

14.51 The symbols for the chemical elements are one- or two-letter abbreviations of the official names of the elements (e.g., lead = *plumbum*). They are used in text as well as in equations, formulas, and tabular matter. These abbreviations are never set with periods. (For the use of mass and molecular numbers with names of the elements, see par. 7.120.)

Actinium	Ac		Mendelevium	Md
Aluminum	Al		Mercury	Hg
Americium	Am		Molybdenum	Mo
Antimony	Sb		Neodymium	Nd
Argon	Ar		Neon	Ne
Arsenic	As		Neptunium	Np
Astatine	At		Nickel	Ni
Barium	Ba		Niobium	Nb
Berkelium	Bk		Nitrogen	N
Beryllium	Be		Osmium	Os
Bismuth	Bi		Oxygen	O
Boron	B		Palladium	Pd
Bromine	Br		Phosphorus	P
Cadmium	Cd		Platinum	Pt
Calcium	Ca		Plutonium	Pu
Californium	Cf		Polonium	Po
Carbon	C		Potassium	K
Cerium	Ce		Praseodymium	Pr
Cesium	Cs		Promethium	Pm
Chlorine	Cl		Protoactinium	Pa
Chromium	Cr		Radium	Ra
Cobalt	Co		Radon	Rn
Columbium	Cb		Rhenium	Re
Copper	Cu		Rhodium	Rh
Curium	Cm		Rubidium	Rb
Dysprosium	Dy		Ruthenium	Ru
Einsteinium	Es		Samarium	Sm
Erbium	Er		Scandium	Sc
Europium	Eu		Selenium	Se
Fermium	Fm		Silicon	Si
Fluorine	F		Silver	Ag
Francium	Fr		Sodium	Na
Gadolinium	Gd		Strontium	Sr
Gallium	Ga		Sulfur	S
Germanium	Ge		Tantalum	Ta
Gold	Au		Technetium	Tc
Hafnium	Hf		Tellurium	Te
Helium	He		Terbium	Tb
Holmium	Ho		Thallium	Tl
Hydrogen	H		Thorium	Th
Indium	In		Thulium	Tm
Iodine	I		Tin	Sn
Iridium	Ir		Titanium	Ti
Iron	Fe		Tungsten	W
Krypton	Kr		Uranium	U
Lanthanum	La		Vanadium	V
Lawrencium	Lr		Xenon	Xe
Lead	Pb		Ytterbium	Yb
Lithium	Li		Yttrium	Y
Lutetium	Lu		Zinc	Zn
Magnesium	Mg		Zirconium	Zr
Manganese	Mn			

COMMERCIAL COPY

14.52   Copy concerned with commerce, especially tabular matter, makes frequent use of many of the abbreviations and symbols given here.

GENERAL ABBREVIATIONS

acct., account
agt., agent
a/v, ad valorem
bal., balance
bbl., barrel
bdl., bundle
bu., bushel
c.l., carload
COD, cash on delivery
cr., credit, -or
cwt., hundredweight

doz., dozen
dr., debit, debtor
f.o.b., free on board
gro., gross
mdse., merchandise
mfg., manufacturing
mfr., manufacturer
pd., paid
pk., peck
std., standard
ult., *ultimo* (last)

SYMBOLS

℔ *or* /, per
#, number; pound
%, percent
c/o, in care of
@, at
$ *or* dol., dollar
c., ct., *or* ¢, cent

©, copyright
Mex.$, Mexican peso
Can$, Canadian dollar
£, pound
A£, Australian pound
s. *or* /, shilling
d., penny, pence

CONSTITUTIONS AND BYLAWS

14.53   In quoting from constitutions, bylaws, and the like, the words *section* and *article* are spelled out the first time they are used and abbreviated thereafter. Caps and small caps are traditionally employed for these words:

SECTION 1. The name of the association . . .
SEC. 2. The object of the association . . .
ARTICLE 234. It shall be the duty of . . .
ART. 235. It shall be the duty of . . .

FOR FURTHER REFERENCE

14.54   No general alphabetical list of abbreviations has been given in this chapter: if it were useful as a reference tool, such a list would have to be too long to print in a general style manual such as this one. An excellent list of this sort, running nearly two hundred close-set, three-column pages is that in *The Complete Dictionary of Abbreviations* by Robert J. Schwartz. Less extensive but still very useful lists are printed in *Webster's New International* and *Collegiate* dictionaries.

336

15   *Notes and Footnotes*

INTRODUCTION

15.1 Almost every work that is neither fiction nor an account based on personal experience relies in part on secondary sources (other publications on the same or related subjects) or primary sources (manuscript collections, archives, contemporary accounts, and so on). A direct quotation from any of these must be identified in a footnote (or in a reference to the bibliographical listing; see par. 16.48). If the quotation comes from a printed source, the original page number(s) must be included in the footnote. Ideas and interpretations attributed to, or facts discovered by, another writer should also be documented.

15.2 Notes documenting the text, and corresponding to reference numbers in the text, are called "footnotes" when they are printed at the foot of the page and "notes" when they are printed at the back of the book or, a rare practice, at the end of a chapter. The University of Chicago Press in most of its publications follows the preference of scholars for footnotes, particularly when the notes contain additional textual material. In a book where the documentation consists entirely of references to sources and is not essential to an understanding of the text, the notes *may* be set at the back of the book, arranged by chapter and provided with running heads giving the page numbers on which the references to the notes appear. (These running heads must, of course, be inserted after all pages have been made up; see par. 1.72.)

LENGTH AND QUANTITY OF FOOTNOTES

15.3 To print notes at the foot of the page presents certain problems in bookmaking not always understood by authors. The makeup man (who rearranges galleys of type into pages) must observe two firm rules: (1) the type pages, including the footnotes, must all be the same length; (2) each footnote must appear on the same page as the reference to it, although the final note on a page may run over to the next page. Thus, a manuscript peppered with footnote references, two or more of which might fall in the last line of text

338

on a page, may well be a printer's nightmare. Similarly, several long footnotes, the references to which fall close together toward the end of a page, present a sometimes insoluble problem in makeup.

15.4 In addition to the printer's problems involved in reproducing heavy documentation there is the matter of appearance. A page of type containing more footnote material than text not only is unpleasant to the eye but may discourage all but the most determined reader. No doubt there will always be some scholarly works where footnotes necessarily outweigh the text, and publisher and printer must understand and cope with the difficulties. In most instances, however, the author, by careful planning, can avoid the pitfalls of excessive documentation without sacrificing his obligations to scholarship.

REDUCING FOOTNOTES

15.5 The author may reconsider a lengthy discursive note amplifying his text. Is *all* of it essential? May some or all of it be included in the text rather than in a note?

15.6 The *number* of footnote references in the text may be cut down by grouping several citations in one note instead of giving each in a separate note. For example, a sentence such as the following requires only one footnote, not five:

> Only when we gather the work of several men—Walter Sutton's explications of some of Whitman's shorter poems; Paul Fussell's careful study of structure in "Cradle"; S. K. Coffman's close readings of "Crossing Brooklyn Ferry" and "Passage to India"; and the attempts of Thomas I. Rountree and John Lovell, dealing with "Song of Myself" and "Passage to India," respectively, to elucidate the strategy in "indirection"—do we begin to get a sense of both the extent and specificity of Whitman's forms.[1]

> 1. Sutton, "The Analysis of Free Verse Form, Illustrated by a Reading of Whitman," *Journal of Aesthetics and Art Criticism* 18 (December 1959): 241–54; Fussell, "Whitman's Curious Warble: Reminiscence and Reconciliation," in *The Presence of Whitman,* ed. R. W. B. Lewis, pp. 28–51; Coffman, " 'Crossing Brooklyn Ferry': Note on the Catalog Technique in Whitman's Poetry," *Modern Philology* 51 (May 1954): 225–32, and "Form and Meaning in Whitman's 'Passage to India,' " *PMLA* 70 (June 1955): 337–49; Rountree, "Whitman's Indirect Expression and Its Application to 'Song of Myself,' " *PMLA* 73 (December 1958): 549–55; and Lovell, "Appreciating Whitman: 'Passage to India,' " *Modern Language Quarterly* 21 (June 1960): 131–41.

15.7 A paragraph containing several short quotations may carry one footnote reference at the end of the paragraph or following the last of the quotations. The corresponding note must, of course, list the citations in order of their appearance in the paragraph. Here, in deference to the reader, the author must be judicious. One footnote listing four references when there are, say, six quotations in the paragraph is unclear. One footnote reference should never apply to material in *more* than one paragraph (except, of course, to a single quotation of more than one paragraph).

15.8 Complicated tabular material, lists, and other entities that are not part of the text should be put in an appendix at the back of the book, not included in footnotes. The footnote may read simply:

> 2. For a list of institutions involved see Appendix A.

RELATION OF FOOTNOTES TO BIBLIOGRAPHY

15.9 In a book containing an alphabetically arranged bibliography, footnotes citing books included in the bibliography should not repeat all the details given in the bibliographical entry. The first reference to a given work in each chapter usually includes the full name of the author, the complete main title of the work (no subtitle), and the relevant page number(s). Subsequent references in the same chapter give a shortened form of the title, as described in pars. 15.35–46 below. A work *not* listed in the bibliography must be cited with full bibliographical details the first time it appears in each chapter, or at least the first time it appears in the book. (It is not necessary to include in the bibliography every work cited in the footnotes, nor, of course, is it desirable that every work listed in the bibliography be cited in the footnotes.)

15.10 In a book containing a discursive bibliographical essay or other nonalphabetical arrangement of sources, footnotes usually include full bibliographical details the first time a work is referred to in each chapter, or at least the first time it appears in the book. When a work is cited repeatedly throughout a book, however, it is wholly unnecessary (indeed pedantic) to repeat bibliographical details in each chapter; the author's name and a short title are sufficient, and sometimes the author's name alone is enough (see par. 15.35).

PLACEMENT OF FOOTNOTE NUMBERS IN TEXT

15.11 Footnote numbers should be typed slightly above the line in the text and should not be enclosed in parentheses or followed by periods or slash marks.

15.12   Footnote numbers should *follow* any punctuation marks (except a dash):

> "This," George Templeton Strong wrote approvingly, "is what our tailors can do."[1]
>
> (In an earlier book he had said quite the opposite.)[2]
>
> This was obvious in the Shotwell series[3]—and it must be remembered that Shotwell was a student of Robinson.

15.13   Wherever possible a footnote number should come at the end of a sentence, or at least at the end of a clause. Numbers set between subject and verb or between other related words in a sentence are distracting to the reader.

15.14   The footnote number *follows* a quotation, whether the quotation is short and run into the text or long and set off from the text in reduced type. The number should not be inserted after the author's name or after matter preceding the quotation.

15.15   The placing of footnote numbers at the end of, or within, a line of display type is to be discouraged. A footnote applicable to an entire chapter, or article, should be unnumbered and should appear on the first page of the chapter, before any numbered notes (see par. 15.21). A reference number that appears at the end of a subhead should be moved to an appropriate spot in the text.

NUMBERING FOOTNOTES

15.16   Footnotes should be numbered consecutively, beginning with 1, throughout a chapter of a book or an article in a journal. Although in scholarly books this sometimes results in three-digit numbers (undesirable particularly from a book designer's point of view), it is far more practical than the old-fashioned system of beginning with 1 on each page. First, manuscript page and printed page are rarely of equal length, and so the footnotes that appear together on a manuscript page will not be those that appear together on the printed page; thus all footnote numbers and references to them must be checked and most of them reset in page proofs, a costly process and one subject to error. Second, any cross-references to notes numbered by page rather than by chapter must include page numbers as well; "see note 2 above" is meaningless when a chapter contains more than one note 2. The latter objection applies also to the (otherwise workable) practice of numbering footnotes up to 9 and starting over.

15.17   The same reference number should not be repeated in the text (in tables this is permissible, often desirable; see par. 12.31). Where a subsequent reference is made to a source cited earlier, the new footnote contains either the shortened form of the citation or, if the citation is exactly the same, a reference to the earlier note:

> 3. See note 1 above.

15.18   If a footnote is added, or deleted, in the typescript, the following numbers throughout the chapter must be changed and any cross-references to footnotes adjusted. Such evidence of negligence as a footnote numbered 4a is unprofessional. If the book is in galleys, any material to be added should be inserted at the end of an existing footnote, or in parentheses in the text. If the book is in page proof, nothing should be added that would alter the length of the type page.

15.19   Footnotes to tables, charts, graphs, or other illustrative material are not numbered with the text footnotes. Symbols or letters, sometimes numbers, indicate notes to such material (see par. 12.30), and the notes are printed below the table, etc., not at the foot of the text page.

DUAL SYSTEM OF NOTES

15.20   It is possible and sometimes helpful in a heavily documented work to separate substantive notes from those largely devoted to citing sources. In such a system the citation notes should be numbered, as footnotes are numbered, and put at the back of the book (see par. 1.61). The substantive notes should be indicated by symbols, beginning with an asterisk for the first note on each page (for sequence of symbols see par. 12.30). If an editor or translator adds his own footnote, it may be numbered with the author's notes or signaled by an asterisk. Such notes should be signed "—ED." or "—TRANS." following the period ending the note.

UNNUMBERED FOOTNOTES

15.21   In anthologies, books of readings, and other collections of previously published material, the source of each chapter, or other division, may be put in an unnumbered footnote and inserted, before any numbered notes, on the first page of that chapter. For material still in copyright from a previous publication the note should include mention of permission from the copyright holder to reprint and a copyright notice (see pars. 2.120–22, 4.28).

342

Source notes

> Reprinted with permission of The Macmillan Company and Geoffrey Bles, Ltd., from *A Guide to Communist Jargon*, by R. N. Carew Hunt. Copyright 1957 by R. N. Carew Hunt.
>
> From Ali al-Giritli, *Tarikh al-sinaᶜa fi Misr* [The history of industry in Egypt] (Cairo, [1952]), pp. 40–51, 97–104, 141–50; reproduced by kind permission of the author.
>
> From Maxim Gorky, *Days with Lenin* (New York, 1932), pp. 3–7, 11–57, by permission of International Publishers Co., Inc.
>
> Reprinted, with changes, from *The Metropolis in Modern Life*, ed. Robert Moore Fisher (New York: Doubleday & Co., 1955), pp. 125–48, by permission of the author and the publisher. Copyright 1955 by The Trustees of Columbia University in the City of New York.
>
> Reprinted from *Geographic Reports*, Series GEO, no. 1, August 1951, pp. 1–3. Washington, D.C.: U.S. Department of Commerce, Bureau of the Census.

Even when the numbered notes are at the back of the book, permission notices should appear on the first page of the chapter. Such notes are, of course, unnecessary when all the permissions are acknowledged together in the front matter of the book.

15.22   In symposia and other multiauthor works the authors of the chapters may be identified in unnumbered footnotes. Such identifying footnotes are unnecessary in books containing a "List of Contributors" in which the authors' affiliations are given. Special acknowledgments may also be given in an unnumbered note.

Notes identifying authors and acknowledging aid

> Philip B. Kurland is Professor of Law, The University of Chicago.
>
> Ramiro Delgado García, M.D., is President, Interdisciplinary Committee, Division of Population Studies, Colombian Association of Medical Schools; Vice-President, Colombian Association for the Scientific Study of Population; and Executive Secretary, University Committee for Population Research, Universidad del Valle, Colombia. This paper represents the personal opinions of the author and has not been officially endorsed by the institutions of which he is a member.
>
> This paper was supported in part by Grant AM-04855, National Institutes of Health, and in part by Grant 5-M01-FR-0047-04, United States Public Health Service.
>
> The author gratefully acknowledges the assistance of Dr. Oscar J. Blunk of the National Cyanide Laboratory in the preparation of this paper.

(For unnumbered notes accompanying scholarly editions and other texts see par. 19.41 and the illustrations therein.)

TYPING FOOTNOTES

15.23   Footnotes accompanying a typescript submitted for publication should be typed consecutively on sheets separate from the text.

They must be *double-spaced*, within each note as well as between notes, and each page, like the text pages, should have generous margins to accommodate necessary editor's and printer's marks. The reason for separating footnotes from text in the typescript is that footnotes are set in a type size smaller than the text type and therefore must be handled separately by the typesetter. Notes to a chapter are headed, for example, "Notes to Chapter 15" and put either at the end of the typescript or at the end of each chapter (preferably the former; see par. 2.9). The pages of notes should be numbered consecutively with the text pages.

15.24 Each note begins with a paragraph indention (in typescript) and ends with a period, whether or not it is a complete sentence. After type has been set and pages are made up, short notes may be grouped together on one line (by the printer), but in typescript each note must begin on a new line.

15.25 The note number should be typed on the line and followed by a period. It used to be common practice to set the number preceding each footnote as a superior number. Modern practice increasingly tends toward setting the number on the line, in the same type size as the footnote. Numbers set on the line are easier to read and less expensive to set.

ARRANGEMENT OF ITEMS

15.26 Like the series of titles given in note 1 (par. 15.6), several references documenting a single fact in the text should be separated by semicolons, the last one followed by a period. Wherever possible, all items in a footnote should be run together in a single paragraph, as in note 1 above.

15.27 When a footnote contains not only the source of a quotation in the text but other related material as well, the source of the quotation comes first. The following material may start a new sentence or may be separated from the first item by a semicolon, depending on the nature of the material.

15.28 When a footnote includes a quotation, or other matter to be documented, the source is given in parentheses, after the quotation and before the final period.

4. One estimate of the size of the reading public at this time was that of Sydney Smith: "Readers are fourfold in number compared with what they were before the beginning of the French war. . . . There are four or five hundred thousand readers more than there were thirty years ago, among the lower orders" (*Letters*, ed. Nowell C. Smith [New York: Oxford University Press, 1953], 1:341, 343).

An acceptable alternative is to give the source following the quotation without parentheses; the quotation then carries terminal punctuation, and the source citation ends with a period:

> . . . among the lower orders." *Letters*, ed. Nowell C. Smith (New York: Oxford University Press, 1953), 1:341, 343.

Consistency in this matter should be observed throughout a book.

"SEE ALSO" AND "CF."

15.29 Authors should keep in mind the distinction between *see* or *see also* and *cf.* (*confer*, "compare"). Cf. is not italicized (except in legal style), and only when it begins a sentence (as here) or a note is it capitalized.

THE FORM OF A NOTE

15.30 The remainder of this chapter is devoted to the form in which references should be arranged in footnotes, or notes. No one manual can hope to protect author and editor from every thorn encountered in the thicket of scholarly documentation. An attempt is made here to provide examples of the most frequently used kinds of sources, together with a sprinkling of uncommon ones. A few guiding principles, kept firmly in mind by an author and his editor, may elucidate the reasoning behind the following strictures and help solve specific problems not covered in these pages. Although it is hoped that authors who use footnotes will follow the style outlined in this chapter, logical variations are permissible. An author who wishes to deviate from the style, however, should make his preferences known to his publisher, before the manuscript has been edited for publication (see par. 2.81).

GENERAL RULES

15.31 A citation should enable the interested reader to find the source with a minimum of effort. Thus, a reference to a book should begin with the element under which the reader may expect to find it in a library catalog, usually the name of the author or of a government agency or corporate body standing in place of an author. The volume number (if any) and date should be given for any periodical publication. The depository, collection, and item number, if any, are essential for unpublished material.

15.32 The dates of publication of printed sources must be included, and dates of manuscript material where possible. The classics, the Bible, commonly used reference books, and other self-evident sources are, of course, exempt from this rule, except that the edition should be specified when page references are given.

15.33 All references to a particular source must be consistent. For example, to specify the volume of a periodical in one note and give only the date in another reference to it is unacceptable.

FULL REFERENCES

15.34 Give each source in full the first time it appears in each chapter of a book (but see pars. 15.9–10). Items to be included in full references are listed below in the order in which they should be given. Amplification of the form for each item is provided in the following pages. References to various kinds of sources that do not conform to these general rules are illustrated in pars. 15.130–40.

BOOK

Author's full name
Complete title of the book
Editor, compiler, or translator, if any
Name of series in which book appears, if any, and volume or number in the series
Edition, if other than the first
Number of volumes
Facts of publication—city where published, publisher, date of publication
Volume number, if any
Page number(s) of the particular citation

ARTICLE IN A PERIODICAL

Author's full name
Title of the article
Name of the periodical
Volume (and number) of the periodical
Date of the volume or of the issue
Page number(s) of the particular citation

UNPUBLISHED MATERIAL

Title of document, if any, and date
Folio number (or box number or other identifying specific)
Name of collection
Depository, and city where it is located

SHORTENED REFERENCES

15.35 After the first reference to a particular work in each chapter, all subsequent references in the same chapter to that work should be shortened. There are two acceptable ways to shorten references to books and articles. The first is the short-title form described in the following paragraphs. The second, commonly used in scholarly journals, is to omit the title of the work and give only the last name of the author followed by a comma and the page number of the reference; when more than one work by the same author has been cited, a short title is necessary, as well as the author's last name.

15.36 A shortened reference to a *book* should omit the facts of publication, series title, edition (unless more than one edition has been cited), and number of volumes. It should include only the last name of the author and the short title of the book, in italics, followed by the page number of the reference.

15.37 A shortened reference to an article in a periodical should omit the name of the periodical, volume number, and date. It should include only the last name of the author and the short title of the article and the page number of the reference.

15.38 A shortened reference to a manuscript collection should omit the name and location of the depository, unless more than one collection with the same name has been cited; where this is true, the depository must be given but the location of it is omitted.

15.39 *Last name of the author.* Only the last name of the author, or of the editor if given first in the full reference, is needed. First names or initials should be included only where two or more authors with the same last name have been cited. "Ed.," "trans.," and "comp." following a name in the first reference may be omitted from subsequent references. If a work has more than one author, the last name of each should be given. Coauthors with the same last name should appear as, for example, Jewkes and Jewkes (not as Jewkes or The Jewkeses), even though the first reference lists them as John and Sylvia Jewkes.

15.40 *Short title.* The short title contains the key word or words from the main title of the work (book or article). Abbreviations or words from the subtitle should not be included unless this fact is noted in the first reference (see par. 15.44). The order of words in the title should not be changed; for example, *Politics in the*

Twentieth Century should not be shortened to *Twentieth-Century Politics.* In foreign language titles one must be careful not to omit a word that governs the case ending of a word included in the shortened title. In general, titles of from two to five words should not be shortened:

Deep South
North of Slavery
Elizabethan and Metaphysical Imagery

For many titles the omission of the initial "The" or "A" is sufficient:

Rise of the West

Examples of shortened titles

FULL MAIN TITLE	SHORT TITLE
Health Progress in the United States, 1900–1960	*Health Progress*
The Culture of Ancient Egypt	*Ancient Egypt*
A Compilation of the Messages and Papers of the Presidents, 1789–1897	*Papers of the Presidents*
Kriegstagebuch des Oberkommandos der Wehrmacht, 1940–1945	*Kriegstagebuch*
"A Brief Account of the Reconstruction of Aristotle's *Protrepticus*"	"Aristotle's *Protrepticus*"

15.41 *"Op. cit." and "loc. cit."* Op. cit. (*opere citato*, "in the work cited") and loc. cit. (*loco citato*, "in the place cited") have long served as space savers in scholarly footnotes. Both, used with the author's last name, stand in place of the title of a work cited earlier in the chapter or article. But consider, for example, the frustration of the assiduous reader on meeting "Wells, op. cit. p. 10" in note 95 and finding the title of the work by Wells back in note 2, or, in a carelessly edited book, finding *two* works by Wells cited earlier, or none at all. To save the reader's nerves, not to mention the editor's, and for greater clarity, the University of Chicago Press has discarded both op. cit. and loc. cit. and in place of them has adopted the short-title form described above.

15.42 *"Ibid."* Ibid. (*ibidem*, "the same") is used to refer to a single work cited in the note immediately preceding. It should not be used if more than one work is given in the preceding note. Ibid. takes the place of the author's name, the title of the work, and as much of the succeeding material as is identical. The author's name is never used with ibid., nor is a title. Ibid. may also be used in place of the name of a journal or book of essays in successive references to the same journal or book within one footnote.

Examples of full and shortened references

> 5. John P. Roche, *The Quest for the Dream: The Development of Civil Rights and Human Relations in Modern America* (New York: Macmillan Co., 1963), pp. 204–6.

> 6. J. H. Hexter, "The Loom of Language and the Fabric of Imperatives: The Case of *Il Principe* and *Utopia*," *American Historical Review* 69 (1964): 945–68.

> 7. Stevens to Sumner, 26 August 1865, Charles Sumner Papers, Harvard College Library, Cambridge, Mass.

> 8. James Losh, *The Diaries and Correspondence of James Losh*, ed. Edward Hughes, 2 vols., Publication of the Surtees Society, vols. 171, 172 (Durham, England: Andrews & Co. for the Society, 1962–63), 2:200–212.

> 9. Roche, *Quest for the Dream*, p. 175.

> 10. Hexter, "Loom of Language," p. 949.

> 11. Stearns to Sumner, 28 August 1865, Sumner Papers.

> 12. Losh, *Diaries and Correspondence*, 1:150.

> 13. Ibid., 2:175.

> 14. Ibid., p. 176. [The same volume number as the preceding note.]

> 15. Ibid. [The same page as the preceding note.]

15.43 "*Idem.*" Idem ("the same," sometimes abbreviated as id.) may be used in place of an author's name in successive references within one note to several works by the same person. It is not used for titles, except in legal references.

> 16. Arthur I. Gates, "Vocabulary Control in Basal Reading Material," *Reading Teacher* 15 (November 1961): 81–85; idem, "The Word Recognition Ability and the Reading Vocabulary of Second- and Third-Grade Children," ibid. 15 (May 1962): 443–48.

15.44 *Abbreviations.* If a work is cited frequently throughout a chapter or a book, its title may be abbreviated after its first appearance. The full title should be given the first time it is cited, followed by an indication in parentheses of the abbreviation to be used for it thereafter. An abbreviated title differs from a shortened title in that words may be abbreviated and the order changed.

> 17. Nathaniel B. Shurtleff, ed., *Records of the Governor and Company of the Massachusetts Bay in New England (1628–86)*, 5 vols. (Boston, 1853–54), 1:126 (hereafter cited as *Mass. Records*).

The parenthetical note giving the abbreviation may be placed directly after the title of the work, but it is easier to find if it comes at the end of the reference.

15.45   When many sources are cited repeatedly—journals, series, manuscript collections, and the like—abbreviations may be alphabetically arranged in a list of abbreviations and printed either in the front matter of the book or as an appendix. It is often helpful to refer the reader to such a list following the first use of an abbreviation.

15.46   In biographies, editorial notes to published correspondence, and other works where a personal name appears frequently, initials, without periods, may be used in place of a name (e.g., JM for James Madison in all notes to *The Papers of James Madison*, or EBB and RB in a work on the Brownings).

SPECIFIC RECOMMENDATIONS

15.47   Most of the recommendations in paragraphs 15.48–128 are applicable to bibliographies as well as to footnotes. The chief differences between the two are that in an alphabetical bibliography the author's name is reversed and punctuation between author's name, title of the work, and the facts of publication consists of periods rather than commas or parentheses.

NAME OF THE "AUTHOR"

15.48   In footnotes the name of the author (or translator, editor, compiler) is given *first name first* and generally followed by a comma. (The last name is given first only in alphabetically arranged material, such as a bibliography or an index.)

15.49   The name should be spelled out as it appears on the title page of the book being cited. Degrees or affiliations following the name should be omitted.

15.50   If only the author's initials are given on the title page but his first name is known, the first name may be supplied, or that part of it not on the title page *may* be enclosed in square brackets: G[eoffrey] A. Cranfield. But if he is a well-known author who always uses only his initials, his preference should be respected and his full name not supplied: T. S. Eliot, J. B. S. Haldane, O. Henry [pseud.], e. e. cummings, F. R. Leavis, C. S. Lewis, G. E. Moore, J. D. Salinger, C. P. Snow, J. M. Synge, A. J. P. Taylor, C. V. Wedgwood, H. G. Wells.

15.51   One initial preceding the surname is inadequate. In a voluminous library catalog many given names are suggested by, for example, the letter "J." If the title page of the book being cited carries only one initial before the last name of an author, it is usually possible to determine the full name by consulting library cards or biographical reference books. Only when the full name cannot be found should the initial alone appear.

15.52 If no author's name appears on the title page but the author is known, the name should be placed in brackets.

> 18. [Antonio de Espejo], *New Mexico: otherwise the voiage of Anthony of Espeio . . . translated out of the Spanish copie printed first at Madreel* [Madrid], *1586, and afterward at Paris, in the same yeare* (London, 1587).

If a work is assumed to be by a specific author, but the fact of authorship cannot be reliably established, the name, followed immediately by a question mark, may be given in brackets.

15.53 If there is no ascertainable "author" (editor, compiler, or other), the reference begins with the title of the work. The use of "Anonymous" or "Anon." should be avoided.

15.54 *Two authors*

> 19. John P. Dean and Alex Rosen, *A Manual of Intergroup Relations* (Chicago: University of Chicago Press, 1955), p. 102.

15.55 *Three authors*

> 20. Richard K. Beardsley, John W. Hall, and Robert E. Ward, *Village Japan* (Chicago: University of Chicago Press, 1959), pp. 303–4.

15.56 *More than three authors.* The name of the first author is used, followed by "et al." (*et alii*, "and others"). No comma should intervene between the author's name and et al., and no more than one author's name should be used.

> 21. Jaroslav Pelikan et al., *Religion and the University*, York University Invitation Lecture Series (Toronto: University of Toronto Press, 1964), p. 109.

(In a bibliography, however, it is customary to give all the authors' names; see par. 16.15.)

15.57 *Omission of author's name.* If an author's full name is given in the text near the reference to, or near a quotation from, his work, the name may be omitted in the footnote. When only the last name is given in the text, the full name should be included in the footnote, if it is the first reference to the work in a chapter. As a convenience to readers, however, the full name, even when it appears in the text, may be repeated in the footnote when the work is to be cited in shortened form in subsequent references.

15.58   *Names of editors, compilers, translators.* If an editor's name is given on the title page of a book, and the book has no single author, the editor's name appears first in the footnote, followed by a comma and "ed." or, for more than one editor, "eds."

> 22. H. H. Rowley, ed., *The Old Testament and Modern Study* (Oxford: Clarendon Press, 1951), p. 50.
>
> 23. Urban T. Holmes and Kenneth R. Scholberg, eds., *French and Provençal Lexicography* (Columbus: Ohio State University Press, 1964), p. 138.
>
> 24. Alexander Dallin et al., eds., *Diversity in International Communism: A Documentary Record, 1961–63* (New York: Columbia University Press, 1963), p. 24.

Names of compilers or translators given on the title page of a book are treated in like manner.

> 25. William Harlin McBurney, comp., *A Check List of English Prose Fiction, 1700–1739* (Cambridge: Harvard University Press, 1960), p. 76.
>
> 26. Maynard A. Amerine and Louise B. Wheeler, comps., *A Check List of Books and Pamphlets on Grapes and Wine and Related Subjects, 1938–1948* (Berkeley and Los Angeles: University of California Press, 1951), p. 121.
>
> 27. Jen Yu Wang and Gerald L. Berger, eds. and comps., *Bibliography of Agricultural Meteorology* (Madison: University of Wisconsin Press, 1962), p. 520.
>
> 28. Boleslaw Szczesniak, ed. and trans., *The Russian Revolution and Religion, 1917–1925* (Notre Dame, Ind.: University of Notre Dame Press, 1959), p. 175.
>
> 29. Mark Graubard, trans., and John Parker, ed., *Tidings out of Brazil* (Minneapolis: University of Minnesota Press, 1957), p. 13.

15.59   In a reference to an edited or translated work that carries an author's name on the title page, the name of the editor or translator follows the title of the work and is preceded by "ed." (here meaning "edited by," and thus never "eds.") or "trans." (meaning "translated by").

> 30. Marc Bloch, *Feudal Society*, trans. L. A. Manyon (Chicago: University of Chicago Press, 1961), p. 69.
>
> 31. James Madison, *The Papers of James Madison*, ed. William T. Hutchinson and William M. E. Rachal (Chicago: University of Chicago Press, 1962–), 1:49.
>
> 32. Edmund Burke, *The Correspondence of Edmund Burke*, ed. Thomas W. Copeland (Cambridge: At the University Press; Chicago: University of Chicago Press, 1958–), vol. 3, *July 1774–June 1778*, ed. George H. Guttridge (1961).

The last is an example of a multivolume work with a general editor—Professor Copeland—and individual editors for each volume. The editor's name follows that part of the work for which he is responsible.

352

15.60 In a work where the editor or the translator is more important to the discussion than the original author, the editor's (translator's) name is given first. For example, in a work on Eliot:

> 33. T. S. Eliot, ed., *Literary Essays*, by Ezra Pound (New York: New Directions, 1953), p. 10.

TITLES

15.61 The title of a *book* (or a pamphlet or any other single publication) should be given exactly as it appears on the title page, except that:

a) It is printed in italics (underlined in the typescript).

b) Capitalization should be altered to conform to Press style (see par. 7.123; for capitalization of foreign language titles see chapter 9).

c) Punctuation may be added where necessary. A colon (not a semicolon, comma, or dash) separates the main title from the subtitle. The initial letter of the word following the colon is capitalized.

15.62 Titles of other works appearing in an italicized title are enclosed in quotation marks:

> 34. A. Rey, *Skelton's Satirical Poems in Their Relation to Lydgate's "Order of Fools," "Cock Lorell's Bote," and Barclay's "Ship of Fools"* (Bern: K. J. Wyss, 1899), pp. 23–30.

15.63 A translation of a foreign language title is enclosed in brackets and set in roman type, without quotation marks. Only the first word and proper nouns or adjectives are capitalized.

> 35. N. Ia. Ivanov, *Kornilovshchina i ee razgrom: Iz istorii bor'by s kontrrevoliutsiei v 1917 g.* [The Kornilov affair and its liquidation: the history of the struggle by the counterrevolutionaries in 1917] (Leningrad: Izdatel'stvo Leningradskogo universiteta, 1965).
>
> 36. A. N. Shcherbatov and Sergei Stroganov, *Kniga ob arabskoi loshadi* [Book on the Arabian horse] (St. Petersburg, 1909).

15.64 Long titles characteristic of books published in earlier centuries are italicized but otherwise follow the original exactly, in punctuation and capitalization (except whole words in capital letters, which should be given an initial capital only) as well as in spelling. These may sometimes be shortened, even in the first reference, and ellipsis dots (three) used to indicate that the title of the original is longer.

> 37. "Ut Pictura Poesis, by Mr. Nourse, late of All-Souls College, Oxon, 1741," in *A Collection of Poems . . . by Several Hands* (London, 1758), p. 95.

15.65   The title of a *periodical publication* (journal, magazine, news-paper) is given in italics and capitalized according to the style used for book titles. Note that the titles of foreign journals, like the titles of foreign books, are capitalized according to rules different from those governing English titles (see chap. 9). An initial "The" is usually omitted, even though it appears on the cover, title page, or masthead of the publication (*American Historical Review; New York Times*).

15.66   Such publications as the *Proceedings of the American Philo-sophical Society* include the name of the organization as part of the title (rather than American Philosophical Society, *Proceedings*).

15.67   In references to English language daily newspapers published in the United States, the name of the city of publication is italicized as part of the title, whether or not it appears officially as such: *St. Louis Post-Dispatch; St. Paul Pioneer Press; San Francisco Chronicle.* (It is of course preferable to cite newspaper titles accurately—that is, to italicize a city name only when it is part of the official title—but few authors are meticulous about the matter, and the editor should not be expected to check every citation to a newspaper in a heavily documented book. But the rare author who consistently makes the distinction in his citations should be permitted to keep it.) The city name is not given with such titles as *Wall Street Journal, Christian Science Monitor, National Intelligencer,* or with titles containing a state name or other geo-graphical designation (*Arkansas Gazette*). When the city may not be widely known or when it might be confused with another of the same name, the abbreviation of the state name may be given in parentheses: *Oneida* (N.Y.) *Observer; Springfield* (Mass.) *Re-publican.* In citing foreign dailies the city of publication may be given in parentheses after the title if it does not form part of the title: the *Times* (London), *L'aurore* (Paris); but *Manchester Guard-ian, Frankfurter Zeitung.* Foreign language dailies published in the United States are similarly cited.

15.68   The title of an *article* in a periodical, a *chapter* or other part of a book, and any *unpublished work*, such as a dissertation, a paper read at a meeting, or a manuscript in a collection, is given in roman type and enclosed in quotation marks. Titles of material issued in mimeographed or other copy-machine form are also quoted. As in book titles, capitalization and punctuation should conform to Press style, and original spelling should be retained.

38. Alan Grob, "Tennyson's *The Lotos Eaters:* Two Versions of Art," *Modern Philology* 62 (1964): 119.

39. W. T. de Bary, "Chinese Despotism and the Confucian Ideal: A Seventeenth-Century View," in *Chinese Thought and Institutions*, ed. John K. Fairbank (Chicago: University of Chicago Press, 1957), pp. 163–203.

40. Pedro Carrasco, "Kinship and Territorial Groups in Pre-Spanish Guatemala" (Paper delivered at the Fifty-seventh Annual Meeting of the American Anthropological Association, Washington, D.C., November 20, 1958), p. 10.

41. René Millon, "When Money Grew on Trees" (Ph.D. diss., Columbia University, 1955), p. 25. [Note that "unpublished" is not necessary, since if the dissertation were published its title would be italicized and, usually, the publisher given.]

42. United States Educational Foundation for Egypt, "Annual Program Proposal, 1952–53," mimeographed (Washington, D.C.: Department of State, 1951), p. 28.

43. "Minutes of the Committee for Improving the Condition of Free Blacks, Pennsylvania Abolition Society, 1790–1803," Papers of the Pennsylvania Society for the Abolition of Slavery, Historical Society of Pennsylvania, Philadelphia, Pa.

15.69   Titles of works issued in microfilm are given in italics:

44. Abraham Tauber's *Spelling Reform in the United States* (Ann Arbor, Mich.: University Microfilms, 1958) is of great value.

15.70   Names of manuscript collections and depositories are given in roman type, without quotation marks. Designations that are not actual titles of manuscripts are also given without quotation marks, for example, the names of letter writers and such terms as *telegram, memorandum, diary*. The word *letter* is not used in citing correspondence; the names of the correspondents and the date of the communication are sufficient. First names of correspondents need be given only if they have not been mentioned in the text or where confusion might result from their omission.

45. Diary of Lewis Tappan, 23 February 1836 to 29 August 1838, Tappan Papers, Library of Congress, Washington, D.C.

46. Owen to Agassiz, 9 December 1857, Louis Agassiz Papers, Houghton Library, Harvard University, Cambridge, Mass.

47. Louis Agassiz, "Report to the Committee of Overseers . . ." [28 December 1859], Overseers Reports, Professional Series, vol. 2, Harvard University Archives, Cambridge, Mass.

15.71   *Series title.* If a book is part of a series, that fact is usually noted in any full reference to the work. If a series title is unnecessary as a finding tool and if, in the author's opinion, it adds nothing to the reader's information on the particular source, it may be omitted. A *series* of publications should be distinguished from a *multivolume* work or a *periodical*. A multivolume work, first, is a work on one subject that occupies two or more volumes. In addition to the title of the whole work, each volume may have its own title, and the volumes may be written all by the same author or each by a different author. The work has a beginning, a middle, and an end; there are only so many volumes in it. In reference to such works the general title is given in italics and so is the title of each volume (see n. 32).

15.72 A periodical is sometimes confused with a series, especially when a single issue, or supplement, is devoted to one complete work. The title of a periodical—annual, semiannual, bimonthly, and so on—should be italicized whether the issue being cited consists of one work (whose title is also italicized; see n. 48) or of a selection of shorter works (see n. 38).

> 48. Helen C. Palmatary, *The Pottery of Marajó Island, Brazil, Transactions of the American Philosophical Society*, n.s., vol. 39, pt. 3 (Philadelphia, 1950).

15.73 A *series* is an open-ended group of individual volumes, or pamphlets, usually on related subjects but not intended as a unified whole. The title of the series may reflect the publishing agency (Smithsonian Miscellaneous Collections), the general subject of the series (Nature of Human Society), or both (Chicago History of American Civilization; Logan Museum Publications in Anthropology).

15.74 A series title in a footnote is in roman type, is capitalized as a title, and is not enclosed in quotation marks or parentheses. It follows the italicized title of the book or pamphlet and is followed by the volume or number of the publication in the series. The name of the series editor is usually omitted.

15.75 Many series do not number their publications. Others use both volume numbers and subsidiary numbers. Any number given with a series is an essential part of the reference.

15.76 If the publisher's name appears in the series title, it is not repeated in the facts of publication.

15.77 Ambiguous series titles should be avoided (Current Report no. 4; Bulletin no. 143; Research Records, no. 4; Anthropological Series, no. 10); such titles should be preceded by the name of the responsible agency.

> 49. Edmund S. Morgan, *The Birth of the Republic, 1763–89*, Chicago History of American Civilization (Chicago: University of Chicago Press, 1956), p. 10.

50. Julian H. Steward, ed., *Handbook of South American Indians*, Smithsonian Institution, Bureau of American Ethnology Bulletin no. 143 (Washington, D.C., 1949), p. 10.

51. Wendell C. Bennett, ed., *A Reappraisal of Peruvian Archaeology*, Society for American Archaeology Memoir no. 4 (Menasha, Wis., 1948), p. 10.

52. *Directorio de librerías y casas editoriales en America latina*, 4th ed., Pan American Union, Bibliographic Series, no. 2, pt. 3 (Washington, D.C., 1958).

53. Robert Wauchope, *A Tentative Sequence of Pre-Classic Ceramics in Middle America*, Middle American Research Records, vol. 1, no. 14 (New Orleans: Tulane University, 1950), p. 10.

54. Arthur H. R. Fairchild, *Shakespeare and the Arts of Design*, University of Missouri Studies, vol. 12 (Columbia, 1937), pp. 104, 109.

55. C. N. Stavron, *Whitman and Nietzsche: A Comparative Study of Their Thought*, University of North Carolina Studies in the Germanic Languages and Literature, no. 48 (Chapel Hill, 1964), p. 139.

15.78 *Edition.* References generally should be to a hardbound edition of a book. When an edition other than the first is used, the number of the edition and the date of its publication should be given in the reference, because the pagination as well as some of the content may differ from that of the first edition. The number of the edition follows the title of the work and is preceded by a comma.

56. John W. Hazard, *The Soviet System of Government*, 4th ed. rev. (Chicago: University of Chicago Press, 1968), p. 25.

15.79 The number of the edition may be found sometimes on the title page of the book, and always on the copyright page. (See also par. 15.102.) A new edition is sometimes called Revised Edition (no number); Second Edition, Revised and Enlarged; or other variants. These should be abbreviated, and placed after the title and before the facts of publication, as "rev. ed.," "2d ed., rev. and enl." Such terms and their abbreviations should be in English, even though the book is in a foreign language.

57. Robert E. Spiller et al., eds., *Literary History of the United States*, rev. ed. in 1 vol. (New York: Macmillan Co., 1953), p. 72.

15.80 Modern editions of the classics must be specified when page numbers are given (see par. 15.130).

58. Horace, *Satires, Epistles, and Ars poetica*, Loeb Classical Library (London, 1932), p. xxvii.

59. John Dryden, *Dramatic Essays*, Everyman's Library (1906), pp. 42, 45.

15.81   *Reprint editions.* To supply libraries in new colleges and universities and to replace worn or lost copies in older libraries, publishers are now reproducing, by offset or other processes, many standard works of scholarship long out of print, in hardbound reprint editions. Although the pagination of such a reprint usually remains the same as that of the original work, the use of the reprint should be noted, as well as the date of the original publication. (Note that a *reprint edition* differs from a *new impression*, or new printing issued by a publisher to keep a book in print after an earlier printing has been sold out; see par. 15.103.)

> 60. Gunnar Myrdal, *Population: A Problem for Democracy* (1940; reprint ed., Gloucester, Mass.: Peter Smith, 1956), p. 15.

Place and publisher of the reprint edition could be omitted from this citation, or, if it would serve a useful purpose, the name of the original publisher (Harvard University Press) might also be given.

15.82   *Paperback editions.* To make scholarly works readily available to students and to a wider public generally, many publishers issue titles—either reproduced from hardbound editions or printed simultaneously with hardbound editions—in quality paperback series, such as the Phoenix Books of the University of Chicago Press. Paperback editions are sometimes abridged or otherwise changed from the original edition and so the pagination may not be the same. Also, a scholar seeking a cited source in a library will usually find only the hardbound edition. For these reasons it is recommended that a hardbound edition be used in scholarly citations (see par. 15.78). If a paperback edition is cited, the fact should be noted. (In books intended primarily for students it is useful to indicate the availability in paperback of works mentioned.)

> 61. Leon F. Litwack, *North of Slavery: The Negro in the Free States, 1790–1860* (Chicago: University of Chicago Press, Phoenix Books, 1965), pp. 53–54.

15.83   *Number of volumes.* For a work of more than one volume (except well-known reference tools, of course) it is desirable to give the total number of volumes. This information follows the title of the work, or the number of the edition if one is given, and is preceded by a comma.

> 62. Ernest Baker, *History of the English Novel*, 10 vols. (New York: Barnes & Noble, 1924–39), 5:62.

If a work is still in progress, the number of volumes so far published *may* be given, but this is generally undesirable because the information becomes obsolete in a year or two.

> 63. Thomas Jefferson, *Papers of Thomas Jefferson*, ed. Julian P. Boyd et al., 17 vols. to date (Princeton: Princeton University Press, 1950–), 10:32.

FACTS OF PUBLICATION

15.84 The facts of publication include the place (city), the publisher, and the date. These are enclosed in parentheses. No comma precedes the opening parenthesis. A colon follows the place name, and a comma follows the publisher's name.

15.85 The facts of publication should be given in full references to printed books and pamphlets and to material issued in mimeographed or other copy-machine form. They are omitted in citing well-known reference sources (see par. 15.125), classical works, and similar material where designations other than page numbers are used.

15.86 References to periodical publications carry only the date of the volume or issue being cited, not the publisher's name or (except in rare instances) the place of publication.

15.87 *Place.* The name of the city where the publisher's main editorial offices are located is usually sufficient: (New York: Macmillan Co., 1965). (For punctuation with city and date alone see par. 15.100.)

15.88 If the title page of the book cited lists two cities with the publisher's name, it is permissible, but not necessary, to use both: (Chicago and London: University of Chicago Press, 1965). (If "London" does not appear on the title page of the book being cited, it must not be given in the reference.) The University of California Press prefers the use of "Berkeley and Los Angeles" in references to its publications.

15.89 If the place of publication is not widely known, the abbreviation of the state name should follow it: (Menasha, Wis.: Banta Publishing Co., 1965); (Englewood Cliffs, N.J.: Prentice-Hall, 1965).

15.90 The distinction between Cambridge, England, and Cambridge, Mass., should be made. In the absence of contrary indications—such as inclusion of the state name or mention of Harvard University—it will be assumed that the English city is meant: it should never be necessary to specify "Cambridge, England." Thus the following are all acceptable. For the English Cambridge: (Cambridge, 1967) or (Cambridge: At the University Press, 1967). For the Massachusetts Cambridge: (Cambridge, Mass.: Harvard University Press, 1967) or (Cambridge: Harvard University Press, 1967).

15.91 Regardless of the title page, the English name, where there is one, should be substituted for the foreign city name in the facts of publication: Vienna (Wien), Cologne (Köln), Turin (Torino), Rome (Roma), Milan (Milano), Munich (München), Brunswick (Braunschweig), Prague (Praha), The Hague ('s Gravenhage).

15.92 Where neither place of publication nor publisher appears on the title page, "n.p." (no place) takes the place of both: (n.p., 1840).

15.93 *Publisher.* The publisher's name may be given either in full, as printed on the title page of the book being cited, or in an acceptable abbreviated form. An initial "The" is omitted even when the full name is given. (Correct spelling of American publishers' names, and acceptable abbreviated forms, are listed in *Books in Print*, published annually by R. R. Bowker Co., and, for Great Britain, in *British Books in Print: The Reference Catalogue of Current Literature*, published by J. Whitaker & Sons and R. R. Bowker Co.) "Inc.," "Ltd.," and "S.A." are generally omitted after the publisher's name. The use of either long or short forms must be consistent throughout a book or journal.

15.94 Punctuation and spelling of publishers' names must be accurate. For example, there is no comma in Houghton Mifflin Co.; there is a comma in both Little, Brown & Co. and the former Harcourt, Brace & Co. There is no capital "M" in the middle of Macmillan; the London firm is Macmillan & Co., and the New York firm is Macmillan Co.

15.95 If the name of the publisher has changed since the book was published, the name on the title page is the one to use, not the present name, e.g., Henry Holt & Co., not Holt, Rinehart, and Winston.

15.96 For books copublished by two different publishers—for example, one in the United States and one in another country—it is permissible, but not necessary, to give both in the facts of publication.

64. Marc Bloch, *Feudal Society*, trans. L. A. Manyon (Chicago: University of Chicago Press; London: Routledge & Kegan Paul, 1961), p. 157.

In a book published in the United States and addressed principally to American readers, a footnote reference should give the American edition of a book, or both—not just the British edition.

15.97   If a book is published by a subsidiary of a publisher—a fact printed on the title page—both names appear: (Cambridge: Harvard University Press, Belknap Press, 1965).

15.98   In a translation the original publisher does not appear in the facts of publication unless the original, foreign language title is also given.

15.99   No part of a foreign publisher's name should be translated, even though the place of publication has been anglicized.

15.100   In some books and in many journals the publisher's name is omitted from footnote references and even from the bibliography. Some publishing houses require the inclusion of the publisher's name in footnotes only if the book cited was published after 1900. When the publisher's name is omitted, the place of publication is followed by a comma instead of a colon: (New York, 1965). In books published by the University of Chicago Press the inclusion of the publisher's name is encouraged, particularly in references to books still in copyright.

15.101   The publisher's name is, of course, essential in footnotes to quoted material for which permission to reprint has been granted by the publisher as holder of the copyright.

15.102   *Date of publication.* In footnotes, as well as in bibliographies, the date of publication of a book means the *year* of publication—not the month or day. Sometimes the date of publication may be found on the title page of a book. More often it appears only on the copyright page and is the same as the date of copyright.

15.103   If a date other than that of the first edition is used, the edition must be specified (see par. 15.78). Copyright pages often list successive *printings* or *impressions*, with the dates of each. These are not new *editions* of the book and therefore should be ignored in determining the date of publication.

15.104   A reference to a work of several volumes published in different years should give inclusive dates.

> 65. Paul Tillich, *Systematic Theology*, 3 vols. (Chicago: University of Chicago Press, 1951–63), 3:45.

If it is desirable to cite only one volume of a multivolume work published over a period of years, the facts of publication should follow the number and title of that volume, and only the year of publication of the particular volume is given.

> 66. Douglas Southall Freeman, *George Washington*, vol. 3, *Planter and Patriot* (New York: Charles Scribner's Sons, 1951), p. 50.

15.105 If the work has not yet been completed, the date of the first volume is followed by an en dash.

> 67. Donald Lach, *Asia in the Making of Europe* (Chicago: University of Chicago Press, 1965–), 1:594.

15.106 Where there is no ascertainable date of publication, "n.d." (no date) takes the place of the date in the facts of publication. Where the date is ascertainable, but not printed in the book, it is enclosed in brackets.

15.107 *Reference numbers.* Following the facts of publication in a footnote come the specific designations necessary for finding the passage referred to in the text. Here the words volume, part, number, book, chapter, page(s), note(s), appendix, folio are abbreviated and lowercased as vol., pt., no., bk., chap., p. (pp.), n. (nn.), app., fol. Plurals add "s" for all but p. and n. The abbreviation l. (ll.) for line(s) should be avoided, except in works containing many such references. (The letter *l* on the typewriter is used also for the arabic figure 1 and may thus confuse the typesetter. If the abbreviation is used, it is helpful to write "ell," and circle it, above the letter, at least the first time it appears in the notes.)

15.108 Arabic numerals are generally used with all the above designations, except, of course, lowercase roman numerals in references to pages numbered in roman numerals in the source being cited. (For volume numbers see par. 15.114.)

15.109 References to a passage extending over several pages should give the first and last page numbers. The use of f. or ff. (and following) after a single page number is discouraged.

15.110 Inclusive page numbers (and other inclusive numbers) are separated by an en dash in print (a hyphen on the typewriter).

15.111 *Passim* ("here and there") should be used sparingly and only after inclusive page numbers indicating a reasonable stretch of text, or after a reference to a chapter, part, etc. Passim, being a complete word, is not followed by a period unless it falls at the end of a citation.

15.112 Whenever possible, foreign language designations, such as *Band, Heft, tome,* should be translated into the English equivalents. Fascicle (fasc.) is an English word and should be retained, although the publishing of books in parts (fascicles) is largely a European practice.

15.113 When volume and page numbers are both given, "vol." and "p. (pp.)" are omitted (see nn. 65, 67). Other designations are never omitted, except in biblical, classical, and other special kinds of material. Both "vol." and "p." must be used when the volume number applies to the series title, not to the title of the individual work being cited (see nn. 53, 54).

15.114 *Volume numbers.* As many of the footnote examples in the preceding pages show, the University of Chicago Press recommends the use of arabic numerals for volume numbers in all footnotes, bibliographies, and other scholarly apparatus in books and journals.

15.115 Most publishers have traditionally printed volume numbers of books and journals in roman numerals, particularly in the footnotes and bibliographies of books in the fields of literature, history, and political science. Roman numerals, especially when set in full capital letters, are large, cumbersome, and typographically unpleasant. Consider LXXXVIII versus 88, for example. Some otherwise literate people cannot count up to C the Roman way. Many learned journals have had their golden anniversaries, and some have passed the century mark; for these, as time goes on, roman volume numbers become more and more unwieldy. Consequently, many present-day writers, editors, and others involved with the printed word are now replacing roman numbers with arabic. For example, dates of publication seldom appear in roman numerals on title pages of books as once they commonly did. All these and other considerations lie behind the Press policy of using arabic numerals wherever possible.

15.116 The distinction between volume and page number must, of course, remain clear. The use of a different typeface for the arabic volume number is one solution. Another, more practical and less expensive way—and the one preferred by the University of Chicago Press—is to put a colon between the volume number and the page number, using the same typeface for each. (See nn. 65, 67, 71, and others.)

15.117   In references to publications appearing annually, semiannually, quarterly, bimonthly, and so on, the volume number comes directly after the title of the publication (no comma). The date (year) of the volume follows the volume number and is enclosed in parentheses.

> 68. Ricardo Quintana, "Situational Satire: A Commentary on the Method of Swift," *University of Toronto Quarterly* 17 (1948): 130–36.

15.118   If the volume is paginated consecutively throughout, it is unnecessary to give the number of the issue or the month of publication. It is acceptable, however, to include one or both of these items. When an author is consistent about what he includes in all his citations to a particular journal, the copy editor should not query him or change his usage. When the number of the issue is given, it should follow the volume number and precede the date. When the month is given, it should precede the year, within the parentheses.

> 69. Perez Zagorin, "Carl Becker on History," *American Historical Review* 62, no. 1 (October 1956): 10.

An alternative form, acceptable if followed consistently, is to give the date after the page number: 62:10 (October 1956).

15.119   When a periodical has published volumes in successive series, each beginning with volume 1, it is desirable to give the series number as well as the volume number and date. "New Series" and "Old Series" are abbreviated as "n.s." and "o.s."

> 70. "Letters of Jonathan Sewall," *Proceedings of the Massachusetts Historical Society*, 2d ser. 10 (January 1896): 414.
>
> 71. G. M. Moraes, "St. Francis Xavier, Apostolic Nuncio, 1542–52," *Journal of the Bombay Branch of the Royal Asiatic Society*, n.s. 26 (1950): 279–313.

15.120   Some periodicals carry only the issue number (no volume number). If the issues are numbered consecutively from the beginning of publication, the number is followed by the date, in parentheses. Here a comma is appropriate after the periodical name and series designation.

> 72. Jean Filliozat, "Les premières étapes de l'Indianisme," *Bulletin de l'Association Guillaume Budé*, 3d ser., no. 3 (1953), pp. 83–96.
>
> 73. Konrad Lorenz, "The Wisdom of Darwin," *Midway*, no. 22 (1965), p. 48.

15.121   If the numbers begin with 1 each year, the year becomes the volume number, is not enclosed in parentheses, and is followed by the issue number.

> 74. M. E. Sergeenko, "Kolumbarii Statiliev Tavrov," *Vestnik drevnei istorii*, 1964, no. 4, p. 399.

15.122 If only the month (or the season) and year of publication are given, the month precedes the year and neither is enclosed in parentheses.

> 75. Lucy Eisenberg, "Scientists vs. Animal Lovers: The Conflict That Never Ends," *Harper's*, November 1966, pp. 101–10.

15.123 References to daily newspapers or weekly publications require only the date of issue—day, month, and year. Volume numbers are unnecessary. In newspaper references it is best to omit page numbers also; in different editions of the same issue a particular news item may not be on the same page in each edition. It is useful, however, to give page numbers for references to the *New York Times* and the *Times* (London), citing the edition consistently used in preparing the indexes to these two newspapers.

> 76. *New York Times*, 11 August 1965, p. 3.
>
> 77. *Times* (London), 25 May 1965, p. 11.
>
> 78. John M. Allison, review of *In My Time* by Robert Strausz-Hupé, *Saturday Review*, 25 September 1965, p. 39.
>
> 79. E. W. Caspari and R. E. Marshak, "The Rise and Fall of Lysenko," *Science*, 16 July 1965, pp. 275–78.

15.124 Names of months may be abbreviated in newspaper references, especially where there are many such references. Consistency in this matter must be observed. (For abbreviations see par. 14.28.)

15.125 In citing well-known reference books the facts of publication (place of publication, publisher, and date) are usually omitted, but the edition if not the first must be specified. References to an encyclopedia, dictionary, or other alphabetically arranged work give the item (not the volume or page number) preceded by "s.v." (*sub verbo*, "under the word").

> 80. *Encyclopaedia Britannica*, 11th ed., s.v. "Prayers for the Dead."
>
> 81. *Webster's New International Dictionary*, 2d ed., s.v. "epistrophe."
>
> 82. *Columbia Encyclopedia*, 3d ed., s.v. "cold war."
>
> 83. *Dictionary of American Biography*, s.v. "Wadsworth, Jeremiah."

15.126 References to the Bible should include book, in roman type and abbreviated (see par. 14.38), chapter, and verse—never, of course, a page number.

> 84. Heb. 13:8.
>
> 85. 1 Thess. 4:11.
>
> 86. Ruth 3:1–18.
>
> 87. Gen. 25:19–37:1.
>
> 88. 2 Kings 11:12.
>
> 89. 1 Sam. 10:24.

15.127 References to plays and poems carrying section and line or stanza numbers may omit edition and facts of publication. (These should not be omitted, of course, where they are essential to a discussion of texts.)

> 90. *The Winter's Tale*, act 5, sc. 1, lines 13–16.
>
> 91. *The Faerie Queene*, bk. 2, canto 8, stanza 14.

In works of literary criticism including many such references, the form of citation may be shortened:

> 92. *WT* 5. 1. 13–16.
>
> 93. *FQ* 2. 8. 14.

When the title of the play or poem is mentioned in the text, it is not repeated in the footnote. References to parts are often inserted in the text in parentheses, or in brackets following quotations set in reduced type (see pars. 10.45–57).

15.128 References to poems or plays that do not carry line numbers must include the page number of the passage quoted, and therefore the edition and the facts of publication must be given in the first reference. Titles of plays and of long poems are italicized even when they are printed as part of a larger volume.

SPECIAL TYPES OF REFERENCES

15.129 Two fields wherein practices in citing sources vary significantly from the general rules outlined above are classics and law. Scholars in these fields have developed workable patterns of documentation that are understood and accepted by their readers. In works predominantly in classics or the law, therefore, it is best to adhere as closely as possible to these patterns.

CLASSICAL REFERENCES

15.130 Abbreviations are used extensively in classical references for the author's name; for the title of the work; for collections of inscriptions, papyri, ostraca, etc.; for titles of well-known periodicals and reference tools. The most widely accepted standard for abbreviations is the comprehensive list in the front of the *Oxford Classical Dictionary*.

15.131 Facts of publication are omitted, but the name of the edition or other identifying information may be inserted in parentheses following the title. The edition *must* be provided when a page number is used.

15.132 Titles of individual works, collections, and periodicals are in italics, whether given in full or abbreviated form. Titles of unpublished collections are in roman, without quotation marks. In Latin and Greek titles only the first word and proper nouns and adjectives derived from proper nouns are capitalized. Abbreviations of Greek titles are usually transliterated.

15.133 In references to individual works there is no punctuation between the author's name and the title of his work or between the title and numerical references to divisions of the work (books, parts, chapters, lines, etc.). The names of these divisions are omitted unless they are needed for clarity. If "ibid." is used in succeeding references, it is followed by a comma, but the preferred classical form is the use of the abbreviated title.

15.134 Different levels of division of a work (book, section, line, etc.) are separated by periods; commas are used between several references to the same level; the en dash is used between continuing numbers. If explanatory abbreviations are necessary before the numerical references for clarity (bk. 1, sec. 3), commas rather than periods are used to separate the different elements.

15.135 Arabic numerals are used for all subdivisions of individual works. (This is a departure from former style, in which lowercase roman numerals were used to indicate books, and is now widely accepted by journals in the fields of classical languages and literatures.)

> 94. Homer *Odyssey* 9. 266–71.
>
> *or:*
>
> 94. Hom. *Od.* 9. 266–71.
>
> 95. Plato *Republic* 360E–361B.
>
> 96. Lucan *Bellum civile* 3. 682.
>
> 97. Cicero *De officiis* 1. 133, 140.
>
> 98. Ovid *Amores* 1. 7. 27.
>
> 99. Thucydides *History of the Peloponnesian War* 2. 40. 2–3.
>
> *or:*
>
> 99. Thucydides 2. 40. 2–3.
>
> *or:*
>
> 99. Thucy. 2. 40. 2–3.
>
> 100. Pindar *Isthmian Odes* 7. 43–45.
>
> *or:*
>
> 100. Pind. *Isthm.* 7. 43–45.
>
> 101. Aristophanes *Frogs* 1019–30.
>
> 102. Sappho *Invocation to Aphrodite*, st. 2, ll. 1–6.
>
> 103. Solon (Edmond's numbering) 36. 20–27.

15.136 In references to volumes in collections of inscriptions, papyri, and ostraca, roman numerals are used for the volume in the collection (in spite of Press preference for arabic volume numbers in other kinds of citations). Commas follow the title of the collection (usually abbreviated) and the volume number. After the volume number of the collection comes the document number, followed by the divisions within it; these should be punctuated according to the classical form described above.

> 104. *IG Rom.*, III, 739. 9. 10, 17.

(*"IG Rom."* = *Inscriptiones Graecae ad res Romanas pertinentes.*)

> 105. *POxy.*, 1485.

Note that in the last example no volume is cited; the number is the document number. (*"POxy."* = *Oxyrhynchus Papyri.*)

15.137 Some collections are cited only by the name of the editor, in roman.

> 106. Dessau, 6964. 23–29.

("Dessau" = H. Dessau, ed., *Inscriptiones Latinae selectae.*)

15.138 Superior figures or letters are used in several ways in classical references. When a superior number is used immediately after the title of a work or after the volume number of a collection and before the following punctuation, it indicates the number of the edition:

> 107. Stolz-Schmalz *Lat. Gram.*^{5} (rev. Leumann-Hofmann; Munich, 1928), pp. 390–91.
>
> 108. *Ausgewählte Komödien des T. M. Plautus*^{2}, vol. 2 (1883).

When a superior number or a letter is placed after a number referring to a division of a work, it indicates a part or section or other subdivision. An acceptable alternative to superior lowercase letters is to put them on the line, in the text type size. Such letters, when set on the line, may be capital or lowercase according to how they appear in the source being cited. (When in doubt, make them lowercase.)

> 109. Aristotle *Poetics* 20. 1456^{b}20. 34–35.
>
> 110. Aristotle *Metaphysics* 3. 2. 996^{b}5–8.
>
> > *or:*
>
> 110. Aristotle *Metaphysics* 3. 2. 996b5–8.
>
> 111. Aristotle *Nicomachean Ethics* 1177b31.
>
> 112. *IG*, II^2, 3274.
>
> 113. Roscher *Lex.* 2. 2223A. 15 ff.

15.139   The form for the classical references may properly be applied to medieval works. It may also be adapted for citations to modern sources occurring in a work where most of the references are classical.

> 114. Augustine *De civitate Dei* 20. 2.
>
> 115. Augustine *City of God* (trans. Healey-Tasker) 20. 2.
>
> 116. *Beowulf* 11. 2401–7.
>
> 117. *Sir Gawain and the Green Knight* (trans. John Gardner), pt. 2, st. 1, lines 21–24.
>
> 118. Abelard *Epistle 17 to Heloïse* (Migne, *PL* 180. 375c–378a).

LEGAL REFERENCES

15.140   Footnotes in a predominantly legal work usually follow the style set forth in detail in *A Uniform System of Citation*, 11th ed., published by the Harvard Law Review Association. *In general*, legal references differ from nonlegal references as follows:

> Only the surname of an author is given (unless more than one author with the same name is cited).
>
> Authors of books and titles of books are given in caps and small caps.
>
> Authors of articles are given in roman caps and lowercase; titles of articles are given in italics; titles of periodicals are abbreviated and given in caps and small caps.
>
> Names of cases are given in roman, as are acts, bills, names of courts, etc.

> 119. HOGAN, ELECTION AND REPRESENTATION 160 (1945).
>
> 120. Smith, *Liability in the Admiralty for Injuries to Seamen*, 19 HARV. L. REV. 418 (1906).
>
> 121. Bridges v. California, 314 U.S. 252 (1941).
>
> 122. United States v. Dennis, 183 F.2d 201 (2d Cir. 1950).

REFERENCES TO PUBLIC DOCUMENTS

15.141   The multitudinous publications of the United States government, governments of other countries, the United Nations, and local governments all over the world, and unpublished materials in the possession of these governments and public organizations, present endless problems in documentation. For a description of the kinds of documents most often cited, the reasons for the form of citation, and the items essential to particular references, see chapter 17.

FOR FURTHER REFERENCE

15.142   Although most publishers' style books contain a section on footnotes, no one, to our knowledge, has compiled a definitive work covering all aspects of documentation ("The Compleat Footnoter"?). *The MLA Style Sheet,* compiled by William R. Parker, offers concise and sensible advice on footnotes in the field of humanities, though it retains roman numerals (in small capitals) for volume numbers of books and journals, which this manual discourages. *A Uniform System of Citation,* published by the Harvard Law Review Association, is a well-indexed small handbook useful for forms of citations and abbreviations in legal works; the forms used therein—especially the use of caps and small caps for names and titles—are often modified in practice.

16 *Bibliographies*

INTRODUCTION

16.1 Most works with any pretensions to scholarship include a list of books and other references bearing on the subject of the work. In the humanities and some other fields, the list is usually titled Bibliography or, if it includes only works referred to in the text, Works Cited. In the natural sciences, a list of cited works is usually headed References. A general bibliographical list is best placed at the end of the book, before the index; shorter lists are sometimes placed at the ends of chapters: convenience to the reader should govern the placement of bibliographical material.

16.2 Convenience to the reader should also govern the nature of the list and the arrangement of works within it. When a bibliography is intended to direct the reader to other works for further reading and study, an *annotated* bibliography is most useful. This is a list of books in alphabetical order (or a series of lists with subject headings if the number of entries is large), with comments appended to some or all of the entries. In the following example[1] comments are set on separate lines, but they are often run in:

> Stang, Richard. *The Theory of the Novel in England, 1850–1870.* New York: Columbia University Press, 1959.
>
> A systematic, impressive study uncovering "modern" doctrines about fiction in forgotten publications before James.
>
> Tillyard, E. M. W. *The Epic Strain in the English Novel.* London: Chatto & Windus, 1958.
>
> A defense of the reality of genres—particularly the epic—and of their usefulness to criticism. The method of definition, based on one quality only, leads to some awkward acrobatics.
>
> Watt, Ian. *The Rise of the Novel: Studies in Defoe, Richardson, and Fielding.* Berkeley and Los Angeles: University of California Press, 1957.

1. Slightly altered from Wayne C. Booth, *The Rhetoric of Fiction* (Chicago: University of Chicago Press, 1961).

Wellek, René, and Warren, Austin. *Theory of Literature.* New York: Harcourt, Brace & Co., 1949.
See especially "The Nature and Modes of Fiction" and Bibliography.

16.3   Sometimes an annotated bibliography takes the form of a bibliographical essay, not alphabetically arranged, in which the writer treats the literature of the field discursively but with full bibliographical details for each title:

> Probably the most readable of the military histories of the Civil War are those of Bruce Catton: *Mr. Lincoln's Army* (1951), *Glory Road* (1952), *A Stillness at Appomattox* (1953), *This Hallowed Ground* (1956)—all published in New York by Doubleday & Co. —and *Grant Moves South* (Boston: Little, Brown & Co., 1960). The previously cited *Civil War and Reconstruction* (1961) by James G. Randall and David Donald remains one of the best accounts of the war as a whole.[2]

16.4   Any long bibliography, whether annotated or not, *may* be broken into sections if division into categories makes the bibliography more useful to the reader (sometimes such division merely makes finding a given item more difficult) and if the division is according to some consistent principle. In a book employing primary sources (unpublished material), it is often best to list these in a separate section because they do not fit well in an alphabetically arranged list of published sources. Again, in a study of the work of one man, it is usually best to list works *by* him separately from works *about* him. In the main, however, the reader of a scholarly book is best served by a straight alphabetical list of the important books and articles bearing on the author's subject. This should certainly include the works frequently cited in the text and may include all works referred to (see pars. 15.9–10). Seldom is there any reason to number the items.

MODE OF CITATION

16.5   The method of citation varies from one field to another. Outside the natural sciences, the text citation typically takes the form of a footnote (see chap. 15). In a footnote the work is often cited briefly, full bibliographical information being given in the bibliography. In the natural sciences, too, footnotes may be used, but two other methods are more common. The clearer of them—and the one preferred by the University of Chicago Press—is by author's last

---

2. Slightly altered from Elbert B. Smith, *The Death of Slavery: The United States, 1837–65* (Chicago: University of Chicago Press, 1967).

name and the date of publication. This information is enclosed in parentheses and inserted in the text at the appropriate point. Another method is to number the works listed in the references and to insert these numbers, enclosed in parentheses, in the text. The latter method saves space where citations are copious, but it is somewhat less kind to the reader and is more susceptible to error. Bibliographical details, of course, are given in the list of references. Citation in scientific books is discussed more fully below (pars. 16.46–50).

16.6   *Consistency the goal.* In bibliographical citations and lists—as in every other aspect of editorial work—one of the chief ends to be pursued is consistency. Although the University of Chicago Press prefers the forms and conventions listed below, it does not insist on rigid adherence to them in every book it publishes. It does insist on consistency, however, and if for weighty reasons an author feels Press style should be departed from, it requests him then to follow consistently the style of an influential journal in his field and to inform the publisher's editor that he has done so.

16.7   *The facts to be noted.* In the main, all scholarly reference lists, whether in the humanities or the natural sciences, include the same information about a published work. For a book, these facts are:

> Name of the author or authors, the editors, or the institution responsible for the writing of the book
> Full title of the book, including the subtitle if there is one
> Series (if any)
> Volume number
> Edition, if not the original
> City of publication
> Publisher's name (sometimes omitted)
> Date of publication

For an article in a periodical, the facts given are:

> Name of the author
> Title of the article (sometimes omitted in scientific bibliographies)
> Name of the periodical
> Volume number or date or both
> Pages occupied by the article

16.8   Note that the physical facts about a work—dimensions, number of pages, number of illustrations, and so on—are not given. Such facts are listed on library catalog cards and on booksellers' lists but are omitted from scholarly bibliographies.

16.9   *Spelling and abbreviation.* Parts of books are spelled with lower-case letters. In running text they are spelled out; in parenthetical references, usually abbreviated (for abbreviations see par. 14.32):

> The author's method can be seen at its most effective in volume 2, parts 3 and 4.
> (see vol. 2, pts. 3, 4)   (fig. 14)   (pl. 7)   (pp. 465–70)
> *but:* (table 4)   (lines 34–36)

16.10   In the facts of publication, publishers' names are usually pruned of "Inc." and "Ltd.," and "Company" is abbreviated to "Co." The ampersand (&) is permissible when used consistently. It is also permissible (and in scientific reference lists, usual) to shorten the name still further. This must be done consistently, however, and should follow the forms of one of the standard book-trade reference works (see par. 16.53).

DIFFERENCES BETWEEN FIELDS

16.11   Although all types of reference lists give roughly the same information, stylistic conventions in presentation differ markedly between the humanities and the natural sciences. This stems partly from the fact that journal articles rather than books make up the bulk of a scientific reference list, partly from the preferred methods of citation, and partly perhaps from tradition. Whatever the causes, however, a great gulf is fixed between the two families of disciplines, and publishers and editors must adjust their practices to the differences. For that reason, the examples that follow are grouped under two headings.

16.12   The forms preferred by the University of Chicago Press, both in the humanities and in the natural sciences, are designed for clarity and economy. The bibliographical facts are presented in what seems to be the most logical order. Arabic numerals are used throughout: vol. 3 or 138, not III or CXXXVIII. A minimum of punctuation is used. And only two styles of type are employed: roman and italic. Additional typefaces are often seen in bibliographies and reference lists. Caps and small caps, for example, are sometimes used for authors' names. Although this practice may add to the attractive appearance of a list, it does more to raise costs than to increase clarity. Again, boldface type is often seen for the volume numbers of journals in scientific lists. It is hard to find any justification for this practice except custom in certain fields.

THE HUMANITIES AND RELATED FIELDS

16.13   The features of a typical bibliographical entry are shown in figure 16.1.

16.14   Note that this brief entry consists of three chief parts: authorship, title, facts of publication. In the styles illustrated in this chapter, these three parts remain the chief entities of an entry, even though a particular part may become very complicated, as the "title" of a book that is part of a series, or even disappear, as the "author" of an anonymous work. If a writer or editor holds in mind this tripartite arrangement, he will usually be able to improvise simple,

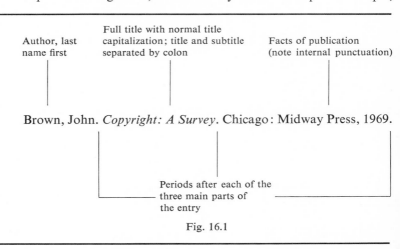

Fig. 16.1

logical styles for bibliographical situations not covered here. For many of these, chapter 15, which gives examples of a great many different types of works, may be helpful. Generally, footnote style can be changed into bibliographical style by transposing authors' first and last names, removing parentheses from the facts of publication, omitting page references, and repunctuating with periods between (and sometimes within) the three parts of the entry.

16.15   *Author's name.* A bibliographical entry gives the author's name in inverse order: Brown, John (*not* John Brown). In cases of multiple authorship the preference of the University of Chicago Press is still to list all names in the same order: Brown, John; Doe, John; and Roe, Richard. The examples in this chapter all follow this principle, and the Press commends it to its authors. Good arguments can be adduced in favor of listing only the first author's name in inverse order, however (Brown, John, John Doe, and Richard Roe), and the Press will allow this system if it is consistently followed.

16.16 The writer or editor may sometimes be in doubt about the most appropriate order when alphabetizing authors' names, particularly when works of multiple authorship are involved. Since these problems arise more frequently in scientific reference lists, they are discussed in a later section of this chapter (par. 16.55).

16.17 *Title of work.* Compiling a bibliography also raises questions of how much editing may be done to the title of a work in applying rules of style. Scholars generally agree that capitalization, punctuation, and the use of italic type may be changed within limits but that the author's spelling must not be altered (see pars. 7.122–43). These rules reflect the realities of the printing and publishing processes, for capitalization, punctuation, and the use of italics on a title page are matters that printers and publishers have always felt were theirs to control. Hence it is pointless to reproduce such variations in a scholarly bibliography. Thus the title page of a book may read:

THOMAS MANN'S
Doctor Faustus
The Sources and Structure of the Novel

Transcribed and reduced to bibliographical form, this will read: *Thomas Mann's "Doctor Faustus": The Sources and Structure of the Novel.* That is, the entire title has been put in italics, the title within the title has been enclosed in quotation marks, and a colon has been introduced between title and subtitle.

16.18 *Facts of publication.* For a bibliographical entry the facts of publication are the same as those given for a footnote (pars. 15.84–128), but somewhat differently punctuated. The University of Chicago Press continues to urge the use of publishers' names for books published in the twentieth century, especially those that could still be in copyright.

SOME TYPICAL BIBLIOGRAPHICAL ENTRIES

16.19 *Book by single author*

Burr, G. L. *Narrative of the Witchcraft Cases.* New York: Barnes & Noble, 1959.

16.20 *Book by two or more authors.* Note that all names appear in inverse order (Press preference). Note also the use of semicolons with three or more names.

> Dean, John P., and Rosen, Alex. *A Manual of Intergroup Relations.* Chicago: University of Chicago Press, 1955.
>
> Adler, J. H.; Schlesinger, E. R.; and Westerborg, E. van. *The Pattern of United States Import Trade since 1923.* New York: Federal Reserve Bank of New York, 1952.
>
> Modell, Walter; Schwartz, Doris; Hazeltine, Louise; and Kirkham, Frederic T., Jr. *Handbook of Cardiology for Nurses.* 4th ed. New York: Springer Publishing Co., 1962.

16.21 *Association as "author"*

> International Statistics Institute. *Proceedings of the 34th Session, International Statistics Institute, Ottawa, 1963.* 2 vols. Toronto: University of Toronto Press, 1964.
>
> Modern Language Association. *International Bibliography, 1963.* New York: New York University Press, 1964.

16.22 *Editor as "author"*

> Whitney, Thomas P., ed. *The New Writing in Russia.* Ann Arbor: University of Michigan Press, 1964.

16.23 *Editor named in addition to author.* The editor's name is set off by periods. In the second example, so also is the number of volumes.

> Cartwright, Peter. *Autobiography of Peter Cartwright, the Backwoods Preacher.* Edited by W. P. Strickland. Cincinnati: L. Swormstedt & A. Poe, 1856.
>
> Dryden, John. *The Works of John Dryden.* Edited by H. T. Swedenberg. 8 vols. Berkeley and Los Angeles: University of California Press, 1956–62.

16.24 *Translator named in addition to author.* In the second example, note the use of quotation marks for a title within a title:

> Ariès, Philippe. *Centuries of Childhood: A Social History of Family Life.* Translated by Robert Baldick. New York: Alfred A. Knopf, 1962.
>
> Baudelaire, Charles. *One Hundred Poems from "Les Fleurs du Mal."* Translated by C. F. MacIntyre. Berkeley and Los Angeles: University of California Press, 1947.

16.25 *Volume in a series*

> Biays, Pierre. *Les marges de l'œkoumène dans l'est du Canada: Partie orientale du Bouclier canadien et île de Terre-Neuve.* Travaux et documents du Centre d'études nordiques. Quebec: Les Presses de l'université Laval, 1964.

378

Note that the series volume number is run in with the series name:

> Caldwell, Helen. *The Brazilian Othello of Machado de Assis: A Study of "Dom Casmurro."* Perspectives in Criticism, vol. 6. Berkeley and Los Angeles: University of California Press, 1960.
>
> Wolf, Theta Holmes. *The Effects of Praise and Competition on the Persisting Behavior of Kindergarten Children.* Child Welfare Monograph Series, no. 15. Minneapolis: University of Minnesota Press, 1938.

The series editor's name may follow the series title:

> Kluckhohn, C. K. M.; Clinchy, Everett R.; Embree, Edwin R.; Mead, Margaret; and Abernathy, Bradford S. *Religion and Our Racial Tensions.* Religion in the Post-War World, edited by W. L. Sperry, vol. 3. Cambridge, Mass.: Harvard University Press, 1945.

If a book within a series is itself a multivolume work, the number of volumes or (if the reference is to a particular volume) the volume number follows the book title and is set off by periods:

> Grattan, C. Hartley. *The Southwest Pacific to 1900: A Modern History.* Vol. 1. University of Michigan History of the Modern World. Ann Arbor: University of Michigan Press, 1963.

Series and volume editors may both be named:

> Burke, Edmund. *The Correspondence of Edmund Burke.* Edited by Thomas W. Copeland. Cambridge: At the University Press; Chicago: University of Chicago Press, 1958–. Vol. 5, *July 1782– June 1789*, edited by Holden Furber, 1965.

16.26   *Pseudonymous and anonymous literature.* In listing a work published under a pseudonym, the author's real name should be used if it is known, since that is how the book will be listed in most library card catalogs. The pseudonym may be enclosed in brackets after the name if desired:

> Beyle, Marie Henri [Stendhal]. *The Charterhouse of Parma.* Translated by C. K. Scott-Moncrieff. New York: Boni & Liveright, 1925.

If only the pseudonym is known, it is used as the author's name but noted as a pseudonym:

> Pushquill, Hacker [pseud.] . . .

16.27   If the author of an anonymous work is known, his name is given in brackets. If it is not known, the work is listed merely by its title (without "Anon." or any such addition):

> [Horsley, Samuel.] *On the Prosodies of the Greek and Latin Languages.* 1796.

> [Haine, William?] *Certain Epistles of Tully Verbally Translated.* 1611.
>
> *True and Sincere Declaration of the Purpose and Ends of the Plantation Begun in Virginia, of the Degrees Which It Hath Received: and Meanes by Which It Hath Been Advanced, A: . . . ,* 1610.

16.28   *Author's name with initials only.* If the author's name appears on the title page of a book or at the head of an article with initials only, in place of his given names, the missing name(s) should be supplied or not, according to how the author is listed in library catalogs:

> Eliot, T. S. *Four Quartets.* London: Faber & Faber, 1944.
>
> Crane, Ronald S. *The Idea of the Humanities and Other Essays Critical and Historical.* 2 vols. Chicago: University of Chicago Press, 1967.

In the latter entry, the author's name could be given as Crane, R[onald] S., but for most scholarly purposes this is a needless refinement.

16.29   *Translation of an anonymous work*

> Zeydel, Edwin H., trans. *Ecbasis cuiusdam captivi per tropologiam—Escape of a Certain Captive Told in a Figurative Manner: An Eleventh-Century Latin Beast Epic.* Studies in Germanic Languages and Literatures, no. 46. Chapel Hill: University of North Carolina Press, 1964.

16.30   *Edition other than first*

> Frank, Tenney. *An Economic History of Rome.* 2d rev. ed. Baltimore: Johns Hopkins Press, 1927.
>
> Bober, M. M. *Karl Marx's Interpretation of History.* 2d ed., rev. Harvard Economic Studies. Cambridge, Mass.: Harvard University Press, 1948.

16.31   *Article in a symposium or volume of conference papers*

> Kaiser, Ernest. "The Literature of Harlem." In *Harlem: A Community in Transition,* edited by J. H. Clarke. New York: Citadel Press, 1964.

Inclusive page numbers may be given if desired:

> Ogilvy, David. "The Creative Chef." In *The Creative Organization,* edited by Gary A. Steiner, pp. 199–213. Chicago: University of Chicago Press, 1965.

16.32   For some kinds of unpublished materials the arrangement of elements normal for published works suffices, as in the following two categories.

16.33   *Dissertation or thesis*

> Trent, James W. "The Etiology of Catholic Intellectualism." Ph.D. dissertation, University of California, 1964.
>
> Ross, Dorothy. "The Irish-Catholic Immigrant, 1880–1900: A Study in Social Mobility." Master's thesis, Columbia University, n.d.

16.34   *Unpublished duplicated material*

> Moore, Philip S. "Academic Development: University of Notre Dame: Past, Present, and Future." Mimeographed. Notre Dame, Ind.: University of Notre Dame, 1960.
>
> Foster, Julian; Stanek, R.; and Krassowski, W. "The Impact of a Value-oriented University on Student Attitudes and Thinking." Mimeographed. Santa Clara, Calif.: University of Santa Clara, 1961.
>
> Rein, Martin, and Miller, S. M. "The Demonstration Project as a Strategy of Change." Paper read at Mobilization for Youth Training Institute Workshop, 30 April 1964, at Columbia University. Mimeographed.

16.35   *Manuscript material.* Here scholarly practice and convenience to the reader dictate a different arrangement of the elements of the entry: city in which the depository is located; name of the depository; collection name or number. If a title exists and if the author is known, these facts may be added.

> Edinburgh. University Library. D.c. 2-392. "Novum organum botanicum" [by John Walker].
>
> Boston. Massachusetts Historical Society. Edward Everett papers.

It is seldom necessary to list an individual item from a manuscript collection in the bibliography of a book, but when it is, the item may be listed as follows:

> Washington, D.C. National Archives. Record Group 77. Lieutenant Colonel R. E. DeRussy to Brevet General J. G. Totten, 15 May 1853.
>
> St. Paul, Minn. Minnesota Governor's Archives. File 355. General Terry, U.S.A., to Governor.

16.36   *Reprint edition of a book.* In listing a latter-day reprint of a book long out of print (see par. 15.81), facts of publication for both the original edition and the reprint may be given, although the date alone should suffice for the original:

> Audsley, George Ashdown. *The Art of Organ Building.* 2 vols. 1905. Reprint (2 vols. in 1). New York: Dover Publications, 1964.

16.37 *Edition with special publisher's imprint.* Some publishers issue certain categories of books through a special publishing division or under a special imprint. In such instances the imprint may be given after the publisher's name:

> Cooper, James Fenimore. *The Letters and Journals of James Fenimore Cooper.* Edited by J. F. Beard. 2 vols. Cambridge, Mass.: Harvard University Press, Belknap Press, 1960.

16.38 If it is necessary to list a book from a paperback series, the entry may be handled similarly:

> Clark, W. E. Le Gros. *History of the Primates.* 5th ed. Chicago: University of Chicago Press, Phoenix Books, 1966.

16.39 *Introduction, etc., to a book by another author*

> Harris, Mark. Introduction to *With the Procession,* by Henry B. Fuller. Chicago: University of Chicago Press, 1965.
>
> Arendt, Hannah. Foreword to *The Future of Germany,* by Karl Jaspers. Chicago: University of Chicago Press, 1967.

16.40 *Book in a foreign language.* A book in a language other than English is treated the same as a book in English except that capitalization in the title follows the conventions of the language of the book. Bibliographical information is translated: "vol.," not *tome* or *Band;* "rev.," not *verb.*; and so on. The publisher's name is given as it appears in the book, of course, although it may be shorn of "S.A." and the like. The city of publication is given in its English form (see par. 15.91):

> Cesbron, Henry. *Histoire critique de l'hystérie.* Paris: Asselin & Houzeau, 1909.
>
> Gundert, Wilhelm. *Japanische Religionsgeschichte: Die Religionen der Japaner und Koreaner in geschichtlichem Abriss dargestellt.* Stuttgart: Gundert Verlag, 1943.

For languages less widely understood than French and German, a translation may be added in brackets:

> Alampiev, Pëtr M. *Ekonomicheskoe raionirovanie SSSR* [Economic regionalization of the USSR]. Moscow: Gosplanizdat, 1959.

16.41 *Article in a journal or magazine.* The simplest way to state the facts of publication is to set down journal name, volume number in arabic figures, colon, and run of pages. Note that no punctuation is used between the journal name and volume number:

> Jacobsen, Thorkild. "The Assumed Conflict between Sumerians and Semites in Early Mesopotamian History." *Journal of the American Oriental Society* 59:485–95.
>
> Dowden, Wilfred S. Review of *The Poetic Voices of Coleridge,* by Max F. Schulz. *Modern Philology* 62:270–72.

Since the title of the journal article is enclosed in quotation marks, an included book title is set in italics and the title of a short story or poem in single quotation marks:

> Brick, Allan R. "*Wuthering Heights:* Narrators, Audience, and Message." *College English* 21 (1959):80–86.
>
> Bowen, Merlin. "*Redburn* and the Angle of Vision." *Modern Philology* 52 (1954):100–109.
>
> Loomis, C. C., Jr. "Structure and Sympathy in Joyce's 'The Dead.'" *PMLA* 75 (1960):149–51.

16.42   As a kindness to the reader, the year of issue is often given in parentheses after the volume number. Anything more than this, however (such as an issue number), is a needless waste of typesetting if the pages of each volume are numbered consecutively:

> Kirsopp Lake, A. "The Origin of the Roman House." *American Journal of Archaeology* 41 (1937):598–601.

If, instead of a volume number, an issue number or a date follows the journal name, it is best set off with commas. Popular magazines, even though they carry volume numbers, should be identified by date of issue:

> Meyerovitch, Eva. "The Gnostic Manuscripts of Upper Egypt." *Diogenes,* no. 25 (1959), pp. 84–117.
>
> Prufer, Olaf. "The Hopewell Cult." *Scientific American,* December 1964, pp. 90–102.
>
> Cohn, Marcus. "Religion and the FCC." *Reporter,* 14 January 1965, pp. 32–34.

If the magazine quoted is one in which an article begins in the front and jumps to the back, inclusive pages are meaningless and should be omitted:

> Gavin, James M. "The Weapons of 1984." *Saturday Review,* 31 August 1968, p. 13.

16.43   The University of Chicago Press discourages the use of abbreviations for journal names in humanistic bibliographies. Except for a few, such as *PMLA, MLN,* and *ELH,* which are almost never spelled out in full, journal names are best left unabbreviated.

16.44   *Forthcoming work.* It sometimes happens that an author needs to list a work that has been accepted for publication but not yet published. In such a case, *forthcoming* (for a book) or *in press* (for a journal article) takes the place of the date of publication:

> Katz, Howland. *Parameters of Social Disintegration.* Chicago: Midway Press, forthcoming.
>
> Lambert, Phineas P. "The Identity of the *Pearl* Poet: Some New Evidence." *Modern Philology,* in press.

16.45   *Public documents.* For the special problems of listing public documents see chapter 17.

THE NATURAL SCIENCES

16.46   As stated at the beginning of this chapter, the University of Chicago Press strongly prefers the author-date method of citation in scientific books. It is less subject to error than the numerical method and permits references to be added or changed up to the final stage of manuscript editing with a minimum of bother.

HANDLING CITATIONS IN THE TEXT

16.47   In the author-date method both elements of the citation typically are enclosed within parentheses:

> Before proceeding with a more detailed discussion of our methods of analysis, we will describe the system of scaling quantitative scores (Guilford 1950).

Preferably, the citation should stand just within a mark of punctuation. If this is impractical, however, it should be inserted at a logical break in the sentence:

> Various investigators (Goldsmith 1958; Jones and Carter 1960) have reported findings at variance with the foregoing.

If the author has just been mentioned, it is not necessary to repeat his name in the citation:

> This coefficient has been taken from the heavy-ion scattering experiments of Bromley, Kuehner, and Almquist (1960).

16.48   When reference must be made to a particular page or section of a book, or to a particular equation or the like, it is best to do this at the point of citation rather than in the reference list. Appropriate abbreviations are used:

> (Brown 1948, p. 178)   (Jackson 1959, sec. 22.6)
> (Fowler and Hoyle 1965, eq. [87])

16.49   For works of multiple authorship use the full form of citation for one to three authors but an abbreviated form for four or more. Thus a work by three authors would be cited:

> (Nordberg, Morinigo, and Barnes 1962)

But a work, for instance, by Zipursky, Hull, White, and Israels would be cited:

> (Zipursky et al. 1959)

If, as sometimes happens, there is another work of the same date that would also abbreviate to "Zipursky et al."—say, a paper by Zipursky, Smith, Jones, and Brown—the only solution is to cite both in full.

16.50   In the absence of any reasons to the contrary, private communications are best handled as footnotes rather than as citations to a reference list. An asterisk should be used (outside any punctuation mark), and in the unlikely event that there are two or more such citations on a page, the regular sequence of asterisk, dagger, double dagger, etc., is used (see par. 12.30).

> Spieth has indicated that some men they studied who had hypertensive drugs were indeed faster in psychomotor speed than non-treated hypertensives.*

---

* Walter Spieth 1962: personal communication.

THE REFERENCE LIST

16.51   Although an entry in a scientific bibliography contains the same information as an entry in, say, a historical bibliography, the elements are usually arranged differently. A typical arrangement, and one representing the preferences of the University of Chicago Press, is shown in figure 16.2.

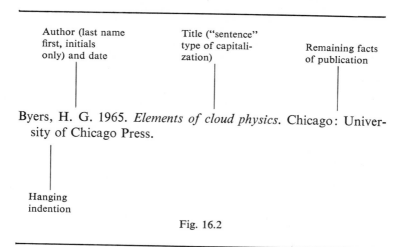

Fig. 16.2

16.52   Entries are alphabetically arranged (chronologically for a particular author or constellation of authors) and unnumbered. In brief, the elements of a bibliographical entry should be in the following order:

Author (last name first) and date, period.

Title (ordinary sentence-style capitalization), period. Book titles are set in italic, article titles in roman type. Article titles may be omitted entirely if this is done consistently.

Facts of publication. For a book: city of publication, colon, publisher's name abbreviated. For a journal article: journal name abbreviated and in italic type, volume number, colon, pages on which article appears.

16.53   Abbreviations must be consistent throughout the reference list. For the names of American publishers, use the list given in *Books in Print*. For British publishers, use *British Books in Print: The Reference Catalogue of Current Literature*. For the names of scientific journals, the University of Chicago Press prefers the abbreviations system used in *Chemical Abstracts List of Periodicals* (1961 [several supplements]).

16.54   Page references should be handled as elsewhere (see par. 8.36). Press style is illustrated by the following sequences:

3–17, 23–26, 100–103, 104–7, 124–28, 1115–20

16.55   Names should be alphabetized as they are in an index. Most other problems of alphabetical arrangement may be solved by observing the following principles:

A single-author entry comes before a multiple-author entry beginning with the same name.

An author's own volume comes before a book he has edited.

Corporate authors (such as associations) are alphabetized according to the first significant word of the name.

SOME TYPICAL ENTRIES

16.56   Press preferences for some common types of references are illustrated by the following examples.

16.57   *Book*

Lehman, H. C. 1953. *Age and achievement*. Princeton: Princeton Univ. Press.

Weber, M.; Burlet, H. M. de; and Abel, O. 1928. *Die Säugetiere*. 2d ed. 2 vols. Jena: Gustav Fischer

16.58   *Article in a journal*

Lewis, E. B. 1957. Leukemia and ionizing radiation. *Science* 125:965–72.

The article title may be omitted:

> Elliot, O., and Scott, J. P. 1961. *J. Genet. Psychol.* 99:3–22.

16.59 *Contribution to a symposium or volume of conference papers*

> Brues, A. M., and Sacher, G. A. 1952. Analysis of mammalian radiation injury and lethality. In *Symposium on radiobiology*, ed. J. J. Nickson, pp. 441–65. New York: Wiley.

As with a journal article, the title may be omitted to save space.

16.60 *Edited volume*

> Landsberg, H., and Van Mieghem, J., eds. 1962. *Advances in geophysics.* New York: Academic Press.

16.61 *Later edition*

> Turner, D. 1965. *Handbook of diet therapy.* 4th ed. Chicago: Univ. of Chicago Press.

16.62 *Public document.* If the author of a governmental report or study is given, the document is treated like any other published work:

> Blair, H. A. 1956. *Data pertaining to shortening of life by ionizing radiation.* U.S. Atomic Energy Commission unclassified report UR-442.

16.63 An anonymous document is usually treated as if the sponsoring body were the author:

> United Nations. 1962. *Report of the United Nations Scientific Committee on the Effects of Atomic Radiation.* General Assembly, Official Records: Thirteenth Session, Supplement no. 17 (A/3838). New York.

16.64 *Unpublished paper*

> Royce, John C. 1968. Finches of Du Page County. Paper read at 2d Annual Conference on Practical Bird-Watching, 24–26 May 1968, at Midland University, Flat Prairie, Illinois.

16.65 *Book in a series*

> Kendeigh, S. C. 1952. *Parental care and its evolution in birds.* Illinois Biological Monographs, vol. 22, nos. 1–3. Urbana: University of Illinois Press.

16.66 *Several works by same author.* If an author or team of authors appears more than once in an alphabetically arranged reference list, it is usual to substitute a 3-em dash for the author's name or names after the first appearance:

> Buettner-Janusch, J. 1962. Biochemical genetics of the primates— hemoglobins and transferrins. *Ann. N.Y. Acad. Sci.* 102:235–48.
>
> ———. 1964. The breeding of galagos in captivity and some notes on their behavior. *Folia Primatol.* 2:93–110.
>
> ———. 1966. *Origins of man.* New York: Wiley.

Buettner-Janusch, J., and Andrew, R. J. 1962. Use of the incisors by primates in grooming. *Am. J. Phys. Anthropol.* 20:129–32.

16.67 If two or more works by the same author bear the same publication date, they are distinguished by letters after the date:

Edwards, G. 1966*a*.
———. 1966*b*.

16.68 When the same authors appear repeatedly in a reference list, a style of arrangement long used by anthropologists and others may well be adopted:

Burney, Charles A.
  1961. Excavations at Yanik Tepe, northwest Iran. *Iraq* 23:138–53.
  1962. The excavations at Yanik Tepe, Azerbaijan, 1961. Ibid. 24:134–49.
  1964. The excavations at Yanik Tepe, Azerbaijan, 1962: Third preliminary report. Ibid. 26:54–61.
Burton Brown, T.
  1951 *Excavations in Azerbaijan, 1948*. London: John Murray.
  1962 Excavations in Shahrigar, Iran. *Archaeology* 15:27–31.

FOR FURTHER REFERENCE

16.69 No sources known to the editors of the University of Chicago Press are particularly useful in supplementing generally the forms recommended in this chapter. The style sheets of influential journals, however, particularly in scientific work, are often helpful in giving forms for listing types of publications frequently cited in their fields. Mentioned earlier were two publications useful for establishing abbreviations for the names of publishers: *Books in Print* and *British Books in Print: The Reference Catalogue of Current Literature*, for American and British publishers, respectively. Also mentioned earlier was the excellent list of abbreviated journal titles in *Chemical Abstracts List of Periodicals*.

17   Citing Public Documents

FORM OF THE CITATION

17.1   The purpose of using a particular form of citation for public documents is to make them accessible to anyone wishing to locate them in a library. Most large institutional libraries in the United States subscribe to the *National Union Catalog: A Cumulative Author List Representing Library of Congress Printed Cards and*

389

Titles Submitted by Other American Libraries and to the Library of Congress printed card service. Accordingly, it is most sensible for authors to conform to the Library of Congress form of citation except in matters of capitalization and punctuation. This form requires the following order of information. First, the country, state, city, town, or other governmental division (for example, United States [commonly abbreviated in footnote references], Illinois, Chicago, Highland Park, Cook County) issuing the document; second, the legislative body, executive department, court, bureau, board, commission, or committee; and third, any further division, regional office, etc.

> U.S., Treasury Department, Internal Revenue Service, District Director

17.2   Following the information about the "author" or issuing agent, the title of the document or collection of documents should be given. The remainder of the citation is largely determined by the nature of the document. For example, the *Congressional Record* requires the number of the Congress, the session, the year, the volume, sometimes the part, and the page number, but no facts of publication; reports require document or report numbers in addition to the Congress and session; and reports prepared by individual persons for the government require those persons' names and the facts of publication. Recommended forms for citation of public documents are grouped at the end of this chapter.

UNITED STATES DOCUMENTS

17.3   Public documents in the United States may be divided into two main types: the congressional (journals of the House and Senate; debates; reports, hearings, and documents of committees; and statutes) and the executive departmental (reports, bulletins, circulars, etc.).

CONGRESSIONAL DOCUMENTS

17.4   *House Journal, Senate Journal.* Motions, actions taken, votes on roll calls or divisions, but no speeches except presidential addresses and messages; published separately for House and Senate at the end of each session.

390

17.5   Until 1874 congressional debates were privately printed.

1789–1824	*Annals of Congress*
1824–37	*Congressional Debates*
1833–73	*Congressional Globe*

In 1874 the government began to print its own record of the debates, in the *Congressional Record*.

17.6   *Statutory material.* The most commonly encountered forms of statutory material are the following:

United States Constitution.

Statutes at Large. Contains all laws passed since the adoption of the Constitution; issued at the close of each Congress or, after 1938, at the end of each calendar year.

Revised Statutes. Most statutes in force as of 1 December 1873; published 1875. Cite by section only.

Revised Statutes (2d ed., 1878). Published to correct inaccuracies; two supplements issued to cover period from 1874 to 1901. Cite by section only.

United States Code. Contains all laws in force. Latest edition: 1964; cumulative supplements issued each year. Cite by title and section (because sections are not continuous throughout a volume).

17.7   Several other compilations of documents that will be encountered less frequently are the following:

Journal of the Congress of the Confederate States of America, 1861–65.

Journal of the Continental Congress.

American State Papers. Legislative and executive, 1789–1838. Organized by class—for example, I. Foreign Relations; II. Indian Affairs; III. Finance; VIII. Public Lands.

Senate Documents (1817–49, 1876–).

Senate Executive Documents (1847–95).

Senate Miscellaneous Documents (1847–76).

Senate Reports (1847–).

State Papers (1817–30). House documents.

Executive Documents (1830–47). House documents.

House Documents (1876–).

House Executive Documents (1847–95).

House Miscellaneous Documents (1847–76).

House Reports (1819–).

Executive Journal of the Senate. Nominations and treaties. Published only when released from injunction to secrecy; latest, 1948. Since 1929 most deliberations on nominations and treaties have been conducted in open session and so can be found in the *Congressional Record*.

EXECUTIVE DEPARTMENTAL DOCUMENTS

17.8 *Example: Department of State.* Each State Department publication is classified in a series. It is given a series number and a publication number, both of which must be included in a citation. Examples of series are the following:

> Treaty Series
> Executive Agreement Series (the first two were replaced by Treaties and Other International Acts Series in 1946)
> Arbitration Series
> Commercial Policy Series
> Conference Series
> European Series
> Far Eastern Series
> Inter-American Series
> Latin American Series
> Map Series

STATE AND LOCAL GOVERNMENTAL DOCUMENTS

17.9 Citations should parallel the form for federal documents.

UNPUBLISHED PUBLIC DOCUMENTS

17.10 Materials in the National Archives in Washington, D.C.—records, films, still photographs, sound recordings—should be cited by "record group" number, a classificatory system developed in the 1940s. A record group commonly consists of the records of a bureau, executive department at the bureau level, or independent agency. Examples are:

> Record Group 55, "Records of the Danish Government of the Virgin Islands"
> Record Group 65, "Records of the Federal Bureau of Investigation"
> Record Group 91, "Records of the Inland Waterway Corporation"
> Record Group 105, "Records of the Bureau of Refugees, Freedmen, and Abandoned Lands"

17.11 A guide to the record groups, arranged in numerical order, is contained in *Guide to the Records in the National Archives* (1948). Supplements are issued quarterly in *National Archives Accessions*.

PUBLIC DOCUMENTS OF GREAT BRITAIN

STATUTES

17.12   The chief collections of statutory material are the following:

The Statutes. Statutes of the period 1235–1948, with the exception of the years 1642–60.

Acts and Ordinances of the Interregnum, ed. C. H. Firth and R. S. Rait, 3 vols. (London, 1911). Includes statutes not listed in the preceding.

Public General Acts. Since 1921, published after every session of Parliament.

17.13   After passage each public bill is given a chapter number. The form of the citation should be as follows: year of reign, monarch's name (abbreviated), and chapter number. Official abbreviations: Car. (Charles), Edw., Eliz., Geo., Hen., Jac. (James), Phil. & M., Rich., Vict., Will., W. & M. Arabic numbers are used throughout—including the ordinals of monarchs' names (Geo. 6, Eliz. 2)—except for chapter numbers, which vary according to the type of bill: public (arabic chapter number), private (roman chapter number), and local (italic arabic chapter number).

PARLIAMENTARY PAPERS

17.14   The *Parliamentary Papers,* sometimes called *Sessional Papers,* are divided into three series: *Accounts and Papers, Bills,* and *Reports.* Both volume number in *Parliamentary Papers* and volume number in series are necessary for a citation; page numbers alone are not very helpful—in fact, are misleading—since volumes are often not paged consecutively throughout. The three series are composed of "command papers," each of which is assigned a number. The following series have been used to date:

1833–68/69	No. 1 to No. 4222
1870–99	C. 1 to C. 9550
1900–1918	Cd. 1 to Cd. 9239
1919–1955/56	Cmd. 1 to Cmd. 9899
1956/57–	Cmnd. 1–

17.15   Various other compilations may be encountered:

House of Lords Journal (successor to the *Rolls of Parliament*)
House of Commons Journal
House of Lords *Papers and Bills*
House of Commons *Papers*
House of Commons *Bills*

DEBATES

17.16   Until 1908 House of Lords and House of Commons debates were published together; since 1908 they have been published in separate series:

> *Hansard Parliamentary Debates*, 1st series (1803–20)
> *Hansard Parliamentary Debates*, 2d series (1820–30)
> *Hansard Parliamentary Debates*, 3d series (1830–91)
> *Parliamentary Debates*, 4th series (1892–1908)
> *Parliamentary Debates*, Commons, 5th series (1909–)
> *Parliamentary Debates*, House of Lords, 5th series (1909–)

Although no longer the official name of the parliamentary debates, *Hansard* is still frequently used in citations to all series of debates.

EARLY RECORDS

17.17   The following are the chief collections of early records:

> *Pipe Rolls* (31 Hen. 1 to 2 Will. 4). Exchequer records.
> *Chancellor's Rolls* (9 Hen. 2 to 2 Will. 4). Exchequer records.
> *Charter Rolls* (1 John to 8 Hen. 8). Most formal letters.
> *Patent Rolls* (3 John to present). Less formal letters.
> *Close Rolls* (6 John to 1903). Letters and deeds directed to specific persons.
> *Fine Rolls* (1 John to 23 Car. 1). Judicial writs and appointments.

Further information may be found in *Guide to the Contents of the Public Record Office*, 2 vols. (London, 1963).

UNITED NATIONS DOCUMENTS

17.18   There are three classes of United Nations documents: Official Records, Treaty Series, and special agency series. The organs of the United Nations (General Assembly, Security Council, Economic and Social Council, Disarmament Commission, etc.) and the special agencies (FAO, GATT, ICAO, UNESCO, ITU, WHO, etc.) all have their own series, numbered consecutively.

RECOMMENDED FORMS OF CITATION

17.19   In the following paragraphs, forms preferred by the University of Chicago Press for citing public documents are given. The examples are far from exhaustive; indeed, only the most commonly cited types of documents are included. For documents not falling in any of the categories illustrated, the general principles given at the beginning of the chapter (pars. 17.1–2) plus common sense should suggest logical forms. It will be noted that the examples here are all in footnote form. These can easily be converted to bibliographical form by following the suggestions in par. 16.14.

17.20   The forms suggested are full citations, which would be shortened after first use in a given book or chapter. A reference to the *Senate Journal*, for example, would be fully cited as follows:

> 1. U.S., Congress, Senate, *Journal*, 16th Cong., 1st sess., 7 December 1819, pp. 9–19.

In shortened form this might read:

> 1. Senate, *Journal* [or *Senate Journal*], 16th Cong., 1st sess., 7 December 1819, pp. 9–19.

In a book with a great deal of documentation of this sort, the shortened form could be abbreviated further:

> 1. *Senate Journal*, 16 Cong., 1 sess., 7 Dec. 1819, pp. 9–19.

UNITED STATES CONGRESSIONAL DOCUMENTS

17.21   *Debates*

> 2. U.S., Congress, Senate, *Congressional Globe*, 39th Cong., 2d sess., 1867, 39, pt. 3:1792.
>
> 3. U.S., Congress, Senate, *Congressional Record*, 77th Cong., 1st sess., 1941, 87, pt. 9:9505.

17.22   *Reports and hearings*

> 4. U.S., Congress, House, Committee on Interior and Insular Affairs, *Fire Island National Seashore, N.Y.: Report to Accompany H.R. 7107*, 88th Cong., 2d sess., 1964, H. Rept. 1638, p. 5.
>
> 5. U.S., Congress, Senate, Committee on Commerce, *Conversion to Metric System: Hearing on S. 1278*, 88th Cong., 2d sess., 7 January 1964, p. 58.
>
> 6. U.S., Congress, Senate, Committee on Aeronautical and Space Sciences, *Soviet Space Programs*, 87th Cong., 2d sess., 1962, p. 301.

17.23   *Statutory material*

> 7. U.S., *Constitution*, Amend. 14, sec. [or §] 1.
>
> 8. U.S., *Statutes at Large*, vol. 65.

UNITED STATES EXECUTIVE DEPARTMENTAL DOCUMENTS

17.24   *Reports*

> 9. U.S., Department of State, *Trade Expansion Act of 1962*, Commercial Policy Series, no. 196, pp. 21–25.

10. U.S., Department of State, *Igbo: Basic Course*, prepared for the Foreign Service Institute by L. B. Swift, A. Ahaghotu, and E. Ugorji (Washington, D.C.: Government Printing Office, 1962), p. 400.

11. U.S., Department of State, *A Plan for the Establishment in Hawaii of a Center for Cultural and Technical Interchange between East and West*, 86th Cong., 2d sess., 1960, p. 28.

17.25 *Early records*

12. Correspondence Relative to the Public Deposits, *American State Papers: Finance*, 4:495–99.

Or, in an alternate form:

12. Correspondence Relative to the Public Deposits, *American State Papers*, Class III, *Finance*, 4:495–99.

13. *American State Papers: Miscellaneous*, 1:725.

14. J. J. Abert, Supplementary Report on the LeMoille Canal, to the Secretary of War, 27 January 1829, Record Group 77, National Archives, Washington, D.C.

PUBLIC DOCUMENTS OF GREAT BRITAIN

17.26 *Papers*

15. Great Britain, *Parliamentary Papers*, vol. 120 (*Accounts and Papers*, vol. 56, August 1906), "Trade and Navigation: Imports," pp. 10–107.

16. Great Britain, *Parliamentary Papers*, vol. 1 (1941/42) (*Bills: Public*, vol. 1), "Finance Bill," pt. 3 (Income Tax), pp. 11–18.

17. Great Britain, *Parliamentary Papers*, vol. 33 (1948/49) (*Accounts and Papers*, vol. 12, October 1949), "Trade and Navigation Accounts: Exports," pp. 131–42.

18. Great Britain, *Parliamentary Papers*, vol. 14 (1961/62) (*Reports from Commissioners, Inspectors, and Others*, vol. 7), "Report of the Midlands Electricity Board," Report no. 286, pp. 295–96.

19. Great Britain, *Parliamentary Papers*, vol. 15 (*Reports*, vol. 5), "Twenty-fifth Annual Report of the Fishery Board for Scotland: Scientific Investigations," Cd. 3682, 1906, p. 20.

20. Great Britain, *Parliamentary Papers* (Commons), "Reports from the Select Committee on the Education of the Lower Orders in the Metropolis" (nos. 427, 469, 495, 497, 498), 1816, 4:100.

21. Great Britain, *Parliamentary Register*, 32 (1792):212–17.

17.27 *Debates*

22. Great Britain, *Parliamentary Debates* (Commons), Standing Committee E, *Official Report*, vol. 4 (Transport Bill), 5 December 1961, pp. 3–7.

23. Great Britain, *Parliamentary Debates* (Lords), 5th ser., 58 (1924): 111–15.

24. Great Britain, *Hansard's Parliamentary Debates*, 3d ser., 249 (1879): 611–27.

25. Great Britain, *Parliamentary Debates* (Commons), 5th ser., 26 (1911):226–27.

26. *Patent Rolls*, 3 Rich. 2, pt. 1, m. 12d (*Calendar of Patent Rolls, 1377–81*, p. 470).

IRISH PUBLIC DOCUMENTS

17.28 *Parliamentary papers*

27. Eire, *Parliamentary Debates* (Senate), 54 (1961) : 106–226.

28. Ireland, *Parliamentary Register* (Commons), 11 (1791) : 1–7.

29. Northern Ireland, *Parliamentary Debates* (Commons), 53 (1962–63) : 1130–35.

UNITED NATIONS DOCUMENTS

17.29 *Papers and reports*

30. United Nations, Economic and Social Council, *Report of the Permanent Central Opium Board* (E/OB/17), December 1961, pp. 40–45.

31. United Nations, Secretariat, *Treaty Series*, 360 (1960) : 200–201.

32. United Nations, General Assembly, *Summary Records* (A/C. 4/S.R. 1232), 1 December 1961, p. 2.

33. United Nations, General Assembly, *Report of the Subcommittee on the Situation in Angola*, Suppl. 16 (A/4978), January 1962, pp. 40–45.

34. Food and Agricultural Organization, *Food Additive Control in Denmark*, prepared by Erik Uhl and Soren C. Hansen (FAO Additive Control Series, no. 5), 1961, pp. 25–30.

35. World Health Organization, *Toxic Hazards of Pesticides to Man: Twelfth Report of the Expert Committee on Insecticides* (WHO Technical Report Series, no. 227), 1962, pp. 6–10.

FOR FURTHER REFERENCE

17.30 Everett S. Brown's *Manual of Government Publications* (1950) is a guide to United States public documents and some foreign documents; helpful information about federal and local documents and archives, and bibliographical listings of guides to these materials, may be found in *Harvard Guide to American History*. Standard guides to archival material are: *Guide to the Records in the National Archives*, with quarterly supplements in *National Archives Accessions; Guide to Archives and Manuscripts in the United States*, edited by Philip M. Hamer, listing the collections of more than one thousand archival agencies, historical societies, libraries, and other organizations; and, for British archival materials, *Guide to the Contents of the Public Record Office*. T. R. Schellenberg's *Modern Archives* contains an explanation of the classification systems of the British, French, and German archives. Philip C. Brooks's *Research in Archives* offers useful suggestions, with examples, on citing unpublished archival materials.

18 Indexes

18.1   Every serious book of nonfiction should have an index if it is to achieve its maximum usefulness. A good index records every pertinent statement made within the body of the text. The key word here is *pertinent*. The subject matter and purpose of the book determine which statements are pertinent and which peripheral. An index should be considerably more than an expanded table of contents and considerably less than a concordance of words and phrases.

DEFINITIONS

18.2   *Kinds of indexes.* Because an index should enable a reader to find every pertinent statement made in a book, it usually includes both proper-name and subject entries. Occasionally, if the material is complex and there is a large cast of characters, two indexes are prepared: one of persons only and the other of subjects and proper names other than those of persons. This division may be particularly helpful to the reader of a large historical work, for instance. An even further division may be useful in a history of literature, art, or music, in which a separate listing of the works of

400

the creators may be provided. For example, an anthology of poetry in several parts with discursive introductions may require a subject index, an author-and-title index, and an index of first lines. Perhaps the rarest is the index that is of subject matter only, as might be called for in a discourse on philosophy, theology, or mathematics. Needless to say, the last-named is the most difficult to prepare, and usually requires a specialist in the particular field.

18.3   *Entries and subentries.* The *entry* is the principal subdivision of an index. A simple entry consists of a *heading* and *page references.* The heading is a concisely phrased statement of one particular subject discussed within the book; it usually includes at least one noun, which may be modified by other parts of speech. The page references, or *folios,* direct the reader to information in the book about the heading; if this information continues for more than one page, that fact must be indicated by the citation of the pages on which the discussion begins and ends. (The abbreviations *f., ff.,* and *et seq.* should never be used in an index; *passim,* to signal scattered references in a sequence of pages, is allowable but should be used sparingly.)

Brest-Litovsk, Treaty of, 469–70, 473, 479

Indefinite article, 53, 175, 187–201 passim

The two examples above are of entries unmodified by subentries. The *subentry,* which usually consists of a *subheading* and page references, enables the reader to find discussion of particular aspects of the principal entry of which it forms a part:

Statistical material, 16, 17, 89; marking of, for printers, 176; months in, 65; proofreading, 183; states, territories, and possessions in, 65–66; time of day in, 64; units of measure in, 63

Indian: ceremonial dances, 20; food, 33, 261–73; handicrafts, 11–17, 134; marriage customs, 84

18.4   Obviously every subheading must bear a logical relationship to the heading. Usually it must also bear a close grammatical relationship; that is, it must be possible to join heading and subheading in normal order and have the combined phrase make sense grammatically as well as semantically. In the example above at left, note how the heading and first subheading join to read "marking of statistical material for printers." In the last example the principal heading, *Indian,* is an adjective and modifies successively the four subheadings. Never, of course, should a word (such as *Indian*) that can be used as either adjective or noun be used in both senses in the same entry.

18.5　Often it is necessary or helpful to use subheadings that are subdivisions or units within a larger category, expressed in the principal heading:

Sacred books: Bible, 77; Koran, 34–37; Talmud, 128–30; Upanishads, 92–96; Vedas, 143–51

Indian tribes: Ahualucos, 140–41; Aztecs, 81–84; Chichimecs, 67–68; Huastecs, 154; Mixe, 178; Olmecs, 90–102; Toltecs, 128–36; Zapotecs, 168–72

In such instances, the relationship between entry and subentry is logical rather than grammatical and need not be expressed in grammatical terms.

18.6　A complete entry consists of the principal entry, all subentries (including page references), and all cross-references.

18.7　*Cross-references.* Cross-references, devices inserted at appropriate places in the index to guide the reader in his search for the complete information contained in the book, are of two general kinds: *see* references, and *see also* references.

18.8　*See* references are used in the following situations:

1. When the indexer has chosen one among several key words or phrases and the reader might refer to another:

Roman Catholic Church. *See* Catholicism
Adolescence. *See* Youth

2. When the subject has been treated as a subentry to a principal entry:

Book of Common Prayer. *See* Church of England, and Book of Common Prayer
Iroquois Indians. *See* Indian tribes, Iroquois

3. When an entry has been alphabetized under another letter of the alphabet:

The Hague. *See* Hague, The
Van Gogh, Vincent. *See* Gogh, Vincent van

4. When a personal name has been alphabetized under the real surname rather than pseudonym, name in religion, earlier name, or married name:

Bell, Currer. *See* Brontë, Charlotte
Louis, Father. *See* Merton, Thomas

Thibault, Jacques Anatole. *See* France, Anatole
Burton, Mrs. Richard. *See* Taylor, Elizabeth

5. When reference is from a popular or shortened form of a term to the "official," scientific, or full form:

Mormon Church. *See* Jesus Christ of Latter-Day Saints, Church of
Baking soda. *See* Bicarbonate of soda

African violet. *See* Saintpaulia
Gray's "Elegy." *See* "Elegy Written in a Country Churchyard" (Gray)

An entry composed of a heading and a *see* reference is termed a *blind entry*.

18.9   *See also* references are used when *additional* information can be found in another entry or subentry:

Elizabethan Settlement, 11–15, 17, 43; and Hooker, 13–14. *See also* Catholicism; Church of England; Protestantism

Maya: art of, 236–43; cities of, 178 (*see also* Chichén Itzá; Uxmal); human sacrifice among, 184–87; present-day, 267. *See also* Quiché Maya; Yucatán, Indians of

18.10   All cross-references that pertain to an entire principal entry should usually appear at the end of the complete entry and be preceded by a period (but see par. 18.91 and the index to this book). Those pertaining only to a subentry should follow that subentry and be enclosed within parentheses. The terms *see* and *see also* should be marked for italic type but may appear in roman type if they are followed by italic type. A cross-reference should be used only if it leads to additional page references.

18.11   In all cross-references, headings of both principal entries and subentries should be cited in full form and exactly as they appear in the index, with inversion and punctuation carefully observed. When more than one principal heading is cited, these should be separated by semicolons; if reference is to a subheading, the corresponding principal heading should be cited first, followed by a comma and the subheading. Cross-references should be given in alphabetical order.

18.12   *Run-in and indented styles.* In most general books the index is set in *run-in* style; that is, the subentries follow one another with no breaks between. All the examples above of entries that include subentries are set in run-in style. Often in reference works such as encyclopedias and occasionally in general books of a highly detailed nature, the index is set in *indented* style; that is, each subentry begins a new line, indented from the left, usually one em.

Orthodentine, 22, 99, pl. 17
   formation of, 60–63
   reticular fibers in, 96, 102
   in subholosteans and holosteans, 90,
      103, pls. 18 and 19
   in teleosts, 95, 96

The latter arrangement makes a very complex index easier for the eye to follow and also allows for the use of sub-subentries. Whichever style is used for the subentries, runover lines are always indented from the left in an index.

THE INDEXER

18.13   The ideal indexer sees the book as a whole—both in scope and in arbitrary limitations—understands the emphasis of the various parts and their relationships to the whole, and—perhaps most important of all—clearly pictures the potential reader and anticipates his special needs. He must make certain that every pertinent statement in the book has been recorded in the index in such a way that the reader will be able to find without difficulty the information he seeks. He must have sufficient knowledge of both publishing and printing practices to be able to present the data he assembles according to editorial amenities and within the mechanical limitations of typography.

18.14   *The author as indexer.* The author most nearly approaches the ideal as indexer. Certainly, he knows better than anyone else both the scope and limitations of his work; and certainly, he knows the audience to which he has addressed himself. At the same time, he can be so subjective about his own work that he may be tempted to include in his index even references to milieu-establishing, peripheral statements and, as a result, may prepare a concordance rather than an efficient index. Invariably, the best scholarly indexes are made by authors who have the ability to be objective about their work, who understand what a good index is, and who have mastered the mechanics of the indexing craft.

18.15   *The professional indexer.* The professional has the advantages of objectivity and experience in many fields of interest and scholarship. His acquaintance is seldom as deep as that of an author in any particular field, and so he may miss some subtleties, but for the author who cannot prepare his own index, the professional indexer is the logical choice for the task. In much of what follows in this chapter it is assumed, for purposes of fuller explanation, that the author and the indexer are not the same person.

18.16   Whoever the indexer is, he should be intelligent, widely read, and well acquainted with publishing practices; he must also be level-headed, patient, scrupulous in his handling of detail, and analytically minded. This rare bird must, at the same time that he is being intelligent, level-headed, patient, accurate, and analytical, work at top speed to meet an almost impossible deadline. Less time is available for the preparation of the index than for almost any other step in the bookmaking process. For obvious reasons, an index cannot be completed until page proofs are available.

404

Typesetters are anxious for those few final pages of copy; printers want to get the job on the press; binders are waiting; salesmen are clamoring for finished books—let's get that index done!

THE PROCESS OF INDEXING

18.17   Indexes are usually prepared from page proofs. Some preliminary work can be done from galleys, particularly if the book is of great length and complexity. From galleys, the indexer can make some decisions about headings, and even subheadings, and prepare index cards accordingly. He cannot complete any entry until page proofs are available, however, and so except in special circumstances it is usual to wait for page proofs before beginning work on an index.

18.18   From the page proofs individual cards are prepared (usually one item to a card) and alphabetized. When all entries, subentries, and suitable cross-references have been made, the cards are edited into final form. Then the entire index is retyped, double-space, on 8½-by-11-inch sheets in a form that can be marked by the editor and set in type by the printer.

PREPARING THE INDEX CARDS

18.19   The indexer should hold in mind that he is preparing a working tool for the one book at hand. By the time of page proofs, decisions have long since been reached between author and editor concerning style and usage. If British spelling has been used consistently throughout the text, so should it be in the index. Shakspere in the text would call for Shakspere in the index. Hernando Cortez should not be indexed as Cortés, Hernán, Cortes, Hernando, or any other variant; Virgil as Vergil; Sir Walter Raleigh as Ralegh, Sir Walter. Similarly, the spelling of place names should agree with the text; if the author used the language of origin ('s Gravenhage, Köln), the name should not be changed in the index to the better-known English form (Hague, The; Cologne). Nor should geographical terms be altered to their present form (Saint Petersburg, Petrograd, Leningrad; Cape Canaveral, Cape Kennedy; Siam, Thailand; Byzantium, Constantinople, Istanbul). The use of accents and other diacritical marks should also be observed (Yucatán, Yucatan; Schönberg, Schoenberg). Only in the rare instance in which confusion might arise in the reader's mind should any cross-reference or parenthetical word or phrase be inserted giving "correct" or more widely used forms. In spelling, capitalization, use of italics, etc., the index should scrupulously reflect the text (but see par. 18.41). The indexer must not attempt to edit the book in page proofs; at the same time, he may indicate, directly on the proofs, obvious typographic or other errors and index according to the correction. (The page proofs he is working on are not the corrected master set, of course, but an unmarked duplicate set.) He should keep a list of these items and call them to the attention of the manuscript editor when he delivers the finished index along with the set of proofs he has been using.

18.20   At the outset, the indexer must familiarize himself with the entire work by reading quickly through the proofs from beginning to end. Only then can he be aware of the scope, chronological or otherwise; the author's approach and self-imposed limitations, historical, philosophical, political, clinical, or other; the "cast of characters," whether human or in the guise of other entities.

18.21   Abundant desk or table space is essential for efficient indexing. Because page proofs are often printed on long sheets with more than one actual book page on each sheet, the indexer may find it convenient to cut the proof sheets into individual pages. He will then find his working space less cluttered, and he will more easily spot page folios by being able to see each page as an entity as it will appear in the finished book.

18.22   Being supplied with three-by-five cards, an alphabetical guide for these cards, and a file box, he is now ready to begin his actual indexing. Cards should be typed, not handwritten, to obviate later errors arising from misinterpretation of the indexer's handwriting. A special platen for index cards speeds typing, but is not really necessary, and the long strips of perforated card stock which tear apart into three-by-five cards are another (and alternate) luxury.

18.23   As each entry is noted on its card, a key word or phrase may be underlined or otherwise indicated on the proof; this will later enable the indexer, on rechecking his cards against the proofs, to make sure that he has indeed included everything that should appear in the final index. On this first trip through the proofs, it is better to make too many entries than later to backtrack and attempt to retrieve material originally overlooked; unnecessary and peripheral items can be eliminated later.

INDEXABLE AND NONINDEXABLE PARTS OF THE BOOK

18.24 Preliminary matter—dedications, epigraphs, forewords, prefaces, acknowledgments, tables of contents, lists of illustrations (including charts, maps, graphs) and lists of tables should not be indexed. An exception is an introduction that for one reason or another is placed among the preliminaries rather than with the text. Nor should most of the back matter be indexed: glossary, bibliography, and so on; appendixes should be indexed if they contain important pertinent material not included in the main body of the text but not if they merely reproduce documents (for example, the text of a treaty) that are discussed in the text.

18.25 Notes, whether at the foot of the page or at the back of the book, may be indexed if they continue or amplify discussion in the text (textual or reading notes); those that merely document statements in the text (reference notes) should not be indexed. Index references to notes should normally be by page number alone; for example, 134 n (thin space between numeral and *n*, no period after *n*). If there are several notes on a page, the note number may be given (in this instance with a period): 134 n.14.

18.26 Matter in tables, charts, graphs, maps, drawings, photographs, and other illustrative material is occasionally listed in the index when it is of particular importance to the discussion. Then too, index references to illustrations may be of great assistance to the reader when he can be referred to a reproduction of a painting being discussed in an art book. References to illustrative material can be by both page number and illustration (pl., fig., chart) or table number.

WHAT GOES ON THE CARD

18.27 Finding an indexable item on a page, the indexer prepares a card. (There should be one card for each heading and only one page reference per card, especially in the early stages.) The card records three facts:

1. A key term, or "subject." (This will probably become the heading for a main entry.)

2. A statement about the key term, or "predicate." (In the final form of the index, some of these statements will become subentries, whereas others will be dropped, as cards are combined and page references grouped under main entries.)

3. The page reference. (If the passage indexed covers more than a single page, beginning and ending pages should be given.)

18.28   Abbreviations should be used sparingly in an index. Exceptions to this general practice might be in scientific, mathematical, or other similar works covering fields in which abbreviations have become part of the accepted language and are used even within the text itself.

18.29   *An example.* In figure 18.1, showing a paragraph from chapter 4 of John A. Wilson's *The Burden of Egypt* (Chicago: University of Chicago Press, 1951), several words have been underlined and one

---

King as a god —70

On the rock plateau of Gizeh, to the north of the capital city at Memphis, rise the three great pyramids of the Fourth Dynasty. Artificial mountains designed to resist decay to the maximum, they are symbolic in two respects. Their enduring shape and construction asserted very successfully an eternal life for the mortal being who was buried within; and the investment in labor and materials in each pyramid was a ringing insistence that the service of the king was the most important task of the state. No other activity visibly and enduringly claimed the energies of the Egyptian people. It was the eternal home of their god-king, which was worthy of their supreme efforts in time, in materials, in manpower, and in craftsmanship. In sublime arrogance the royal pyramids dominated the Old Kingdom and sent their shadows down the ages.

Fig. 18.1. One paragraph from page proof as marked by indexer

---

phrase written in the margin as possible index headings. These might be handled as follows on cards (the paragraph appears on page 69 of the text):

```
Gizeh            site of pyramids         69
Dynasty, Fourth  pyramids built in        69
God-king         concept behind pyramids  69-70
King as god      exemplified in pyramids  69-70
Old Kingdom      pyramids produced under  69-70
```

18.30   The cards reflect earlier, as well as on-the-spot, decisions of the indexer. As a result of his quick perusal of the pages, he had decided that the many references to dynasties might best be grouped under a main heading, *Dynasty.* He had discovered too that the theme of the divinity of the king ran through long stretches of the book, thus meriting special attention. At this point he had not decided whether *King as a god* would be a main entry or not and if so whether it might better be *Divinity of king.* As it turned out, the main heading was *King,* and *as a god*—with several other page references—a subheading. Also, since other references to *God-king* were few and (as here) equivalent to *King as a god*, this became a blind entry:

> God-king. *See* King, as a god

CHOOSING TERMS FOR ENTRIES

18.31   As nearly as possible, the indexer should imagine himself the eventual reader and try to anticipate needs and expectations. Under what headings would he be most likely to look for information? How full should these headings be? Should they be expanded, modified, or broken down? What should be included? What omitted?

18.32   The wording for all entries should be clear, concise, logical, and consistent throughout. Terms should be chosen according to the author's usage as far as possible. If, for example, the author of a philosophical work uses the term *essence* to mean *being*, *essence* should be used in the index, with perhaps a cross-reference. If the same author has used the same terms interchangeably, only one should be chosen for use in the index; in the latter instance, suitable cross-reference is essential:

> Essence (being), 97, 109, 119, 246, 359
> Being. *See* Essence

Considerable thought should be given to the choice of key words in all entries. If the terminology of the author cannot be used in brief form in the index, a widely known equivalent should be substituted. Here is where the indexer must, above all, put himself in the place of the eventual reader and choose words that will most readily come to mind. Common sense is often the best guide. If the indexer is faced with a choice between two equally cogent words or phrases, he can simply choose one and indicate by a cross-reference the choice he has made.

WHEN TO INDEX PROPER NAMES

18.33   An entry should be made for every proper name about which a pertinent statement is made. For example, a book on city planning in California might include the statement, "Los Angeles is the third most populous city in the United States, being exceeded only by New York and Chicago." In this context, only one proper name should be indexed at this point: Los Angeles. New York and Chicago are mentioned only to give a point of reference and should not be indexed here even though the names of these two cities may occur in other, more significant contexts elsewhere in the book. Again, a Spanish grammar might say, "Between 1585 and 1588, Cervantes wrote and produced more than twenty plays, of which only two survive, *La Numancia* and *El trato de Argel*," to illustrate a discussion of tense. The indexer would make no entries from this sentence for an index to the grammar. If, however, the same sentence appeared in a biography or critical study of Cervantes, the index for the latter book should certainly include more than one reference to the sentence. Then too, scene-setting statements to establish historical milieu, particularly in opening sequences, should be carefully considered before they are indexed. For example, the first sentence of John M. Rosenfield's introduction to his *Dynastic Arts of the Kushans* (Berkeley and Los Angeles: University of California Press, 1967) reads: "In the first three centuries of the Christian era, a great inland empire stretched from the Ganges River valley into the oases of Central Asia. This empire was created by a nation of former nomads whose ruling princes gave themselves the dynastic name Kushan. Opulent and powerful men, cast in much the same mold of Iranian princely ideals as Darius the Great, Timur, or Akbar, they governed a land which lay at the junction of three culture spheres—the Indian subcontinent, Iran and the Hellenized Orient, and the steppes of Central Asia." Fine scene setting, impressive cast of characters—but the indexer should simply pass it by without making a single entry.

HOW TO INDEX NAMES OF PERSONS AND THINGS

18.34 Names of one sort or another make up the greater part of most indexes, and the index composed only of names is by no means unusual. Yet the handling of names probably causes more trouble for the uninitiated, would-be indexer than any other aspect of indexing craft. Therefore it will be discussed in some detail in the paragraphs that follow.

18.35 *Familiar forms of personal names.* Personal names should be indexed as they have become widely and professionally known:

> Lawrence, D. H. [*not* Lawrence, David Herbert]
> Poe, Edgar Allan [*not* Poe, E. A., *or* Poe, Edgar A.]
> Bizet, Georges [*not* Bizet, Alexandre César Léopold]
> Cervantes, Miguel de [*not* Cervantes Saavedra, Miguel de]

(Note, however, that in a biography or critical study of Lawrence, Bizet, or Cervantes, the full name should appear in the index.)

18.36   *Pseudonyms.* Persons who use pseudonyms professionally should be listed under their real names, with suitable cross-references:

Ouida. *See* Ramée, Marie Louise de la

Ramée, Marie Louise de la [pseud. Ouida]

Æ. *See* Russell, George William

Russell, George William [pseud. Æ]

18.37   *Persons with same names.* Persons with the same names, both surnames and given names, should be further identified:

Field, David Dudley (clergyman)
Field, David Dudley (lawyer)

If many persons with the same surname appear in the same book, particularly if they are members of the same immediate family, suitable parenthetical identifications should be furnished in the index. For example, the index to *O'Neill* by Arthur and Barbara Gelb (New York: Harper & Bros., 1962) contains the following entries:

O'Neill, Edmund Burke (brother)
O'Neill, Edward (grandfather)
O'Neill, Mrs. Edward (Mary) (grandmother)
O'Neill, Mrs. Eugene (Agnes Boulton O'Neill Kaufman)
O'Neill, Mrs. Eugene (Carlotta Monterey O'Neill)
O'Neill, Mrs. Eugene (Kathleen Jenkins O'Neill Pitt-Smith)
O'Neill, Eugene Gladstone
O'Neill, Eugene, Jr.
O'Neill, Mrs. Eugene, Jr. (Elizabeth Green)

O'Neill, Eugene, III (son of Shane)
O'Neill, James (father)
O'Neill, Mrs. James (mother) (Mary Ellen "Ella" Quinlan)
O'Neill, James, Jr. ("Jamie") (brother)
O'Neill, John (godfather)
O'Neill, Oona (daughter by Agnes) (Mrs. Charles Chaplin)
O'Neill, Shane Rudraighe (son by Agnes)
O'Neill, Mrs. Shane (Catherine Givens)

18.38   *Married women.* Many married women are widely known by their maiden names, and should usually be indexed accordingly. References to married names can, if necessary in the context, be supplied in parentheses or by means of suitable cross-references:

Sutherland, Joan (Mrs. Richard Bonynge)
Bonynge, Mrs. Richard. *See* Sutherland, Joan

Marinoff, Fania (Mrs. Carl Van Vechten)
Van Vechten, Mrs. Carl. *See* Marinoff, Fania

Many others, better known by their married names, should be indexed under their married names, with references to their maiden names, husbands' full names, familiar names, and the like supplied within parentheses or by cross-references if needed:

Besant, Annie (neé Wood)
Wood, Annie. *See* Besant, Annie
Browning, Elizabeth Barrett

Roosevelt, Eleanor (Mrs. Franklin D.)
Truman, Mrs. Harry S. (Bess)

Occasionally, a woman may play two roles of importance within the confines of a single book—as an unmarried person and later as a wife. For example, in a study of the Barrett family, the following index entries might be needed for one person:

Barrett, Elizabeth (later Elizabeth Barrett Browning), 12, 18–36, 79–82. *See also* Browning, Elizabeth Barrett

Browning, Elizabeth Barrett, 128, 143–45, 162–67. *See also* Barrett, Elizabeth

18.39   *Monarchs, saints, popes.* Monarchs, saints, popes, should be listed according to their "official," not personal, names:

John (king of England)   Leo XIII (pope)
Xavier, Saint Francis

18.40   *Obscure persons.* Persons referred to in the book by surname or given name only should be further identified:

Thaxter (family physician)   John (Smith's shipmate on *Stella*)

18.41   *Full form of name.* Proper names should be indexed in full, even though the author may use shortened forms in the text:

TEXT	INDEX
"the president" or "Nixon"	Nixon, Richard M.
"the lake"	Michigan, Lake
"the bay"	San Francisco Bay
"Shasta"	Shasta, Mount
"the Village"	Greenwich Village

18.42   *Confusing names.* Proper names about which there might be some confusion should be clearly identified within parentheses:

New York (city)   Mississippi (state)
New York (state)   Mississippi (river)

18.43   *Acronyms and abbreviated forms of proper names.* Certain governmental, international, and other organizations that have become widely known under their abbreviated names, usually consisting of capital letters, should be indexed according to the abbreviations, particularly if the full names are cumbersome and little known. Abbreviations of organizations not widely known by abbreviations may appear in parentheses following the full name in the index, especially if the author has used the abbreviations anywhere in the text:

AFL   NATO   UNESCO
CIO   SEATO   UNICEF

but:

United Nations (UN)   World Health Organization (WHO)
National Labor Relations Board (NLRB)

18.44   *Daily newspapers.* Most daily newspapers in English should be indexed under the name of the city of publication regardless of how the name appears on the masthead:

> *Chicago Sun-Times*
> *New York Daily News* [not *Daily News* or *Daily News, New York*]
> *New York Times*
>
> *but:*
>
> *Christian Science Monitor*
> *PM*
> *Times* (London)
> *Wall Street Journal*

A foreign language newspaper should be alphabetized according to the first substantive in its title; the place of publication may be included in parentheses:

> *Aurore, L'* (Paris)
> *Dziennik Zwiazkowy Zgoda* (Chicago)
> *Jewish Daily Forward* (Chicago)
> *Prensa, La* (Buenos Aires)

18.45   *Periodicals.* Periodicals are indexed according to the full title, disregarding any article that may appear at the beginning:

> *Nation*
> *Observer*
> *Saturday Review* [present American periodical]
> *Saturday Review* [British periodical]
> *Saturday Review of Literature* [American before 1952]

18.46   *Titles of artistic works.* A reference to a work by an author (or composer or painter) is usually indexed both as a main entry under its title and as a subentry under the main entry for the author. Most books cite the works of many authors, and so the author's name should be included, in parentheses, in the main entry for the individual work; if, however, the work is by the principal subject of a biographical or critical study, for example, such identification is not needed:

Wolfe, Thomas: childhood of, 6–8; early literary influences on, 7–10; literary reputation of, in 1939, 44; *Look Homeward, Angel*, 34–37; and Maxwell Perkins, 30–41

Look Homeward, Angel (Wolfe), 34–37

It has been assumed that the two entries above are from the index to a book of essays about American novelists of the 1930s and 1940s; hence the "(Wolfe)" after *Look Homeward, Angel*. If these had been from the index to a biography of Thomas Wolfe, the identification within parentheses would have been unnecessary.

413

18.47   If there are citations to many works by the same author, the titles of these works as subentries to the main entry for the author can be grouped, for easy reference, at the end of the other subentries:

Shelley, Percy Bysshe, 167–68, 193–96; and atheism, 195–96; and Blake, 196; and Coleridge, 193–94, 196; and Keats, 194–95; and Platonism, 167, 194–95; and religion, 167. Works: *Adonais*, 194–95, 200; *Defence of Poetry*, 194–96; *Mont Blanc*, 193–94; *Prometheus Unbound*, 196; *Queen Mab*, 193

Works and authors that are discussed in the text should be indexed as shown above; those that are cited in notes only as documentation should not usually be indexed in any form.

ALPHABETIZING THE CARDS

18.48   There are two ways of handling the physical job of arranging the raw index cards in alphabetical order. One is to hold them temporarily in page-number order until the indexer has gone completely through the proofs and then to alphabetize them all at once. The advantages of this method are (1) it gives the indexer a final opportunity to verify page references while his mind is not on other things as well and (2) it is usually faster in terms of net time spent in alphabetizing. The second way is to alphabetize the cards as he goes along. The chief advantages here are (1) the indexer can add page references to an already existing card if he remembers that he has a card with the heading he needs and (2) headings can be changed and cards refiled as he goes along if it becomes obvious that this should be done. Professional indexers use both methods, but probably incline more strongly to the second. Inexperienced indexers are best advised to use the first method because it tends to eliminate careless errors that result from doing several things at once.

18.49   There are different approaches also to the theoretical side of alphabetizing. The two chief approaches are called the *letter-by-letter* mode of alphabetizing and the *word-by-word*. All alphabetizing is letter by letter in one sense: in arranging a series of words in alphabetical order, one considers first the initial letter of the word, then the second letter, the third letter, and so on:

aardvark
aardwolf
Aaron
Ab
aba
abaca

The need to make a choice among different modes arises when one is alphabetizing not a set of single words but a set of headings, some of which consist of more than one word. How far does one carry the letter-by-letter principle? In the letter-by-letter mode one alphabetizes up to the first mark of punctuation; that is, one ignores spaces and hyphens between words. In the word-by-word mode, one applies the principle through the end of the first word and then stops, using second and subsequent words only when two or more headings begin with the same word. The differences should be apparent in the following series:

LETTER BY LETTER	WORD BY WORD
Newark	New Bern
New Bern	New England
Newborough	New Jersey
New England	New York
New Jersey	New Zealand
Newmarket	Newark
Newport	Newborough
New York	Newmarket
New Zealand	Newport

18.50   Letter-by-letter alphabetizing is strongly preferred by the University of Chicago Press, and any index prepared for a Chicago book should be so arranged. The letter-by-letter approach cannot be followed slavishly, of course. Exceptions are the handling of names beginning with *Mc* (see par. 18.59) and the alphabetizing of subentries, in which unimportant words are skipped over (see par. 18.54). Also, when the name of a person is the same as the name of a place, the person comes first (i.e., *London, Jack,* before *London, England*).

GENERAL RULES

18.51   The letter-by-letter approach should be followed in alphabetizing arbitrary combinations of letters, acronyms, and most abbreviations (see par. 18.57). Further identification may be furnished within parentheses:

ACTH (adrenocorticotropic hormone)
ASCAP (American Society of Composers, Authors, and Publishers)
UNESCO (United Nations Educational, Scientific and Cultural Organization)
WFMT (Chicago radio station)
XYZ affair

18.52   Numerals should be alphabetized as though spelled out:

> 10 Downing Street (alphabetized under *Ten*)
> 42d Street (alphabetized under *Forty-second*)

Years are alphabetized according to their usual spoken forms:

> 1066 (alphabetized as though spelled *ten sixty-six*)
> 1492 (alphabetized as though spelled *fourteen ninety-two*)

18.53   Umlauted vowels are alphabetized along with unumlauted vowels.

18.54   In alphabetizing headings of subentries, introductory articles, prepositions, and conjunctions are disregarded:

> Marinoff, Fania (Mrs. Carl Van Vechten); caricatured by Covarrubias, 128; childhood of, in Boston, 45; marriage of, 83; in *Spring's Awakening*, 133; at Stage Door Canteen, 145; as Trina in *Life's Whirlpool*, 137

18.55   Occasionally, arrangement of subheadings is according to chronological, mathematical, or other sense, rather than alphabetical (see par. 18.76):

> Dynasties, Egyptian: First, 10; Second, 12, 141; Third, 45; Fourth, 47–49
>
> Flora, alpine: at 1,000-meter level, 46, 130–35; at 1,500-meter level, 146–54; at 2,000-meter level, 49, 163–74

PERSONAL NAMES

18.56   *Names with particles.* Family names containing particles often present a perplexing problem to the indexer. Both the spelling and the alphabetizing of these names should follow the personal preference of, or accumulated tradition concerning, the individual, as best exemplified in *Webster's Biographical Dictionary.* Note the wide variations in the following list of actual names arranged as they should appear in an index:

> à Beckett, Gilbert Abbott
> Becket, Thomas à (*or* Becket, Saint Thomas)
> Broek, Jacobus ten
> D'Annunzio, Gabriele
> Da Ponte, Lorenzo
> de Gaulle, Charles
> De La Rey, Jacobus Hercules
> Deventer, Jacob Louis van
> de Vere, Aubrey Thomas
> De Vries, Hugo
> Gogh, Vincent van
> Guardia, Ricardo Aldolfo de la
>
> Hindenburg, Paul von
> La Fontaine, Jean de
> Lafontaine, Louis Hypolite
> La Guardia, Fiorello H.
> Linde, Otto zur
> Ramée, Marie Louise de la
> Robbia, Luca della
> Thomas a Kempis
> Vandervelde, Emile
> Van Devanter, Willis
> Van Rensselaer, Kiliaen
> Velde, Jan van de
> Von Schrenk, Hermann

18.57   *Names with "Saint."* A personal name in the form of a saint's name should be spelled according to the preference of the person himself. If spelled with the abbreviation, such names should nevertheless be alphabetized as if spelled out. In the names of saints, the

word *saint* should always be spelled out; an entry referring to a
saint, however, should be alphabetized according to the personal
name:

St. Denis, Ruth	St. Laurent, Louis Stephen
Sainte-Beuve, Charles Augustin	Saint-Saëns, Camille
Saint-Gaudens, Augustus	Sebastian, Saint

18.58 *Compound names.* Alphabetize compound surnames, with or without hyphens, according to preferences of individuals or established usage:

Ap Ellis, Augustine	Larevellière-Lépeaux, Louis Marie
Bannerman, Henry Campbell-	Lloyd George, David
Castelnuovo-Tedesco, Mario	Machado de Assis, Joaquim Maria
Diniz da Cruz e Silva, Antônio	Mendes, Frederic de Sola
Fénelon, François de Salignac de	Mendès-France, Pierre
La Mothe-	Merle d'Aubigne, Jean Henri
García Calderón, Francisco (*whose*	Merry del Val, Rafael
father is Calderón, Francisco García)	Ortega y Gasset, José
	Pinto, Fernám Mendes
Gatti-Casazza, Giulio	Vaughan Williams, Ralph
Ippolitov-Ivanov, Mikhail	

18.59 *Names with "Mac," etc.* Personal names beginning with "Mc," or "M'," the abbreviated forms of "Mac," should be indexed under "Mac," as though the full form were used:

Mabie, Hamilton W.	Macaulay, Rose
McAdoo, William G.	McAuley, Catharine
Macalister, Donals	MacMillan, Donald B.
McAllister, Alister	Macmillan, Harold
MacArthur, Douglas	

18.60 *Hungarian names.* In Hungarian, personal names appear with the surname first, followed by the given name (Bartók Béla). In English, however, Hungarian names are usually written in English order and reinverted—with the comma—in alphabetizing:

Bartók, Béla

18.61 *Arabic names.* Romanized Arabic names containing the elements *Abd* (which may be combined, as in *Abdul, Abd-el-*), *abu-*, and *ibn* are usually alphabetized under those elements:

Abd-al-Muttalib	abu-al-Ala al-Maarri
Abd-el-Krim	ibn-Khaldun
Abdul Kerim Pasha	ibn-Saud

Those beginning with *al-* (equivalent of *the*) are alphabetized under the element following this particle:

Battani, al-
Khansa, al-
Khwarizmi, al-

417

18.62   *Chinese names.* In the romanized form of most traditional Chinese names, the family name usually appears first, followed by the pre-name (usually hyphenated). Therefore, no inversion should be made in alphabetizing:

Chiang Kai-shek   Mao Tse-tung
Chia Shih-ku   Sun Yat-sen
Lin Yutang   Su Tung-p'o

Many Chinese names, particularly from earlier times, consist of only two elements. In the romanized forms, there is little consistency about the use of hyphens. These names too should be alphabetized without inversion:

Lao-tzu
Li Po
Sun Fo

Many twentieth-century Chinese with ties to the West have adopted the practice of giving the family name last (Tang Tsou, H. H. Kung, T. V. Soong, etc.). These names should be inverted in alphabetizing:

Kung, H. H.
Soong, T. V.
Tsou, Tang

18.63   *Japanese names.* Most Japanese names consist of only two elements—a single prename followed by the family name—and should be inverted in alphabetizing:

Hayakawa, Sessue
Tojo, Hideki
Yoshida, Shigeru

18.64   *Indian names.* Most modern Indian names appear with the surname last and should be inverted in alphabetizing. Note too that, as in other countries, personal preference of the individual as well as usage should be observed:

Gandhi, Mohandas Karamchand
Krishna Menon, V. K.
Nehru, Jawaharlal

18.65   *Burmese names.* Most Burmese names consist of only one element. The *U* that often accompanies the name is a term of respect:

Nu, U
Thant, U

18.66   *Indonesian names.* Most Indonesian names consist of only one element—which the person chooses for himself:

Suharto
Sukarno

18.67   *Vietnamese names.* Most Vietnamese names appear with the surname last and should be inverted in alphabetizing:

> Dong, Pham Van
> Thieu, Nguyen Van

18.68   *Other Asian names.* Throughout Asia, many names derive from the European languages and from Arabic, Chinese, and other, less widely used, languages, regardless of the places of birth of the persons bearing these names. The language from which the name derives may thus often be the determining factor in alphabetizing. Then too, in India, the many languages (Kannada, Malayalam, Tamil, Telugu), religions, and castes, all may affect the form of personal names. The entire matter seems to be undergoing great change in many parts of Asia at the present time. The indexer's immediate problem can perhaps best be solved by querying the author whenever the "rules," traditions, or standard reference works do not answer specific questions.

PLACE NAMES

18.69   *Geographic names.* Geographic proper names beginning with *Mount, Lake, Cape, Sea,* and the like which actually refer to the names of mountains, lakes, capes, and seas should be alphabetized according to the rest of the name following this element:

> Everest, Mount   Mendocino, Cape
> Japan, Sea of   Titicaca, Lake

If, however, this first element is thought of as part of the complete name, the name should be alphabetized according to the first element:

> Cape of Good Hope   Lake of the Woods

Names of cities or towns beginning with these same elements should be alphabetized according to the first element:

> Cape Girardeau, Mo.   Mount Vernon, N.Y.
> Lake Forest, Ill.   Sea Girt, N.J.

18.70   *Names beginning with articles.* Names beginning with non-English articles are usually alphabetized under the article:

> El Dorado   Le Bourget
> El Ferrol   Les Eyzies
> El Paso   Los Angeles
> La Coruña   Los Michis
> La Crosse   's Gravenhage
> LaPorte

Names beginning with *the* are alphabetized under the principal element:

> Dalles, the
> Hague, The
> Lizard, the

18.71   *Names with "Saint."* Place names beginning with *Saint* or *Sainte* should be spelled out in full:

> Saint Louis, Mo.
>> *not*
> St. Louis, Mo.

Note also that in French place names the saint's name is invariably hyphenated (though not when applied to the saint himself)—Ile Saint-Louis, Rue Saint-Honoré, Saint-Cloud.

EDITING THE COMPLETED INDEX CARDS

18.72   When the indexer reaches the end of the page proofs and has prepared cards for all entries and subentries he has deemed necessary, he should turn back to the proofs once again for another quick reading of the entire work. At this time, the marks he has made on the proofs to indicate that he has prepared cards for the signaled passages will assist him in making certain that his index is as full as it should be. He may find that unmarked items prove indexable in the light of later sections that develop a theme, at first mention seeming only peripheral, into a point of considerable importance to the work as a whole. In such instances, he will of course prepare new cards or add to those already made. Completely overlooked items may also be noticed at this time. When he has completed this final examination of the proofs and is satisfied that he has prepared cards for all indexable items, he should then examine every card to make sure that all necessary information has been included in proper form.

18.73   It is at this crucial stage that the index really takes shape. Editing the cards, grouping entries, determining subentries, and furnishing an adequate but not excessive number of cross-references—all these together make the difference between an index that is an efficient, truly complete key to the material within a book and one that is merely a collection of words and page numbers.

GROUPING CARDS AND DETERMINING SUBENTRIES

18.74   From the indications of "subject" and "predicate" on the cards, the indexer should now make final decisions about principal entries and subentries. Here he makes his final choice among closely synonymous terms—emperors, kings, rulers; agriculture, farming, crop raising; clothing, costume, dress; clan, tribe, group; life, existence, being—and prepares suitable cross-references to indicate that choice. Here he decides whether certain entities should be treated as principal entries or as subentries under a comprehensive, inclusive principal heading—Mohawk; Iroquois; Hopi; Kwakiutl; *or* Indian tribes: Hopi, 00; Iroquois, 00; Kwakiutl, 00; Mohawk, 00. Pottery making; Weaving; Painting; Wood carving; *or* Handicrafts: painting, 00; pottery making, 00; weaving, 00; wood carving, 00—again with cross-references if needed in the context. His main concern here, as everywhere in the preparation of an index, should be to make sure that every pertinent piece of information within the book is recorded, as either principal entry or as subentry, and that the reader will be able to find it easily.

18.75   *When to furnish subentries.* Main entries unmodified by subentries should not be followed by an extensive row of page numbers. Such an entry forces the reader to run through many pages before he finds the exact information he needs. A general rule of thumb—if such exists about any aspect of indexing—is to try to furnish at least one subentry if there are more than five or six references to any single subject. Subentries can be overdone, of course. An entry consisting of four or five subentries, each with one page reference, is as undesirable as a long, unanalyzed entry.

18.76   *Arrangement of subentries.* Subentries should be arranged alphabetically according to the first important word or chronologically according to the order of appearance of the material within the book. The University of Chicago Press prefers the former arrangement, but the latter also is widely used, especially for historical studies and others in which the text itself is structured on a chronological basis (see par. 18.55).

18.77   *The problem of sub-subentries.* Sub-subentries are difficult or impossible to use in run-in indexes but can often be avoided by repeating a word or phrase in the subentry:

> Eskimos: language, 18; pottery, 432–
>   37; tradition of, in Alaska, 123;
>   tradition of, in California, 127

The indexer should assume that his index will be set in run-in style unless he is informed differently by the manuscript editor. Therefore he should not use sub-subentries without getting a specific OK. Almost never should sub-sub-subentries be used.

18.78 *Punctuation.* An inverted phrase for the title of the main entry is of course punctuated to show the inversion:

> Balance of payments
>
> *or*
>
> Payments, balance of

If the title is followed immediately by page references, a comma should appear between the title and first numeral and between subsequent numerals:

> Payments, balance of, 16, 19

If the title is followed immediately by subentries, a colon precedes the title of the first subentry:

> Payments, balance of: definition of, 16

All subsequent complete subentries are followed by semicolons:

> Payments, balance of: definition of,
>   16; importance of, 19

Note that there is no punctuation at the end of any complete entry. Discussion of a single point may begin, be interrupted, and then continue on subsequent, widely scattered pages. These facts must be indicated by appropriate punctuation within both main entries and subentries:

> Education, higher, 16, 36–38, 64–67,
>   119–20; at Cambridge, 37–38, 119;
>   at Harvard, 16, 64–65

A *see also* cross-reference is preceded by a period, and two or more cross-references are separated by semicolons:

> Learning capacity, 332, 352–53. *See
>   also* Performance; Training

Inclusive numbers (see par. 8.36 for preferred forms) are separated by en dashes.

CROSS-REFERENCING

18.79 Most cross-references are added at this point in the indexing process, after the final form of entries and subentries has been determined and after the principal headings and subheadings have been edited. Cross-references that have been inserted earlier, during the preparation of the cards, should be carefully examined to make certain that they agree with the final form of headings and subheadings. Blind entries should be added if for good reason information has been indexed under a heading that would not easily come to a reader's mind. But to add many entries on the pattern of

> Psychology, depth. *See* Depth psychology

or

> Magazines. *See* Periodicals

is to be overkind to the reader to the point of cluttering the index with useless headings. The indexer should also consider whether it is not easier to duplicate references under a second heading than to make a cross-reference to an entry with only two or three references. That is, not

> Youth movements. *See* "Jeunesse" organizations
> "Jeunesse" organizations, 45, 67–68

but simply

> Youth movements, 45, 67–68
> "Jeunesse" organizations, 45, 67–68

TYPING THE INDEX

18.80   After the alphabetic arrangement has been completed and carefully rechecked, the entire index should be typed—double space and in one column—in final form on 8½-by-11-inch sheets so that it can be marked by the editor or designer and easily followed by the typesetter. Only the final index typed on sheets should be delivered to the publisher. The indexer should hold the cards, however, until he knows that the index has been typeset, proofread, and printed.

TYPOGRAPHICAL CONSIDERATIONS

18.81   *Type size and column.* Indexes are usually set in smaller-sized type than the body of a book, often two sizes smaller. That is, if the body copy is set in 10-on-11-point type and the extracts, bibliographies, and appendixes in 9 on 10, the index would probably be set in 8 on 9. Usually, too, indexes are set in two columns; if the type page is 27 picas wide (as is this book), the index columns are 13 picas wide, with a 1-pica space between. In large-format books, however, the index is often set in three columns or even four.

18.82 *Justification.* Body copy for most books at present is set in a *justified* column; that is, the right side of the column is straight and even, just like the left. This effect is achieved by varying the amount of space between words to make all lines the same length. The shorter the lines the more awkward this is to do, and in a column the width of some index columns the result is sometimes ludicrous. So it is increasingly the practice to set index columns *ragged right* (see the text examples in this chapter and the index to this book). This is not only better looking (according to many typographers) than a narrow justified column but is cheaper to set and easier to correct in proof (see par. 19.25).

18.83 *Indention.* The distinction between the indented and run-in styles of setting subentries has been mentioned earlier (par. 18.12). If the indented style is adopted, and if there are sub-subentries (perhaps even—though this is discouraged—sub-sub-subentries), the editor or designer should figure maximum indentions before marking up copy for the typesetter. Subentries might be indented 1 em, sub-sub-entries 2 ems, sub-sub-subentries 3 ems, and runover lines 4 ems. This may mean, however, that the runover lines are too short for efficient setting and that something else must be done. Indentions could be reduced to 1 en (also called *nut space*), 1 em, 1½ ems, and 2 ems, or the index set in two columns instead of three, or the sub-sub-subentries run into the sub-subentries. Whatever the solution, the point is that problems like this should be solved before any type is set.

18.84 What cannot be solved before setting type are the problems connected with page and column breaks. A line consisting of one or two page numbers only should not be left at the top of a column, for example. A single line at the end of an alphabetic section (followed by a blank line) should not head a column, nor should a single line at the beginning of an alphabetic section be allowed to stand at the foot of a column. Blemishes like these (called *bad breaks* by editors and printers) are eliminated by transposing lines from one column to another, by adding to the white space between alphabetic sections, and sometimes by lengthening or shortening all columns on facing pages by one line. Another kind of bad break is more easily corrected. In a long index, it often happens that an entry breaks in the middle at the foot of the last column on a right-hand page. Then the first column on the following (left-hand) page begins with the indented part of the entry, a confusing situation for the reader. This is corrected by repeating the main heading above the carried-over part of the entry followed by the word *continued* in parentheses:

Ingestive behavior, 65–71	Ingestive behavior (*continued*)
definition of, 13, 15	network of causes underlying, 68
in dog, 93–94	physiology of, 69–70, 86–87
in hydra, 20–21	in rat, 100
and manipulative ability, 61	in sheep, 22
metabolic processes cause stimulation of, 71	in starfish, 45, 52–62

18.85   *Special typography.* An index to a complicated book can often be simplified if special typography is used to differentiate headings, references, or both. If, for example, two kinds of personal names need to be distinguished in an index—perhaps authors and literary characters—one or the other might be set in caps and small caps. Page references to illustrations might be in italic and references to the principal treatment of a subject in boldface. Before settling on such a system, however, the author or editor should confer with a representative of the typesetter to make sure the scheme is practicable. He should also remember to provide a key to the significance of the different kinds of type at the head of the index (for example see par. 18.89).

GAUGING THE LENGTH OF AN INDEX

18.86   An inexperienced indexer may wish to have guidance on the appropriate magnitude of the index he is undertaking. The desirable length of the index of course will vary according to the nature of the book, scholarly books generally needing longer indexes than popular books. For a typical scholarly book this might be from one-fiftieth to one-twentieth the length of the text. That is, a book of, say, three hundred pages might need an index of from six to fifteen pages, depending upon how closely written the book is. (One page of a two-column index generally accommodates about one hundred lines.)

18.87   What does this mean in terms of index cards? Again, much depends upon variables such as the typeface chosen for the index and the width of the column in which it is set. But as an extremely rough working figure, the indexer may assume that an average of five references per text page will yield a short index (one-fiftieth the length of the text) whereas fifteen or more references per text page will yield a fairly long index (perhaps one-twentieth the length of the text). As a running check on his work, then, the indexer can examine his page proofs or count references on his accumulating cards from time to time and from that figure estimate the relative size of the finished product.

EXAMPLES OF INDEX FORM

18.88   *Example A.* A typical scholarly index for a long (450-page) study of Soviet industrialization. Note the alphabetization of the run-in subentries. Note also what are essentially run-in sub-subentries under "Annual plans: functioning of." This can occasionally be done without confusion if the sub-subentries are all identical in construction (here, "for such-and-such year") and attach themselves obviously to the preceding subentry. In most circumstances, sub-subentries are possible only in an indented-style index, such as the one in example *C*.

A. AN EXTENSIVE SCHOLARLY INDEX

Agriculture, 6, 7, 35, 176, 308–58; during *All-out Drive*, 83–85, 96–97, 139; investment in, 84–85, 137, 191, 192, 238, 304; labor in, 310–12, 320, 384–86; during NEP, 41–42; during *Post-Stalin*, 329, 432–33; and price system, 287–88, 293; during *Purge Era*, 177, 195–98; during *Stalin Has Everything His Way*, 238, 239, 241–42, 309–10, 343–44; during *Three "Good" Years*, 139–42, 156–58, 176; during *Warming-up*, 55–56. *See also* Acreages, sown; Animal products; Crop production; Farm output; Farm products; Kolkhozy; Livestock; Peasants; Sovkhozy; *and names of individual commodities*
"All-citizen statistical ration," 282, 384, 410
Annual plans: functioning of, 27, 125–26; for 1931, 73, 77–79, 120; for 1932 and 1933, 120–21; for 1935 and 1936, 129–32; for 1937, 184–85; for 1947, 254–56; targets of, 120, 130–32, 183. *See also* Control figures
Arden Conference, 178 n

18.89   *Example B.* Index in run-in style for a book on animal behavior, showing the use of references in boldface and italic type to distinguish illustrative material.

426

B. Index Employing Boldface and Italic References

References to drawings are printed in boldface type. Numbers in italics refer to the photographic inserts; the first number is that of the location of the insert, the second that of the page in the insert

Goose: allelomimetic behavior of, **18**; imprinting in, 178, *148–2*

Grasshopper population fluctuations, 216

Gravity as related to tactile sense, 34

Ground squirrel. *See* Prairie dog

Group formation, 160–61

Growth curve, 224–26, **225**

Growth of populations, 224–32, *212–2*

Guinea pig: female sexual behavior of, 80–81; limited motor capacity of, 32–33; male sexual behavior of, 81–82

Gull: nesting territories of, 222; primary stimulus in, 142

Gynandromorph, behavior of, 126

Habitat selection in deermouse, 243–44, **243**

Habit formation, 98; decreases variability, 156; makes behavior consistent, 122; in organization of behavior, 150; versus variability, 108

Habrobracon, behavior of gynandromorphs of, 126

Hand-rearing, effects of, 113–15, 235–36; of chimpanzees, 197–98; of sheep, 24

Hands of vertebrates, 46–47

Hardy's law, 240–41; conditions seldom met in natural populations, 249; and human populations, 251

Harvard University Laboratory of Social Relations, 105

18.90 *Example C.* Index in indented style for a book on astronomy. Note the use of sub-subentries, as well as the use of italic type for references to pages upon which definitions occur (the index is called "Index to Subjects and Definitions").

C. Index in Indented Style

Page numbers for definitions are in italics

Brightness temperatures, 388, 582, 589, 602

Bright rims, 7, 16, 27–28. *See also* Nebular forms

B stars, 3, 7, 26–27, 647

Bulbs (in nebulae). *See* Nebular forms

Cameras, electronic, 492, 499

Carbon flash, 559

Cassiopeia A (3C461). *See* Radio sources; Supernovae

Catalogs
 of bright nebulae, 74
 of dark nebulae, 74, 120
  Lundmark, 121
  Lynds, 123
  Schoenberg, 123
 Herschel's (of nebulae), 119
 of planetary nebulae, 484–85, 563
  Perek-Kohoutek, 484, 563

Vorontsov-Velyaminov, 484
 of reflection nebulae, 74
 3C catalog of radio sources, revised, 630

Central stars. *See* Planetary nebulae

Cerenkov radiation, 668, 709

Chemical composition, 71. *See also* Abundances; *names of individual elements*
 of stars and nebulae, 405

Clark effect, *756, 758,* 765

Clouds. *See* Interstellar clouds

Cluster diameters, 170, 218
 angular, 184
 apparent, 167, 168

Cluster distances, 167, 168, 171, 173, 174, 215–16

Clusters, 172–73, 181–82
 absolute magnitudes, 181

18.91   *Example D.* The use of one-em dashes before subentries in this index represents a compromise between indented and run-in styles. Each subentry starts a new line, but sub-subentries are run in, and so the indention is no more than that for a normal run-in index such as example *A* or *B*, above. This style is most satisfactory for an index in which there are a few entries requiring rather elaborate breakdown, the rest being simple entries.

D. USE OF THE DASH

Argos: cremation at, 302; and Danaos of Egypt, 108; Middle Helladic, 77; Mycenaean town, 204, 233, 270, 309; painted tomb at, 205, 299; shaft graves at, 84
Arkadia, 4; Early Helladic, 26, 40; Mycenaean, 269, 306
Armor and weapons. *See also* Frescoes, battle; Metals and metalworking
—attack weapons (general): Early Helladic and Cycladic, 33; Mycenaean, 225, 255, 258–60; from shaft graves, 89, 98–100; from tholos tombs, 128, 131, 133
—body armor: cuirass, 135–36, 147, 152, 244, 258, 260, 311; greaves, 135, 179, 260; helmets, 101, 135, 147, 221, 243, 258

—bow and arrow, 14, 99, 101, 166, 276
—daggers, 33, 98, 255, 260
—shields, 98–99, 135, 147, 221, 260
—sling, 14, 101, 260
—spears and javelins, 33, 195, 210, 260
—swords: in Crete, 147; cut-and-thrust, 228, 278; Middle Helladic, 73; Mycenaean, 175, 255, 260, 279; from shaft graves, 98; from tholos tombs, 128, 131, 133, 135
Arne. *See* Gla
Asine: Early Helladic, 29, 36; Middle Helladic, 74; Mycenaean town and trade, 233, 258, 263; seals from, 38; shrine at, 166, 284–88; tombs at, 300

18.92   *Examples E, F, and G.* The first example, from a beautifully edited anthology, *Poetry of the English Renaissance, 1509–1660,* ed. J. William Hebel and Hoyt H. Hudson (New York: F. S. Crofts & Co., 1929), combines indexes of authors, titles, and first lines. Such a combination, probably easiest of all on the reader, is less usual for an anthology than separate indexes—one of authors and titles, set narrow measure, and another of first lines, set wide measure, with leaders (examples *F* and *G*).

E. THREE TYPES OF ENTRIES COMBINED

Authors' names are printed in CAPITALS, *titles of poems in italics, and first lines of poems in ordinary* roman *type*

Come, my way, my truth, my life, 743
Come over the bourn, Bessy, 408
Come, pass about the bowl to me, 872
Come sleep! O sleep, the certain knot of peace, 112

Come, sons of summer, by whose toil, 665
Come, spur away, 693
Come then, and like two doves with silv'ry wings, 647
Come, we shepherds whose blest sight, 768

Come, worthy Greek, Ulysses, come, 280
Come, you whose loves are dead, 394
Coming homeward out of Spain, 73
Commendation of her beauty, stature, behavior, and wit, 208
Compare me to the child that plays with fire, 224
Comparison of the sonnet and the epigram, 521
Complaint of a lover rebuked, 29
Complain we may, much is amiss, 47
Confined love, 463
Conscience, 739
CONSTABLE, HENRY, 229
Content, not cates, 661
COOPER, ROBERT, 42

Cooper's Hill, 844
CORBET, RICHARD, BISHOP OF OXFORD AND NORWICH, 633
Coridon and Melampus' song, 386
Corinna's going a-maying, 654
CORNISH, WILLIAM, 42
Corpse, clad with carefulness, 80
Corydon, arise my Corydon, 199
Could not once blinding me, cruel, suffice, 766
Country men of England, 426
Courage, my soul! now learn to wield, 859
COWLEY, ABRAHAM, 829
CRAIG, ALEXANDER, 228
CRASHAW, RICHARD, 758, 1025

F. AUTHOR-TITLE INDEX

McCord, David, 27, 51, 130
MacLeish, Archibald, 55, 62, 180
"*Man Is But a Castaway*," 125
Man Said to the Universe, A, 139
Martial, 119
Masefield, John, 136
Masked Shrew, The, 105
Master, The, 185
Masters, Edgar Lee, 166
Mathematics or the Gift of Tongues, 72
Melville, Herman, 128
"*Men Say They Know Many Things*," 124
Message from Home, 99
Metropolitan Nightmare, 115
Millay, Edna St. Vincent, 75, 133
Moore, Marianne, 67, 84, 147
Moss, Howard, 181
Motion of the Earth, The, 38
Mr. Attila, 177
My Father's Watch, 24

Naked World, The, 69
Nash, Ogden, 120
Newton, 158
New York—December, 1931, 149
Nicholl, Louise Townsend, 26, 36, 52, 142
Nicholson, Norman, 38
Non Amo Te, 119
"*No Single Thing Abides*," 9
Numbers and Faces, 91

Ode to the Hayden Planetarium, 29
Once a Child, 21
Our Little Kinsmen, 107

Physical Geography, 52
Plane Geometry, 87
Pleiades, The, 31
"*Point, The*," 89
Pope, Alexander, 121, 157
Prelude, The; Book VI, 85
Princess, The, 33
Progress, 130

G. INDEX OF FIRST LINES

God sends his teachers unto every age................ 388
Good-bye, my Fancy.............................. 474
Good-bye, proud world! I'm going home............. 309
Gusty and raw was the morning.................... 436

Hark! hark! the bugle's lofty sound................. 75
Has there any old fellow got mixed with the boys?...... 385

FOR FURTHER REFERENCE

18.93   Readers whose questions are not answered by this short chapter may find additional help in one or more of the following (fully listed in the Bibliography): Sina Spiker, *Indexing Your Book;* G. V. Carey, *Making an Index;* Robert L. Collison, *Indexes and Indexing*, and, by the same author, *Indexing Books.*

Part 3

Production and Printing

19   *Design and Typography*

19.1   The purposes of a chapter on design and typography in this manual are two. First, it is intended to give editors some basic facts about bookmaking so that they may work more knowledgeably with professional designers, production personnel, and printers. Second, it aims to give helpful suggestions to those editors, copywriters, and others who must plan the design and typography of a book, pamphlet, or brochure without the guidance of an expert. It is *not* intended to serve the needs of professional designers, typographers, production people, etc. For these reasons it deals only with the bare essentials of designing and producing a letterpress book.

19.2   The design of a book ideally complements and enhances the subject of the book. A textbook usually requires a complex design (not to be undertaken by an amateur), a scholarly monograph a less complex design but one that will accommodate footnotes, bibliographies, glossaries, and other aspects of scholarly communication.

PRELIMINARY PLANNING

19.3   At the initial stage of planning a design the editor can greatly assist the designer by explaining the nature of the work and the audience for whom it is intended. The editor should also stipulate the placement of notes, the kind and number of illustrations to be included, the number of tables, graphs, or charts, how many levels of subheads are necessary, what the running heads will consist of, what material is to be in the preliminary pages and what in the back matter, and any other special problems peculiar to the work. Many publishing houses, the University of Chicago Press among them, provide the editor with a form transmittal sheet upon which to list such information; the sheet goes with the copy of the manuscript to the production and design department. Such fact sheets are often not enough, however, and subsequent conferences between designer and editor are helpful and productive.

434

19.4   Before he can design a book, the designer must know not only the nature of the subject and the contents of the book but also its length. The editor's rough estimate of the number of words is not usually enough, nor is the number of manuscript pages. The designer must have an accurate *castoff* (or *character count*), prepared by the production department (in some publishing houses by the editor), giving him the number of characters in (*a*) text, (*b*) extracts, (*c*) footnotes, (*d*) appendixes, glossary, bibliography, etc. Physical size as well as the nature of the book will determine the width and length of the type page and the typeface, type size, and leading between lines to be specified.

19.5   It should be emphasized that the manuscript used by the designer should be *final* (at least so far as the title and the number and nature of the parts are concerned) and *complete* in all essentials. In some publishing houses it is the practice to complete the editing phase of preparation before turning the manuscript over for design. In others (including Chicago), to save time, the book is designed from a carbon copy of the manuscript while the original is being edited. If the latter system is used, the editor should quickly inform the designer of any editorial changes affecting the design of the book, such as the addition of a subtitle to the book title or an increase in the number of levels of subheadings, or warn him that such changes *may* be made.

CASTOFF

19.6   The most accurate way to determine the exact length the printed work will be is to count each *character*, meaning each letter, mark of punctuation, and space between words. With heavily edited material this may be the only way. The less time-consuming and more usual way is to count (*a*) the characters in an average line of the manuscript and (*b*) the number of lines, and then to multiply *a* by *b*. If different typewriters have been used in preparing the manuscript—one with elite type, another with pica, for example—the number of characters per line will of course also be different. A separate estimate should then be made for each type size in the manuscript and the results added together for the total number of characters.

19.7   The designer needs, however, not just a total character count of the work but a count broken down by kinds of material in it. Each kind of material will be set in its own specified type size, in part determined by the amount of material in a given category. For material such as bibliographies and glossaries, where each item begins a new line, the number of lines, including runover lines, is often more helpful than a character count. A typical character count might read as follows:

	CHARACTERS	NUMBER OF LINES
Text	700,000	. . . .
Extracts	50,000	. . . .
Appendix	85,000	. . . .
Bibliography	. . . .	240

The number and any peculiarities of size of tables and illustrations should be included with the character count, although characters in tables and legends need not be counted.

19.8 The designer, with the manuscript and its character count in hand, will determine the typeface, the type sizes for each category, and the size of the type page. He will then be able to figure how many characters of each type size will fit on a single printed page. Dividing the figures in the character count by the relevant number of characters per printed page will give him an accurate estimate of the length of the finished book.

LAYOUTS

19.9 The designer *lays out* his plans for a particular book, usually on one of various kinds of special drawing paper, the result being the *layout* of the book's design. He rules off the exact size of the trimmed page and of the type page and shows how display type and text matter will fit within it. On his layout he writes all type sizes and measurements and specifies the typeface to be used.[1]

19.10 A normal layout will include all the preliminary pages where display type is used; a chapter opening; two facing pages showing text, with extracts, subheads, footnotes, and running heads and page numbers; back matter, such as appendixes, glossary, bibliography; and index. The designer should include all his specifications on the layout. Marks on the manuscript may be missed by the editor, especially if the designer has used a second copy of the manuscript.

1. See sample layouts following par. 19.65.

19.11   From the designer's layout the editor (or a production person) will mark the manuscript for the printer.[2] The layout is eventually sent with the edited, marked manuscript to the printer.

TEXT TYPE

TYPE PAGE

19.12   The type page, also called *text page* or *text area*, is commonly measured in picas: the width of a printed line and the length of the space occupied by the (usually specified) number of lines on a page, including footnotes. *Trim size* refers to the size of the whole page, including all margins.

19.13   *Width.* As a rule, text matter intended for continuous reading (as opposed to reference material) should be set in lines neither too wide nor too narrow for comfortable reading. Ideally the line should accommodate 65 to 70 characters. Depending upon the size of type chosen, this means a line 22 to 27 picas wide.

19.14   In addition to reference materials, such as dictionaries, various other kinds of books are more economically set in double columns—books of readings, lengthy proceedings, and the like. A double-column format will accommodate considerably more words per page. First, the text page may be wider than 30 picas (often the widest measure practical for Linotype setting). Second, the shorter reading line in a double-column format permits the use of smaller type and less leading, without impairing readability, than a typical one-column line. The width of the type page of a double-column format will include the space necessary between the two columns, usually 1 pica. Thus, if the type page is 31 picas wide, each column will be 15 picas wide.

19.15   *Length.* The length of the type page is determined not so much by readability as by conventional relationships between width and length. Margins set off and enhance the type area in much the same way as does the mount for a drawing or picture. There should, generally speaking, be more margin at the bottom of a page than at the top to avoid the appearance of type falling off the page. The inner margins should be narrower than the outer margins, as a double-page spread is the entity and not two single pages.

2. See example of marked manuscript, page 454.

19.16   Which of the many available typefaces to use and what sizes of type to use for text, notes, and other apparatus in a given book are perhaps a designer's most important decisions. Since every printing house does not own every available typeface, the designer should know, if possible, which printer is to set the book and should consult that printer's type book for what he can provide. Next, the designer-typographer considers the nature of his material. Is it peppered with foreign words requiring a variety of diacritical marks? Is it highly technical, containing mathematics or other material requiring symbols? In the field of mathematics, for example, a limited number of typefaces in a limited number of sizes are available with all the necessary characters.

19.17   *Alphabets.* The usual font (all the type characters of one face and size) contains five alphabets: roman capitals, roman lowercase letters, italic capitals, italic lowercase letters, and small capitals. Some works, however, require seven alphabets, the additions being boldface capital and lowercase letters. For such works a typeface (such as Times or Baskerville) with a related boldface in the appropriate sizes must be chosen.

19.18   Authors and editors will aid the bookmaking process, both economically and aesthetically, by avoiding wherever possible the use of boldface letters or other characters not commonly found in a five-alphabet font. It is not necessary, for example, to introduce boldface numerals in bibliographies or reference lists (see par. 16.12), or in section numbers or subheadings in the text.

19.19   The following remarks apply to space between words, between letters, and between lines in the text.[3]

19.20   *Between words.* Spacing between printed words is largely a matter of the mechanics of composition. The operator puts a space after each word, and when the line is justified, the space is expanded to accommodate the line of type within the specified line length. Spacing between words will vary slightly from line to line, but all word spacing in a single line should be the same. Unequal word spaces in a line should be marked by the proofreader. A line with

---

3. For suggestions about spacing and sinkage with display type see pars. 19.53–63 and sample layouts (par. 19.65).

narrow spacing is called a *close* line, one with wide spacing an *open* line. Excessively wide spacing detracts from readability, is unsightly, and is thus to be avoided. Also, a number of successive open lines may produce the printing phenomenon called a *river*—white spaces meandering vertically down the page and distracting the eye of the reader. Modern composition methods in general, therefore, aim for close word spacing.[4]

19.21   *Between letters.* In display matter (title pages, chapter headings, etc.) and in subheads set in full caps or caps and small caps, *letterspacing*—additional space between letters—is often specified by the designer. For subheads in the text the amount of space is likely to be standard; but for large display lines the designer may ask for *optical,* or *visual,* spacing. This means that the typesetter is to insert varying amounts of spacing material between letters, depending upon their form: more, for example, between N and E, less (or none) between L and A. Except where so specified, letterspacing should be avoided by the compositor. All letters within words of a given typeface should be separated from each other by the same amount of space. Authors and editors should be aware, however, that some combinations of letters, particularly in the italic alphabets, give the illusion of more space between them.[5]

19.22   *Between lines.* The space between lines of type is called *leading,* or *leads,* because in hand or Monotype composition it is often created by strips of lead inserted between lines of type. To make more space between lines of text is to *lead it,* or to *lead it out.* To *close up* lines—less space between them—is to *delete leads.* Leading is measured in *points* and is always specified by a designer for each type size used in a book.[6] Where increased leading is necessary—before and after extracts, for example—the number of points is usually also specified. When an author wishes "more space" to indicate a new section in his text, the words *blank line* circled in the margin or in the space itself will indicate to the compositor how much space is to be inserted. A space mark (#) is usually sufficient to indicate extra space between alphabetical sections in indexes.

4. For word spacing in unjustified material see par. 19.26.

5. Garamond gives good examples of this.

6. If 2 points of leading are wanted between lines of a 10-point Linotype face, the usual designation is *10 on 12* (10-point typeface cast on a 12-point body). In Monotype or handset type, the usual designation is *10 pt. ld. 2,* because, generally, separate leads are inserted between lines.

19.23   To determine an appropriate amount of leading requires consideration of a number of factors. The first of these, for text matter at any rate, is readability, and this is largely dependent upon the type measurements. The larger the type size, the more leading is required to prevent the eye from being distracted by the lines above and below the one being read. Also, the wider the line of type, the greater the leading needed, because the eye in moving from the end of one line to the beginning of the next takes a long jump, and in closely set material the eye may easily jump to the wrong line. Another factor often considered is economy. A relatively small type size and reduced leading allows more words per page, making a thinner book and cutting costs of paper, mailing (weight), and so forth, although the cost of composition remains the same. The opposite of this is the desire to make a short work into a longer book. More than the usual number of points between lines will obviously result in fewer lines per page and thus more pages in the book.

19.24   The designer's ultimate concern, in specifying leading as in every other facet of planning a book, is the nature of the material and the audience for whom it is intended.[7]

JUSTIFICATION

19.25   A page of type is conventionally rectangular, its left and right edges neatly aligned. To make a line of type, regardless of the words in it, exactly the same length as its fellows is to *justify* the line. This is still common practice in bookmaking (less so in advertising material), and even some typewriters are equipped to justify lines in typescript. Since words in a language, unlike bricks in a building, are not all of the same length and since a word cannot be divided at the end of a line without regard for the rules of word division, the spacing between words in justified lines cannot be exactly the same in each line. The shorter the line, the more acute the problem becomes for the compositor. In an index, for example, when an entry runs for two or more lines, the runover lines must be indented under the first line, thus making the runover line even shorter. Sometimes there is room for only two medium-sized words on a line, with enough space between them to accommodate another, shorter word, because the next word in the entry is too long to fit on the line and cannot be divided (*through* or *passed*, for example).

7. For examples of specifications appropriate to various kinds of material see sample layouts (par. 19.65).

19.26   A solution to this problem, now becoming acceptable in book-making as in other kinds of printed material, is simply *not* to justify lines of type. The width of the type page, or of the type column, is taken as the maximum. The left edge is even—that is, each line begins directly under the line above—but the right edge runs *ragged* (*ragged right*, the designer calls it). Word spacing is the same in every line, and the line ends with the word nearest the maximum length of the type line. No word except a very long one has to be divided at the end of a line, and thus the reader is not distracted by vertical rows of hyphens.

SUBHEADS

19.27   The typeface and type size used for all subheads (see pars. 1.50–57) are ideally the same as those used for the text. The typesetter can then set them at the same time as he sets the text. Differentiation of levels is brought about by various combinations of the available five-alphabet font and by placement on the page. For example, *A*-level subheads might be set in caps and small caps (or in full caps), *B*-level in small caps, and *C*-level in italics (lowercase except the first word and proper names) at the beginning of a paragraph (often called *run-in side heads*). *A*- and *B*-level subheads may be letterspaced 1 or 2 points. *A*-level heads might be centered and *B*-level flush left, or both may be indented, say, 2 ems (or 2 picas) from the left. Space above and below each subhead should be inserted to set them off from the text.[8] A subhead should never be set at the bottom of a page with no text following it on the page. Instead, the page should run short and the subhead should be set at the top of the following page. The first line of text following a subhead may begin flush left or be indented more than the usual paragraph indention.

19.28   *A*-level:

NOMENCLATURE USED IN EASTERN AFRICA

B-level and text following:

BASIC ASSUMPTIONS

The first Pan-African Congress on Prehistory . . .

8. Such spacing should be so specified that the subhead plus the white space above and below it exactly equals a whole number of text lines. If, for example, the text is being set on a 12-point body, a 12-point subhead might be leaded 8 points above and 4 points below. The subhead and its white space thus equal two lines of text.

C-level:

> *The Kalomo industry.* The Kalomo industry, which represents
> the Iron Age occupation of the Batoka Plateau . . .

19.29   In a work where the number of levels of subheads varies from
chapter to chapter—for example, three levels in some chapters
and only one or two in others—the designer will specify the type
sizes and placement for all three levels but may suggest use of
B-level specifications for the most important level in chapters containing only one or two levels.

EXTRACTS

19.30   Extracts are commonly intended to illustrate points made in the
text and are therefore considered part of the text proper.[9] They
must, however, not only be identifiable as extracts but also be
readable. There are various typographic ways to accomplish both
purposes. Whichever method is used, extra space—at least 2 or
3 points—should be inserted both above and below each extract.
The amount of space should be specified for the printer.

19.31   *Reduced type.* The traditional and still common method for indicating extracts is to set them in a type size 1 point smaller than
that of the text. Leading is also reduced at least 1 point. The
extract is usually set to the same measure (width) as the text (except a verse extract, which is usually centered), the extra space
above and the reduced type serving notice to the reader that this
is quoted material. For example, if the text is set 11 on 13, the
extracts may be set 10 on 12, or 10 on 11. To set extracts in reduced type, however, adds to the cost of composition because the
compositor must deal with them separately from the text.

19.32   *Indention.* A more economical way of indicating extracts is to set
them in the same type size as the text but indented at least 2
picas from the left. They may also be indented from both left and
right. The width of the type page and the length and number of
the extracts are considerations here. The smaller the type page,
the less feasible indention from both sides becomes.

9. For length and nature of quoted material, here called extracts, see chapter 10.

NOTES

19.33   Notes set at the bottom of the page (footnotes) add to the cost of makeup but by most scholars are considered preferable to notes at the back of the book. Where notes are to be placed in a given book is usually an editorial decision, not to be arbitrarily changed by a designer without consultation.[10]

19.34   *Type size.* Footnotes are set in type at least two sizes smaller than that of the text, but no smaller than 8-point solid.[11] In most typefaces, 8 on 9 is a good and readable size for footnotes.

19.35   *Space.* There must be enough space between the notes and the text—at least 4 points—so that they are clearly differentiated. Spacing between notes and text is not an entirely rigid matter. In the same book it may of necessity vary, say, between 4 and 6 points to accommodate the exigencies of particular pages in makeup.

19.36   *Hairline rules.* In closely set text it is sometimes desirable to insert a 3- or 5-pica hairline rule flush left above the notes on each page. This device is optional. When a footnote must continue on a following page, however, a 3-pica or full-measure hairline rule should always be inserted above the continuation.

19.37   *Continued notes.* When a note is continued on a following page, not only should a hairline rule be used above it but the continuation should never begin with a full sentence because the reader may very well think he has finished the note on the first page and miss the continuation. This is of course a problem in page makeup and can be checked by the editor or proofreader only in page proofs. The length of the page or the footnote material itself can usually be adjusted easily to avoid such breaks.

19.38   *Footnote numbers.* Numbers in the text referring to footnotes are always superior figures. Traditionally, the corresponding numbers introducing each footnote have also been superior numbers, a practice still followed by many designers. The University of Chicago Press prefers the more modern and more convenient practice of setting footnote numbers on the line, in the same type size

10. For numbering and placement of notes see par. 1.17.

11. Notes to tables and the like are often set in 6-point.

as that of the footnotes, and followed by a period. The larger number makes for easier identification by the reader, and the avoidance of superior figures lessens the cost of setting footnotes.

19.39 *Paragraphing.* The paragraphing of notes and footnotes should be in keeping with the design of the rest of the book. They may be set flush (like the footnotes in this manual), in regular indented paragraph style, or in flush-and-hang style.

19.40 *Notes at back of book.* When notes are placed at the back of a book or (what is rarely done) at the end of a chapter, they are usually set in a type size smaller than that of the text but not so small as that of footnotes. The degree of difference between text and notes is not important here, since the two kinds of printed matter do not appear on the same page. Each note usually begins with a paragraph indention, and note numbers, as in footnotes, are set on the line (not superior) and followed by a period.

19.41 *Unnumbered notes.* In some works—translations and editions of the classics, for example—it is desirable to omit note numbers in the text. Any notes—consisting of variants, definitions or identifications, or other editorial explanations—must then be keyed to the text by line or page number, usually followed by the word being explained in the note. In a scholarly edition such notes usually appear at the foot of the page; in a work designed for a wider readership they are often placed in the back of the book so that the reader need not be distracted by scholarly apparatus on the text pages. In the accompanying examples (figs. 19.1, 19.2, 19.3) the notes in the first two are keyed to lines and are set at the foot of the page; the first consists of variants, the second of editorial explanation. The third example shows one way to set notes in the back of the book, keyed to the text by page numbers, because the text lines are not numbered.

INDEXES

19.42 Indexes are usually set in two columns. To determine the width of a column, subtract 1 pica from the width measurement of the text page (to account for the space between the columns) and divide by 2. For example, if the type page is 24 picas wide, the index will be set in columns 11½ picas wide, with a 1-pica space between them.

O sweete soule Phillis w'haue liu'd and lou'd for a great while,   45
(If that a man may keepe any mortal ioy for a great while)
Like louing Turtles and Turtledoues for a great while:
One loue, one liking, one sence, one soule for a great while,
Therfore one deaths wound, one graue, one funeral only
Should haue ioyned in one both loue and louer Amintas.   50
   O good God what a griefe is this that death to remember?
For such grace, gesture, face, feature, beautie, behauiour,
Neuer afore was seene, is neuer againe to be lookt for.
O frowning fortune, ô death and desteny dismal:
Thus be the poplar trees that spred their tops to the heauens,   55
Of their flouring leaues despoil'd in an houre, in a moment:
Thus be the sweete violets that gaue such grace to the garden,
Of their purpled roabe despoyld in an houre, in a moment.
   O how oft did I roare and crie with an horrible howling,
When for want of breath Phillis lay feintily gasping?   60
O how oft did I wish that Phœbus would fro my Phillis
Driue this feuer away: or send his sonne from Olympus,
Who, when lady Venus by a chaunce was prickt with a
    bramble,
Healed her hand with his oyles, and fine knacks kept for a
    purpose.
Or that I could perceiue Podalyrius order in healing,   65
Or that I could obtaine Medæas exquisite ointments,
And baths most precious, which old men freshly renewed.
Or that I were as wise, as was that craftie Prometheus,
Who made pictures liue with fire that he stole from Olympus.
Thus did I cal and crie, but no body came to Amintas,   70
Then did I raile and raue, but nought did I get by my railing, [C4ᵛ]
Whilst that I cald and cry'd, and rag'd, and rau'd as a mad
    man,

45 for] *omit* C E
49 Therfore] Thefore A
58 roabe] roabes B C D E
59 roare and crie] cry, and roare D

62 this] that D
64 his] *omit* E purpose.] purpose:
C E; purpose? D
70 Amintas,] Amintas. C E;
Amintas: D

Fig. 19.1. From Abraham Fraunce's translation, *The Lamentations of Amyntas* (1587), edited by Franklin M. Dickey, in Publications of the Renaissance English Text Society, vol. 2 (Chicago: University of Chicago Press for The Newberry Library, 1967), p. 63.

Florimell. What's that? 115

Celadon. Such an Ovall face, clear skin, hazle eyes, thick
brown Eye-browes, and Hair as you have for all the
world.

Flavia. But I can assure you she has nothing of all this.

Celadon. Hold thy peace Envy; nay I can be constant an' 120
I set on't.

Florimell. 'Tis true she tells you.

Celadon. I, I, you may slander your self as you please; then
you have, ——— let me see.

Florimell. I'll swear you shan'not see. ——— 125

Celadon. A turn'd up Nose: that gives an air to your face:
Oh, I find I am more and more in love with you! a
full neather-lip, an out-mouth, that makes mine water
at it: the bottom of your cheeks a little blub, and two
dimples when you smile: for your stature 'tis well, and 130
for your wit 'twas given you by one that knew it had
been thrown away upon an ill face; come you are
handsome, there's no denying it.

Florimell. Can you settle your spirits to see an ugly face,
and not be frighted, I could find in my heart to lift up 135
my Masque and disabuse you.

Celadon. I defie your Masque, would you would try the
experiment.

Florimell. No, I won'not; for your ignorance is the Mother
of your devotion to me. 140

Celadon. Since you will not take the pains to convert me
I'll make bold to keep my faith: a miserable man I am
sure you have made me.

Flavia. This is pleasant.

Celadon. It may be so to you but it is not to me; for ought 145
I see, I am going to be the most constant *Maudlin.* ———

116 *Ovall face*] probably a description of Nell Gwyn. See the
illustration facing p. 31; one incongruous detail, the turned-up nose,
may have been included as a joke, like the ironic description of King
George in the person of the Emperor of Lilliput (*Gulliver's Travels*, I, ii).

128 *out-mouth*] i.e., having full lips.

129 *blub*] swelling.

134 *Can*] if you can.

146 *Maudlin*] melancholy lover. See the quotation from Scudéry's
Ibrahim in the general introduction.

Fig. 19.2. From *Secret Love*, in *John Dryden: Four Comedies*, edited
by L. A. Beaurline and Fredson Bowers (Chicago: University of
Chicago Press, 1967), p. 41.

446

19.43   Index matter is usually set in 8- or 9-point type—8 on 9 (1-point leading) being a common specification in most typefaces.

19.44   Each main entry begins flush left, and runover lines are indented—*flush-and-hang* style. The amount of indention for runover lines should be specified. When the index contains no indented subentries, runover lines are indented 1 em. When subentries are separated from the main entry, they are indented 1 em and all runover lines are indented 2 ems. When sub-subentries are also set separately, they are indented 2 ems and all runover lines are indented 3 ems. (See also chap. 18.)

P. 42   LYNCEUS: The keen-eyed Argonaut.

P. 43   OUR BIRD-WATCHER CAROLS . . . : Horace's three and a half lines in the Latin text constitute a clever paraphrase of a six-line epigram by Callimachus (*Anthologia Palatina,* xii. 102).

P. 44   TO DISTINGUISH BETWEEN . . . : Horace says, "to distinguish between the solid and the void" (*inane abscindere soldo*), with reference to Epicurean physics, where the atoms or matter (*solidum*) move in the void or empty space (*inane*).

To QUOTE PHILODEMUS . . . : Horace here alludes to an epigram of Philodemus, a celebrated Greek Epicurean philosopher and writer of erotic epigrams (*ca.* 110—*ca.* 40–35 B.C.).

ILIA: The mother of Romulus.

EGERIA: Tutelary nymph and consort of Numa.

P. 46   TIGELLIUS: The Sardinian singer.

HIS FATHER'S: Julius Caesar, the adoptive father of Octavian.

P. 47   MAENIUS: Name of an unidentifiable individual, like others in this satire, Novius, Balbinus, Hagna, Ruso, Labeo, whose conduct typifies their excesses.

P. 48   THE DWARF SISYPHUS: An amusing freak, not quite two feet tall, kept by Mark Antony and given this overwhelming mythological nickname.

Fig. 19.3. From *The Satires and Epistles of Horace*, translated by Smith Palmer Bovie (Chicago: University of Chicago Press, 1959), p. 297.

447

TEXT OTHER THAN PROSE

VERSE

19.45   Works such as poems and verse plays differ from prose in that the length of a line is determined by the author, not, as in prose, by the designer. The designer must do his best to reproduce the author's intention within a stipulated width of the printed page.

19.46   The size of type, and the width of the type page, should wherever possible accommodate the longest line—allow it to be set on one line—so that the shape of the poem on the page helps the reader to understand its rhythmic nature; if more than a few lines must be run over, the shape of the poem is lost.

19.47   In most books of poetry the individual poems will vary one from another in the length of lines, and, generally speaking, the best way to place them on the page is to center each poem optically within the given measure of the text. No hard and fast rules can be laid down here; each book must be considered with its own problems in mind.

PLAYS

19.48   *Cast of characters.* For the reader's convenience a list of the characters appearing in a play (often called *dramatis personae*) is frequently given before the beginning of the play. This list usually appears on a page by itself, the verso of the title page introducing the play, facing the first page of the play proper. Such a list may be arranged either in alphabetical order or in order of appearance or in order of importance. Any identifying remark about a character, if less than a sentence, follows the name and is separated from it only by a comma (if a sentence or more, it is separated from the name and set as a sentence or several sentences). Both names and remarks are commonly set in the same typeface as the text of the play, in roman or in italics.

19.49   *Act and scene numbers.* Act and scene numbers may be designed in the manner described above (par. 19.27) for setting the first two levels of subheads in prose works. A new act does not necessarily begin on a new page, but there should be at least 12 points above and 6 points below the new act number. A new scene should have about 8 points above and 6 points below the scene number. If, however, an act or scene ends so close to the bottom of a page that at least two lines of text of the following act or scene cannot be accommodated on the page, the bottom of the page should be left blank (short page) and the new division should begin on the following page. Either arabic or roman (capitals for act, lowercase for scene) may be used to designate these divisions.

19.50 *Speakers' names.* Because the name of each speaker in a play must be easily identifiable, must stand apart from the words he speaks, names are commonly set in a manner different from that of the text—for example, in italics or in caps and small caps or all in small caps—but in the same typeface as the text so that they can be composed by the typesetter at the same time. They may be placed on a separate line, either centered or flush left, where they are most easily identified. This method, of course, takes more space, and where space is a consideration, especially where speeches are short and change of speaker frequent, it is better to set the name in the left margin of the text page, followed by a colon or a period (see fig. 19.2 and example in par. 19.51). Speakers' names may be abbreviated to save space, but abbreviations must be consistent throughout a volume and the speaker easily identifiable by the abbreviation used (an editorial consideration).

19.51 *Stage directions.* Like the speakers' names, stage directions must also be differentiated from the text by means of the type. They are usually set in italics and enclosed in brackets (sometimes parentheses). Introductory material setting the scene is also set in italics but not enclosed in parentheses.

Scene iii. Bohemia. A desert country
near the sea

Enter Antigonus, *with the* Babe, *and a* Mariner

Ant. Thou art perfect then, our ship hath touch'd upon
The deserts of Bohemia?
Mar.   Ay, my lord; and fear
We have landed in ill time: . . .

. . . .

Ant. . . .
There lie, and there thy character; there these,
Which may, if Fortune please, both breed thee, pretty,
   [*Laying down the babe, with a paper and a bundle*]
And still rest thine. . . .

. . . .

Well may I get aboard! This is the chase;
I am gone for ever.
         [*Exit, pursued by a bear*

449

19.52   *Line numbers.* In verse plays, especially when there are notes or other references to particular lines, it is common practice to provide line numbers for every fifth or tenth line. Such numbers are set in the outside margins—the left margin on verso pages, the right on recto pages.

DISPLAY TYPE

19.53   *Display type* means the typeface(s) used for preliminary pages (half title, series title, title page, copyright, dedication, epigraph, etc.), for part and chapter titles, for running heads, and sometimes for subheads (when they are not set in the same typeface as the text). Display type need not be the same typeface used for the text and its appurtenances but should be compatible with it.[12]

19.54   Like other art forms and fashions, type styles have changed radically over the years, as the most cursory comparison of eighteenth- and mid-twentieth-century title pages will show. The modern designer, while avoiding faddishness, will keep abreast of current styles and possibilities of display type to enhance the aesthetic appeal of a book. In a serious book, however, he will eschew practices more suitable for magazine articles or advertising material, such as dropping a chapter title into the middle of the text or running it vertically.

19.55   The untrained person faced with planning a title page is well advised to keep it simple. Each item should be set on a separate line; all should be centered or all flush left or all flush right: main title, subtitle, author's name, publisher's imprint.

CHAPTER OPENINGS

19.56   Some books carry only chapter titles, but in most books chapters are also numbered. Any book that contains cross-references in the text to other chapters (like this manual) must of course have numbered chapters. The University of Chicago Press prefers arabic figures to roman numerals for chapter numbers, and the figure alone, not preceded by the word *chapter*. The figure should be at least as large as the type size used for the chapter title and is generally set on the line above the title.

19.57   The chapter title should be set in a type size larger than that of the text but not so large as to dwarf the reading matter below it. The designer considers the length of each chapter title in a book

12. For content and sequence of preliminary pages see par. 1.1.

before choosing a typeface and type size suitable for chapter titles. If titles require more than one line, as frequently happens, he will usually specify how many characters are allowed in each line and ask the editor to mark the breaks accordingly. But note that titles (and other display type) are never justified even where text lines are so treated, and word breaks should be avoided. When titles are set in full capitals, letterspacing will make them easier to read. In books in which each chapter is by a different author the author's name is included in the display type.

19.58 The beginning of the text in each chapter is also a consideration in chapter openings. It is a common practice, for example, to omit the paragraph indention, setting the first line flush left. (This is often done after subheads also.) When the first line begins flush left, the first letter may be a display initial—either a *stickup initial* or a *drop initial* (if it is a three-line drop initial, for example, the second and third lines of text will be set shorter to accommodate it). If a display initial is used, the following letters—article and noun, single long word, prepositional phrase, etc.—are usually set in small capitals.

19.59 Chapter display type generally is set lower than the top of the type page. The amount of space between it and the top of the page is called *sinkage*. The amount of sinkage (in picas) is specified by the designer, and, in page proofs if possible, the chapter openings should be checked for uniformity in this matter.

19.60 Titles of parts of the book other than chapters—preface, contents, bibliography, index, etc.—are usually set in the same type size as the chapter titles. In special instances, however, a designer may choose a different type style for them. Sinkage is generally the same for them as for the chapter openings.

19.61 In a work with one appendix the word *Appendix* precedes the title of the appendix, usually on a line by itself and in smaller type. Where there is more than one appendix, each is given a number or a letter (Appendix A, Appendix B, etc.) and the word *Appendix* is generally retained in the display type to avoid confusion with chapters and other parts of the book.

RUNNING HEADS

19.62 Running heads must be readable at a glance and distinct from the text.[13] In choosing the type size for running heads, the designer

13. For selection of material to be used in running heads see par. 1.45.

will consider the length of all possible running heads in the particular work, with the understanding that the editor may be able to shorten the overlong ones (see par. 2.108). There must also be allowance for sufficient space—at least 2 picas—between the running head and the page number.

FOLIOS

19.63 Page numbers (folios) in the text are commonly given at the top of the page, left on verso pages, right on recto pages. If the typeface provides a choice, old style (O.S.) or modern (lining or aligning) figures are specified. *Drop folios* (at the foot of the page) are used on the first page of a chapter and other opening pages (appendix, index, etc.) and may be used throughout the book. When used only on pages that have display matter at the top, drop folios are often smaller than the regular folios.

FOR FURTHER REFERENCE

19.64 Nonprofessionals seeking further help in book design may find it in *Bookmaking*, by Marshall Lee, or in the short work by Stanley Morison, *First Principles of Typography*, in the series of Cambridge Authors' and Printers' Guides. Both books are listed in the Bibliography.

SAMPLE LAYOUTS AND MARKED MANUSCRIPT

19.65 The following six pages show (1) a layout for a chapter opening (p. 453), (2) a page of manuscript marked by the editor from specifications provided by the designer and an uncorrected proof of the same page set in type (pp. 454–55), (3) a layout for a two-page spread of text, with reduced matter, subheads, footnotes, and running heads (pp. 456–57), and (4) a layout for a page of text set in two columns (p. 458).

[*Text continued on page 459*]

12

The Individual and His Property

Each individual should keep to what is his own —Cicero

(A) SELF INTEREST

Margin annotations:

4 PICAS

3 PICAS

CHAP. NO.:
← 24 PT. CASLON NO. 540 (ARABIC)

CHAP. TITLE
← 24 PT. CASLON AMERICAN ITALIC u.l.c. CENTERED.

← 11 PT. BASKERVILLE ITALIC u.l.c.

TEXT:
11/13 BASKERVILLE × 27 PICAS

← C. & S.C.
← 1 LINE #

VARIABLE # BETWEEN TEXT AND FOOTNOTE. MINIMUM 6 PTS.

FOOTNOTES:
8/9 BASKERVILLE. USE ALIGNING FIGURES.

1

00

New page, verso
or recto

Text: 11/13 Baskerville × 27

1 2

~~Chapter XII~~

24 Caslon
no. 540 etr

lc
THE INDIVIDUAL AND HIS PROPERTY

24 Caslon American
italic ulc etr

11 Baskerville
italic ulc etr

Each individual should keep to
what is his own.—Cicero

A head - 11/13 esc
etr

flush
par.

Self=Interest /\ The characteristic problems of modern political theory
are not "political" problems. They are not problems of the state itself
but problems of the relation between the individual and the state. Even
to translate _polis_ as "state" obscures the change which took place when
the individual emerged as the theoretically significant unit of political
behavior, for this change involved not only ~~nriyx~~ a changed conception
of his human nature but also a changed conception of his "political"
relations to other men.

It is true that Mill, in _On Liberty_, will find that his "principle
of individuality" is illustrated by "the whole stream of Greek history,"
as a "series of examples of how often events on which the whole destiny
of subsequent civiliaztion turned were dependent on the personal character
for good or evil of some one individual." But whatever may have been
the role of the individual in Greek history, he does not play any decisive
role in Plato's or Aritotle's political theory. Cicero's _Republic_ is
                     surviving
the earliest/political theory which is largely composed of examples of
how much depends on the personal character for good or evil of some one
individual.

The changed conception of human nature which is usually correlated
with the emergence of the individual in modern political theory is the
conception that "Human nature is essentially selfish, and that the

454

12

The Individual and His Property

Each individual should keep to what is his own.—Cicero

SELF INTEREST

The characteristic problems of modern political theory are not "political" problems. They are not problems of the state itself but problems of the relation between the individual and the state. Even to translate *polis* as "state" obscures the change which took place when the individual emerged as the theoretically significant unit of political behavior, for this change involved not only a changed conception of his human nature but also a changed conception of his "political" relations to other men.

It is true that Mill, in *On Liberty,* will find that his "principle of individuality" is illustrated by "the whole stream of Greek history," as a "series of examples of how often events on which the whole destiny of subsequent civilization turned were dependent on the personal character for good or evil of some one individual." But what ever may have been the role of the individual in Greek history, he does not play any decisive role in Plato's or Aristotle's political theory. Cicero's *Republic* is the earliest surviving political theory which is largely composed of examples of how much depends on the personal character for good or evil of some one individual.

The changed conception of human nature which is usually correlated with the emergence of the individual in modern political theory is the conception that "human nature is essentially selfish, and that the effective motives on which a statesman must rely are egoistic." In his *History of Political Theory* Sabine detects this individualistic assuption "behind nearly everything that Machiavelli said about political

VERSO →
RUNNING
HEAD:
11/13
BASKERVILLE
ALL SMALL
CAPS
CENTERED.
2 POINTS
LETTERSPACE.

(A) HEAD:
11/13 C. & S.C.
CENTER
TO OCCUPY
3 LINES
IN TEXT.

(B) HEAD:
11/13 ITALIC.
TO OCCUPY
2 LINES
IN TEXT.

(A) THE ROMAN MIND

(B) *Machiavelli*

456

RECTO
RUNNING
HEAD + FOLIO:
11/13 BASKERVILLE
ITALIC u.l.c.
(CENTER)
FOLIO,
MODERN
FIGURES.

← 6 PTS #

EXTRACTS:
10/12
BASKERVILLE
X 27 PICAS

← 6 PTS #

457

FOLIOS AND
RUNNING
HEADS:
10/11 BASK (MOD)
FIGURES AND
ITALIC u.l.c.

TEXT:
10/11
BASKERVILLE
X 15 PICAS,
TWO
COLUMNS

TABLES:
8 PT. BASK
SOLID WITH
6 PT. BOX
HEADS AND
FOOTNOTES.
CENTER IN
TWO COLUMN
WIDTH

(A) HEAD:
10/11 C+S.C.
CENTERED.
TO OCCUPY
2 LINES
IN TEXT.

(B) HEAD:
10/11 ITALIC
u.l.c
RUN-IN,
WITH
PARAGRAPH
INDENTION.
1 LINE # ABOVE.

000

Author's Name

TABLE 3   ← CAPS

TITLE:

(———) ← ROMAN u.l.c.

(A) MARITIME SPACE

(B) Waterways

1.

↑
FOOT NOTES:
8/9 PT. WITH
ALIGNING FIGURES

458

[*Text continued from page 452*]

TYPE SPECIMENS

19.66   The following twenty pages illustrate ten typefaces commonly used in bookmaking. The characters (alphabets) available in each typeface are listed on the verso page, and examples of the type set in 12-, 10-, 9-, and 8-point are given on the recto page, along with the number of characters per pica for each type size. Note that the number of characters per pica in a given type size varies from one typeface to another.

Baskerville

ABCDEFGHIJKLMNOPQRSTU
VWXYZ&

abcdefghijklmnopqrstuvwxyz
fl ff fi ffi ffl

$1234567890
1234567890

ABCDEFGHIJKLMNOPQRSTUVWXYZ

*ABCDEFGHIJKLMNOPQRSTU
VWXYZ&*

abcdefghijklmnopqrstuvwxyz fl ff fi ffi ffl

$1234567890
1234567890

.,-:;[]()?!''?!;:

12 POINT

LINOTYPE

460

12 point
2 point
leaded
2.26
characters
per
pica

LITTERA SCRIPTA MANET. LITERATURE IS THE WRITTEN expression of those who believe they have something to say that is worth recording and reading by others. It has occupied the mind of men and women to an extent *greater than all the other arts summed together. Hence,* the importance of the study of all the means, in their several respects and aspects, by which the thought of mankind has been recorded and transmitted. By far the MOST POTENT OF ALL THESE MEANS IS THE TYPOGRAPHIC BOOK.

10 point
2 point
leaded
2.61
characters
per
pica

THE PRINTER'S OBJECT IS THAT HIS AUTHOR'S WORK SHALL BE read, and not for the day only; and for this purpose both author and printer must submit wholeheartedly to the customs of their *public. If a given author has few readers, and expects fewer, he* may experiment as capriciously as he will; and only then. Those who wish their books to be read tomorrow as well as today will RESPECT TRADITION. THIS APPLIES WITH PECU-LIAR FORCE TO LETTERS AND TYPE.

9 point
1 point
leaded
2.88
characters
per
pica

LITTERA SCRIPTA MANET. LITERATURE IS THE WRITTEN EXPRESSION OF those who believe they have something to say that is worth record-ing and reading by others. It has occupied the mind of men and *women to an extent greater than all the other arts summed together.* Hence, the importance of the study of all the means, in their several respects and aspects, by which the thought of mankind has been re-CORDED AND TRANSMITTED. BY FAR THE MOST POTENT OF ALL THESE MEANS IS THE TYPOGRAPHIC BOOK.

8 point
2 point
leaded
3.15
characters
per
pica

THE PRINTER'S OBJECT IS THAT HIS AUTHOR'S WORK SHALL BE READ, AND NOT for the day only; and for this purpose both author and printer must submit wholeheartedly to the customs of their public. If a given author *has few readers, and expects fewer, he may experiment as capriciously as* he will; and only then. Those who wish their books to be read tomorrow AS WELL AS TODAY WILL RESPECT TRADITION. THIS APPLIES WITH PECULIAR FORCE TO LETTERS AND TYPE.

461

Bembo

ABCDEFGHIJKLMNOPQRSTU
VWXYZ&

abcdefghijklmnopqrstuvwxyz
fl ff fi ffi ffl

$1234567890
$1234567890

ABCDEFGHIJKLMNOPQRSTUVWXYZ

*ABCDEFGHIJKLMNOPQRSTU
VWXYZ &*

abcdefghijklmnopqrstuvwxyz fl ff fi ffi ffl

$1234567890
1234567890

.,-:;[]()?!''?!;:

12 POINT

MONOTYPE

462

Littera scripta manet. Literature is the written expres-sion of those who believe they have something to say that is worth recording and reading by others. It has occupied the mind of men and women to an extent greater than all the other *arts summed together. Hence, the importance of the study of all the* means, in their several respects and aspects, by which the thought of mankind has been recorded and transmitted. By FAR THE MOST POTENT OF ALL THESE MEANS IS THE TYPOGRAPHIC BOOK.

The printer's object is that his author's work shall be read, and not for the day only; and for this purpose both author and printer must submit wholeheartedly to the customs of their public. If a given author has few *readers, and expects fewer, he may experiment as capriciously as he will; and only* then. Those who wish their books to be read tomorrow as well as today WILL RESPECT TRADITION. THIS APPLIES WITH PECULIAR FORCE TO LETTERS AND TYPE.

Littera scripta manet. Literature is the written expression of those who believe they have something to say that is worth recording and reading by others. It has occupied the mind of men and women to an extent greater *than all the other arts summed together. Hence, the importance of the study of all the* means, in their several respects and aspects, by which the thought of mankind HAS BEEN RECORDED AND TRANSMITTED. BY FAR THE MOST POTENT OF ALL THESE MEANS IS THE TYPOGRAPHIC BOOK.

The printer's object is that his author's work shall be read, and not for the day only; and for this purpose both author and printer must submit wholeheartedly to the customs of their public. If a given author has few readers, and expects fewer, *he may experiment as capriciously as he will; and only then. Those who wish their books to* BE READ TOMORROW AS WELL AS TODAY WILL RESPECT TRADI-TION. THIS APPLIES WITH PECULIAR FORCE TO LETTERS AND TYPE.

463

Bodoni Book

ABCDEFGHIJKLMNOPQRSTU
VWXYZ&

abcdefghijklmnopqrstuvwxyz
fl ff fi ffi ffl

$1234567890

ABCDEFGHIJKLMNOPQRSTUVWXYZ

*ABCDEFGHIJKLMNOPQRSTU
VWXYZ*

abcdefghijklmnopqrstuvwxyz fl ff fi ffi ffl

$1234567890

.,-:;[]()?!''*?!*;:

12 POINT

LINOTYPE

464

12 point
2 point
leaded
2.46
characters
per
pica

LITTERA SCRIPTA MANET. LITERATURE IS THE WRITTEN expression of those who believe they have something to say that is worth recording and reading by others. It has occupied the mind of men and women to an extent greater *than all the other arts summed together. Hence, the im-*portance of the study of all the means, in their several re-spects and aspects, by which the thought of mankind has been recorded and transmitted. By far the most potent of ALL THESE MEANS IS THE TYPOGRAPHIC BOOK.

10 point
2 point
leaded
2.78
characters
per
pica

THE PRINTER'S OBJECT IS THAT HIS AUTHOR'S WORK SHALL BE read, and not for the day only; and for this purpose both author and printer must submit wholeheartedly to the customs of their *public. If a given author has few readers, and expects fewer, he* may experiment as capriciously as he will; and only then. Those who wish their books to be read tomorrow as well as today will RESPECT TRADITION. THIS APPLIES WITH PECULIAR FORCE TO LETTERS AND TYPE.

9 point
1 point
leaded
2.96
characters
per
pica

LITTERA SCRIPTA MANET. LITERATURE IS THE WRITTEN EXPRESSION OF those who believe they have something to say that is worth recording and reading by others. It has occupied the mind of men and women to *an extent greater than all the other arts summed together. Hence, the* importance of the study of all the means, in their several respects and aspects, by which the thought of mankind has been recorded and trans-MITTED. BY FAR THE MOST POTENT OF ALL THESE MEANS IS THE TYPOGRAPHIC BOOK.

8 point
2 point
leaded
3.27
characters
per
pica

THE PRINTER'S OBJECT IS THAT HIS AUTHOR'S WORK SHALL BE READ, AND NOT for the day only; and for this purpose both author and printer must submit wholeheartedly to the customs of their public. If a given author has few *readers, and expects fewer, he may experiment as capriciously as he will;* and only then. Those who wish their books to be read tomorrow as well as TODAY WILL RESPECT TRADITION. THIS APPLIES WITH PECU-LIAR FORCE TO LETTERS AND TYPE.

465

Caledonia

ABCDEFGHIJKLMNOPQRSTU
VWXYZ&

abcdefghijklmnopqrstuvwxyz
fl ff fi ffi ffl

$1234567890
1234567890

ABCDEFGHIJKLMNOPQRSTUVWXYZ

*ABCDEFGHIJKLMNOPQRSTU
VWXYZ*

abcdefghijklmnopqrstuvwxyz fl ff fi ffi ffl

$1234567890
1234567890

.,-:;[]( ) ?!''?!;:

12 POINT

LINOTYPE

466

12 point
2 point
leaded
2.23
characters
per
pica

LITTERA SCRIPTA MANET. LITERATURE IS THE WRITTEN expression of those who believe they have something to say that is worth recording and reading by others. It has occupied the mind of men and women to an extent *greater than all the other arts summed together. Hence,* the importance of the study of all the means, in their several respects and aspects, by which the thought of mankind has been recorded and transmitted. By far the MOST POTENT OF ALL THESE MEANS IS THE TYPOGRAPHIC BOOK.

10 point
2 point
leaded
2.61
characters
per
pica

THE PRINTER'S OBJECT IS THAT HIS AUTHOR'S WORK SHALL BE read, and not for the day only; and for this purpose both author and printer must submit wholeheartedly to the customs of their *public. If a given author has few readers, and expects fewer, he* may experiment as capriciously as he will; and only then. Those who wish their books to be read tomorrow as well as today will RESPECT TRADITION. THIS APPLIES WITH PECULIAR FORCE TO LETTERS AND TYPE.

9 point
1 point
leaded
2.83
characters
per
pica

LITTERA SCRIPTA MANET. LITERATURE IS THE WRITTEN EXPRESSION of those who believe they have something to say that is worth record-ing and reading by others. It has occupied the mind of men and *women to an extent greater than all the other arts summed together.* Hence, the importance of the study of all the means, in their several respects and aspects, by which the thought of mankind has been re-CORDED AND TRANSMITTED. BY FAR THE MOST POTENT OF ALL THESE MEANS IS THE TYPOGRAPHIC BOOK.

8 point
2 point
leaded
3.06
characters
per
pica

THE PRINTER'S OBJECT IS THAT HIS AUTHOR'S WORK SHALL BE READ, AND not for the day only; and for this purpose both author and printer must submit wholeheartedly to the customs of their public. If a given author *has few readers, and expects fewer, he may experiment as capriciously as* he will; and only then. Those who wish their books to be read tomorrow AS WELL AS TODAY WILL RESPECT TRADITION. THIS APPLIES WITH PECULIAR FORCE TO LETTERS AND TYPE.

467

Granjon

A B C D E F G H I J K L M N O P Q R S T U
V W X Y Z &

a b c d e f g h i j k l m n o p q r s t u v w x y z
fl ff fi ffi ffl

$1234567890
1234567890

A B C D E F G H I J K L M N O P Q R S T U V W X Y Z

A B C D E F G H I J K L M N O P Q R S T U
V W X Y Z

a b c d e f g h i j k l m n o p q r s t u v w x y z fl ff fi ffi ffl

$1234567890
1234567890

., - : ; [ ] ( ) ? ! '' ? ! ; :

12 POINT

LINOTYPE

468

12 point
2 point
leaded
2.44
characters
per
pica

Littera scripta manet. Literature is the written expression of those who believe they have something to say that is
worth recording and reading by others. It has occupied the
mind of men and women to an extent greater than all the
other arts summed together. Hence, the importance of the
study of all the means, in their several respects and aspects, by
which the thought of mankind has been recorded and trans-
MITTED. BY FAR THE MOST POTENT OF ALL
THESE MEANS IS THE TYPOGRAPHIC BOOK.

10 point
2 point
leaded
2.85
characters
per
pica

The printer's object is that his author's work shall be read, and
not for the day only; and for this purpose both author and printer
must submit wholeheartedly to the customs of their public. If a given
author has few readers, and expects fewer, he may experiment as
capriciously as he will; and only then. Those who wish their books to
be read tomorrow as well as today will respect tradition. This ap-
PLIES WITH PECULIAR FORCE TO LETTERS AND TYPE.

9 point
1 point
leaded
3.06
characters
per
pica

Littera scripta manet. Literature is the written expression of those
who believe they have something to say that is worth recording and reading by others. It has occupied the mind of men and women to an extent
greater than all the other arts summed together. Hence, the importance of
the study of all the means, in their several respects and aspects, by which
the thought of mankind has been recorded and transmitted. By far the most
POTENT OF ALL THESE MEANS IS THE TYPOGRAPHIC BOOK.

8 point
2 point
leaded
3.41
characters
per
pica

The printer's object is that his author's work shall be read, and not for
the day only; and for this purpose both author and printer must submit wholeheartedly to the customs of their public. If a given author has few readers, and
expects fewer, he may experiment as capriciously as he will; and only then. Those
who wish their books to be read tomorrow as well as today will respect tra-
DITION. THIS APPLIES WITH PECULIAR FORCE TO LETTERS AND TYPE.

469

Janson

ABCDEFGHIJKLMNOPQRSTU
VWXYZ&

abcdefghijklmnopqrstuvwxyz
fl ff fi ffi ffl

$1234567890
1234567890

ABCDEFGHIJKLMNOPQRSTUVWXYZ

*ABCDEFGHIJKLMNOPQRSTU
VWXYZ*

abcdefghijklmnopqrstuvwxyz fl ff fi ffi ffl

$1234567890
1234567890

.,-:;[]()?!''?!;:

12 POINT

LINOTYPE

470

12 point
2 point
leaded
2.26
characters
per
pica

LITTERA SCRIPTA MANET. LITERATURE IS THE WRITTEN expression of those who believe they have something to say that is worth recording and reading by others. It has occupied the mind of men and women to an extent *greater than all the other arts summed together. Hence,* the importance of the study of all the means, in their several respects and aspects, by which the thought of mankind has been recorded and transmitted. By far the MOST POTENT OF ALL THESE MEANS IS THE TYPOGRAPHIC BOOK.

10 point
2 point
leaded
2.55
characters
per
pica

THE PRINTER'S OBJECT IS THAT HIS AUTHOR'S WORK SHALL BE read, and not for the day only; and for this purpose both author and printer must submit wholeheartedly to the customs of their *public. If a given author has few readers, and expects fewer, he* may experiment as capriciously as he will; and only then. Those who wish their books to be read tomorrow as well as today will RESPECT TRADITION. THIS APPLIES WITH PECU-LIAR FORCE TO LETTERS AND TYPE.

9 point
1 point
leaded
2.74
characters
per
pica

LITTERA SCRIPTA MANET. LITERATURE IS THE WRITTEN EXPRESSION OF those who believe they have something to say that is worth record-ing and reading by others. It has occupied the mind of men and *women to an extent greater than all the other arts summed together.* Hence, the importance of the study of all the means, in their several respects and aspects, by which the thought of mankind has been RECORDED AND TRANSMITTED. BY FAR THE MOST POTENT OF ALL THESE MEANS IS THE TYPOGRAPHIC BOOK.

8 point
2 point
leaded
3.01
characters
per
pica

THE PRINTER'S OBJECT IS THAT HIS AUTHOR'S WORK SHALL BE READ, AND NOT for the day only; and for this purpose both author and printer must submit wholeheartedly to the customs of their public. If a given author *has few readers, and expects fewer, he may experiment as capriciously as* he will; and only then. Those who wish their books to be read tomorrow AS WELL AS TODAY WILL RESPECT TRADITION. THIS AP-PLIES WITH PECULIAR FORCE TO LETTERS AND TYPE.

471

Optima

ABCDEFGHIJKLMNOPQRSTU
VWXYZ&

abcdefghijklmnopqrstuvwxyz
fl ff fi

$1234567890

ABCDEFGHIJKLMNOPQRSTU
VWXYZ&

abcdefghijklmnopqrstuvwxyz fl ff fi

$1234567890

. , - : ; [ ] ( ) ? ! ' ' ' ? ! ; :

12 POINT

12 point
2 point
leaded
2.10
characters
per
pica

Littera scripta manet. Literature is the written expression of those who believe they have something to say that is worth recording and reading by others. It has occupied the mind of men and women to an *extent greater than all the other arts summed together.* Hence, the importance of the study of all the means, in their several respects and aspects, by which the thought of mankind has been recorded and transmitted. By far the most potent of all THESE MEANS IS THE TYPOGRAPHIC BOOK.

10 point
2 point
leaded
2.51
characters
per
pica

The printer's object is that his author's work shall be read, and not for the day only; and for this purpose both author and printer must submit wholeheartedly to the customs of *their public. If a given author has few readers, and expects* fewer, he may experiment as capriciously as he will; and only then. Those who wish their books to be read tomorrow as WELL AS TODAY WILL RESPECT TRADITION. THIS APPLIES WITH PECULIAR FORCE TO LETTERS AND TYPE.

9 point
1 point
leaded
2.78
characters
per
pica

Littera scripta manet. Literature is the written expression of those who believe they have something to say that is worth recording and reading by others. It has occupied the mind of men and women *to an extent greater than all the other arts summed together.* Hence, the importance of the study of all the means, in their several respects and aspects, by which the thought of mankind has been RECORDED AND TRANSMITTED. BY FAR THE MOST POTENT OF ALL THESE MEANS IS THE TYPOGRAPHIC BOOK.

8 point
2 point
leaded
3.12
characters
per
pica

The printer's object is that his author's work shall be read, and not for the day only; and for this purpose both author and printer must submit wholeheartedly to the customs of their public. If a given author has few *readers, and expects fewer, he may experiment as capriciously as he will;* and only then. Those who wish their books to be read tomorrow as well AS TODAY WILL RESPECT TRADITION. THIS APPLIES WITH PECULIAR FORCE TO LETTERS AND TYPE.

Palatino

CHARACTERS IN THE FONT

ABCDEFGHIJKLMNOPQRSTU
VWXYZ&

abcdefghijklmnopqrstuvwxyz
fl ff fi

$1234567890
1234567890

ABCDEFGHIJKLMNOPQRSTUVWXYZ

*ABCDEFGHIJKLMNOPQRSTU
VWXYZ*

abcdefghijklmnopqrstuvwxyz fl ff fi

*$1234567890
1234567890*

.,-:;[]()?!''?!;:

12 POINT

LINOTYPE

12 point
2 point
leaded
2.15
characters
per
pica

LITTERA SCRIPTA MANET. LITERATURE IS THE WRITTEN EX-
pression of those who believe they have something
to say that is worth recording and reading by others.
It has occupied the mind of men and women to an
extent greater than all the other arts summed to-
gether. Hence, the importance of the study of all the
means, in their several respects and aspects, by which
the thought of mankind has been recorded and trans-
MITTED. BY FAR THE MOST POTENT OF ALL
THESE MEANS IS THE TYPOGRAPHIC BOOK.

10 point
2 point
leaded
2.57
characters
per
pica

THE PRINTER'S OBJECT IS THAT HIS AUTHOR'S WORK SHALL BE READ,
and not for the day only; and for this purpose both author and
printer must submit wholeheartedly to the customs of their
public. If a given author has few readers, and expects fewer, he
may experiment as capriciously as he will; and only then. Those
who wish their books to be read tomorrow as well as today will
RESPECT TRADITION. THIS APPLIES WITH PECULIAR
FORCE TO LETTERS AND TYPE.

9 point
1 point
leaded
2.78
characters
per
pica

LITTERA SCRIPTA MANET. LITERATURE IS THE WRITTEN EXPRESSION OF
those who believe they have something to say that is worth recording and reading by others. It has occupied the mind of men and
women to an extent greater than all the other arts summed together.
Hence, the importance of the study of all the means, in their several
respects and aspects, by which the thought of mankind has been
RECORDED AND TRANSMITTED. BY FAR THE MOST PO-
TENT OF ALL THESE MEANS IS THE TYPOGRAPHIC BOOK.

8 point
2 point
leaded
3.01
characters
per
pica

THE PRINTER'S OBJECT IS THAT HIS AUTHOR'S WORK SHALL BE READ, AND NOT
for the day only; and for this purpose both author and printer must submit wholeheartedly to the customs of their public. If a given author has
few readers, and expects fewer, he may experiment as capriciously as he
will; and only then. Those who wish their books to be read tomorrow
AS WELL AS TODAY WILL RESPECT TRADITION. THIS APPLIES
WITH PECULIAR FORCE TO LETTERS AND TYPE.

Scotch Roman

A B C D E F G H I J K L M N O P Q R S T U
V W X Y Z &

a b c d e f g h i j k l m n o p q r s t u v w x y z
fl fi ff ffi ffl

$1234567890

A B C D E F G H I J K L M N O P Q R S T U V W X Y Z

A B C D E F G H I J K L M N O P Q R S T U
V W X Y Z &

a b c d e f g h i j k l m n o p q r s t u v w x y z fl fi ff ffi ffl

$1234567890

. , - : ; [ ] ( ) ? ! ' ' ? ! : ;

12 POINT

MONOTYPE

12 point
2 point
leaded

2.18
characters
per
pica

Littera scripta manet. Literature is the writ-ten expression of those who believe they have some-thing to say that is worth recording and reading by others. It has occupied the mind of men and women *to an extent greater than all the other arts summed to-gether.* Hence, the importance of the study of all the means, in their several respects and aspects, by which the thought of mankind has been recorded and trans-MITTED. BY FAR THE MOST POTENT OF ALL THESE MEANS IS THE TYPOGRAPHIC BOOK.

10 point
2 point
leaded

2.61
characters
per
pica

The printer's object is that his author's work shall be read, and not for the day only; and for this purpose both author and printer must submit wholeheartedly to the customs of their *public. If a given author has few readers, and expects fewer, he* may experiment as capriciously as he will; and only then. Those who wish their books to be read tomorrow as well as today will RESPECT TRADITION. THIS APPLIES WITH PECU-LIAR FORCE TO LETTERS AND TYPE.

9 point
1 point
leaded

2.88
characters
per
pica

Littera scripta manet. Literature is the written expression of those who believe they have something to say that is worth record-ing and reading by others. It has occupied the mind of men and women *to an extent greater than all the other arts summed together. Hence, the* importance of the study of all the means, in their several respects and aspects, by which the thought of mankind has been recorded and TRANSMITTED. BY FAR THE MOST POTENT OF ALL THESE MEANS IS THE TYPOGRAPHIC BOOK.

8 point
2 point
leaded

3.24
characters
per
pica

The printer's object is that his author's work shall be read, and not for the day only; and for this purpose both author and printer must submit wholeheartedly to the customs of their public. If a given author has few readers, *and expects fewer, he may experiment as capriciously as he will; and only then.* Those who wish their books to be read tomorrow as well as today will respect TRADITION. THIS APPLIES WITH PECULIAR FORCE TO LETTERS AND TYPE.

Times New Roman

ABCDEFGHIJKLMNOPQRSTU
VWXYZ&

abcdefghijklmnopqrstuvwxyz
fl ff fi ffi ffl

$1234567890

ABCDEFGHIJKLMNOPQRSTUVWXYZ

*ABCDEFGHIJKLMNOPQRSTU
VWXYZ*

abcdefghijklmnopqrstuvwxyz fl ff fi ffi ffl

$1234567890

.,-:;[]()?!''?!;:

12 POINT

LINOTYPE

12 point 2 point leaded 2.26 characters per pica	LITTERA SCRIPTA MANET. LITERATURE IS THE WRIT-ten expression of those who believe they have something to say that is worth recording and reading by others. It has occupied the mind of men and women to an extent *greater than all the other arts summed together. Hence,* the importance of the study of all the means, in their several respects and aspects, by which the thought of mankind has been recorded and transmitted. By far the MOST POTENT OF ALL THESE MEANS IS THE TYPOGRAPHIC BOOK.
10 point 2 point leaded 2.67 characters per pica	THE PRINTER'S OBJECT IS THAT HIS AUTHOR'S WORK SHALL BE read, and not for the day only; and for this purpose both author and printer must submit wholeheartedly to the customs of their *public. If a given author has few readers, and expects fewer, he* may experiment as capriciously as he will; and only then. Those who wish their books to be read tomorrow as well as today will RESPECT TRADITION. THIS APPLIES WITH PECULIAR FORCE TO LETTERS AND TYPE.
9 point 1 point leaded 2.83 characters per pica	LITTERA SCRIPTA MANET. LITERATURE IS THE WRITTEN EXPRESSION of those who believe they have something to say that is worth record-ing and reading by others. It has occupied the mind of men and *women to an extent greater than all the other arts summed together.* Hence, the importance of the study of all the means, in their several respects and aspects, by which the thought of mankind has been re-CORDED AND TRANSMITTED. BY FAR THE MOST POTENT OF ALL THESE MEANS IS THE TYPOGRAPHIC BOOK.
8 point 2 point leaded 3.06 characters per pica	THE PRINTER'S OBJECT IS THAT HIS AUTHOR'S WORK SHALL BE READ, AND not for the day only; and for this purpose both author and printer must submit wholeheartedly to the customs of their public. If a given author *has few readers, and expects fewer, he may experiment as capriciously as* he will; and only then. Those who wish their books to be read tomorrow AS WELL AS TODAY WILL RESPECT TRADITION. THIS APPLIES WITH PECULIAR FORCE TO LETTERS AND TYPE.

479

Words set in SMALL CAPS are defined elsewhere in the Glossary

---

A As. *See* ALTERATION.

AGATE LINE. A unit of measurement for newspaper advertising space, 1/14 of a COLUMN INCH.

ALPHABET LENGTH. The horizontal measurement, in POINTS, of the lowercase alphabet set in type of a particular face and size.

ALTERATION. A change from the manuscript copy introduced in proof, distinguished from a *correction* made to eliminate a printer's error. Alterations are billed as a separate item (above the charge for original composition). Alterations made by the author (*author's alterations*—colloquially, "AAs"), or some part of them, are customarily charged against his royalties.

AMPERSAND. The name for the character "&."

ARTWORK. (1) Illustrative material (photographs, drawings, etc.) intended for reproduction. (2) Additions or corrections made by hand on etch proofs (see PROOF) or other reproduction copy.

ASCENDER. The part of such letters as *d, f, h,* and *k* that extends above the X-HEIGHT, or top of the letter *x*.

BACKBONE. The SPINE of a book.

BACK MATTER. *See* END MATTER.

BASE LINE. In type, a line connecting the bottoms of the capital letters. *See also* X-HEIGHT.

BASIS WEIGHT, *or* BASIC WEIGHT. The weight in pounds of a ream of paper cut to a standard size; or, when the letter *M* is used in the designation, the weight of one thousand such sheets. Basis weight is also called *substance;* thus, "substance 80" means the same as "80-pound paper."

BASTARD TITLE. *See* HALF TITLE.

BENDAY PROCESS. A method of laying a screen (dots, lines, or other textures) on line plates by the use of gelatin films, to give the printed image an appearance of tone. Named for the inventor, Benjamin Day (1838–1916). The same effects can be produced by an artist working directly on the original artwork with transparent adhesive printed screens, such as Zip-a-tone, or with Craftint, a chemically treated drawing paper. *See also* HALF-TONE.

BEVEL. The sloping edge of an ELECTROTYPE or STEREOTYPE, by which the plate is attached to the base with catches while being printed.

BIBLIOGRAPHY. In its larger sense, the science of describing books and recording their history; in a restricted sense, a list of books on a particular topic or by a particular author.

BINDER'S BOARD. The pasteboard stiffening in a book cover over which the cloth, paper, or leather is applied.

BINDING. (1) A covering for the pages of a book. (2) The process by which such a covering is attached. Materials include leather, cloth, paper, and plastic. Processes include *case binding* and *perfect binding*, as well as such processes (seldom used for ordinary books) as *spiral*, *comb*, *ring*, and *post* binding.

In case binding, sewn signatures plus end papers are enclosed in a rigid cover. *Smyth sewing* passes the thread through the fold of each signature and locks it at the back. *Side sewing* passes the thread through the entire book from the side. *Side wiring* is essentially the same, except that wire staples are used instead of thread. At this stage the book is referred to as *unbound signatures* and (with the addition of a jacket or other protective wrapping) may be sent to reviewers. The last step, *casing in*, sees the signatures glued into the rigid case.

Perfect binding is a method of holding together the pages of a book without stitching or sewing. After folding and collating, the backs of the signatures are cut off; the cut edges are then roughened to produce a surface of intermingled fibers to which an adhesive is applied. The books are usually finished with a wraparound paper cover.

BLACK LETTER. *See* TYPE STYLES.

482

BLEED. An illustration that continues off the page when the edge of the paper has been trimmed away in binding is said to *bleed*.

BLIND FOLIO. A page number counted but not actually expressed in the makeup of a book.

BLIND STAMP. An impression from a die on a cover, letterhead, certificate, or other piece of printing without the use of color.

BLOCK. A CUT.

BLOCK LETTER. *See* TYPE STYLES.

BLOCK QUOTATION. *See* EXTRACT.

BLOW UP. To enlarge photographically. A photograph, chart, figure, etc., subjected to such treatment is termed a *blowup*.

BLUEPRINT. *See* PROOF.

BLURB. Descriptive material on a book's jacket.

BOARDS. Rigid material, usually pasteboard, used to make the case of a book (*see* BINDING).

BODY. The part of a piece of metal type that serves as a base for the raised printing surface. *Body size* (measured in points) is the dimension corresponding to the height of the printed letter and is the same for all characters in the font. In machine composition type may be cast on a larger body than that of the font (as a 10-point face on a 12-point body—"10 on 12") to obtain an effect of leading between lines. *Body width* is the dimension corresponding to the width of the printed letter and varies from character to character. *See also* FONT; MEASUREMENT; SORT; TYPE SIZES.

BODY TYPE. *See* TYPE STYLES.

BOLDFACE. *See* TYPE STYLES.

BOOK. Publishers distinguish between a *book*—a unified, isolated product of an author or editor, usually of some length—and a *journal*—a collection of diverse articles appearing at regular intervals. The two receive different editorial and production treatment, although they grade into each other with such publications as yearbooks and annual reviews. The *pamphlet* differs from the book chiefly in size; it is usually paper-covered.

BOOK CLOTH. Cotton cloth, sized, glazed, or impregnated with synthetic resins, used for book covers and available in a large variety of weights, finishes, colors, and patterns.

BOOK NUMBER. *See* STANDARD BOOK NUMBER.

BOOK PAPER. Paper made principally for the manufacture of books, pamphlets, and magazines as distinguished from newsprint and from writing and cover stock. *See also* PAPER.

BOXHEADING. *See* HEADING.

BRACKETS. A device for enclosing material [thus]. In British usage, ( ) are known as brackets; [ ] as *square brackets*.

BROADSIDE. A broadside page is one designed to read normally when the book is turned 90 degrees (also called *landscape*). Wide tables and illustrations are often run broadside. In University of Chicago Press practice the *left* side of a broadside table or illustration is at the *bottom* of the page.

BUCKRAM. A heavy book cloth much used for library bindings or for binding large, heavy books.

BULK. The thickness of paper in numbers of sheets per inch; also used loosely to indicate the thickness of a book, excluding the BOARDS.

BULKING DUMMY. Resembles the finished book in every respect except that the pages and cover are blank. Such a dummy is used by the designer as a final check on the appearance and "feel" of the book, as a guide for the size and position of elements on the jacket, and as a positive indication of the width of the spine (for the stamping).

BUTT SLUGS. To joint two short LINOTYPE slugs with no space between them, making one long line of type or spacing material.

CALENDER. To pass paper between steel rollers to give it a smooth finish.

CAMERA-READY COPY. Artwork, type proofs, typewritten material, etc., ready to be photographed for reproduction without further alteration.

CANCEL. A new leaf or signature replacing a defective one or one containing errors; any material substituting for deleted material. To cancel is to cut out blank or printed pages.

CAPS. An abbreviation for "capital letters."

CAPS AND SMALL CAPS. Two sizes of capitals made on the same body size (as used for subject entries in this glossary).

CAPTION. The title for an illustration or chart, table, etc., and traditionally set above it. To be distinguished from a *legend*, which usually appears below.

CARDING. Inserting strips of heavy paper or extra leads between lines to lengthen a page or column. Sometimes called *faking*.

CARET. A sign directing the printer to insert the correction or additional material written immediately above the line (in manuscript) or at the side (on galley).

CASE. A cover or binding, made by a casemaking machine or by hand and usually printed, stamped, or labeled before it is glued to a book. The process of applying such a ready-made cover is called *casing in*.

CASE, TYPE. A container with individual compartments for each SORT of a font of type. In older cases, capitals were kept in the upper rows of compartments, lowercase letters in the lower rows (hence the terms *uppercase* and *lowercase*). In the *California job case* they are kept side by side.

CASTING OFF, *or* CASTING UP. *See* COPYFITTING.

CENTERED DOT. A heavy dot, ●, used as an ornament before a paragraph. Familiarly called a *bullet*. A lighter centered dot is used in mathematical composition as a multiplication sign.

CENTERED HEAD. *See* HEADING.

CHAPTER HEADING. The number and title of a chapter, usually treated as DISPLAY MATTER.

CHARACTER. A letter, numeral, symbol, or mark of punctuation. In printing type, characters vary in width, as they do on a *variable-spacing* typewriter. On an ordinary typewriter characters are all the same width.

CHARACTER COUNT. In COPYFITTING, a character count is made by computing the number of characters and spaces in an average line of the manuscript and multiplying by the number of lines in the manuscript.

CHASE. A metal frame in which type is locked up for printing.

CLOTHBOUND. A book protected by a rigid cover, usually cloth wrapped around boards, is called *clothbound* (sometimes the wrapping is paper of a distinctive pattern). *See also* PAPERBOUND.

COATED PAPER. *See* PAPER.

COLD TYPE. Any process that produces a photographic image of the material set, for OFFSET PRINTING. Metal type (which comes hot from casting) is not used; hence the name.

COLLAGE. An illustration made by pasting photographs, line cuts, type, etc., in combination.

COLLATE. In bookmaking, to examine the folded signatures of a book to make sure that they are in proper sequence for binding. *See also* GATHER.

COLLATING MARK. A short rule is positioned on the press so as to print the collating mark on the outside of the fold of each SIG-NATURE. When the signatures are collated in the proper order, these marks will appear in stepwise fashion. A miss means an omitted signature; two side by side mean a duplication. Instead of a rule, letters, figures, or a shortened book title may be used. Sometimes a small letter or figure is printed at the bottom of the first page of each signature (chiefly a British practice).

COLLOTYPE. A method of printing from a plane surface of hardened gelatin treated so that a greasy ink adheres to the parts of the plate bearing the image and from there is transferred to paper. The process embraces the principle of lithography, the non-printing areas retaining moisture which repels ink, leaving the printing areas ink-receptive. Collotype is used principally for the reproduction of pictorial copy. *See also* GRAVURE PRINTING; LETTERPRESS PRINTING; OFFSET PRINTING.

COLOPHON. (1) The trade emblem or device of a printer or publisher (such as the University of Chicago Press's phoenix). (2) A statement placed in former times at the end of a book, giving the information now usually included on the title page. (3) In modern bookmaking, a statement recording the names of the designer and printer, the kinds of type and paper used, and sometimes the size of the edition and other information about the production of the book.

COLOR PRINTING. *See* PROCESS COLOR PRINTING.

COLUMN INCH. A unit of measurement for newspaper advertising space, one inch deep and one column wide.

COMBINATION PLATE. A printing plate combining HALFTONE matter with line ENGRAVING, as when lettering appears on a photographic illustration.

COMPOSITION. Setting a manuscript in type. *See* COLD TYPE; LINOTYPE; MONOTYPE; TYPEWRITER COMPOSITION.

COMPOSITOR. Colloquially, "comp," a highly skilled person who makes corrections in type by hand and performs other hand operations, particularly in constructing tables and other technical matter. *See also* OPERATOR.

COPY EDITOR. *See* EDITOR.

COPYFITTING. The process of estimating the space required to print a given quantity of copy in a desired type size or of producing a quantity of manuscript which, when printed, will fill a given space. The former process is also called *casting off* copy. The usual method is to estimate the number of characters in the manuscript (*see* CHARACTER COUNT) and divide (1) by the *characters per pica* for the typeface and size to be used (this information appears with the sample in the printer's specimen book), (2) then by the measure of the typeset line, and (3) finally by the number of lines of type per page. The result is an estimate of the number of printed pages the manuscript will occupy when set and made up.

COPYHOLDER. A person who reads the manuscript aloud to the proofreader, who checks the PROOF.

COPYRIGHT. The purpose of copyright is to protect certain kinds of property, among them literary property. The protection that the law gives is to reserve to the author or proprietor the exclusive right to make, or have made, copies of his work. Unpublished material is protected under *common law* copyright, published material under *statutory* copyright.

COPYRIGHT PAGE. The VERSO of the title page of a book, bearing the copyright notice, publisher's imprint, and often other information, for example, the STANDARD BOOK NUMBER and the LIBRARY OF CONGRESS CATALOG CARD number.

COVER. The two hinged parts of a book binding, front and back; also the four surfaces making up the covers in this sense, when used to carry printed matter. In a journal or magazine these are often designated *covers 1, 2, 3,* and *4:* cover 1 carries the journal's name and sometimes the contents; covers 2, 3, and 4 may carry information about the journal or advertising.

CRAFTINT. *See* BENDAY PROCESS.

CROPPING. Cutting down an illustration, such as a photograph, in size to improve the appearance of the image by removing extraneous areas. Cropping is performed not by physical cutting but by masking, and *crop marks* are placed on the photograph or drawing as a guide to the engraver's cameraman.

CROSS-REFERENCE. An instruction to the user of an index or similar material (such as this glossary) to look under a synonym for the information he seeks or to look under an additional entry for further information. Also a reference from the text of a book to some other part of the book (figure, table, map, etc.) or to another page.

CUT. A term originally referring to a *woodcut* but now generally used to denote a zinc etching, halftone engraving, or other illustrative matter (*see* ENGRAVING).

CUT-IN HEAD. *See* HEADING.

CYLINDER PRESS. *See* FLATBED PRESS.

DECKLE EDGE. The untrimmed edge of paper as it comes from the machine or the rough natural edge of handmade paper. A deckle edge is sometimes artificially produced on machine-made paper to give a handmade effect.

DELETE. To remove (type) or to direct the compositor to do so. Also, on manuscript, to strike out.

DELIVERY DATE. The date on which the printer delivers bound books to the publisher's warehouse, usually several weeks before PUB-LICATION DATE.

DESCENDER. The part of such letters as *p, q,* and *y* that extends below the *base line*, or bottom of the capitals.

DIE, STAMPING. A die of brass or other hard metal used for stamping the case of a book (*see* BINDING; CASE). The case may be stamped with ink or metallic foil; if the impression is without color, the case is said to be *blind-stamped.*

DIE-CUTTING. The process of cutting regular or irregular shapes out of paper by the use of specially fashioned steel knives. The result may be a "door" that can be folded back or a hole in the paper.

DISCOUNT. A fixed rate (15, 20, or 40 percent, for example) off the retail, or *list,* price of a book which the publisher allows the bookseller or wholesaler. *Discount schedules* are made available to retailers and wholesalers by the publisher.

DISPLAY. Telling the printer to *display* part of the copy means that it will be set on its own line, apart.

DISPLAY MATTER. Matter distinguished by being set in larger or different type and on lines by itself. Examples are the title page, chapter headings, and subheadings within the chapter.

DISPLAY TYPE. *See* TYPE STYLES.

488

DISTRIBUTE. To distribute type formerly meant to take the individual pieces of type out of the CHASE one by one and distribute them to their proper compartments in the case to be used again; foundry type is still treated in this fashion. Used in connection with machine-set type, the expression now means the same as *kill*, that is, to melt down type and Linotype slugs after they have served their purpose.

DOTS. *See* ELLIPSIS POINTS.

DOUBLE NUMERATION. A system of numbering text sections, tables, charts, and figures with the chapter number and their own serial number within the chapter. A type of double numeration is used in this manual.

DROP FOLIO. A page number printed at the foot of the page.

DROP SHIP. To send a book to one address and the bill for it to another.

DUMMY. An unprinted or partially printed or sketched sample of a projected book, pamphlet, book cover, or other material to suggest the final appearance and size of the completed work. *See also* BULKING DUMMY.

DUOTONE. A two-color HALFTONE reproduction from a black-and-white original.

DUST WRAPPER. *See* JACKET.

EDITION. An edition consists of all the copies of a book printed from the same type or the same plates, plus subsequent copies printed from offset plates prepared photographically from the original typography. An edition may go through successive *impressions* as warehouse stocks are exhausted and the book is reprinted in its original or slightly altered form. In University of Chicago Press practice a new edition of a book, as distinct from a new impression, is (1) an extensively revised version of a book (as this edition of the *Manual of Style*), (2) a book wholly reset (as an edition of a classic), (3) an old book of enduring value reissued with new apparatus, such as a scholarly introduction, or (4) a book differently bound and intended for a different audience from the original (as a Phoenix paperback edition).

In the terminology of the rare-book trade the terms *edition* and *impression* are used synonymously, because the early printer distributed his type after each printing.

EDITOR. (1) One who selects and prepares for publication the work of another, as: W. H. Auden and Norman Holmes Pearson, eds., *Romantic Poets: Blake to Poe*. (2) In a book-publishing house, one who procures manuscripts for publication (a *procurement* or *sponsoring editor*—at the University of Chicago Press, a *house editor*) or one who prepares manuscripts for publication (a *copy editor* if his duties are confined to routine correction and imposition of house style; a *manuscript editor* if they include substantive revision). (3) In a large publishing house often an individual exercising purely executive functions.

ELECTROTYPE. A metal printing plate cast from a wax, lead, or plastic mold of type or illustrations, on which has been deposited by electrolysis a copper, nickel, or steel shell, which thus forms a hardened metal face on the soft lead backing. Because of durability and ease of storage, electrotypes are used instead of original type and cuts for printing a large edition or subsequent impressions of a book.

ELHI. Elementary and high school (textbook publishing).

ELITE TYPE. Typewriter type that runs twelve characters to the inch. *See also* PICA TYPE.

ELLIPSIS POINTS (DOTS). Spaced periods used to indicate omission in quoted matter.

EM. In printing, a unit of linear measurement equal to the point size of the type in question; i.e., a 6-point em is 6 points wide. An *en* is equal to one-half an *em*. *See also* MEASUREMENT; SPACING.

ENAMEL PAPER. Coated paper. *See also* PAPER.

END MATTER. The material printed at the end of a book, after the text proper, including appendixes, bibliographies, glossaries, indexes, etc. Also called *back matter* and *reference matter*.

END PAPER. A folded sheet pasted or, rarely, sewed to the first and last signatures of a book, one leaf of which is pasted down to the inside of the front and back covers for the purpose of securing the book within the covers.

ENGRAVER'S PROOF. *See* PROOF.

ENGRAVING. (1) In fine arts, a print from an *intaglio plate* prepared by cutting below the surface with a graver, or burin. (2) In the graphic arts, short for *photoengraving*, a metal plate with a relief printing surface prepared by acid etching. (Here the term is a double misnomer because etching rather than engraving is used,

490

and the result is a relief rather than an intaglio surface.) (3) Also, an illustration printed from such a plate.

A photoengraving is classified as a *line engraving* (*zinc*, or *zinc etching*), used for reproduction of material containing only solid blacks and whites (*see* LINE COPY), or a *halftone engraving*, used for reproduction of continuous-tone copy (*see* HALFTONE).

EPIGRAPH. A quotation (usually short) displayed at the head of a chapter, on a part-title page, or in the preliminaries; often aphoristic and suggestive of the matter to come.

ERRATA (*sing.* ERRATUM). Errors caught only after a book has gone to press, considered sufficiently serious to deserve correction by an *errata slip*, usually tipped in the front or back of the book.

ETCH PROOF. *See* PROOF.

EXTRACT. Printer's term for *block quotation*, a long quotation marked off from the text by being set in smaller type or on narrower measure than the body copy.

FACE. *See* TYPE STYLES.

FIGURE. (1) An illustration printed with the text (hence also called a *text figure*) in distinction to a PLATE, which is printed separately. (2) A numeral.

FLAT. In offset printing, a large sheet of paper with the negatives or positives taped into position for printing. The offset plate is made from it (*see* OFFSET PRINTING).

FLATBED PRESS. Printing press with a flat bed (horizontal or vertical) to hold the type. In a cylinder press *ink rollers* and the *impression cylinder* carrying the paper pass alternately over the type. In old screw-type presses, the paper was laid on the inked type and a flat platen was pressed down from above.

FLUSH. The term *flush* designates the absence of INDENTION. Flush lines of type begin at the left margin. The term *flush right* indicates that type aligns at the right.

FLUSH BLOCKING. Mounting a CUT on a wooden block with a double-sided adhesive. This has replaced the older method of tacking, which required a margin of wood all around.

FLYLEAF. Any blank leaf at the front or back of a book, except the end sheet pasted to the inside of the cover.

FOLDOUT. An oversize leaf, often a map, an illustration, or a table, folded to fit within the trim size of the book and tipped in.

FOLIO. (1) A page number, usually placed at the outside of the running head at the top of the page. If placed at the bottom of the page, the number is a *drop folio.* A folio counted in numbering pages but not printed (as on the title page) is a *blind folio;* any folio printed is an *expressed folio.* (2) Formerly, a book made from standard-size sheets folded once, each sheet forming two leaves or four pages.

FONT. A complete assortment of a given size of type, including capitals, small capitals, and lowercase, together with figures, punctuation marks, ligatures, and the commonly used signs and accents. Many special signs and accents are available but are not included in the regular font. The *italic* of a given face is considered a part of the equipment of a font of type but is spoken of as a separate font.

FOREWORD. A short introductory piece, part of the preliminaries of a book, usually by someone other than the author. Also, a variant term for PREFACE, a use discouraged by the University of Chicago Press.

FORM. The pages of a book intended to print on one side of the sheet and arranged in proper order within the signature. A form usually contains a multiple of eight pages. *See also* IMPOSITION.

FORMAT. The shape, size, style, and general appearance of a book as determined by type, margins, etc. Formerly, the size and proportion of a book as determined by the number of times the sheets have been folded, as FOLIO, QUARTO, OCTAVO, etc.

FORWARDING. In bookbinding, the processes between folding the sheets and casing in, such as rounding and backing, putting on headbands, reinforcing backs, etc.

FOUNDRY PROOF. *See* PROOF.

FOUNDRY TYPE. Certain typefaces are available only from a foundry—that is, the printer cannot order matrices but must buy the pieces of type. Foundry type is usually reserved for display material or other small jobs.

FRACTION. The printer will have the commoner fractions (e.g., $\frac{1}{2}$, $\frac{1}{2}$) set on one SORT; these are called *piece fractions*. Others may be *built up*, either with full-size lining figures and a solidus (7/8) or with SUPERIOR and INFERIOR FIGURES (*split fractions*) ($1, -, 2 ; \frac{1}{2}$).

FRAKTUR TYPE. *See* TYPE STYLES.

FRONTISPIECE. An illustration, often a tip-in plate, facing the title page.

FRONT MATTER. *See* PRELIMINARIES.

FULL MEASURE. *See* MEASURE.

FURNITURE. *See* LEADING; MEASUREMENT.

GALLEY. *See* PROOF.

GATEFOLD. A FOLDOUT leaf in a book or periodical.

GATHER. To assemble the signatures of a book in proper sequence for sewing. *See also* COLLATE.

GILDING. The application of gold leaf to the edges of book paper for the purpose of decoration. *See also* STAINING.

GLOSSY. Short for *glossy print*, a photograph with a hard, very shiny finish, preferred for reproduction work.

GOTHIC. *See* TYPE STYLES.

GRAIN. The arrangement of direction of the fibers in a sheet of paper. Paper resists bending and folding against the grain. For this reason printers take care to make sure that the grain will run vertically in the completed book, so that the folds within the binding will be neat and that the book pages will lie flat when the book is opened.

GRAVURE PRINTING. A method of printing in which the impression is obtained from etched *intaglio* plates, differing from letterpress plates in that the image to be printed lies below the surface of the plate in ink-filled depressions or wells. When the inked plate is wiped clean, the ink remaining in the depressions is left for transfer to the paper by adhesion. *See also* COLLOTYPE; LETTERPRESS PRINTING; OFFSET PRINTING.

GUTTER. The two inner margins (back margins) of facing pages of a book.

HALF TITLE. A brief title standing alone on a separate page preceding the text of a book. When it appears on a page preceding the main title page, such a title is properly called a *bastard title*. *See also* PART TITLE.

HALFTONE. A *photoengraving* process (*see* ENGRAVING) whereby a *screen*, an extremely fine pattern of raised dots (in good-quality work 120 or more to the inch), prints as a continuous tone. Used for the reproduction of photographs, wash drawings, paintings, and other kinds of continuous-tone copy.

HANGING INDENTION. *See* INDENTION; PARAGRAPHS.

GLOSSARY OF TECHNICAL TERMS

HEADING (HEAD). A general term referring to type set apart from (usually above) a section of the text and serving as a title or description of what follows.

A *boxheading* is similar to a cut-in head but has a rule around it; or it is a head for a column in a ruled table.

A *centered head* is a headline placed at equal distances from both margins of the page or column.

A *chapter heading* consists of the chapter number and title and sometimes a brief quotation, description, etc. In multiauthor volumes the author's name is part of the chapter heading.

A *cut-in head* is a head placed in a box of white space cut into the side of the type page. It is usually set in type different from that of the text and placed under the first two lines of the paragraph; also, a head cutting across the body of a table.

A *running head* is a headline placed at the top of a page of a book. Running heads are an aid to the reader and ideally reflect the subdivisions of the work in the most useful way possible.

A *side head* is a headline placed at the side of the page or column. It may either be set as a separate line, in which case it is usually set flush with the margin of the type page, or it may be run in, i.e., in a line continuous with the paragraph to which it belongs.

A *subhead*, or *subheading*, is a head of any description making a subdivision of a chapter.

HOUSE STYLE. *See* STYLE.

IMPORT. A book imported and distributed by a domestic house, usually designated copublisher with the foreign publisher.

IMPOSITION. The process of arranging the made-up pages of a FORM so that, when the sheets are printed and folded, the pages will be in the proper order.

IMPRESSION. (1) All the copies of a book printed at one time; *see also* EDITION. (2) The degree of pressure on a sheet on the printing press; *see also* MAKEREADY.

IMPRINT. The name of a publisher on the title page of a book, generally with the place (and sometimes the date) of publication and sometimes also including a COLOPHON.

INDENT. To set a line of type so that it begins or ends inside the normal margin. In *paragraph-style* indention the first line is indented from the left-hand margin and the following lines are set full measure. In *hanging* indention the first line is set full measure and the following lines are indented.

494

INFERIOR FIGURE. A small numeral that prints partly below the BASE LINE: A_2. *See also* SUBSCRIPT.

INITIAL. A large letter used to begin a chapter or section. A *two-line* or *three-line* initial cuts down into the text two or three lines; a *stickup* initial aligns at the bottom with the first line of text but sticks up into the white space above. *Swash* initials are available in some faces. They are a florid version of the standard italic capital letters.

INK. The material with which the printed impression is formed on the page (except that used in GRAVURE PRINTING) is a thick, sticky substance, available in a great range of colors and compositions.

INSERT. An extra printed leaf, sometimes folded, usually of different paper from the text, which is tipped in or placed loosely between the text pages. Also, additional matter typed on a separate page and pinned to the proof, to be set in type and run in.

INTAGLIO. *See* GRAVURE PRINTING.

INTERTYPE. A slug-casting machine, similar to the LINOTYPE but manufactured by a different company. Matrices for the two machines are interchangeable.

INTRODUCTION. An introduction to a book, unlike a foreword or preface, is usually considered part of the text.

ITALIC. *See* TYPE STYLES.

JACKET. A protective wrapping, usually paper, for a clothbound book; it carries the BLURB on its *flaps*, which fold around the front and back covers. In the rare-book trade usually called *dust wrapper* (*abbr.* d.w.).

JUSTIFY. To space out lines of type to a specified measure.

KEEP TYPE STANDING. *See* STANDING.

KERN. *See* SORT.

KILL. To omit, purposely, text or illustrations in revision of manuscript or printed matter. Also, an order to the printer to break up pages and melt down type (*see also* STANDING).

KTS. "Keep type standing" (*see* STANDING).

LATIN ALPHABET. The ancestor of our alphabet, consisting of twenty-one letters (*j*, *u*, *w*, *y*, and *z* lacking). It is the parent of alphabets used in printing western European languages, including the Old English, German *Fraktur*, and Irish forms of letters. *Latin* is also used to distinguish an alphabet like ours from such forms as the Greek, Cyrillic, or Semitic alphabets.

LAYOUT. A designer's conception of the finished job, including spacing and type specifications.

LEADERS. A row of dots, evenly spaced, designed to carry the reader's eye across the rows of a table, from the chapter title to its page number in a table of contents, etc.

LEADING. Extra spacing between lines of type, in addition to that provided by the shoulders of type sorts. A *lead* (*pron.* lĕd) is a thin strip of metal the length of the line, 1, 2, or 3 points thick. Ordinarily the word *lead* alone means a 2-point lead, and *leaded matter* therefore refers to matter in which there are 2 points between lines. A *slug* is a strip of metal 6 or 12 points thick, used where wider blank spaces are necessary. Spacing material of greater thickness than 12 points is known as *furniture* and is ordinarily made in multiples of 12 points.

The amount of space appearing between lines is called *visual space*. For a typeface that is *small on its body* this may be considerable and should be taken into consideration when leading is specified.

LEAF. One of the hinged pieces of paper making up a book or pamphlet, consisting of two pages.

LEGEND. (1) The lines of descriptive matter accompanying an illustration, distinguished from the *caption*, a title that appears above the illustration or at the head of the legend. (2) The key to the symbols and conventions of a map or chart.

LETTERPRESS PRINTING. Printing from raised surfaces, such as type, photoengravings, and wood or linoleum cuts. The paper is pressed against the inked surface to form an impression. *See also* COLLOTYPE; GRAVURE PRINTING; OFFSET PRINTING.

LETTERSPACING. *See* SPACING.

LIBRARY OF CONGRESS CATALOG CARD. A card printed by the Library of Congress, giving bibliographical information on a publication and assigning call numbers according to two systems, made available to libraries for their own catalogs. The Library of Congress catalog card number (familiarly, "LC number"), which must be used in ordering the card, is now usually printed on the copyright page of any serious book, having been assigned in advance of publication. (The LC number should not be confused with the call number, mentioned above, used by libraries to show where a book is shelved.)

LIGATURE. Two or more connected letters cast on the same body, such as œ, fi, ffi, etc. Older, more decorative forms (as * et*) are known as *quaint characters. See also* LOGOTYPE.

LINE COPY. Copy for reproduction which contains only solid blacks and whites, such as a type proof or a pen-and-ink drawing.

LINE NEGATIVE. *See* NEGATIVE.

LINING FIGURES. *See* NUMERALS.

LINOTYPE. A typesetting machine invented by Ottmar Mergenthaler (1854–99) and developed in the decade before 1886. By use of a keyboard, *matrices* of various letters and signs are arranged and spaced out automatically in a line. The line of matrices is then brought in contact with molten type metal, and the entire line is cast as one *slug*. Because of its speed, this machine was originally used in newspaper composition; however, it is now also in widespread use for book and magazine work and general printing. *See also* INTERTYPE; SPACING.

LITHOGRAPHY. *See* OFFSET PRINTING.

LOCK UP. In letterpress, to wedge the type pages firmly within the CHASE, or frame, by means of *quoins (pron.* coins) opened and closed with a *quoin key.*

LOGOTYPE. Familiarly, "logo"; one or more words, or other combination of letters, cast as one SORT. Often used for company names, trademarks, etc.

LOWERCASE. The uncapitalized letters of the alphabet (*abbr.* lc).

LUDLOW. A slug-casting machine for composing lines of type—principally in display sizes of 18 points or larger. Matrices are assembled by hand and locked in a frame, then placed over a slot in the machine; molten metal is brought in contact with the matrices, thereby casting a solid line, or slug.

MACHINE FINISH. *See* PAPER.

MAKEREADY. In letterpress printing, the operation of putting the type form on the press and getting it ready for printing. It includes the leveling up of the impression so that all parts will print clearly. This process requires a varying amount of time, from a comparatively short period for plain type forms to many hours when halftone illustrations are involved.

MAKEUP. The arranging of type lines and illustrations into page form.

MARGINS. The white space around the printed page, called *head, outside, foot,* and *back margins.* The proper balancing of the width of margins has much to do with the pleasing effect of a book page.

MASTER PROOF. *See* PROOF.

MATRIX (MAT). In Linotype and Monotype, the mold in which the letters are cast; in cold-type processes, the image of the character is sometimes referred to as the *mat.* Also, the paper mold from which a STEREOTYPE is made.

MEASURE. The length of the line (width of the column) in which type is set. *Full measure* refers to copy set full width. *Narrow measure* refers to a block of copy (such as a long quotation) indented from one or both margins to distinguish it from surrounding full-measure copy, or to copy set in short lines for two-column makeup.

MEASUREMENT. The printer's basic unit of measurement is the *point,* approximately 1/72 of an inch; 12 points equal 1 pica, approximately 1/6 of an inch.

Within a font of type of one size the printer commonly measures by *ems.* In 9-point matter, to mark the copy for 1-em paragraph indention means to indent each paragraph 9 points (*see* EM).

MISPRINT. Typographical error, printer's error (PE).

MODERN. *See* TYPE STYLES.

MONOTYPE. A composing machine invented by Tolbert Lanston (1844–1913) and developed about 1890. In this machine a ribbon of paper, which is perforated on a keyboard, operates a casting machine by bringing the single matrices in contact in the proper order with a mold, so that the letters are cast one at a time and arranged in lines automatically spaced to the proper length. This machine is in general use for book and magazine work. *See also* SPACING.

MONTAGE. A photograph in which several images are combined photographically. Often mistakenly used for COLLAGE.

MORTISE. A space cut into a mounted printing plate so that type matter may be inserted.

MULTILITH. A printing machine, often used as an office duplicator, which operates on the offset principle.

NEGATIVE. Used in preparing an *offset plate. See also* PHOTO-OFFSET.

498

NUMERALS. By *arabic numerals* is meant the familiar series 1, 2, 3, 4, 5, 6, 7, 8, 9, 0, making up part of every font of type. Arabic numerals are available in italic (*1, 2, 3, 4, 5, 6, 7, 8, 9, 0*), and some fonts offer both lining figures (illustrated above) and *old-style* (O.S.) *figures,* which resemble lowercase letters in having ascenders and descenders: 1, 2, 3, 4, 5, 6, 7, 8, 9, 0.

By *roman numerals* is meant the series I, II, III, IV, V, VI, VII, VIII, IX, X, . . . , L (50), C (100), D (500), M (1,000). In fifteenth- and sixteenth-century printed books, IƆ is sometimes seen for 500 and CIƆ for 1,000. Roman numerals are made up from either the capital or lowercase letters of the font. In general editorial practice today, roman numerals are little used except (in lowercase) for numbering the preliminary pages of a book.

NUT. Printer's term for an en (*see* EM).

OCTAVO. An old term for a book made from sheets which have been folded three times, each sheet forming eight leaves or sixteen pages. Sometimes applied to any book measuring about 6 by 9 inches.

OFF ITS FEET. Type knocked askew on the proof press is said to be off its feet.

OFFPRINT. An article, chapter, or other excerpt from a larger work printed from the original type or plates and issued as a separate unit; also called *reprint.*

OFFSET (SETOFF). The accidental transfer of an impression from a freshly printed sheet to the back of the next sheet. Also a colloquial term for OFFSET PRINTING.

OFFSET PRINTING. An adaptation of the principles of stone lithography in which the design or page is photographically reproduced on a thin flexible metal plate. For photo-offset, a *negative* is used. If especially fine quality is wanted, a *positive* is used to prepare a deep-etch plate. The plate is curved to fit one of the revolving cylinders of the printing press. The design on this plate is transferred to, or *offset* on, the paper by means of a rubber blanket that runs over another cylinder. Other terms for this process are *planograph* and *lithoprint. See also* COLLOTYPE; GRAVURE PRINTING; LETTERPRESS PRINTING; MULTILITH; PHOTO-OFFSET.

OLD STYLE. *See* TYPE STYLES.

OLD-STYLE FIGURES. *See* NUMERALS.

OPAQUE. In photoengraving, to paint out on the negative those areas that are not wanted on the plate.

OPERATOR. The person who sets copy at the keyboard in one of the mechanical typesetting processes.

OUTLINE HALFTONE. A HALFTONE engraving in which all or part of the background has been eliminated to provide a clearer view of objects meant to be emphasized.

OUT OF PRINT. The publisher's stock of the book is exhausted and there is no present plan to reprint (*abbr.* OP).

OUT OF STOCK. The publisher's stock of the book is temporarily exhausted (*abbr.* OS).

PAGE. The pieces of paper making up a book are called *leaves*. One side only of such a leaf is called a *page*.

PAGE PROOF. *See* PROOF.

PAPER. Book papers are generally described in terms of the following quantitative and qualitative factors.

1. The *printing method* for which the paper is intended. Papers prepared for offset printing generally require more critical manufacture than letterpress papers. Offset papers carry a sizing which binds the fibers more closely together to prevent picking on the press (*see* PICK); also they must maintain certain tolerances in moisture content.

2. The *material* of which the paper is made. The principal element in the book printing paper is cellulose fiber derived from wood. However, clays, sizing glue, dyes, and other chemicals are added to shape the finished product.

3. Although the *color* of book paper can generally be described as white, many subtle variations exist, ranging from pure white to a yellow white. These are further affected by opacity and brightness. Both factors are accurately measured in the manufacture of paper.

4. *Finish.* The finishes of book printing papers range from *antique* (rough) to *gloss enamel* (highly polished). Between these are such finishes (in order of increasing smoothness) as eggshell, regular finish, English finish, pigmented, dull enamel, and machine finish.

5. The *weight* of book printing paper is commonly defined in terms of *basis weight*. The basis weight of any given sheet of paper is the weight of one ream (500 sheets) of that paper trimmed

to a sheet size of 25 by 38 inches. A specific lot of paper might be described as 38 × 50–100 lb. Lakeview eggshell. Its basis weight would be 50 pounds. *See also* BASIS WEIGHT.

6. The *bulk* or thickness of a sheet is expressed in thousandths of an inch.

7. *Price* is another dimension of evaluating book printing papers. Roughly speaking, prices range from 14¢ to 25¢ per pound. (Printing papers are always sold by the pound, not by the sheet or ream.)

It should be noted that papers are received by printers from the paper manufacturer in one of two forms. Rolls, which are less expensive per pound, are ordered when a job is to be put on a web-fed press. Paper is ordered for delivery in flat sheets on a skid or pallet when the press to be used is a sheet-fed press.

PAPERBACK. A book bound in paper and sold at a lower price than a comparable clothbound book. *Quality* paperbacks are sold through bookstores and other normal bookselling channels, *mass* paperbacks through newsstands, drugstores, supermarkets, etc.

PAPERBOUND. Bound with a paper rather than a cloth-and-board cover (*see* CLOTHBOUND). A paperbound book is often called a PAPERBACK.

PARAGRAPHS. There are two kinds of ordinary paragraphs. A *plain* paragraph has the first line indented and the other lines flush. A *hanging* paragraph, or paragraph with *hanging indention*, has the first line set flush and all others indented.

PART TITLE. The title of a division of a book, usually printed alone on a separate *part-title page* preceding the text to which it pertains.

PASTEUP. The assembling of the various elements of type and illustration as a guide to the printer for makeup. Also, preparing CAMERA-READY COPY.

PE. Abbreviation for *printer's error*, used in correcting proof (*see* TYPOGRAPHICAL ERROR).

PENALTY COPY. Copy difficult to compose (heavily corrected, faint, much in a foreign language, etc.) for which the typesetter charges a certain percentage over the regular rate.

PERFECT BINDING. *See* BINDING.

PERFECTOR PRESS. A press designed to print both sides of the paper in one pass through the press.

PERMISSIONS. Documents giving an author or publisher formal permission to reproduce something—a poem, passage in a book, photograph, chart, map, table, etc.—in another work.

PHOTOCOMPOSITION. *See* COLD TYPE.

PHOTOENGRAVING. *See* ENGRAVING.

PHOTO-OFFSET. An offset printing process in which a negative print of the copy is used in the photochemical preparation of the metal plate. Photo-offset is known also as *offset lithography, photolithography*, and, loosely, as *planography* and *lithography*.

PI. To mix up type accidentally.

PICA. Twelve points.

PICA EM. Twelve-point em.

PICA TYPE. Typewriter type that runs ten characters to the inch (*see also* ELITE TYPE).

PICK. *Picking* is the pulling loose of paper fibers by heavily inked type; such fibers collectively are called *pick*.

PICK UP. To reuse previously printed matter as part of a new work, either by printing from the original type or by photo-offset. As a direction to the printer or artist, sometimes abbreviated P.U.

PLANOGRAPH. *See* MULTILITH; OFFSET PRINTING; PHOTO-OFFSET.

PLATE. The term refers both to the surface from which a print is made and to the print itself. Thus a plate may be any solid surface bearing a reproduced illustration or type form to be used in printing, such as a halftone engraving, etching, electrotype, etc. The term *plate* also refers to a full-page illustration on smooth or coated paper, printed separately and inserted in a book as a TIP-IN or WRAPAROUND or in a separate signature.

PLATE PROOF. *See* PROOF.

POINT. The printer's basic unit of type measurement—0.0138 inch (approximately 1/72 of an inch).

POSITIVE. A photographic image on paper or film which corresponds to the original subject in all details.

PREFACE. A preliminary element of a book containing the author's formal statement of the purpose of the book and often the acknowledgments, unless these are long enough to go into a separate section. *See also* FOREWORD; INTRODUCTION.

PRELIMINARIES. The opening pages of a book, including the title page and other pages used to identify and explain the text, usually folioed with lowercase roman numerals.

502

PRESSWORK. In bookmaking, the actual printing of the book, as distinct from *composition* and *makeup*, which precede, and *binding*, which follows.

PRINTER'S ERROR. *See* TYPOGRAPHICAL ERROR.

PROCESS COLOR PRINTING. Halftone reproduction of full-color art or photographs through use of several plates (usually four), each printing a different color. *Process colors* are *cyan* (also called *peacock*), *magenta, yellow,* and *black.*

PROGS. Progressive proofs of process color plates, showing the colors individually and progressively combined, as the plates will print.

PROOF. A *galley proof* is an impression of the type as it stands in a long, shallow metal tray known as a *galley.* Such proofs are used by the proofreader and author for reading, and errors are corrected by the printer while the type remains in this form. After corrections have been made in a galley, a *revised proof* is taken for checking them.

A *page proof* is an impression of the type after it has been made into page form.

A *foundry proof* is an impression taken of a type page after it is locked up for the casting of book plates. The black border on such proof is made by the *bearers* in which the type is enclosed in locking up.

A *plate proof* is an impression taken of the completed plate for final comparison before printing.

An *etch proof* (or *reproduction proof*—"repro") is the proof of a type page or other matter to be reproduced by photo-offset.

Master proof is the set of galley or page proof carrying all corrections and alterations, both printer's and author's; it is usually so stamped by the printer.

An *engraver's proof* is a proof of a line or halftone ENGRAVING.

Blueprints, vandykes, and *silver prints* are photographic prints prepared from text or art copy intended for offset reproduction. They serve the same purposes as page proof and engraver's proof in letterpress work.

PROOF PRESS. A small, hand-operated press for pulling proofs.

PROOFREADERS' MARKS. A system of marking errors on proofs evolved over many years and (with minor variations) internationally understood.

P.U. *See* PICK UP.

PUBLICATION DATE. The date upon which booksellers are formally authorized by a publisher to offer a book to the public. *See also* DELIVERY DATE.

QUAD. A large space to be used in setting a line of type; if not otherwise designated, an *em quad*, equal in width to the point size of the type. *En quads* are half that width and 2- and 3-em quads are also available. (In printer's parlance, a *3-to-em space*, that is, one-third of an em—is abbreviated to *3-em space*.) In speech an en quad is often called a *nut* to avoid confusion with "em quad."

QUAINT CHARACTERS. *See* LIGATURE.

QUARTO. An old term for a book made from sheets which have been folded twice, each sheet forming four leaves or eight pages. Sometimes applied to any book measuring about 9 by 12 inches.

QUERY. On manuscript or proof, a question addressed to the author or editor (*abbr.* qy).

RAGGED RIGHT. Set with the right-hand margin unjustified. *See also* JUSTIFY.

RANGE. *Range right* and *range left* are equivalent to *flush right* and *flush left*—chiefly a British usage. *See also* FLUSH.

REAM. The number unit on the basis of which paper is handled—now usually 500 sheets. The weight per ream, or *basis weight*, is the means by which the price is fixed. But a unit of 1,000 sheets is also used as a basis for handling paper, in which case the letter *M* is used with the weight designation. *See also* BASIS WEIGHT; PAPER.

RECTO. A recto page is a right-hand page, and to "start recto" is to begin on a recto page, as a preface or an index does. *See also* VERSO.

REFERENCE MARKS. Numerals, letters, or symbols such as asterisks and daggers used at the point of reference in text and at the head of a note or footnote.

REFERENCE MATTER. *See* END MATTER.

REGISTER. To print an impression on a sheet in correct relationship to other impressions already printed on the same sheet, e.g., to superimpose exactly the various color impressions in PROCESS COLOR PRINTING. When such impressions are not exactly aligned, they are said to be *out of register*.

REMAINDER. To sell off remaining publisher's stock of a slow-moving book at a reduced price. A book so sold.

REMAKE. To alter the makeup of a page or series of pages.

REPRINT. (1) To print a work a second or subsequent time without significant changes (*see* EDITION). (2) As a noun, often used for OFFPRINT.

REVERSE OUT. When an image of type or of a drawing appears in white surrounded by a solid block of color or black, the copy is said to be *reversed out*. This technique makes possible the use of the white paper as a "color."

REVISED PROOF. *See* PROOF.

RIVER. In widely spaced composition an undesirable streak of white space running down through several lines of type, breaking up the even appearance of the page.

ROMAN. The ordinary type style, distinguished from *italic*.

ROUT. To cut away or deepen the blank, or nonprinting, areas in a printing plate with a special engraver's tool, so that they will not become inked and make a mark on the paper during printing.

RULE. A strip of brass or type metal, type high, by the use of which a line may be printed. Such lines vary in width and character.

RUNAROUND. Type set in narrow lines to fit around an illustration or a box.

RUN BACK. In reading proof, to move material from the beginning of one line to the end of the one above it (*abbr.* rb).

RUN DOWN. In reading proof, to move material from the end of one line to the beginning of the next (*abbr.* rd).

RUN IN. (1) To merge a paragraph with the preceding one. (2) To insert new copy (whether an omission of the operator or an author's addition) into the text.

RUNNING HEAD. *See* HEADING.

RUNOVER. (1) In flush-and-hang material (*see* INDENT), all lines after the first of a particular entry (also called *turnover* lines); (2) the continuation of a heading on a second line; (3) a large amount of reset material.

SANS SERIF. *See* TYPE STYLES.

SCREEN. (1) The dot pattern applied to the image in HALFTONE printing. (2) A uniform pattern of dots applied to line copy to obtain an effect of tone (*see* BENDAY PROCESS).

SERIF. A short, light line projecting from the top or bottom of a main stroke of a letter, originally, in handwritten letters, a beginning or finishing stroke of the pen. Gothic and sans serif faces lack serifs.

SET. The horizontal dimension of type. It is expressed in units on composing machines and is generally spoken of as *condensed* or *extended, thin* or *fat*.

SETOFF. *See* OFFSET.

SEWING. *See* BINDING.

SHEETWISE. A method of printing in which a different form is used for each side of the sheet, as distinct from WORK-AND-TURN.

SHILLING MARK. *See* SOLIDUS.

SIDE HEAD. *See* HEADING.

SIGNATURE. A sheet of a book as folded ready for sewing. It is often 32 pages but may be only 16 or even 8 pages if the paper stock is very heavy, or 64 pages if the paper is thin enough to permit additional folding. The size of the press also regulates the size of the signature.

SILVER PRINT. *See* PROOF.

SLANT. *See* SOLIDUS.

SLASH. *See* SOLIDUS.

SLIPCASE. A protective box in which a book or set of volumes fits. When shelved, the spines of the books are visible.

SLUG. A line of type or spacing material cast by a Linotype machine; also similar spacing material used with other kinds of composition. *See also* LEADING.

SMALL CAPS. Capital letters that are smaller than the regular caps of a font (*abbr.* sc). Small caps are usually equal to the X-HEIGHT of the font.

SOLID. A term referring to type matter which has no added leading between the lines other than that provided by the shoulder of the type itself (*see* SORT).

SOLIDUS. A type sort consisting of a slant line (/), used between the parts of a fraction (5/8), to separate lines of poetry when quoted in run-in fashion, to separate shillings and pence in prices (2/6), etc. Also called *virgule, shilling mark, slant,* and *slash.*

SORT. Body of metal with a character in relief cast at one end. Each sort is *type high to paper*—that is, 0.9186 inch high, wide in proportion to the width of the character (*i* is narrow, *m* wide, and *a* intermediate), and a certain number of points deep. The nonprinting area (less than type high) of the sort above and below the character is called the *shoulder*. Part of the character extending beyond the body of the sort is called a *kern*.

SPACING. By *spacing* is meant lateral spacing between words, sentences, or columns, and paragraph indentions. (Vertical spacing between lines is called LEADING.) The meaning of technical names for spaces and methods of spacing depends on whether *foundry* type (type cast for hand composition) or machine-set type is being used. An *em quad* is a block of metal the top of which forms a square (*see* QUAD). A 12-point em quad is thus 12 points square. The term *em* is often used, the qualifying word *quad* being understood, in any given size of type, as a unit of measurement. Thus in 8-point matter "indent 2 ems" means that the line should be indented 16 points. Two- and 3-em quads are multiples cast as one block and are used for spacing out the last lines of paragraphs or filling other blank spaces. Spaces smaller than the em quad are *en quads* and *3-to-em, 4-to-em,* and *5-to-em spaces,* equaling one-half, one-third, one-fourth, and one-fifth of an em, respectively. Spaces 1 and 2 points thick are available, and a *hair space* is a very thin space, usually about one-half point thick. *Letterspacing* involves the use of thin spaces between letters, when words are set entirely in capitals. Most lines of capitals are made more readable by judicious letterspacing, but lowercase letters should rarely be letterspaced except when necessary to fill out very narrow columns.

In MONOTYPE composition a variable unit of measurement is used, and therefore the spacing material is less uniform than it is in foundry type. The system is too complicated for a full explanation here. There are 18 units in a quad, which, while approximately an em quad, may be more or less, according to whether the type face is "fat" or "thin." There are also a *9-unit,* a *6-unit,* a *5-unit,* and a *4-unit space,* equaling approximately an en quad, a 3-to-em space, a 4-to-em space, and a 5-to-em space, respectively. These are all fixed spaces, varying only with the variation of the *set* (meaning width) of the typeface. The *justifying space,* by which the line is spaced out to the proper width, is normally a 5-to-em space and is automatically expanded in the casting machine to lengthen the line to the width of the page.

In the case of the LINOTYPE machine, the system is again different. Normal spacing or word separation is provided automatically by *spacebands,* sliding steel wedges which spread the composed line of type matrices to its predetermined width. Extra-thin spacebands, recommended for good bookwork, have a minimum width of 2 points and a maximum spread of 6½ points (approximately 0.028–0.091 inch). Fixed spaces, for requirements other than line justification, include matrices for the em quad, the en quad (or *figure space*), and some nineteen widths of thin spaces and hair spaces. The finest hair space is 0.0035 inch, or one-quarter of a point thick, thus providing Linotype composition with the utmost flexibility in spacing.

SPINE. The part of a book binding visible when the book is shelved. In University of Chicago Press practice the spine title reads either across the short dimension of the spine or from top to bottom (so that it reads normally when the book is lying face up on a table).

STAINING. The coloring of the edges of book pages for decorative effect. *See also* GILDING.

STANDARD BOOK NUMBER. A Standard Book Number (SBN) uniquely identifies the particular book to which it is assigned. The number consists of nine digits broken into three parts, usually separated by hyphens. The first part, the *publisher prefix*, identifies the publisher; the second part, the *title number*, identifies the particular title or edition; and the third part, always a single digit (*check digit*), serves as an arithmetic check against errors in transcription of the whole number. The SBN system, which originated in England, is coming into use in the United States and other English-speaking countries.

STANDING. *Standing type* is type that has been set and is (more or less) ready for printing. To print from standing type is to print from the type that was set, in distinction to printing from an ELECTROTYPE or STEREOTYPE made from that type, or printing by PHOTO-OFFSET. "Keep type standing" (*abbr.* KTS) is an order to the printer to hold the made-up pages for a possible subsequent printing (*see* KILL).

STEREOTYPE. A printing plate cast from a papier-mâché matrix ("mat") made by forcing the latter into the face of type matter and drying it by baking. Used in printing newspapers and books in the same manner as ELECTROTYPES.

STUB OF A TABLE. The guiding entries in the left-hand column of a table.

STYLE. Rules of uniformity in matters of punctuation, capitalization, word division, spelling, and other details of expression—many of which may vary according to custom. *House style* is the set of rules adopted by a particular publishing or printing house.

SUBHEADING. *See* HEADING.

SUBSCRIPT. In mathematics, a small numeral, letter, fraction, or symbol that prints partly below the BASE LINE.

SUBSCRIPTION BOOK. A book or set of books intended for marketing by door-to-door agents or by mail. *See also* TEXTBOOK; TRADE BOOK.

SUBSTANCE. *See* BASIS WEIGHT.

SUPERIOR FIGURE. A small numeral that prints above the X-HEIGHT: A^2. *See also* SUPERSCRIPT.

SUPERSCRIPT. In mathematics, a small numeral, letter, fraction, or symbol that prints above the X-HEIGHT.

SWASH LETTERS. Capital letters of peculiar or unusual character introduced into a font of type for ornamental purposes. *See also* INITIAL.

TEXTBOOK. A book or special edition of a book intended for quantity sales to schools or colleges. *See also* SUBSCRIPTION BOOK; TRADE BOOK.

TIP-IN. A separately printed leaf pasted, or *tipped,* into a book. *See also* WRAPAROUND.

TOOL. To alter the surface of a printing plate with engraver's tools, as when making a "tooled line" to separate one illustration from another engraved on the same halftone plate.

TRADE BOOK. A book intended for sale to the general public through bookstores. *See also* SUBSCRIPTION BOOK; TEXTBOOK.

TURNOVER. *See* RUNOVER.

TYPE HIGH. Exactly as high as a piece of metal type (0.9186 inch).

TYPE SIZES. Before the adoption of the point system, which became general about 1878, type sizes were known by distinguishing names. The sizes to which these names referred lacked uniformity among different typefounders, particularly in different countries; this confusion led to the immediate popularity of the point system, which originated in France and was developed in the United States (*see also* MEASUREMENT). Types of various sizes formerly bore names, such as Great Primer for 18-point type. For a complete list of these see any large dictionary under "Type."

The designation of type sizes by points refers to the vertical size of the SORT and has no definite reference to the size of the typeface itself. All the different styles of 12-point faces, for instance, are approximately the same size, but there is considerable variation. The designation *12-point*, as referring to a particular typeface, means that it is ordinarily cast on a 12-point body. In Monotype and Linotype composition the size of the body is often increased to enlarge the space between the lines without having to insert leads for that purpose. Thus a face ordinarily cast on a 10-point body may be cast on a 12-point body to give the appearance of 2-point leading; it is then referred to as "10 on 12."

TYPE STYLES. The type commonly used in books and all classes of ordinary reading matter is known as *roman*. Although all roman types are essentially the same in form, there are two fairly well-defined divisions or styles. The older form is called *old style* and is characterized by strength and boldness of feature, with strokes of comparatively uniform thickness and with an absence of weak hairlines. The serifs are rounded, and the contour is clear and legible. *Caslon* is an example of an old-style face. The other style is called *modern* and is characterized by heavier shadings, thinner hairlines, and thin, straight serifs. *Bodoni* is an example. Although a few typefaces combine certain characteristics of the two styles, and are thus called *transitional*, it is usually comparatively easy to classify any particular face as *old style* or *modern*. Aside from the *roman*, there are four other general classes, known as *italic*, *script*, *gothic*, and *text*. *Boldface* versions of all the commonly used faces (sometimes in both roman and italic) are also available, and many faces are also available in both *extended* and *condensed* versions.

The slanting letter mainly used for emphasis and display is known as *italic*. It is cut to match all roman typefaces, and a font of roman type for book and magazine work would be considered incomplete without a corresponding font of italic.

Script types are imitations of handwriting. Their widest use is in the printing of announcements, invitations, and stationery.

Gothic or *sans serif* is perfectly plain, with lines of uniform thickness and without serifs. It is sometimes known as *block letter*.

510

Text is a survival of the first types cast and was originally an imitation of the hand-lettering which prevailed before movable types were invented. It is often known as *black letter.* German *Fraktur* resembles it closely.

Body type is a common name for type used for reading matter as distinguished from *display type*, which is used for advertisements, title pages, part and chapter headings, etc.

TYPEWRITER COMPOSITION. Material specially typed for reproduction. With "book" typefaces and a variable-spacing typewriter such composition closely resembles machine-set work.

TYPOGRAPHICAL ERROR. Colloquially, "typo," an error made by the compositor or operator; also called *printer's error.*

VANDYKE. *See* PROOF.

VERSO. A verso page is a left-hand page; specifically, the verso of a given right-hand page is the back of that page. *See also* RECTO.

VIRGULE. *See* SOLIDUS.

WIDOW. A short line ending a paragraph at the top of a page, avoided when possible by changes in wording or spacing which either remove the line or lengthen it; also, less strictly, a word or part of a word on a line by itself at the end of any paragraph.

WOODCUT. *See* CUT.

WORD DIVISION. Dividing words at the end of a line; *Webster's New International Dictionary* gives the divisions used by most printers and publishers.

WORK-AND-TURN. To print *work-and-turn*, a form is arranged (imposed) so that a sheet may be printed on one side, turned end for end, and printed on the other side, to give two copies of the pages when cut in half. *See also* SHEETWISE.

WORK-UP. A mark or smudge on a printed page, caused when a piece of spacing material in an improperly locked form works up into printing position.

WRAPAROUND. A folded sheet of smooth or coated paper, bearing printed illustrations, slipped around the outside of a signature before sewing as a means of adding such illustrations to a book without the necessity of tipping in single leaves. Thus, when a wraparound is placed on a 16-page signature, the two leaves of the wraparound sheet appear 16 pages apart in the finished book. *See also* TIP-IN.

WRONG FONT. A type of different size or face from that of the context in which it accidentally appears (*abbr.* wf).

X-HEIGHT. In type, a vertical dimension equal to the height of the lowercase letters (such as *x*) without ascenders or descenders. *See also* BASE LINE.

ZINC ETCHING. *See* ENGRAVING.

ZIP-A-TONE. *See* BENDAY PROCESS.

Bibliography

American Institute of Physics. *Style Manual for Guidance in the Preparation of Papers.* 2d rev. ed. New York: American Institute of Physics, 1967.

Intended to assist authors in the preparation of articles published by the American Institute of Physics and its member societies.

American Mathematical Society. "Manual for Authors of Mathematical Papers." Reprinted from *Bulletin of the American Mathematical Society,* vol. 68, no. 5 (September 1962).

Advises mathematicians preparing papers for publication on how to improve the readability and appearance of the printed article; and how to eliminate unnecessary delay, trouble, and expense in printing.

American Medical Association. Scientific Publications Division. *Style Book and Editorial Manual.* 3d ed. Chicago: American Medical Association, 1965.

Written for authors preparing copy for the *Journal of the American Medical Association,* this manual is often helpful to editors working on medical copy.

Ashley, Paul P. *Say It Safely: Legal Limits in Publishing, Radio, and Television.* 3d ed. Seattle and London: University of Washington Press, 1966.

An up-to-date discussion of the legal aspects of libel in the field of communications.

Bartlett, John. *Familiar Quotations: A Collection of Passages, Phrases, and Proverbs Traced to Their Sources in Ancient and Modern Literature.* Edited by Emily Morison Beck. 14th ed. revised and enlarged. Boston: Little, Brown & Co. 1968.

The first source to consult in checking a familiar quotation.

Bernstein, Theodore M. *The Careful Writer: A Modern Guide to English Usage.* New York: Atheneum, 1965.

An alphabetically arranged list of usages, good and bad, with graceful discussion of why they should be embraced, tolerated, or shunned. A particularly helpful ally of the manuscript editor.

Books in Print: An Author-Title-Series Index to the "Publishers' Trade

513

List Annual." 2 vols. New York and London: R. R. Bowker Co. Published annually.

The standard annual listing of books issued by American publishers. Indispensable for checking bibliographies and footnotes. An editorial office should have the current edition plus at least a selection of earlier volumes.

British Books in Print: The Reference Catalogue of Current Literature. London and New York: J. Whitaker & Sons and R. R. Bowker Co. Published at intervals of 2 to 4 years.

Serves the same purpose for British books as *Books in Print* (which see) does for American. Supplemented by *Whitaker's Cumulative Book List,* published in quarterly parts and an annual volume.

Brooks, Philip C. *Research in Archives: The Use of Unpublished Primary Sources.* Chicago: University of Chicago Press, 1969.

A manual for researchers in archives, especially United States presidential papers, with helpful suggestions for citing references.

Brown, Everett S. *Manual of Government Publications.* New York: Appleton-Century-Crofts, 1950.

A general guide to United States public documents, with material on foreign documents as well.

Carey, Gordon V. *Making an Index.* Cambridge Authors' and Printers' Guides, no. 3. 3d ed. Cambridge: At the University Press, 1963.

A slim pamphlet offering excellent advice on making a useful index. Some of the style recommendations are at variance with the preferences of the University of Chicago Press.

Chemical Abstracts List of Periodicals. Washington D.C.: American Chemical Society, 1961.

Gives standard abbreviations (preferred by the University of Chicago Press) for the titles of thousands of scientific journals, in the biological as well as the physical sciences. There are several supplements.

Collison, Robert L. *Indexes and Indexing: Guide to the Indexing of Books, and Collections of Books, Periodicals, Music, Gramophone Records, Films, and Other Material, with a Reference Section and Suggestions for Further Reading.* London: Ernest Benn, 1959.

As the baroque subtitle indicates, this book covers a good deal more than the indexing of scholarly books and may usefully be consulted by an indexer with problems of indexing nonbook materials. Regarding the mechanics of indexing, the method taught by Collison here is ingenious, fast, and economical but should not be attempted by anyone making his first index.

514

————. *Indexing Books.* Rev. ed. Tuckahoe, N.Y.: John de Graff, 1967.

A fuller treatment of book indexing than that included in the preceding entry. Most of the preferences of the University of Chicago Press are reflected at least as alternatives.

Columbia Lippincott Gazetteer of the World, The. Edited by Leon E. Seltzer. New York: Columbia University Press, 1952.

Sometimes supplies information not found in *Webster's Geographical Dictionary* (which see). Later editions include a 1961 Supplement.

Concise Dictionary of American History. Edited by Thomas C. Cochran and Wayne Andrews. New York: Charles Scribner's Sons, 1962.

A convenient desk book for editors of historical works. Authoritative articles carefully selected and abridged from the five-volume original.

Conference of Biological Editors. *Style Manual for Biological Journals.* 2d ed. Washington, D.C.: American Institute of Biological Sciences, 1964.

The standards of the "AIBS *Manual*" are followed by a great many journals and are acceptable to most publishers of scientific books. Except in a few details its recommendations and those of the University of Chicago Press *Manual* are identical. A good feature is a discussion of effective writing that could be studied profitably by authors in any field.

Dictionary of American Biography. 21 vols. New York: Charles Scribner's Sons, 1928–36. 2 supplements, 1944, 1958.

A standard reference work (does not list living persons).

Dictionary of National Biography. Edited by Leslie Stephen and Sidney Lee. 21 vols. 1885–1901. Now published by Oxford University Press. 6 supplements. A volume of corrections and additions (Boston: G. K. Hall, 1966).

A standard source book for British biography.

Fowler, H. W. *A Dictionary of Modern English Usage.* 2d ed. revised by Sir Ernest Gowers. Oxford: Clarendon Press, 1965.

The classic work on English usage for discriminating writers. A necessity in any university press editorial office.

Gill, Robert S. *The Author-Publisher-Printer Complex.* 3d ed. Baltimore: Williams & Wilkins Co., 1958.

A short, clearly written exposition of the relations among author, printer, and publisher—what each can reasonably expect from the other and how these demands are best met—covering more or less the same ground as part 1 of this manual.

Great Britain. Public Record Office. *Guide to the Contents of the Public Record Office.* 2 vols. London: H. M. Stationery Office, 1963.

The standard guide to British archival materials. It has superseded M. S. Giuseppi's *Guide to the Manuscripts Preserved in the Public Record Office* (London, 1923).

Hamer, Philip M., ed. *Guide to Archives and Manuscripts in the United States.* New Haven: Yale University Press, 1961.

A standard guide to archival materials in the United States.

Handbook of Physics and Chemistry. 48th ed., edited by Robert C. Weast and others. Cleveland: Chemical Rubber Co., 1967.

Useful for an editor handling material in physics or chemistry or general material involving names of chemical compounds.

Hart's Rules for Compositors and Readers at the University Press, Oxford. 37th rev. ed. London: Oxford University Press, 1967.

Reflects the typographical usages of a prestigious and conservative scholarly press. It is much briefer than the present manual and sometimes at variance with it, but it is nonetheless useful to American editors. The section on setting foreign languages is particularly helpful.

Harvard Guide to American History. Cambridge, Mass.: Harvard University Press, Belknap Press, 1954.

Contains helpful information, accessibly arranged, on public documents and other historical source materials.

Hattery, Lowell H., and Bush, George P., eds. *Reprography and Copyright Law.* Washington, D.C.: American Institute of Biological Sciences, 1964.

Explores the conflict of copyright protection and the growing practice of copying by photographic and other processes. Material is derived from presentations at a symposium by the American University in 1963, with the addition of a summary chapter, appendixes, and bibliography.

Lee, Marshall. *Bookmaking: The Illustrated Guide to Design and Production.* New York: R. R. Bowker Co., 1965.

A well-written, clearly illustrated, and easily understood book on the mechanics of bookmaking (composition, engraving, platemaking, printing, etc.) for authors, editors, designers, and production people. The best book on the subject.

Literary Market Place (LMP). New York: R. R. Bowker Co. Published annually.

A handy, paperback directory of current publishing personnel and services, including lists of book publishers, book clubs, literary awards, reviewers, translators, and trade events of the year.

516

McCartney, Eugene S. *Recurrent Maladies in Scholarly Writing.* Ann Arbor: University of Michigan Press, 1953.

Informative and entertaining essays on editing, by a former Latin teacher turned editor (University of Michigan Press, 1922–52).

Mathematics in Type. Richmond, Va.: William Byrd Press, 1954.

Contains information on methods of composition; rules for setting and spacing; suggestions for preparation and marking of manuscripts; and a showing of symbols. Chapter 1 ("Factors Affecting Difficulty of Composition") and chapter 5 ("Preparing and Marking the Manuscript") of particular interest and value to editors and authors.

Menzel, Donald H.; Jones, Howard Mumford; and Boyd, Lyle G. *Writing a Technical Paper.* New York: McGraw-Hill Book Co., 1961.

An excellent brief treatment of the subject.

MLA Style Sheet, The. Compiled by William Riley Parker. Rev. ed. New York: Modern Language Association of America, 1951.

A brief guide to bibliographical style preferences of *PMLA.* Adopted by many other journals and recommended by many modern language departments.

Morison, Stanley. *First Principles of Typography.* Cambridge Authors' and Printers' Guides, no. 1. Cambridge: At the University Press, 1951.

A pamphlet offering assistance to the nonprofessional faced with the problem of designing a piece of printed matter or selecting typefaces.

Nicholson, Margaret. *A Manual of Copyright Practice: For Writers, Publishers, and Agents.* 2d ed. New York: Oxford University Press, 1956.

The standard handbook in its field.

Perrin, Porter G. *Writer's Guide and Index to English.* 4th ed. Glenview, Ill.: Scott, Foresman & Co., 1968.

A widely used college textbook on expository writing, including chapters on sentence and paragraph construction, spelling, punctuation, and various types of papers.

Phillips, Arthur. *Setting Mathematics: A Guide to Printers Interested in the Art.* Printed for the Monotype Corporation Ltd. Bristol: John Wright & Sons, 1956.

Especially written to help users of Monotype machines but an excellent reference for mathematical authors and editors. Sections particularly helpful: "The Mathematical Manuscript: The Author's Responsibility"; "Names or Descriptions of Mathematical Signs"; "Abbreviations"; and "Glossary."

517

Schellenberg, Theodore R. *Modern Archives: Principles and Techniques.* Chicago: University of Chicago Press, 1956.

A work on archival principles and techniques that contains a helpful explanation (pp. 195–204) of the classification systems of the British, French, and German archives.

Schwartz, Robert J. *The Complete Dictionary of Abbreviations.* New York: Thomas Y. Crowell Co., 1955.

A long (194 three-column pages), extremely inclusive list of abbreviations alphabetically arranged. Useful for identifying a rare or unfamiliar abbreviation in copy.

Skillin, Marjorie E.; Gay, Robert M.; and others. *Words into Type.* Rev. ed. New York: Appleton-Century-Crofts, 1964.

An excellent manual of printing practice for authors and editors. The chapters on grammar and use of words are particularly helpful.

Spiker, Sina. *Indexing Your Book: A Practical Guide for Authors.* Madison: University of Wisconsin Press, 1953.

The author confines herself to describing the construction of an analytical index to a serious book of nonfiction and addresses herself primarily to the nonprofessional making his first index. There is a fuller description of the mechanics of indexing than that in the corresponding chapter of this *Manual.* The "chronological" arrangement of subentries illustrated is not that recommended by the University of Chicago Press.

Statesman's Year-Book, The: Statistical and Historical Annual of the States of the World. Edited by S. H. Steinberg. New York: St Martin's Press. Published annually.

Particularly valuable to the editor for its up-to-date information on Commonwealth countries and international organizations, including the United Nations.

Strunk, W., Jr., and White, E. B. *The Elements of Style.* New York: Macmillan Co., 1959.

A short classic offering excellent, practical advice on achieving a clear and graceful expository style.

Turner, Mary C. *The Bookman's Glossary.* 4th ed. New York: R. R. Bowker Co., 1961.

Definitions of technical terms relating to the editing, printing, and marketing of books—a useful supplement to the short glossary included in this *Manual.* For anyone struggling with the translation of a foreign business letter, the list of Foreign Book Trade Terms at the end of the volume is particularly helpful.

Uniform System of Citation, A: Forms of Citation and Abbreviations. 11th ed. Cambridge, Mass.: Harvard Law Review Association, 1967.

518

Handbook, widely used in law review and legal writing in general, of style for citing sources in footnotes—books, articles, statutes, cases, etc. Lists accepted abbreviations of legal terms and publications. Well indexed.

United States Government Printing Office. *Style Manual.* Rev. ed. Washington, D.C.: Government Printing Office, 1967.

An exhaustive treatment of typographical style as practiced by the Government Printing Office. The "GPO *Manual*" is most useful as a supplement to manuals such as this one, particularly in the handling of governmental material and foreign languages.

U.S. Geological Survey. *Suggestions to Authors of the Reports of the United States Geological Survey.* 5th ed. Washington, D.C.: Government Printing Office, 1958.

Useful to editors of geological material of any description.

U.S. National Archives, *Guide to the Records in the National Archives.* Washington, D.C.: Government Printing Office, 1948.

An indispensable tool for anyone working with archival materials in United States history. Includes a numerical list of the record groups by which materials are classified in the National Archives. Quarterly supplements are issued in *National Archives Accessions.*

Webster's Biographical Dictionary: A Dictionary of Names of Noteworthy Persons with Pronunciations and Concise Biographies. Springfield, Mass.: G. & C. Merriam Co., 1956.

A single-volume reference work, indispensable for checking spelling and alphabetization of personal names.

Webster's Geographical Dictionary: A Dictionary of Names of Places with Geographical and Historical Information and Pronunciations. Rev. ed. Springfield, Mass.: G. & C. Merriam Co., 1966.

The first source to consult in checking the spelling or alphabetization of place names.

Webster's Third New International Dictionary of the English Language, Unabridged. Springfield, Mass.: G. & C. Merriam Co., 1964.

The standard for spelling of English words and a basic reference work for any editorial library. "Webster 3" has been criticized for abandoning the attempt to define the "standing" of English words (bookish, colloquial, substandard, etc.) and to suggest that usages are "good" or "bad." Whether it is the province of a dictionary to do so is a separate question, but the 1935 *Second International* did and is still useful for those purposes. Other big dictionaries are available, but the *Third International* is, in the opinion of the editors of the University of Chicago Press, the best American dictionary on the market.

519

Webster's Seventh New Collegiate Dictionary. Springfield, Mass.: G. & C. Merriam Co., 1963.

Based on *Webster's Third New International Dictionary,* the *Collegiate* is the best desk dictionary for author or editor to have at elbow. Actually, the *Collegiate* rather than the big dictionary should be followed for word division whenever possible: prepared after the parent work, it represents the later thinking of the editors on the principles of word division and frequently departs from the divisions given in the unabridged dictionary.

Who's Who: An Annual Biographical Dictionary. New York: St Martin's Press.

A useful annual listing of living notable persons, mainly British.

Who's Who in America: A Biographical Dictionary of Notable Living Men and Women. Chicago: A. N. Marquis Co. Revised and reissued biennially.

A useful listing of living Americans.

Wittenberg, Philip. *The Law of Literary Property.* Cleveland and New York: World Publishing Co., 1957.

A lucid and generally nontechnical exposition of statutory and common-law rights regarding literary property.

World Almanac, The, and Book of Facts. Published annually by Newspaper Enterprise Association, Inc. (hardbound edition, Doubleday & Co.).

An enormous compilation of names and facts about the world—government agencies, population figures, laws, events, etc.—with a comprehensive general index.

Zweifel, Frances W. *A Handbook of Biological Illustration.* Chicago: University of Chicago Press, 1961.

A highly useful guide for authors, editors, and nonscientific artists on preparation of various kinds of illustrative materials for scientific publication.

520

Index

References are to paragraph numbers except where specified otherwise (fig., table, p.). Paragraph numbers consist of chapter number followed by the number of the paragraph within the chapter. Running heads in text carry paragraph numbers of first and last paragraphs on each two-page spread to facilitate finding the items. Page numbers are drop folios. Definitions of technical terms may be found in the Glossary of Technical Terms (pp. 481–511).

Foreign names. *See also* Personal names
  of buildings, streets, etc., 7.45, 9.17
  of place of publication, translated, 15.91
Foreign words. *See also* Word division
  adjectival phrase in, table 6.1 (p. 134)
  familiar, in roman type, 6.42
  in italics, 6.39–42
  plural of, 6.4
  translation of, 6.40–41
  translation of, in footnote references,
    15.112
Foreword
  author's name with, 1.33
  defined, 1.33
  place and date with, 1.36
  placement of, 1.1, 1.33
For example (e.g.)
  punctuation with, 5.50, 5.70, 5.81, 5.96
  in text, 14.31
Forthcoming, for date of publication,
  16.44
Fractions
  breaking, at end of line, 13.25
  decimal, zero with, 13.13
  difficult, in text, 13.21, 13.24
  in figures, 8.6, 8.9
  hyphenated, table 6.1 (p. 133)
  plural of, 8.33
  split, table 13.2 (p. 311)
  of sums of money, 8.10
French
  capitalization, 9.17
  diacritical marks, 9.31
  direct discourse, 5.87, 9.22
  ligature, 6.35
  personal names, 7.8
  place names, 7.45, 18.71
  punctuation, 5.11, 9.18–23
  word division, 9.24–30
Frontispiece, 1.8
  in list of illustrations, 1.29
  tipped in, 11.4
Front matter. *See* Preliminaries
Führer, 7.18

Galley proofs. *See also* Typewriter
  composition
  correcting, 3.8–35
  foul, 3.37
  illustrations in, 3.51–53
  master, 3.6, 3.16
  numbers of, 3.36
  omission of, 3.2 n
General, compounds with, table 6.1
  (p. 133)

General (rank), 7.19
Genus and species names, 7.99–103
Geological terms, 7.108–9
German
  apostrophe and *s,* 9.33
  capitalization, 9.4, 9.32
  diacritical marks, 9.41
  letters, in mathematics, 13.32,
    table 13.2 (p. 310)
  personal names, 7.9
  punctuation, 9.33–34
  word division, 9.35–40
Glossaries
  content and arrangement of, 1.62
  estimating length of, 19.7
  placement of, 1.1, 1.62
  typing, 2.29
God, 7.75–77
Gothic letters
  in mathematics, table 13.2 (p. 311)
  for shape, 6.59
Government, 7.53
Governmental organizations, 7.47–49, 7.53
Government documents. *See* Public
  documents
Governments, numbers with names of, 8.25
Governor, 7.18
Grades, academic, 8.9
Graphs. *See* Line drawing
Great-, compounds with, table 6.1 (p. 133)
Great Britain. *See* Public documents,
  of Great Britain
Greek, 9.110–24
  alphabet, table 9.2 (p. 231)
  alphabet, setting, 10.59 n
  letters, in legends, 11.29
  letters, in manuscript, 2.17
  letters, in mathematics, 13.38, table
    13.1 (pp. 308–9), table 13.2
    (p. 310)
  ligatures, 6.35
  numbers, 9.118, table 9.3 (p. 233)
  punctuation, 9.117
  titles, in classical references, 15.132
  transliteration, 9.111, table 9.2 (p. 231)
  word division, 9.119–24
Guillemets. *See* Quotation marks, in
  French text

Half-, compounds with, table 6.1 (p. 135)
Half title (bastard title), 1.1, 1.2
  epigraph on, 1.24
  second, 1.42 n
  second, page number of, 1.78

Republic, 7.37
  with number, 8.25
Restrictive elements, punctuation of,
    5.27–28, 5.33
Reverend, 7.20, 14.7
Rhyme schemes, letters for, 6.60
Rights, for distribution of published
    material, 4.9, 4.24. *See also* Copyright
River (in type), 19.20
Rivers, names of, 7.38–39, 7.42
Roman Catholic titles, 7.20. *See also*
    Church; Religions
Roman numerals
  in classical references, 15.135–36
  for musical chords, 6.57
  with names, 8.22–24
  in outline style, 8.40
  for page numbers, 1.75–76, 1.78
  in references to pages so numbered,
    15.108
  table of, 8.37
  for volume numbers, 15.115
Royalties. *See* Author's alterations;
    Permission to reprint, fees for
Rules (metal), with footnotes, 19.36–37.
    See also Tables, rules in
Running heads, 1.67–73
  checking in page proofs, 3.43–45
  content of, 1.68–71
  omission of, 1.68, 1.73
  preparing copy for, 2.108–10
  publisher's responsibility for, 2.2
  type specifications for, 19.62
Runover lines. *See also* Flush-and-hang style
  in footnotes, 19.37
  in indexes, 18.83, 19.44
  in manuscript, bibliographies, 2.30
  in manuscript, glossaries, 2.29
Russian
  alphabet (*see* Cyrillic alphabet)
  capitalization, 9.82–84
  letters, in mathematics, table 13.2 (p. 311)
  personal names, 7.13
  punctuation, 9.85–87
  transliteration, 9.81, table 9.1 (p. 224)
  word division, 9.88–96

Sacred writings, names of, 7.84–88
Saint, with names, 14.16, 14.18, 18.57,
    18.71
Saints
  capitalization of appellations of, 7.78
  indexing, 18.39, 18.57
Sans serif type, in mathematics, 13.32
Scaling. *See* Illustrations, scaling

Schedule
  affected by author's alterations, 3.33
  for edited manuscript, 2.54, 2.96
  for index, 3.50
  for multiauthor books, 2.129
  for proofs, 3.4
Scientific terms, 7.98–120, 8.5–9
Screening. *See* Halftone, screen
Script letters, in mathematics, 13.32,
    table 13.2 (p. 311)
Scriptural passages. *See* Bible,
    references to
Scriptures. *See* Sacred writings
Sculpture. *See* Art, works of
Seasons, 7.71
Sections. *See* Subheads
See
  in footnotes, 15.29
  in indexes, 18.7–10, 18.78
Self-, compounds with, table 6.1
    (pp. 133, 134)
Semicolon, 5.61–67
  in compound sentence, 5.61–63
  with elliptical constructions, 5.57–58
  in index entries, 18.78
  with other punctuation marks, 5.67
  preceding *that is,* etc., 5.50
  replacing colon, 5.68
  to separate references, 5.65, 15.26
  with series, 5.48, 5.64
Senator, 7.18
Sentence. *See also* Question
  within another sentence, 5.5, 5.35,
    5.41, 5.60
  compound, punctuation of, 5.24–26,
    5.61, 5.63, 5.68
  incomplete, 10.34
Series. *See also* Paperback editions; Series
    of words or other elements
  New Series (n.s.) and Old Series (o.s.),
    in footnotes, 15.119
  number, in footnotes, 15.119
  title, in bibliographies, 16.25
  title, capitalization of, 7.137
  title, in footnotes, 15.71–77
  title, placement of, 1.4
  title, in scientific bibliography, 16.65
  volume number in, 15.113
Series editor, name of. *See also* Volume editor
  in bibliographies, 16.25
  in footnotes, 15.74
  facing title page, 1.4
Series of words or other elements
  colon introducing, 5.70
  enumeration of, 5.97, 8.38